For further volumes:
http://www.springer.com/series/5175

Christoph Meinel · Harald Sack

Digital Communication

Communication, Multimedia, Security

 Springer

Christoph Meinel
Hasso Plattner-Institute for IT Systems
  Engineering
Potsdam
Germany

and

Harald Sack
Hasso Plattner-Institute for IT Systems
  Engineering
Potsdam
Germany

ISSN 1612-1449
ISBN 978-3-662-51500-6   ISBN 978-3-642-54331-9   (eBook)
DOI 10.1007/978-3-642-54331-9
Springer Heidelberg New York Dordrecht London

Preface

What should still be something pretty amazing seems just like a part of everyday life to a lot of people today. In recent decades, the old dream driving human development toward a mobility spanning time and space has become unprecedented reality. And this without a single physical law being broken. Instead we have learned to handle a surprising number of things in life in dematerialized, digitalized form. Dematerialized in the sense that instead of dealing with the things themselves directly we deal with their digital "shadows" - essentially their images - coded into a series of zeros and ones and then transported at the speed of light via electromagnetic signals to be processed at any computer. Two technological developments have made this possible. First, *computers* in all their forms provide the cosmos to give these so-called digital shadows complete expression. Here, they can be formed anew, processed, linked and stored. Second, the *Internet* offers the possibility of transporting "digital shadows" to another computer almost anywhere in the world in an instant, where they can take effect.

The computer and Internet rank among those very few technological developments in human history that have intrinsically changed people's lives and actions. The industrial revolution of the 19th and 20th centuries expanded our physical mobility in ways that had been unparalleled up to that time. Just as cars, airplanes and spaceships have dramatically increased the radius of human physical activity, the drivers of the *digital revolution* - computers and Internet technology - have expanded our intellectual mobility to an extent that had been previously unimaginable. Our range of mental activity has been freed from (almost) every physical limitation. While it is likely that even the most modern physical transportation medium will continue to need several hours to bring a person from one continent to another, it is possible for him or her to bridge this distance almost immediately with the help of the Internet. Feelings, thoughts and instructions can be sent within seconds as we respond to the wishes and needs of those far away. And, in contrast to physical transportation, this can be done without significant costs.

The Internet has now turned forty and the WWW only just come of age. Because of this young history and the continuously rapid development of the computer and network technologies, the changes triggered by the digital revolution affecting society, business and private life can now only be foreseen in their vaguest manifestation. This makes it all the more interesting to look behind the scenes and gain an understanding of the technical basics of how the Internet and the WWW really work. This book entitled "Digital Communication" seeks to do just that. Along with the two other volumes of the trilogy: "Internetworking" and "Web Technologies," we aim to offer the reader an understandable, comprehensive, trustworthy, informative and detailed guide.

This present volume is devoted to the foundations of digital communication and offers an extensive look back at the history of communication and its technical resources. It covers the fundamentals of communication in computer networks, presents the diversity of digital media and its characteristics and coding and gives an overview of the security issues in the new digital world. The multi-dimensional organization of the material follows a format of accessible descriptions, complemented by numerous technically detailed excursus and glossaries, which offer chapter-related indexed commentaries, as well as bibliographic references providing an invitation for further research and reading. The reader is thus assisted in gaining the easiest entry into the fullness of the available material and also guided in making an interest or topic-based selection.

Based on this book, the Internet and web technologies are introduced comprehensively and in detail in the two volumes that follow: "Internetworking" and "Web Technologies." We get to know the current computer network technologies, the different layers of the Internet, the TCP/IP protocol suite, the WWW, as well as various web technologies, such as URL, HTTP, HTML, CSS, XML, web programming, search engines, Web2.0 and the Semantic Web.

We have made every effort in the hope of inspiring you who are interested laypeople with a fascination for the new digital world. We also aim to provide students - who don't shy away from a bit of hard work and effort - with a useful and comprehensive textbook. Furthermore, we hope to present readers who are seasoned professionals with a dependable, handy reference book that serves to classify areas of specialization easily and reliably within the context of the huge complex of digital communication.

Many thanks to our colleagues at the Hasso Plattner Institute, "Chair of Internet Systems and Technologies" for every imaginable support in research and teaching, as well as to Springer Verlag and, in particular, Hermann Engesser and Dorothea Glaunsinger for their trust in the success of this book project and their patience in its realization. For the translation of our book we are very thankful to Sharon Nemeth. Sharon you did a really excellent job. For the English version we have purged some of the original German bibliographical references and provided some matching English references.

Last but not least we are thankful to Ivana and Anja for the forbearance and tolerance they have shown when we disappeared into our offices on countless weekends and holidays and for your love which accompanied us there.

Potsdam, January 2014   *Christoph Meinel*
                                                                          Harald Sack

Table of Contents

Chapter 1
Prologue

"Whatever is created by the mind is more alive than matter."
– Charles Baudelaire (1821–1867)

The third millenium has begun and new forms of communication such as the Internet have rapidly become a permanent fixture of our everyday life, culture and the foundation of modern society's infrastructure. The World Wide Web, which is often erroneously confused with the Internet itself, supplies us with all types of information and services. The latest news, up-to-the minute stock market quotes, important travel information, flight bookings and knowledge from every imaginable field is only a mouse click away. Today anyone can publish a personal weblog worldwide. The most varied services can be enjoyed via the Internet and information exchanged by interest groups who convene to discuss their shared topics in forums. While scientists of all disciples advance their research with the help of electronic communication, others order gifts and send birthday greetings to their loved ones online.

This chapter serves as a prologue to "Digital Communciation," the first volume of our trilogy: "Digital Communication," "Internetworking," and "Web Technologies." It provides a brief outline to the advance of the dematerialized digital goods that have changed all areas of society in such a fundamental way. The dissemination of digital goods has taken place via new digital communication channels, without which our modern civilization would be impossible to imagine.

1.1 Digital Goods

We can no longer imagine modern civilization without computers, mobile phones, the Internet and the World Wide Web. New machines for processing information at an unimaginable speed for human comprehension, along with new channels of information and data exchange, have opened up brand-new horizons for the ongoing development of human society. Innovative technologies have made it possible to conquer the fundamental borders of time and space in a measure that seemed impossible in the past. No physical laws have

C. Meinel and H. Sack, *Digital Communication*, X.media.publishing,
DOI: 10.1007/978-3-642-54331-9_1, © Springer-Verlag Berlin Heidelberg 2014

been broken, rather we have learned to handle many things in life in dematerialized form. Dematerialized in the sense that instead of dealing with the thing itself, we deal solely with its digital description. These descriptions consist of coded information in the form of electromagnetic signals that can be transported at the speed of light and processed. Our children's generation has already grown up in a new world of computer games, text messages, emails and other modern communication technology and they have a self-evident, intrinsic trust in the blessings of the "digital world." While older people often approach this highly complex technology from a critical distance expressed in mistrust.

The first computers of the mid-twentieth century – which could just manage to perform simple mathematical operations – required floor space the size of a gymnasium and several hours of computing time to make calculations. It was taken as a given that acquisition costs would run into millions of dollars. Today, thanks to the exponential growth of computing performance and the fact that hardware costs have been falling at a comparable rate, computing capacity is virtually unlimited and extremely economical.

IT systems are pervasive today, i.e., they have become an integral part of our environment. Cars, airplanes, televisions and household appliances are all software-driven. At breakneck speed, purely electrically-based designs are being transformed into computer-driven, "ever smarter" models.

The extensive digitalization of information and goods that makes it possible to generate, process, copy, and execute texts, images, videos, vacation tickets, subscriptions, financial transactions and other information, takes places without a loss of quality and at a rapid speed. This is the foundation of the new digital world and its trade and business processes – the so-called **Internet Economy** (or Net Economy) [139].

But also business processes dealing with classic economic assets are carried out for the most part dematerialized in the digital world. **Electronic Business** (E-Business), **Electronic Commerce** (E-Commerce) and **Electronic Procurement** (E-Procurement) were the source of the euphoria and "gold rush mood" that marked the last two decades. Only the burst of what came to be known as the **Dot-com bubble**, just after the end of the century, was able to slow it down somewhat. The development continues – in spite of the current financial crisis (see Fig. 1.1).

It comes as little surprise that the electronic, or more precisely the digital, business field holds the promise of unimaginable potential. The range of the new digital economy extends over multiple areas: from the optimization of supply chain management, to cost reduction in commercial transactions, to the development of new markets and new methods of product design, through to an individualization of the market.

The spread of digitalization has caused the pulse of the world to quicken rapidly. Our world first seemed to get a lot smaller during the course of the Industrial Revolution in the nineteenth century. Distances shrunk both in terms of time and space, sparked by the development of transportation mo-

Definition of terms

E-Business: Describes all company activities that support business processes and relationships with business partners (Business-to-Business, B2B) or between employees
and customers (Business-to-Customer, B2C) carried out with the help of digital
media.

E-Commerce: Electronic commerce is that part of electronic business concerned with
the agreements and processing of legally binding business transactions between business partners (B2B) and customers (B2C, C2C). E-commerce usually includes three
transaction phases: information, agreement and processing.

E-Procurement: Refers to all activities directly connected to and in support of procurement activities (sales). These involve business partners and suppliers (B2B) and
are a component of electronic business.

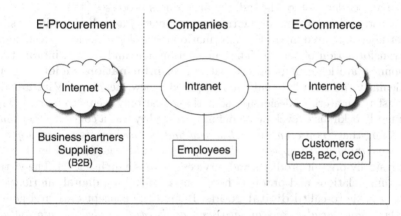

Fig. 1.1 E-Business – business processes and relationships.

des and the electrical communication media. Throughout the world today,
digitalization is responsible for opening up possibilities to what is essentially
delay-free communication. Digitalization has established its role as the pace-
setter and synchronizer of globalization and the worldwide electronic trade.
Possibilities to earn money in electronic trade present themselves in a variety of ways. On the one hand, traditional commodities transactions (sale
of produced goods) are supported by allowing the initiation of business and
customer relationships electronically (offline transaction).
On the other hand, a significant proportion of the commodity transactions
themselves (sale of products and information) is already being carried out
directly online on the Internet (online transactions) and thus contributing
significantly to overall economic revenues. Intangible goods are gaining an
increasingly important foothold in this market.

A case in point is the search engine operator Google[1]. Google is a "classic example" of a globally active major enterprise of the net economy that generates the bulk of its revenues directly from marketing intangibles.

Generally, electronic trade offers a variety of cost benefits for a company. Transaction costs, i.e., costs incurred during the course of a business transaction, can be lowered considerably due to the promise of electronic marketing's saving potential and higher marketing efficiency.

Even the costs accrued prior to initiating the business transaction itself – the transaction initiation costs – can be dramatically reduced when necessary information is acquired from the WWW. Transaction initiation costs are part of the communication costs, which also include customer support and product information. These costs can likewise be lowered through the use of digital media. Besides decreasing costs there is also a huge savings in time due to an acceleration of the individual business processes [213].

The constant development of information technology as well as the increasing importance of related innovative information technology, has led to a structural transformation of society. The information age, and related information economics, are leading us on the path of an **information society**, where particularly the term "virtual" has acquired a new meaning. "**Virtual**" in contrast to "material" designates something that only seems to be real. The German Brockhaus encyclopedia defines "virtuality" as a concept describing something that *"is present in such a way that is based on its essential qualities; something which appears to be real, but is not"* Via the real level, with its physically present products and services, there is a digital level. The virtual trading relations and products here consist solely of a digital information content – the so-called **digital goods**. Behind the concept of digital goods lies the *"immaterial means of satisfying needs, which aided by information systems can be developed, marketed and implemented. With the assistance of electronic media (such as the Internet or mobile phone networks), digital goods are transmitted and by means of information systems displayed and applied"* Numbering first and foremost (also historically) among digital goods are all forms of software and digitalized media such as music, film, books and newspapers. In the meantime, these forms also include tickets, reservations, cash cards, credit cards, stocks, forms, applications, contracts, letters, files, text messages and phone calls.

If we compare the market models of the net economy – where digital goods play a crucial role – and the traditional market models, significant differences immediately come to light. The duplicating and copying of digital goods can be done at a much lower cost than is required for the production of material goods. There are practically no expenses involved in distributing a digital copy via digital information channels. While a traditional, material product depreciates in value over time through use, digital goods are not subject to this phenomenon and, in fact, can even gain in value the more they are used.

---

[1] http://www.google.com/

The value of a material product drops when it is shared. The sharing of a digital product (duplication and transfer to third parties) on the other hand does not decrease in value. What happens is actually quite the opposite: the more a digital good is shared, the higher the value for the individual user becomes.

A popular (historical) example is the purchaser of the very first fax machine (or email system). Because no one shared this technology with the user, he could derive little added value from it. Yet the higher the number of fax or email service users, the more the value increased for the user. This was simply because the number of potential communication partners had risen. This effect is known as the **network effect**. The more users who employ a software system, the greater the possibilities to exchange information and experience, not to mention the decreasing acquisition costs that follow as a consequence. Therefore, a software system becomes that much more attractive with the more users it has.

Digital goods are intangible goods. Logistics and distribution can mostly be carried out today via digital and electronic information channels at virtually no cost. Tangible goods, on the other hand, require a special and usually expensive distribution infrastructure. In determining the value of a good there are further differences. In the case of material goods, a price can be set even without taking the production process into account. However, the value of intangible, digital goods, must be assessed based on the effort expended in producing them. When we take into account the absence of costs for duplication and distribution, the price of digital goods falls steadily with increasing dissemination (see Table 1.1).

Table 1.1 A comparison of the properties of tangible and digital goods.

Tangible goods	Digital goods
High duplication costs	Low duplication costs
Decrease in value through use	Increase in value through use
Individual ownership	Multiple owners possible
Value depreciation by sharing	Value appreciation by sharing
Identification and protection possibilities	Problems with data protection and data security
Challenging dissemination (logistics and distribution)	Simple dissemination
Value / price easily determinable	Value/price only subjectively determinable
Costs easy to identify	Costs difficult to identify
Price setting mechanism known	Price setting mechanism largely unknown
Inventory evaluation possible	Inventory evaluation problematic
Economic theories and models established and available	Theories and models rare

The difference between development costs (fixed costs) and duplication costs (variable costs) for digital goods is huge. In the production planning of traditional, material goods, a parabolic curve is the normal result when the unit price is determined. With increasing production, the unit price falls until it reaches a minimum and increases again with a rise in production as new production capacity must consequently be created. However, in the case of digital products, the unit price sinks as the number of produced (duplicated) products grows (see Fig. 1.2).

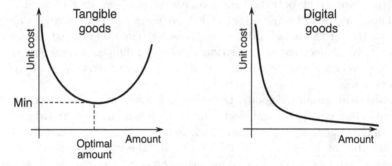

Fig. 1.2 A comparison of production costs for tangible and digital goods.

This possibility of essentially free and instantaneous reproduction has turned the digital good into a **mass product**. With good reason a significant portion of the development costs for digital goods is invested in mechanisms to ensure copy protection. There are many different models of "Digital Rights Management". Digital goods should be restricted to individual users or to a specific digital device to prevent unauthorized transfer and duplication. A constant battle is going on between the industry, who want to develop the safest possible copy protection, and "hackers" (joined by "crackers"), who attempt to bypass and break the current security measures. Once copy protection has been broken, a rapid process begins with the end result being the massive illegal dissemination of a previously protected digital product. A classic example of this occurrence is in the music industry, where this phenomenon has been blamed for huge revenue losses in the past years. Since the introduction of the compact disc (CD) almost 30 years ago, music has been distributed almost exclusively in digital form. As soon as the first CD recording device became available to home users at an affordable price in the 90s, a rash of illegal copying and duplication began which continues up to today. With the emergence of modern audio compression methods and faster Internet connections this phenomenon has become even more virulent.

Digital goods are saved on files or made available on the Internet. Electronic devices are essential for their processing and display. The central element of these devices is normally a **computer**, even when it not always recognizable as such today.

Let us first take a look at the digital product **software**. Software, in the sense of application programs, is only effective if it can be successfully executed on a computer. Application programs initiate the computer to execute predefined functions. The spectrum of these range from those involving the operating system – the basic software of every computer – to computer games, word processing or email. Today, it is often the case that software "only" offers pure information collections for the input in an application program. The route planers on navigation devices use geographic data and road network maps for the calculation of the shortest path between two predefined endpoints. As streets change their course, new data is periodically required to guarantee the most accurate navigation.

Digital **texts** have been an established part of everyday life for quite some time. Up to now it has not been possible for the new medium of "Internet" to squeeze out the traditional print media completely, while at the same time the publishing and newspaper branches have secured their place in the digital market. Every well-known daily newspaper maintains a more or less detailed digital counterpart of their print edition, providing us instantly with the latest news. **Email, instant messaging** and **weblogs** have become an integral part of our text-based, electronic communication cannon. The flood of digital texts that confronts us everyday has long since passed up traditional publication forms in terms of the volume of information offered. Popular literature can now be read comfortably on "eBooks" – irrespective of time and place. These book-like devices in pocket format are loadable with electronic texts and equipped with innovative and easy to read display technology.

In the early 1980's, **music** recordings and playback technology had already pushed out the established media of (vinyl) record albums and magnetic tapes. Innovative coding and compression technologies were able to shrink the digital audio-data volume to such an extent that a transfer of this digital data to the Internet became possible and profitable. Duplicated on a massive scale and distributed via (at the beginning illegal) file sharing, the music industry found itself at the mercy of a serious threat. The playback devices of this compressed digital audio data were themselves small enough to be the owner's constant companion throughout the day – even when playing sports. Traditional radio faced a new competitor in the form of **Internet radio**, which allowed its listeners a much more personalized program format.

Digitalization and compression also include the media of **film** and **television**. Uncompressed digital video data requires an immense storage capacity, which initially prevented the electronic transfer of copyright protected material. However, modern video compression technologies also make a delay-free and viable exchange of moving images via the medium of Internet possible. Methods of video compression demand a high level of computing capacity that has only become a reality through the continuous development of computer hardware. Digital television, Internet TV and video-on-demand support the growing popularity of electronic data links. As conventional analog recording and distribution practices are becoming increasingly replaced with modern, digital recording and sales methods via electronic communication media.

While becoming more powerful, computer hardware has simultaneously become cheaper. The storage capacity and computing performance of a simple mobile telephone today far surpasses that of a university or large company's computer thirty years ago, and the advance of miniaturization continues. The expensive scientific instrument called a "computer" has evolved into a cheap mass market product and information processing has become more popular than ever. The so-called **Moore's Law**, named after *Gordon Moore*, stating that the number of transistors that can be integrated on a microchip doubles every 18 to 24 months [169], can be applied today with amazing accuracy. Simply put, this means the power of microprocessors doubles approximately every 18 months while at the same time they are getting smaller and less expensive. While this trend appears to be slowing down, it is sure to continue for the next 10 to 15 years.

The great proliferation of digital goods today in our modern world is grounded in their intangible nature and in the possibility to duplicate them free of charge and without delay in almost unlimited form. But without an appropriate electronic transport medium, which frees these goods to physical existence outside of the computer, this dissemination could never have taken place so rapidly. **Internet** and the **World Wide Web** have thereby become the quintessence of modern digital communication technology.

Nearly all traditional analog media, such as post, telephone, newspaper, radio or television, have taken up a digital variation of their form (email, voice-over-IP, news, Internet radio, Internet TV etc.). Over the years digital communication technology has made tremendous strides, continually reporting higher data transmission rates and volumes. Especially important is the possibility of direct access to personal, digital information with the help of wireless communication. Mobile communication networks of the third generation and WLAN networks are already considered standard today. New technologies such as Ultra Wide Band (UWB) and ZigBee are waiting in the wings and promise even greater data transmission rates, combined with the simultaneous miniaturization of the required end devices.

1.2 Digital Communication and Its Foundation

We are witnesses to the beginning of a new age characterized by the central role of digital goods and their meaning for economy, science and society. Information is available today via digital channels everywhere, anytime and in every imaginable form, whether it be word, image or sound. The Internet and the WWW play a central part because without them digital goods could not develop their omnipotent meaning. For this reason, digital communication assumes a classic dual role on the path of this new era. On one hand it is the driving force and catalyst for the wide variety of changes we are now experiencing and which also lie ahead of us. On the other hand, digital communication helps us to navigate through our age – distinguished by extreme acceleration, flexibility and dynamism. Digital communication aids us in seizing the opportunity that presents itself and using it accordingly.

What we today call "the Internet" – the infrastructure of our virtual world – is a global network amalgamation made up of the most different computer networks, company networks, science networks, military networks and networks of local or regional operators. These are based on many different kinds of transmission media, whether copper cable, optical fibers, radio waves and network technologies. It only took three decades for what began as an an experimental network consisting of just four computers in 1969 – the year of the moon landing – to evolve into a web of hundreds of millions of computer and multiple networks. Thanks to the Internet technology behind it, we perceive it as a single global network. The technology called **internetworking** enables digital communication across borders via a multiple number of non-compatible networks. This is governed by a fixed set of rules known as **communication protocols**. Internet technology is capable of completely concealing details of the physical network hardware used. This means that the connected computers can communicate with each other irrespective of their individual physical connection to the Internet.

One of the reasons that lead to the Internet's huge dissemination is its **open system architecture**. It is open in the sense that all required Internet specifications are available publicly and accessible to everyone – in contrast to the proprietary networks of certain providers. The entire design of the Internet communication protocol is intended to enable the most different computers and networks to communicate with each other, independent of their various operating systems and application programs.

To be able to explore the possibilities of digital communication, one must understand its foundation and functionality. But let us first take a look at communication and the communication process itself before looking more closely at its digital expression. Communication refers to the process of information exchange between two or more communication partners. The communication could be between people as well as technical systems. The partners code the information to be exchanged in the form of a **message**. In our daily communication, for example, a person forms a verbal utterance from a thought. This utterance must follow specific rules of shared syntax and semantics so that the communication partners "understand" the message. In other words, it is necessary that the receiver is able to reconstruct the contents of the thought out of the acoustic signals.

We will cover a wide spectrum in our examination of digital communication – from the (digital) coding of information up to the technical level of the (digital) communication channel. Various scientific disciplines play a part in this process. The actual information to be sent is generally in analog form. Therefore an analog to digital information conversion (AD conversion) must first

take place. Here, methods from physics, mathematics and computer science
are applied. Afterwards, an efficient encoding of the digital data needs to be
carried out. This is oriented on both the characteristics of the media data as
well as on the nature of the communication channel. The messages to be sent
have to be constructed according to a fixed **syntax**. Each individual communication protocol specifies what this is. We understand a language syntax as
the rules that determine whether or not a sequence of characters forms the
correct words and sentences of a language. The syntax is either specified by a
complete enumeration of all valid words and sentences or with a mix of gene-
rative rules, the so-called **grammar**, or with a mixture of both [41]. Building
on syntax, **semantics** (the theory of meaning) determines the contextual
meaning of words and sentences that are properly formed with the help of
the syntax. The rules of semantics establish how the meaning of complex,
composite character strings is derived from simple character strings. Beyond
semantics, linguistics also assigns a pragmatic aspect to language (**pragmatics**). This refers to the meaning of a character or a character string within
the framework of a certain context and action. The line between semantic and
pragmatics is fluid. For this reason, semantics and pragmatics will hereafter
be discussed together.

The message is transmitted from the **sender** to the **receiver** via a **communication channel**. The communication channel functions as the carrier of
the transmitted message. In its various forms it is referred to as the **communication medium**. In the case of a verbal utterance, this is the air between
both communication partners where the language is transmitted by sound
waves that pass from the sender to the receiver. When the message reaches
the receiver via the communication channel, the receiver must decode the
message in order to gain access to the encoded information. The sound waves reach the ear of the receiver and are recognized as the verbal utterances
of his communication partner. They are then interpreted based on the rules
of syntax and semantics. If the interpretation was successful then the receiver understood the message. Fig. 1.3 shows a schematic representation of
this communication process, based on the information theory, sender-receiver
model of the mathematical theory of communication (information theory). It
was developed in 1949 by *Claude E. Shannon* (1916 – 2001) for the purpose
of improving the technical transfer of signals [217, 219].

But just how a message is interpreted by a receiver depends on the context of
the message. In a conversation, a verbal message is also accompanied by non-
verbal information, such as the speaker's facial expressions, gestures and body
language. A speaker can whisper, stutter, or shout; while speaking she can
look her partner in the eye or blush. According to psychologist *Friedemann
Schulz von Thun*, besides the factual information that is being expressed,
every personal conversation includes a self-revelation by the speaker. This is
an indicator of the relationship between the communication partners and an
appeal to the receiver of the message [241].

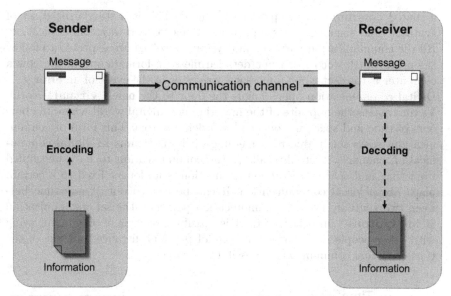

Fig. 1.3 Communication model seen from the information theory perspective.

Digital communication is located somewhere between communication science and computer science. Its distinguishing characteristic is that communication is carried out through an exchange of a series of signals. These signals are composed of just two different basic signals, typically symbolized by 0 and 1. Digital communication only needs a digital communication channel to carry out the communication process. By means of this channel – for example, the Internet – the two basic signals can be transmitted. Information is translated (encoded) from its original analog form into a digital message format and in this way may be transmitted over the digital communication channel. Depending on the type of media (text, image, sound, video, etc.) various specialized encoding procedures and media data formats are used.

Depending on the communication channel, special communication protocols are implemented. These control the reliability of the communicated content formats and the process of communication itself.

The majority of Internet users have no idea of the technical challenges that must be mastered, for example, just to send a simple email to the other end of the world with a mouse click. Nor are users aware of the application programs required to carry this out. In this case it is the the so-called email client, which appears to the user as the "the email program" on his computer. There are the multiple intermediate systems controlling the email's path to the receiver and, once at the receiver, the email server – which is usually installed at a remote computer – is responsible for the correct distribution and delivery of the incoming and outgoing email messages. In order that the different intermediate systems and email servers understand each other, a shared **communication protocol** is used. This is a standardized set of syntactic and semantic rules and mechanisms for two-way communication. All the communication partners and systems involved are expected to follow the protocol. Protocols describe detailed message formats and define how a computer is to react when a message arrives or in the event of an error.

Digital communication opens for us the door to the new, "**virtual**" world. Virtual means the opposite of the material, non-digital world where the borders of time and space no longer play a defining role. This form of communication exists solely due to a merging of data streams in digital communication channels. Virtuality allows the communication to be a decoupled from time and space. Digital communication is no longer fixed to a certain place like physical communication. It can be carried out at any time between two spatially remote communication partners. Digital communication is "**ubiquitous**," in other words it is possible everywhere. Communicating with other people is no longer an issue of physical distance, but one of the type of virtual communication possibility desired.

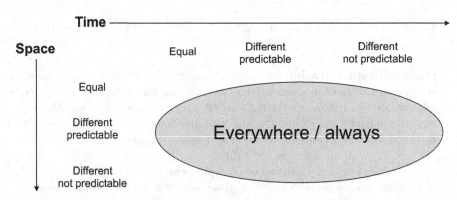

Fig. 1.4 Virtual communication.

Nowadays, the virtual communication possibilities are seldom subject to any limitation. For a large variety of the different of types of media – whether text, image, audio or video – there are various media data formats available. This palette of media types transforms the digital network into a "multi-medium," whose various forms are referred to as **multimedia**. In contrast to traditional "one-dimensional" media, it is now possible to display and convey complex contents more efficiently through the simultaneous use of complementary media building blocks. The communication effect achieved through multimedia technology is therefore higher and results in a overall improvement of information transfer. Although virtual and intangible, the information exchange is transformed to a level that is clearer and intuitively easier to understand. On this level, virtual communication relationships are at least as intense as the traditional ones that are fixed within the borders of time and space.

But at the same time this new digital communication is also responsible for creating a gulf between people. The promise of a connectedness extending beyond the borders of time and space have not been fulfilled for everybody. Participants are those who join by virtue of their educational background and financial resources. A "digital gap" (**digital divide**) can thus result between the rich and the poor, separating people into groups who have no access to the network and those who are themselves a part of the network. Chances of network access are distributed unfairly globally and strongly dependent on social factors. At the same time, this difference of opportunity reinforces social development. Therefore, whoever has access to modern communication technology has a better chance of improving socially and economically. The digital divide exists in our society in the sense that the affluent have more possibilities than the poor or that the young use the Internet more frequently than seniors. The divide can be carried over to the international level where industrial countries are seen as having more possibilities than developing countries. Numerous initiatives have appeared in an attempt to bridge the gap (e.g., "Bridging the Digital Divide,[2]", "One Laptop per Child,[3]") [48, 216]. Rather than focusing further on this complex topic here, we have chosen to take the optimistic view that this gap can be bridged successfully, with the hope that one day this will happen.

1.3 A Guide through Digital Communication

To explore the possibilities of digital communication presented in this book, it is first essential to understand the basics of how it works. We have already discussed the term **communication** itself as well as reflecting on the communication process associated with it.

In the scope of this book, we would like to first take a look at communication from a historical perspective and the **development of communication media**. This will take us from the first cave paintings up to the Internet of the future. Closer attention will be paid to the medium of writing. This pillar of culture became the first "mass medium," its huge proliferation triggered by the invention of the printing press. Telecommunications is not just an invention of the last century. Its origin extends back to ancient times. Relay messengers and fire signal telegraphy had already made it possible for the Romans to effectively manage their world empire. In the course of the Industrial Revolution, the electric telegraph and the telephone were responsible for a previously unimaginable acceleration of everyday life. This progress conti-

---

[2] http://www.digitaldivide.net/
[3] http://www.laptop.org/

nued into the twentieth century – the so-called Information Age – with the development of the computer and the globally-spanning digital Internet.

Computer networks serve today as the transport medium and communication channel of digitally transmitted information. These networks range from the piconet, linking several small devices in the immediate vicinity of the user, to the general global Internet. Basic principles of computer networking will be the focus of the next chapter. We will begin with the classic point-to-point connection, then look at the basics of packet-switched networks and continue on with the diverse communication protocols of the Internet, including an examination of their tasks and organization.

The communicated information is encoded for the purpose of transport and storage. **Encoding** is carried out in accordance with the modality of the transported information. Depending on the type of media sent (text, image, audio, video, etc.), different specialized data formats are used. These digital media data formats are the focus of a further chapter. Beginning with the fundamentals of coding, where the concept of redundancy takes center stage, we will see how appropriate encoding facilitates a minimization of the unimportant part of a message from the actual content itself, thereby compressing the original data. Modern methods of compression go even one step further. They take advantage of the shortcomings in our human sense of perception, purposely removing details from images or audio data whose absence is barely perceptible to us. In this way, JPEG image encoding, MP3 audio encoding and MPEG video encoding, among others, make an important contribution to the popularity of the modern data network and the Internet. In the 90s it first became possible to transmit images, music or even videos via the then limited Internet resources thanks to these techniques.

The aspect of **security** stands in the focus of public interest in a much greater way and in a higher dimensionality and drama than in traditional analog communication. Today, the ubiquitous network enables anonymous access to information and at the same time opens the door to numerous opportunities to carry out manipulation and fraud. The global Internet is an open network. Open means unlimited and accessible to everyone. However, this open entry, which was the basic tenet for the huge popularity of the Internet in past decades, also has its price. There is no central control authority to prevent unauthorized third parties from gaining access to the communication of other's and thus protecting the Internet user's private sphere. In order to maintain confidentiality and protect the private sphere, cryptography techniques must be implemented. The identity of the communication partner can also be proven with cryptography methods. This helps prevent an intruder with a false identity from wreaking havoc on the Internet. No longer do communication partners stand face to face and have the possibility of identifying each other based on outward appearance. They can now be easily located on opposite ends of the world. The methods of cryptography that allow us to have a safe and reliable Internet communication is the subject of the closing chapter of this book, the first volume of a trilogy that deals with the Internet and the World Wide Web.

The epilogue at the end of the book takes a short look ahead to the next two trilogy volumes. Volume 2 is dedicated to the topic "Internetworking" and is a guide through the basic technologies of the global Internet. Volume 3 forms the trilogy's conclusion. Entitled "Web Technologies," it summarizes the technical fundamentals of the World Wide Web and the most important web applications.

1.4 Glossary

Digital: (digitus=[lat.] Finger), Term for data technologies that use only discrete discontinuous, i.e., stepped, mathematical variables. The basis for the digital technique is the binary (two value) numeral system that contains only the states "true" and "false," or the numerical values "1" and "0". These binary numerical values are known as **bits (binary digits)** and represent the smallest possible units of information.

Digital goods: Digital goods are understood as intangible resources that with the help of digital information systems are developed, displayed, distributed and applied. Digital goods may be transmitted with the help of electronic digital media (e.g., the Internet or mobile communications networks) and be displayed and used with the help of information systems.

Digital divide: The term digital divides or digital gap, which arose in the mid-1990s, expresses the fear of those at different socioeconomic levels having unequal access to the Internet and other (digital) information and communication technologies. Disparate opportunity is highly dependent on social factors.

Digital communication   Digital communication designates the exchange of digital messages via digital communication channels set up specifically for this purpose. The data format of the message is determined by the respective media type (text, image, audio, video, etc.). The message is transmitted via a digital communication channel (e.g., Internet or WWW), based on the requirements stipulated by the communication protocol implemented.

Dot-com bubble: The term dot-com bubble was coined by the media to describe a worldwide phenomenon that came about when the "stock market bubble"burst in March 2000. So-called dot-com entrepreneurs were especially hard hit by the crisis, which led to considerable losses for small investors in industrial countries. Technology companies whose field of business involves Internet services fall under the category of dot-com companies. The name, originating from the ".com"syllable of these business domain names, was first used in stock market jargon and then adopted by the media.

Electronic business (also e-business):   The term electronic business describes all activities that support the business processes and relationships with business partners, co-workers and customers of a company conducted with the help of digital media.

Electronic commerce (also e-commerce):   Electronic Commerce describes that part of e-business that concerns the agreements and execution of legally binding business transactions. E-commerce normally covers the three transaction phases: information, agreement and execution.

Electronic procurement (also e-procurement):   Electronic procurement refers to all activities taking place in connection with and in support of procurement transactions (sales) and an integral part of electronic business.

Internet: Internet is the worldwide largest virtual computer network. It consists of many networks and computer systems that are linked together via the Internet protocols.
Numbering among the most important Internet tasks – the so-called "services"– are electronic mail (email), hypermedia documents (WWW), file transfer (FTP) and discussion
forums (usenet /newsgroups). The global network has gained its great popularity primarily through the introduction of the World Wide Web (WWW). Although often seen as
synonymous with the Internet, the WWW is actually only one of many services offered
by the Internet.

Communication: Communication is understood as the one or two-way process of delive-
ring, transmitting and receiving information by humans or technical systems.

Communication protocol: A communication protocol (or simply "protocol") is a set of
rules and regulations specifying the data format of the message to be sent as well as
its means of transmission. Protocols contain agreements about the data packet, the
establishment and termination of a connection between the communication partners
and the manner of the data transmission.

Medium: The type of transport channel used for message transmission between sender
and receiver. To make information exchange possible a carrier medium must be set up
between the sender and the receiver.

Multimedia: When several different kinds of media (e.g., text, image, and sound) are used
for the displaying of information one speaks of a multimedia presentation of information.

Network effect: The network effects occur when the benefits of an object depend on
how many other individuals or organizations use it. A typical example of the network
effect are digital goods, such as software systems, whose use grows as the number of
users increases.

Semantics: Semantics describes a branch of linguistics concerned with the theory of
meaning. It addresses the meaning of language and linguistic signs. The focus is on the
question of how the sense and meaning of complex concepts can be derived from simpler
concepts. Semantics is based on the rules of syntax.

World Wide Web: Designation for the "worldwide data network" (also known as WWW,
3W, W3, and Web). The most successful service on the Internet, characterized by high
user-friendliness and multimedia elements. The WWW actually describes a technology
that implements a distributed, Internet-based hypermedia document model. While today
the terms Internet and World Wide Web (WWW) are often used interchangeably, the
WWW is actually only one of the special services of the Internet that is transmitted
with the HTTP protocol.

Chapter 2
Historical Overview

"He who cannot account for 3,000 years of history remains in the dark, living from one day to the next."
– Johann Wolfgang von Goethe (1749–1832)

Probably nothing has impacted the advance of humankind more significantly than its ability to communicate and exchange information with one another. The knowledge of how to retain the contents of communication and to pass it on – also over great distances – has given communities a significant advantage, assured them of survival and cemented their position of supremacy. The development of writing and paper, as a transportable communication medium, soon led to the establishment of regular messenger services and the first postal system. Already in ancient civilizations optical telegraphic media, such as smoke or torch signals, were used. These enabled the fast transport of messages over large distances with the help of relay stations. The Industrial Revolution, and the heightened need for information and communication accompanying it, accelerated the development of the optical and electrical telegraph, both of which appeared at the same time. Initially available only to the military, government and business, this long-distance communication media gained increasing importance in private communication. The development of the telephone started a huge demand for private communication, also to far-off locations, and led to rapid growth. Development surged in the 19th and 20th centuries thanks to the invention of the phonograph, gramophone, photography, film, radio and television. Mass media was born and continues to shape our society. On the road to total networking the world has became a global village with Europe, America and Asia only a mouse click from each other in the WWW.

2.1 The Development of Writing

To truly be able to understand the spectacular nature of digital communication and the possibilities it offers, it is worthwhile to take a brief look back at the history of communication and its media forms, or in other words *from Homo sapiens to Homo surfiens*. Testimonies to the medium of communica-

C. Meinel and H. Sack, *Digital Communication*, X.media.publishing,
DOI: 10.1007/978-3-642-54331-9_2, © Springer-Verlag Berlin Heidelberg 2014

tion can be found dating back 30,000 years, for example the **cave paintings** from the prehistorical time. With language as the innate means of direct and indirect communication between people (more about that in Excursus 1), the human memory was initially the only aid in keeping and fixing communicated information. However, just as today, the human memory was far from being a reliable or permanent means of storage. Early humans first leave the dark pages of history when they begin recording their sensory impressions in pictorial form. If they were protected from the elements, these rock carvings and paintings, as well as stone engravings and reliefs, remain with us until today. Besides the ritual and religious significance of these prehistoric drawings, they had a communicative purpose above all – namely to preserve messages in a visually. These pictorial representations of our ancestors' lives, were however not intended purely as depictions of reality, but, more importantly, memory aids in supporting the oral tradition. According to the beliefs of Aboriginal Australians, who have preserved their ancient culture up to today, rock paintings retain the souls of the painted image. Through the act of painting itself, the act of touching the depiction, or through rituals performed in the caves, the souls are inspired to a new incarnation and fertility. Additionally, cave paintings provided the people valuable information. They warned about dangerous animals living in the area, gave information about hunting or even hunting instructions. These testimonies to the life of prehistoric, nomadic hunters are called petroglyphs. The actual meaning of these pictures still often remains hidden from the modern viewer. The cultural background in which these depictions were created is simply not known.

Cave paintings are found on all continents. The greatest number of sites in Europe are in France, Spain and Italy. Everyone who looks at these pictures gets the same message, even if they express it in different words. To refresh the viewer's memory about the content, the image only needs to be seen again. Communities who recorded information in the form of drawings were more competitive than those who didn't. But pictures can only express information related to appearance. Sensory impression cannot be shown, for example the scent of a flower, or even abstract qualities such as the content of a law. The development of **language** was a necessary prerequisite to storing this kind of information. It allowed people independence from the here now of a situation as well as the ability to talk about the past and the future or what happens somewhere else. This basic power of human language was perfected with the development of **writing**.

The decisive step leading from the pictograph of the **icon** to the phonetic characters we know today can first be carried out when the information to be transmitted is recorded with the help of visual script characters. The nature of these characters is no longer purely pictorial but directly related to the language of the script user. The characters should thus not only indicate meaning, but also the articulation of the object they describe, such as words, syllables or individual sounds (see Fig. 2.1).

From Pictograms to Phonograms – The Formal Development of Written Characters

- **Pictograms**:
  Pictorial signs used to represent objects, people or animals. Pictograms are often used today to give general information and on traffic signs. For example, the stylized image of a man designates the men's restroom or a knife and fork a restaurant. Simple pictograms are the starting point for the next level of the development of writing.

- **Ideograms**:
  Pictorial signs or a combinations of pictorial signs used to identify intangible expressions. Among other things, these can be activities, abstract terms or feelings. In contrast to pictograms, the meaning of ideograms cannot be construed by the image alone but must be learned. Ideograms are always used within a cultural group and in the framework of a strict formal system. Today ideograms are used, for example, in cartography to show streets or points of interest.

- **Rebus**:
  Rebus spelling is based on the existence of **homonyms**. These are words that sound the same or are linguistically identical to the characters for which they can be replaced. Today rebus spelling can be found, for example, in puzzles. The use of phonetic symbols evolved directly from a rebus type of spelling.

- **Phonograms**:
  Phonograms do not stand for concepts but represent only a specific articulation. Until the development of a complete **alphabet**, phonograms were often used together with the older pictograms, as in the case of Egyptian hieroglyphics.

Fig. 2.1 From pictograms to phonograms.

Excursus 1: The Development of Language

The pictorial representation is older than language, which is on a higher level of abstraction. In the evolutionary process intuition and imagination come before understanding and reporting. People can communicate with each other through language, unlike other creatures. Culturally speaking, it is in fact **language** that has an exceptional meaning for human communication. Language is not only a means of mutual understanding, but also promotes the development of standards and the handing down of values and culture. Language is therefore seen as a prerequisite for any kind of cultural development. The formation of communities and the emergence of a network of cultural relationships within these communities is based on the verbal communication of its members. Since ancient times language has been considered the ultimate "conditio humana" – the thing that distinguishes humans from animals.

As to the origins of language, we have to rely largely on guesswork. Even languages that might be seen as primitive from a linguistic point of view possess a complex set of rules based on syntax and semantics. They have already reached an advanced stage of development considering the huge span of human evolution. Our whole thought process and every thought transfer uses the tool of language. The human, according to *Johann Gottfried Herder* (1744–1803), is a "Sprachgeschöpf"(product of language). Language serves as a means of opening up the world. A person expresses the objects he or she perceives in concepts and signs and in this way is able to explain the world.

The origins of language remain hidden in the darkness of early human history. Only since the invention of writing (see Chap. 2.1) is it possible at all to conserve language and thus to obtain insight into its evolution. But precisely for this reason there is no lack of hypotheses about the history of language.

Anatomists attempt to determine the existence of the speech center in the brain using casts of the fossilized remains of the inside of the skull with its impression of the long decayed cerebral cortex. By comparing the different areas of the brain in humans and in primates, neurobiologists seek to discover clues to the language ability of our ancestors, while linguists attempt to reconstruct a "protolanguage" of all languages and language families known today.

Paleoanthropologists are split on the issue of the **origin of language**. One faction views language as a very old feature of the history of human evolution, believing it to have been developed over a million years ago. The second group holds that language is a young phenomenon that came into existence about 100,000 years ago in a sudden "creative explosion." Based on anatomic prerequisites necessary for the development of a phonetic language, many scientists see a parallel between language evolution, early technological developments (the use of tools) and human social development. The production of complex tools involves the planning and organization of work processes as well as a visualization of the finished product. The transfer of such techniques, with their increasing complexity, requires verbal instruction – for planning the production processes – besides simply imitating (see also Fig. 2.2). Language demands the highest effort from the brain and vocal apparatus. Variation-rich combinations of basic sounds must be created and understood in milliseconds. The exact wording of what has been said generally remains in our memory for only for a short time.

The search for the origins of language begs the question of the first, commonly spoken protolanguage. Through a linguistic comparison of living languages based on similar grammatical characteristics and constructions, it is possible to recognize similarities suggesting a common historical origin. Step by step it has been possible to develop a kind of tree model. Just as with the genealogical tree model, it is possible to draw conclusions about migration and propagation patterns.

Today there are more than 6000 different living languages worldwide, which can be assigned to the approximately 20 largest language families. Their distribution throughout the individual continents is however quite heterogeneous. This means that, in the meantime, about 12% of the 6 billion people who live in Europe speak only 3% of all languages. Sixty percent of the world's population lives in Asia, with about a third of all languages spoken there. In contrast, only about 1% of the world's inhabitants live on the Pacific Islands, but almost 20% of all languages are spoken there. Mandarin Chinese is spoken by nearly a billion people. In Europe a single language is spoken by about three million people, whereas the 850 languages in New Guinea are spoken by an average of only 4,000 people. Half of all languages today have little more than 50 speakers and are therefore threatened with extinction. The majority of linguists now believe that the human ability to speak in any form is not really learned but acquired instinctively. Every healthy child has the ability to learn his native language perfectly at a breathtakingly fast pace – regardless of social environment or intelligence. As an adult, a comparable performance in learning a foreign language is impossible in terms of speed, perfection and apparent ease.

Further reading:

Crystal, D.: Dictionary of Linguistics and Phonetics, John Wiley & Sons, Hoboken, NJ, USA (2011).

Cavalli-Sforza, L., Menozzi, P., Piazza, A.: History And Geography Of Human Genes, Princeton University Press, Princeton, NJ, USA (1994).

Deutscher, G.: The Unfolding of Language: The Evolution of Mankind's greatest Invention, Henry Holt and Company, New York (NY), USA (2006).

Powel, B. B.: Writing: Theory and History of the Technology of Civilization, John Wiley & Sons, Hoboken, NJ, USA (2012).

Theories About the Origin of language

Miracle theory: God created language and gave it to humankind. This occurred either instantaneously at the moment of creation or afterwards following a certain period without language. Evaluating this theory is a religious issue.

Invention theory: Humans invented language. Language proved to necessary at some point in time and consequently the first language was devised. The problem with this theory is its self-reference: the essential condition for the invention of language is that a person can already speak.

Imitation theory: Humans imitated noises in their environment (e.g., the barking of a dog, the sound of the wind, etc.) in naming the object connected with the sound. This type of linguistic rendition of sounds has been retained in our vocabulary up to today. These constructions are called **onomatopoeia**. Yet onomatopoeia differs considerably from language to language even when referring to the same object. Moreover, it does not explain the phonetic inventory of our vocabulary.

Natural sound theory: Humans produced spontaneous exclamations or **interjections**. These formed the starting point for the meaningful creations of sound. An argument against this theory – just as with the onomatopoetic imitation theory – is that interjections differ greatly from language to language.

Reaction theory: An imitative reaction expressed as an utterance in response to environmental stimuli. In this way the word "mama," for example, could be traced back to the movement of an infant's lips prior to nursing. The argument against this theory is the same as in the natural sound theory.

Contact theory: Language is based on the general need for reassurance. The need for contact automatically led to voiced declarations of affection or common song.

Work and tool-making theory: Language arose from rhythmic vocalizations during the course of collective labor (common folk variation). Tool-making and tool use require a division of labor and a transfer of skills and, consequently, language as well. The development of tools cannot be separated from the development of language.

None of the above-named theories has succeeded in convincing linguists and anthropologists completely. However, when the reaction, contact and tool-making theories are combined it is possible to create a coherent, overall picture to some degree. From this, a possible scenario for the evolution of language may be derived.

Further reading:

Deutscher, G.: The Unfolding of Language: The Evolution of Mankind's greatest Invention, Henry Holt and Company, New York (NY), USA (2006).

Fig. 2.2 Theories about the origin of language.

The divergent development of symbols and characters can be understood as an increasingly linear arrangement in accordance with the drawing materials implemented. The reason for this evolution stems from the necessity of carrying out and retaining mathematical calculations that were crucial for the administration of developing societies. While the icon could generally be read by everyone, the written character was separate from the collective memory and could only be understood by those who had mastered the art of reading and writing.

The birthplace of the culture of writing is considered to be the ancient Near East in Mesopotamia, the land between the Euphrates and Tigris rivers. While recent discoveries indicate the existence of even older testimonies of writing, such as from the ancient European Danube culture in the 6th millennium BC, the invention of the **cuneiform** in Mesopotamia around 3500 BC is considered the most important breakthrough in the development of writing. The cuneiform is thought to be the earliest complete writing system, developed by the Sumerian people who had lived in Southern Mesopotamia since the beginning of the 4th millennium BC. At first they used a purely pictographic script (pictogram), but by 3000 BC it had already been transformed into completely abstract forms through extensive phonetization. In the 4th millennium BC, the first city-states appeared in Mesopotamia. With its sacral monarchy and tightly organized and hierarchical temple bureaucracy, the Mesopotamian culture was strictly separated from others. Writing, which was initially implemented in temple administration, quickly became popular as an effective instrument in the area of taxation. It would however be a mistake to assume that in ancient cultures the knowledge and practice of writing was open to the masses as it is today. In all archaic cultures, writing was initially only available to the elite and used exclusively for special purposes, such as in rituals and the sphere of religion (see Fig. 2.3) [37].

Fig. 2.3 Sumerian cuneiform cylinder with an inscription of King Nabonidus from Ur, 555 – 539 BC.

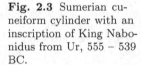

Around 2700 BC, the Akkadians penetrated the territory of the Sumerians, subsequently adopting the word and syllabic writing into their own semitic language. The wedge-shaped characters grouped vertically, horizontally and diagonally resulted in a new script. The cuneiform script, further developed and transformed by the Assyrians and Babylonians, quickly spread and be-

came the writing for traffic in the entire ancient Orient. Just as quickly, the
functional spectrum of writing developed. Writing now became focused on
practical purposes. These included purchasing contracts and certificates as
well as literary and scientific works. Starting in the eighth century BC, cuneiform writing was gradually replaced by other systems of writing such as
the Greek or Phoenician phonetic spelling.Serving as writing material for the
cuneiform were clay and stone tablets and, from 1000 BC on, wax tablets.
Knowledge of the cuneiform writing system was later lost and it was not until 1802 that the German philologist *Georg Friedrich Grotefend* (1775–1853)
took the first successful steps toward deciphering it.

Through a combination of pictures and characters it now became possible to
fix other sensory impressions besides visual information. But even with the
the introduction of phonetic writing, symbols hardly became superfluous.
With their inherent powerful expression, they continue to also be used today
whether in pictograms or advertising. The most remarkable feature of writing,
however, lies in its ability to save and transfer language in uncorrupted form.
The ancient Egyptian **hieroglyphics** (*hieros*=[Gk.]holy, *glyphein*=[Gk.]in-
scribe) passed through a similar development as the cuneiform. This pictographic writing consisting of syllables and single consonants can be traced back
to 3000 BC. The script received its commonly known name "hieroglyphics"
in ancient times from Greek visitors.

In their native language, the Egyptians called their script *"medu netjer*,
"which translates roughly as "the words of God." Carved with a chisel in stone, the script initially adorned monuments, grave chambers and other mostly
religious places of worship (see Fig. 2.4). Hieroglyphics were written on ves-
sels or on the surfaces of walls with a brush and with a reed pen on trade
documents composed of papyrus rolls. From the characters first used for purely ritualistic purposes developed a simplified, easier to write script that was
independently used in profane writing from about 2500 BC. The hieroglyphics themselves were not subject to any kind of changes over the millennia
because the Egyptians considered them sacred. They remained in use up to
the fourth century AD until Greek writing, which had already been introduced in Egypt in the second century BC, evolved into Demotic and Coptic
writing. In the Roman empire, knowledge of the hieroglyphics was lost. First

Fig. 2.4 Ancient Egyptian hieroglyphic writing.

with the discovery of the famous Rosetta Stone (1799) in Egypt by *Napoleon
Bonaparte's* (1769–1821) expeditionary forces did it became possible for the

French Egyptologist, *Jean Francois Champolion* (1790–1832) to decipher the hieroglyphics in 1822.

It was mainly the **Greek alphabet**, whose original form dates back to the Phoenicians, that decisively shaped our western intellectual culture. The **Latin alphabet** succeeded it and continues to be used today, albeit in a slightly expanded and modified form. The first evidence of this phonetic alphabet can be found in inscriptions on clay pottery fragments and bronze statuettes from the eighth century BC. The addition of vowels to the Phoenician characters, which consisted of 22 consonants, was the decisive step in the development of the Greek script. Vowels already existed in the Mesopotamian cuneiform script, or in the Mycenaean-Minoan "Linear B" script , but the Greeks were the first to make a clear distinction between vowels and "pure" consonants. This meant that reading – which amounts to decoding the written message – was made dramatically easier. The reader can rely on a strictly linear sequence of characters and this allows an unambiguous reproduction of the vocalizations. A rich literary culture flourished with the Greek script from the fifth century BC on. It was inherited by the West and has survived to a large degree until today (see Fig. 2.5).

Fig. 2.5 Phoenician and ancient Greek script.

Beyond the European cultural heritage, and independent of it, an early writing culture also developed in Asia. The earliest evidence of Chinese script appears around the time of 1400 BC. This script of the Shang Dynasty has mainly been found carved on so-called **oracle bones** and served primarily in rituals and ceremonies. Both tortoise plastrons and the flat side of an ox scapula served as oracle bones. Used for predicting the future, they were heated with a red hot bronze pin until cracks appeared in the bone material. These cracks were then read by a diviner. In addition to questions and answers, an interpretation of the cracks and fissures was written on the oracle bones.

A great obstacle along the evolutionary path of writing was the much later development and structural design of **grammar**. Grammar as the rules and science of language originated in about the sixth century BC in the Indo-European areas of India and in Greece. Both developments were independent of each other.The first scientific study of language and therefore the oldest surviving grammar can be traced back to the Indian grammarian *Panini*. His work of grammar, the "*Ashtadhyayi*" (=[Sanskrit] eight books of grammatical rules), was composed in the fifth century BC. It contains more than 4000 rules about word formation in Sanskrit in addition to exact phonetic descriptions.

In the Greek culture it was *Plato* (427–348 BC) who was the first to report on the origin of language in his dialogue, "*Cratylus, or On the Correctness of Words.*" The focus of his discussion was on the essence of words themselves and their meaning.Since the Middle Ages grammar has numbered among the seven liberal arts (grammar, rhetoric, dialectic, arithmetic, geometry, astronomy and music). This late development of grammar, as a structural regulator of language, in contrast to the historical darkness shrouding the origin of speech can be viewed with an analogy from technology. A great void stretches between the creation of modern technology at the time of the Industrial Revolution, in the eighteenth and nineteenth centuries, and the emergence of an internationally regulated norm. This time period extends up to the middle of the twentieth century. It was then that a suitable standardization committee was formed in 1946: the ISO (International Standardization Organization).

As only a few people could read and write initially, books and scrolls were available to just a limited group of people for more than a thousand years. In Christian cultures this was the clergy and later the higher nobility. The act of spontaneously capturing one's thoughts in writing or looking something up in a book on the spur of the moment was strictly reserved for a select few. Writing was a long way from being a mass medium. The development of writing as a new medium had a huge effect society and was accordingly also the subject of criticism. For example, in the following story from his dialogue with *Socrates* (470 – 399 BC), "*The Phaedrus,*" the Greek philosopher *Plato*, who himself left no written records behind, gives a vehement critique of writing.

> *Thamus, the king of Egypt, had been imparted by the god Thoth with all the scientific disciples, including the art of writing. This made it possible for people to preserve their thoughts, which they would otherwise have quickly forgotten. But the pharaoh (alias Socrates) was anything but happy. Memory, said the pharaoh, is a wonderful gift, but it can only can survive when it is constantly exercised. With the new invention, people no longer need to use their memory. From now on instead of exerting themselves they only serve the new invention. Writing is therefore very dangerous for it exchanges a memory carved in stone with a weakening of the mind's strength* [185].

Therefore, according to Plato, those who make a written notation are simply too lazy to use their own memory. This complaint against writing, which ironically is only known to us today because it was written down by Plato's pupil Socrates, reminds us in an amazingly similar way of the complaints by modern media critics about television causing human talents to atrophy.

Of course we know today that books don't think independently nor do they make decisions without us. On the contrary, rather then dulling the human spirit books challenge it to strive toward ever greater perfection.But the Socratic warning of not placing too much trust in the written word seemed to ring true all too soon in 48 BC. It was at this time that the library of Alexandria (see also Fig. 2.6), was destroyed in a devastating fire during the wars led by *Gaius Julius Caesar* (100 – 44 BC). The library's size was estimated

at 700,000 scrolls, making it the largest library in the ancient world. When
these works were lost a large part of the collected knowledge of that time was
gone forever. The little that remained was destroyed by Christian zealots in
the early days of Christianity. Practically the entire cumulative knowledge of
antiquity vanished and the long period of the "Dark Ages" began.

2.2 First Communication Network

The variety of materials used to pass on information in written form seems
unlimited in the course of nearly 70,000 years of writing history. Besides inor-
ganic materials, such as stone, clay, metal or even plastic, a large number of
organic materials have also been put to use. These include bone, shell, wood,
leather, palm leaves, papyrus, paper or textiles. Witnesses of the oldest traces
of human culture are found on stone, whether carved, chiseled, or painted.
The first evidence of written characters also appears in fired **clay tablets**
and in tiles of fired clay. Once fired, the clay tablets were also protected from
forgery to a large degree. Unlike the early writing materials of papyrus or
parchment, such tablets were resistant to destruction by fire. In fact, some
archaeologists even believe that the majority of preserved clay tablets were
burned unintentionally in a fire rather than being fired in a kiln. An added
benefit of such material was its exceedingly cheap production .
As the preservation of writing evolved into a more permanent state, so did the
difficulties of sharing and transporting this information across great distances. Despite the durable nature of rock drawings, cave paintings and rock
carvings, their messages could only be transferred indirectly via the often
unreliable memory of the viewer. The transport of inscribed stone, clay or
later wax tablets turned out to be easier, but also in this case the size of the
transferred message was strictly limited. The first step toward a flexible and
easy to transport information carrier was made by the Egyptians with the
development of **papyrus**. This writing material was made out of the pith of
marsh grass plant *Cyperus papyrus* and its production method was a long
held secret.The Egyptians developed a black ink for writing that was composed of soot and a gum arabic solution and applied with a brush made of
rushes.
In about the third century BC, **parchment** is mentioned as a writing material for the first time in ancient Greece. The raw material used for parchment
was hides cured in a lye solution. The hides were cleaned by scraping off any
remnants of flesh and hair and finally stretched on frames to dry. In contrast
to papyrus, parchment could be written on from both sides and mistakes corrected by rescraping. While expensive to produce, unlike papyrus, parchment
was especially durable and resistant in hot, humid climates. It consequently
developed into the most important writing material in the ancient world.

The Library – Its Mission and History

The concept of the "library" was mentioned for the first time by the Greek comic poet *Cratinus* (520 – 423 BC) and refers to a collection of writings. The Middles Ages refined the the concept to mean a collection of books and furthermore as the building housing the collection. In contrast to an "archive,"whose main focus is the documentation of writings of a political and economic nature, the task of libraries today can be divided into three areas: acquiring books and written documents, archiving and cataloging book collections (whose verification proceeds via a bibliography) as well as facilitating the accessibility to the book collection for the purpose of education and information dissemination.

In Egypt, Pharaoh *Ramses II* (approx. 1290 – 1224 BC) had one of the first libraries set up as part of his tomb in around 1250 BC. Allegedly, it contained about 20,000 scrolls. The library of the Assyrian king *Assurbanipal* (approx. 669 – 627 BC), which was started in around 650 BC, is considered the oldest library in world history. Located in Nineveh, it contained over 20,000 clay tablets. Each clay tablet from the library bore the king's insignia of ownership and an army of scribes was hired by the king to make copies of Assyrian, Sumerian and Akkadian texts.

The most important book collection of antiquity is considered to the **Great Library of Alexandria**. Various sources estimate the collected inventory at between 400,000 and 700,000 scrolls. Given the task of collecting all of the writings of the world at that time, it was a central meeting place for researchers and scholars. Affiliated with the great library was the "museion,", a unique research institute dedicated to the muses, where scientists and their students found an ideal place to discuss and immerse themselves in the knowledge of the time. It is all the more tragic for us today that the library was destroyed and its vast collection of writings lost. The actual events of the destruction remain a source of argument up to today. Ancient sources speak about a fire during Caesar's conquest of Alexandria in 48 BC. Further Roman attacks on Alexandria followed in the third century under Emperor *Aurelian* (214 – 275 AD). In the course of these attacks the buildings of the library were gradually destroyed.

Afterwards, a branch of the library, was relocated further inside the city in the so-called "Serapeum." Approximately 40,000 scrolls were stored in this temple. On orders of the Christian emperor *Theodosius I* (346 – 395 AD), *Theophilus* (†412), the patriarch of Alexandria had all pagan temples destroyed, including the Serapeum. And thus an almost 700 year period of library history came to an end. When Alexandria was conquered by the Arabs under Caliph *Omar of Damascus* (592 – 644) the library no longer existed. Widespread versions of Arab destruction were propagated during the medieval crusades.

The Great Library of Alexandria is thought to be the precursor of the modern **National Library**, which had its beginnings in 1536 with the "Bibliothèque du Roi." This library was established by the French king *Francis I* (1494 – 1547). All booksellers were ordered by decree to deliver a mandatory copy of each work published in France to the library of the king. Even today national libraries, in their function as a central state library, have the right to a mandatory copy of each book published in order to archive and catalog all the books of a country.

Further reading:

Michael H. Harris: History of Libraries of the Western World, Scarecrow Press, Lanham, MD (1991).

Fig. 2.6 A brief history of the library.

The decisive step in the evolution of writing materials – up to the point where they became a cheap, simple medium that could be produced in large quantities – was bridged by the Chinese with the invention of **paper.** This event occurred in about 105 AD at the time of the eastern Han Dynasty. In the year 794 the first paper mill in the Arabic world began its operation Thus paper reached Egypt at the end of the eighth century and quickly pushed out papyrus, which had been used for thousands of years. The Arabs carefully guarded the secret of paper production for almost five centuries. They carried on a busy paper trade and via Spain, which was under Arab occupation, western Europeans were soon introduced to paper. The key role of the Islamic culture in the production and distribution of paper can for example still be seen in the Arabic word derivation "ream." A ream of paper means a quantity of 500 identical sheets of paper. The first paper mills in Europe were founded 1144 in Valencia, Spain and 1276 in the city of Fabriano, Italy. In Germany a water-powered mill began operation at a rail mill on the Pegnitz River in 1390. Just 200 years later there were 190 paper mills operating in Germany alone. They were usually located near a flowing water source as paper production required enormous amounts of water. Water power also served as an ideal source of energy.

Fig. 2.7 "The Paper-maker,"(woodcut by Jost Amman, 1568). [6]

Easily transportable information carriers were indispensable for reliable communication across great distances. The disadvantages of a memorized oral message carried by a messenger are obvious: slow transmission speed, short range and a lack of reliability concerning the message transmitted. Additionally, it took a long time for the answer to a message to return – if one ever came back at all. Misunderstandings and mistakes in interpreting the message, such as we know ourselves, were the order of the day.

The history of message transmission is a long and rich one. Already the Egyptians had used the Nile as the main channel of communication sending messages via boat passengers. The Egyptian pharaohs also used numerous foot messengers to keep in touch with their far-flung provinces. They had to be able to cover large distances in as short a time as possible. However nothing existed in the way of a functioning postal system as we know it today. First in the New Kingdom, from approx. 1500 BC onwards, were there official postal messengers in Egypt along with foot messengers and mounted postal messengers.

Besides acoustic telecommunications, for example in the form of relay chains of oral messengers such as in ancient Greece and Persia, drum telegraphy was also used. It remains today a form of communication among indigenous peoples. Having originated foremost in Africa, drum languages soon became widespread. The transmitted message is based on the rhythm and pitch of natural language syllables and "copied" in drum beats.

There is evidence of well-organized **relay messengers** as early as the fifth century BC in the Persian Empire and later also in the Roman Empire. Greek historian *Herodotus* (approx. 484 – 424 BC) reported that King *Cyrus II* (550 – 529 BC Chr.) had his own postal stations set up at regular intervals along the most important traffic routes of the Persian Empire. They were each located about a day's journey from one another by horse, and also served as intermediate rest stations for the messengers. In ancient Greece itself, there were initially no postal system due to the many and often warring city-states. However, foot messengers did exist; the so-called *hemerodrom*. Because of the terrain in Greece they often proved to be even faster than mounted messengers. The most famous of these messengers is *Pheidippides*. In 490 BC, he is said to have traveled the distance from Athens to Sparta (about 240 km) in two days to deliver news of the Battle of Marathon.

The Roman Empire used the *cursus publicus*. This messenger service, operated by means of mounted relay, stretched along the roads of the Roman Empire from Britain to North Africa and from Spain to Arabia and the Black Sea. It is often regarded as the prototype of today's postal service. At the time of its greatest expansion the cursus publicus had a road network of over 90,000 km. On these roads there were stations set at intervals of between 7 and 14 kilometers where mounted messengers could change horses,. This institutionalized messenger service, established under Emperor *Augustus* (31 BC – 14 AD) in the year 15 BC, offered a communication infrastructure only for the ruling elite in the service of public administration and the military.When the Roman Empire declined in the turmoil of the period of migration, this precursor to the postal system gradually fell apart until it came to a complete standstill in the sixth century. For private mail it was necessary to choose another means of transport in the Roman Empire. One way was transporting mail via traveling friends or acquaintances. If only short distances had to be bridged, Romans sent slaves who were especially assigned to this duty and could cover distances of up to 75 km per day.

The regular conveyance of messages was inseparable with the expanding traffic and transport systems. Without traffic there was no flow of messages and with traffic there was not only the need to exchange goods over great distances but also the latest news. Even before the Roman Empire's massive road network system in the European Bronze Age, the so-called Amber Road existed between Italy and Denmark via Austria. In China caravans transported precious goods along the route of the Silk Road, from China's Middle Kingdom to the West.

During the Middle Ages a number of different, and often socially anchored **courier systems** existed: monastery couriers, couriers of the Teutonic Order, merchants, city and university messengers and, unique to the area of southern Germany, the so-called butcher couriers. The butcher's trade made it necessary to travel across the country from cattle market to cattle market. Therefore, transporting letters on the journey was not only natural but also a brilliant business idea. These more or less organized courier services existed either as a one-man operation or as a relay system conveying letters as well as memorized messages. The postal route led through already existing commercial and and political paths of connection. Monastery messengers maintained a communication link between individual abbeys and Rome. The couriers were usually monks who took messages along with them on their travels.

Homing pigeons, which had already been domesticated by the Egyptians five thousand years ago, must also be mentioned here. Their airworthiness (average flight speed of around sixty kmph, with a top speed of up to 120 kmph and a range of up to one thousand km) and excellent sense of direction were responsible for ensuring their place early in the transportation of messages. Because of the iron minerals in their beak, pigeons can orient themselves using the earth's magnetic field and therefore determine their geographical position. In Egypt and other Middle Eastern countries they were introduced as early as 1000 BC, and the Greeks and Romans also kept pigeons for information delivery. *Nur-Ed Din* (1118–1174), emir of Damascus, was the first to establish and develop a carrier pigeon messenger service for state purposes. This means of communication helped him to administer the long embattled empire of Egypt and further to the Iranian highlands.Carrier pigeons were first used in Europe starting in the sixteenth century. They had a fixed place as an important communication medium until the advent of the telegraph. According to one legend, the London banker *Nathan Mayer Rothschild* (1777 – 1836) is said to have received the news of Napoleon's defeat at Waterloo via a carrier pigeon. Aided by this message, it was possible for Rothschild to make a considerable profit at the London Stock Exchange and to thus lay the cornerstone for his fortune.The news agency Reuters used carrier pigeons to communicate stock market quotes between Brussels, Aachen and Cologne until 1851. The Swiss Army also maintained their own carrier pigeon service until 1997.

The first **modern postal service** was established in 1490 by King *Maximilian I* (1459 -1519) between his court in Innsbruck and the Burgundian Netherlands in Mechelen. It was administered by the Thurn and Taxis (formerly spelled Thassis) family. Maximilian was motivated by the need to manage his widely scattered dominions in Tyrol and Styria. He also sought to manage the territory in modern-day Belgium gained through his 1477 marriage to Maria, the daughter and heiress of Charles the Bold of Burgundy. Already in the 15th century numerous members of the Lombard lineage, from Bergamo in Upper Italy, there had been occupied in the papal courier service. As early as 1451, Roger de Thassis was commissioned by Friedrich III to set up a postal service via intermediate stations in Tyrol and Styria for the army and administration.

When Maximilian's son Philip became the king of Castile in 1504, the postal route, installed under *Francis of Taxis* (1459 – 1517) extended to Spain. In the postal contract between Maximilian I and Francis of Taxis the transport times were laid down for the first time with variation depending on the season. Thus, the conveyance of a letter between Brussels and Toledo took 12 days in the summer and 14 days in the winter. A European-wide, fee-based message transport system quickly developed offering a regular and reliable service. It became available for private mail as early as the beginning of the sixteenth century. The tightly organized changing of rider and horse at specially set up stations made it possible to have a daily postal route averaging around 166 km. From the travel report of the Venetian merchant's son *Marco Polo* (1254 – 1324) it is known that China had an excellently structured postal system as early as the thirteenth century. A well-organized system of hostels and stables was maintained for mounted couriers along the main roads of the Chinese Dynasty. It is said to have been comprised of nearly 1, .000 stations. Emperor *Rudolf II of Habsburg* (1552–1612) placed the German postal system under a status of imperial sovereignty in 1597. Its exclusive use was based on the hereditary vassal relationship transferred to the Taxis family. The family was elevated to the status of count of the imperial state in 1615. The post virtually became nationalized and this ultimately meant that the general conveyance of mail was open to everyone. Over time, thanks to special inherited rights – the so-called privilege – the Thurn and Taxis postal service quickly developed into a kind of European state-wide service. By the end of the sixteenth century it already employed an army of around 20,000 couriers.The Thurn and Taxis family achieved a position of indispensability throughout the course of centuries. It was not until 1867 that they were forced to turn over their postal system to Prussia because of the fragmentation of the German Empire into many small states. Article 10 of the constitution of the North German Confederation, the basis for the German Empire, then ended the Thurn and Taxi postal service. Another form of mail transportation was carried out via waterways. The first postal service by ship in Europe

was established in England in 1633 for the carriage of mail between Dover
and Calais, as well as to Dublin.

2.3 The Development of the Printing Press

While the establishment of modern postal systems enabled the transfer of
messages over large distances, this was limited to individual messages between (one) sender and (one) receiver. In order to spread messages quickly
and in large number a simpler way of duplication had to be found. Copying
longer messages manually was bound by quantity and time limits. This changed dramatically with the development of the printing press. The history of
printing can be traced back to ninth century China, with the oldest surviving print discovered in the Buddhist monk caves of Dunhuang, in western
Chinese Turkestan. The print was made in 868, 100 years after books (now
lost) had already been printed in Japan.

Wooden printing blocks exist dating back to sixth century China. These
blocks were made by Buddhist priests who carved religious images in wood,
colored them and used them to print on silk or rag paper. Wooden blocks
or tablets served as stamps. This technique of the **woodcut** (xylography)
is just one relief printing processes and is thought to be the oldest form
of graphic printing. Hallmarks, stamps and seals are also considered to be
much older predecessors of printing. Stamped impressions have been found on
Mesopotamian clay tiles that date back to the third millennium BC. During
the Chinese Tang Dynasty (615 – 906), the idea of printing entire books first
came to fruition in the ninth century. Printing with movable clay letters can
be traced back to the Chinese alchemist and printer *Bi Sheng* (†1052) who
practiced his art in the years between 1041 and 1049. He came up with the
idea of developing a set of standard font letters that could be produced in a
series.

In the western world, the development of the **printing press** is often regarded as the crucial event leading people into a period of generally accessible
information that could be distributed in mass quantities. The impact of this
event cannot be underestimated. For people living then, particularly ecclesiastical and secular leaders, it was a great sensation to be able to duplicate
information thousands of times over at lightning speed. The son of a merchant, *Johannes Gensfleisch zum Gutenberg* (1397 – 1468), was an ingenious
goldsmith who lived at the court "zum Gutenberg", in Mainz, Germany. With
his invention of a casting method for movable type he succeeded in creating
the required norm for a script. Gutenberg became familiar with so-called
block books during his time as a book-copying scribe. These books were
printed using the woodcut technique: both the text and illustration were cut
into wooden blocks. The production of every single page required tremendous effort and for this reason was not superior to the traditional calligraphy

carried out by hundreds of writers. Gutenberg approached the problem of mechanically duplicating written works via printing techniques analytically. He realized that if a block could be broken down into into sufficiently small, individual elements, it would be possible to express what the human spirit could put into words using the 24 known Latin letters and a few punctuation marks. Gutenberg's revolutionary solution to the printing problem involved making a large number of the same stamps for each character, with the necessary low error tolerance. After one printing they could then repeatedly be used for other printings in a different order. Gutenberg succeeded in mechanically producing texts in identical form and – in comparison with the number of handwritten copies – in huge numbers. The first mass medium was born.

Fig. 2.8 "The Printer,"(woodcut by Jost Amman, 1568), [6]

Gutenberg succeeded in casting his first printing type in 1445. It was made of an alloy of lead, antimony and tin, with the addition of bismuth for pouring. As no type from Gutenberg's time has survived, the exact mixture remains unknown. The target mixture distinguishes itself through its fast hardening properties. This made the rapid production of uniform type possible. Gutenburg's casting instrument was able to produce up to 100 letters of uniform type in one hour. The first printed document attributed to him was produced at the same time: a poem about the Last Judgement, written in German in 1360 and based on a Sibylline Book from Thuringia. Only a small fragment of it still survives. His first prestigious printed work – the one that has made him famous until today – is the forty-two line Latin Bible. It was produced in the years 1452 – 1456 in a print run of 185 copies. Of these, 49 copies still exist today, when also only as fragments[1]. Although the Gutenberg Bible can be considered the first mass-produced item of printing technology, it was anything but a cheaply produced and mass-distributed print product. With the production of his superbly printed Bible, Gutenberg's aim was to outdo the craftsmanship skills of calligraphers and copyists. He not only wanted to produce first-rate books but also to deliver them in a consistent quality. Every one of his Bibles consisted of two volumes, each with 648 and 643 pages. Approximately, thirty of the copies were printed on parchment.If Gutenberg had decided to print the entire circulation on parchment, the skins of up to 50,000 calves would have been necessary. In 1450, German paper mills were still not capable of producing the amount of paper needed, therefore the lion's share was imported from Italy. While Gutenberg did not invent the art of printing – and for the present-day viewer his Bible can barely be distinguished from other manuscripts of the time – through a combination of the then known techniques and the masterful engineering of his innovative casting method, he became the founder of a new industry.

Before the invention of printing, text duplication meant tedious manual labor. For the most part it was performed by monks in monasteries. Their painstaking work in the preservation and reverse translation of antique manuscripts should not be underestimated. Students and teachers needed enormous amounts of time to transcribe texts – undoubtedly a reason why the progress of science was very slow during this period. In cities with universities, a regular writing industry developed. At the University of Angers, scribes in the fifteenth century were capable of making copies of lectures in a month's time at relatively low prices. Sometimes it was even possible to complete these manuscripts before the start of the next lectures. At the time Gutenberg was attempting to produce his first typographical work, there were forty professional scribes in his hometown of Mainz alone and additionally those transcribers who were monks or students. While medieval monks needed at least a year for the handwritten copy of a book, Gutenberg could print up to 300 pages per day with his innovative technology .

Even if Gutenberg's role could be better described as a skilled technician than a creative genius, his invention of the movable-type printing press heralded a new age in the entire Western world. Whereas before 1456 there had been approximately 5000 handwritten books on the worldwide market, fifty years later there were nearly 10 million printed copies. Although only a minority of the population could read, the more books entered the market the more the interest in reading grew. The use of writing became part of the public domain thanks to Gutenberg's printing press. Gutenberg himself was however unable to capitalize on his development. He died in 1468, blind and bankrupted by a lawsuit against his financier Mainz banker, *Johannes Fust* (1400–1466). Furst demanded return of the money he had lent the inventor, which finally led to

---

[1] In 1987 one of these books sold for the price of 9.75 million German marks (approx. five million euros), the highest price ever paid for a printed work.

the confiscation of Gutenberg's printing house including the rights to all of his works.

The newly-developed printing technology was being used for political purposes early on. In 1455 the so-called Turkish Calendar ("*A Warning to Christendom Against the Turks*") appeared in which a crusade was called against the Turks who had conquered Constantinople a short time before. The Catholic Church used the new technology for the high-volume publication of **indulgences**. The sale of these documents improved the finances of the Church in the 15th century. In exchange for a fee an indulgence (forgiveness) was granted for a sin committed and verified with an official seal. This practice was one of the main points of criticism of the reformers – especially *Martin Luther* (1483–1546). The indulgence itself was printed in advance. Later, the sinner's name, the date and the signature of the indulgence seller were added by hand. This document was well-suited for mass distribution and reached a circulation of several thousand to over one hundred thousand.

The books printed in the 15th century – at the time the printing process was still in its infancy – are called **incunabula** (early printed works). The year 1500 is documented as the end of the incunabula for purely bibliographic reasons. It is assumed that at this time approximately 30,000 titles with a total publication of 9-10 million books were printed. Of these books about 500,000 survive until today. Because of the predominant use of Latin as the print language, this printed matter was accessible to a Europe-wide market, notwithstanding regional language borders. Besides pamphlets, also street ballads, church and secular calenders, political and inflammatory speeches as well as theological manuscripts were include among the first printed works.

The **Frankfurt Fair** developed as a hub for the new, printed products from Germany, France, Italy and the Netherlands. Mainly raw prints were sold, i.e., unbound, printed sheets of paper. These were transported and distributed by print workshops in barrels. The bookbinding and artistic design of the prints, including section headings and illumination, were dictated by the buyer. Initially, almost exclusively large-format folios were printed, intended for use in the Church liturgy or universities. A significant reduction in the size of the print format could first be seen at the beginning of 1480. Until this time it had been usual practice to add a colophon in hand-written manuscripts and printed works with the details of the scribe or printer as well as the place of printing. For practical reasons, this information and the book's title were moved to the front of the book, appearing there on a separate **title page**. The use of page numbers (**pagination**) also originated at this time as did the first printed advertising posters for the sale of books.

As a mass-produced media, the book had a tremendous influence on modernization in all areas of science, administration, education, religion and art. "Social knowledge" was put on paper, recorded and published to an extent that had never been witnessed before that time. In the beginning the new media was slow to catch on and it was only in the 16th century that the printing press fully emancipated itself from the prevailing culture of handwritten manuscripts. The technology then spread quickly and was known by some as the "black art"– a name that stemmed from the printer's ink but also alluded to an underlying secret knowledge behind the method. As a new craft, the art of printing was not subject to the same limitations that traditional guilds were forced to comply with. Wandering journeyman printers could establish themselves wherever they desired. By the year 1500 there were already 300 printeries in 60 German cities and in Italy there were 150.

The printed book had just begun to inspire the mass spread of ideas when the fear arose of the widespread dissemination of unwelcome or even dangerous thoughts via the printed word. *Berthold von Henneberg* (1441–1504), archbishop and elector of Mainz, was the first German prince to impose a **censor**, with his edict of March 22, 1485, on all "books translated into Greek, Latin or another language" into German. The aim was to prevent certain knowledge and opinions, until that time only discussed among scholars, from gaining a popular audience.

In addition, the bishop ordered the Frankfurt city council, together with church officials, to inspect all of the printed books at the spring fair and to prohibit works, if necessary. A translation of the Bible from Latin into the vernacular was also suppressed. Henneberg believed that the "the Order of the Holy Mass" would be desecrated by its translation into the German vernacular. Pope *Leo X* (1475–1521) strengthened this ban in 1515 for fear of a rampant "spread of falsehoods about the faith." The fear that the Bible would be desecrated if it were available to the general public was coupled with apprehension of a threat to the sole supremacy of clerics to interpret the scriptures.

Because both church and state recognized the consequences of the fast and large-scale dissemination of printed matter, censorship soon became a commonplace practice. On one hand, **preventative censorship** called for a close examination of documents by censorship authorities prior to printing. On the other hand, **repressive censorship** focused on already printed documents, whose further dissemination was regulated by ban or confiscation. These practices were institutionalized in papal bulls by Pope *Innocent VIII* (1432–1492) and Pope *Alexander VI* (1430–1503). It was necessary that every book approved by the Catholic Church be given an **imprimatur** (=[Lat.] it may be printed) by church authorities. Violators were threatened with severe punishments including excommunication, extreme fines and even professional disbarment. The famous **Index librorum prohibitorum** – the blacklist of banned books – first appeared In 1559. It remained in existence until being officially lifted by the Second Vatican Council in 1967.

In the wake of the book's development into a mass medium, cultural criticism was expressed early. The French poet *Victor Hugo* (1802–1885) called the art of printing "the greatest event in human history." Yet a scene in his novel "Notre Dame de Paris" (or "The Hunchback of Notre-Dame") describes the priest, Claude Frollo, as he points his finger at a book and then at the towers and paintings of his beloved cathedral and says: „Ceci tuera cela", – the book

Table 2.1 Milestones in the History of Communication Media

30.000 BC	Cave paintings, first pictographs and proto-writing
3500 BC	Ancient Sumerian inscriptions on unfired clay tablets in Uruk
3200 BC	Cuneiform writing in Mesopotamia
3000 BC	Egyptians develop hieroglyphic writing
3000 BC	The abacus used as a calculating device in Babylon
3000 BC	Papyrus invented as a writing material in Egypt, becomes the forerunner of paper
1500 BC	Ugaritic (Phoenician) cuneiform writing with 27 main characters
1400 BC	Oracle bones provide first evidence of Chinese writing
1000 BC	Carrier pigeons used in Egypt and in the Middle East for message transport
9th c. BC	First record of Greek writing
ca. 650 BC	Assurbanipal founds the first large library in Ninive
6th c. BC	First recorded grammar in India and Greece
6th c. BC	Persian courier postal system established under King Cyrus II
6th c. BC	Darius I, king of Persia, sets up courier relay systems
5th c. BC	Telegraphy with arranged fire signals used in the Peloponnesian War
450 BC	Torch telegraphy used for message communication in Greece
3rd c. BC	Parchment invented as a writing material
288 BC	The Library of Alexandria established by Ptolemy II
1st c. BC	"Cursus publicus", relay courier service set up in the Roman Empire
63 BC	"Acta diurna", first newspaper in the Western World founded in Rome
105 AD	Paper invented by the Chinese
8th c.	Woodcut invented as the first printing method in China
794	First paper mill in Bagdad
1041	First print made with movable clay letters in China
12th c.	Nur-Ed-Din, emir of Damascus, sets up state postal service via carrier pigeon transport
ca. 1440	Johannes Gensfleisch zum Gutenberg develops the printing press with movable type
1455	First printed pamphlet for political propaganda
1485	First state-ordered book censorship enacted by Berthold von Henneberg, archbishop and elector of Mainz
1490	Maximilian I establishes the first modern postal service, administered by the Thurn and Taxis family
1502	The "Newe Zeitung", an early form of the present-day daily newspaper, is published
1536	Francis I founds the "Bibliotèque du Roi", predecessor of the modern national library
1571	First newspaper correspondent agency set up in Augsburg – the "Nouvellanten"
1633	First postal service by ship between Dover and Calais
1647	First European coffee house opens in Venice
1650	First regularly published daily newspaper in Leipzig
1710	Jakob Christof Le Blon develops four color printing
1764	Pierre Simon Fournier standardizes typography
1796	Aloys Sennefelder invents lithography, creating the foundation for modern offset printing

means the end of the cathedrals. The story takes place in the 15th century shortly after the invention of book printing. The ability to read manuscripts was the privilege of a small elite ruling class. The broad population only had the possibility to gain information and knowledge about Bible stories from the paintings and reliefs in churches and cathedrals, the so-called "pauper's Bible" (Biblia pauperum). In this way it was possible to learn about moral principles as well as history and geography.

Pope *Gregory II* (669–731), who settled the dispute about veneration of sacred images in the Catholic church on the basis of the quote from the Bible „Thou shalt not make unto thee any graven image" forbade Eastern Roman Emperor *Leo III* (685–741) in the year 726 any type of image-worship in his empire. He invented the ingenious compromise formulation: „The pictures are for the laity what the written word is for the literate". In contrast, the book would incite the masses to turn away from their most important virtues and possibly to interpret the Bible freely or to even develop more unhealthy curiosity.

2.4 The Birth of the Newspaper Industry

A prototype of the newspaper can be considered the ancient Roman annuals or yearbooks. The most important events to receive the publics' attention were recorded here by the head of the priest quorum – the pontifex maximus. Before the time of Julius Caesar, the pontifex maximus was also responsible for the **calendar**. The calendar date, which today still remains the "first news" every newspaper presents, was relatively complicated to calculate at the time of the Julian calender. Because the lunar year shifted constantly according to to the season, the high priest needed to establish a certain number of additional so-called intercalary days. Upon the inauguration of Julius Caesar, in 63 BC in Rome, the so-called "*acta diurna*" or "*acta urbis*"– the first public gazettes – were created.

These forerunners of our modern newspaper were carved in stone or on metal plates long before the invention of paper. Caesar had the minutes of the Roman senate sessions taken in shorthand. Directly afterwards they were edited and then published on the same day. Originally, there were three such official journals: the senate acts (*acta senatus*), which were not available to the public prior to the time Caesar took office, the people's acts (*acta populi*) and the state acts (*acta urbana*). The acta urbana often had the additional designation *diurna* (daily), although its publication did not yet strictly occur on a daily basis. The official version of the news in the Roman Forum was presented to the public on a white message board and circulated throughout the whole of Rome and the provinces. This forerunner of the newspaper was published until the year 235 AD, although a strict periodicity was not maintained during this time.

The **newspaper industry** with its previously described beginnings in antiquity, had already established a niche in the sixteenth century even before the printing press came on the scene. Written newspapers existed in the form of hand-written notes containing the latest news added as an attachments to commercial and private letters. An example of these were the so-called "Fuggerzeitungen" (Fugger newspapers), established between 1568 and 1605 as a collection of hand-written news items. The Augsburg trading house Fugger had these news pieces compiled from their correspondences and other sources. Since the Fugger business had an extensive network throughout Europe and the world, it organized the first news service and were thus able to stay on top of political events. Jeremias Crasser and Jeremias Schiffle were professional news dealers, whose services were gladly used by the Fugger trading house. Together they founded the first newspaper correspondence office in Augsburg in 1571 and called themselves the "Nouvellanten". The trade with news as a commodity had already begun in the 14th century between Italian cities with Venice as the hub of news transmission. Correspondents and news dealers were mainly representatives in the areas of diplomacy/politics and business. In their reports they inserted special news letters containing general information. Event-focused, one page broadsheets called **leaflets**, which were politically or commercially motivated, appeared with the invention of the printing press. These leaflets usually served less the purpose of political agitation – in the sense of the modern-day protest leaflet – and more the announcement of merchandise offered by barkers and traveling merchants at fairs and outside church doors.

The leaflet authors remained anonymous most of the time. Large illustrations, usually produced as woodcuts, had a dominant place in leaflets. They were intended to motivate purchase as well as to make the content accessible to those who were not able to read. Besides political, religious or military news there were also stories that were pure sensationalism. These topics included exorcisms, comets, people with birth defects or heretics. The leaflet is considered the first means of mass communication. The irregularly published **pamphlet** is the direct predecessor of our daily newspaper. In contrast to a leaflet, a pamphlets consists of several printed pages.

The German word for newspaper, **Zeitung**, appeared at the beginning of the fourteenth century as "*zidunge*" and meant "customer" or "news." Used in the vicinity of Cologne, it describe oral and written messages. On December 4, 1501, the so-called "Newe Zeitung" appeared as the title of a transcribed and Germanized report from Doge *Leonhard Lauredan* (1459–1516). It quickly became the generic name for irregularly appearing published pamphlets and journals in the sixteenth and seventeenth centuries. The newspaper as a printed periodical containing the latest news first came into fashion at the beginning of the seventeenth century. One of these was the first German-language weekly newspaper called "Avisa, Relation oder Zeitung." It was printed in Wolfenbüttel in 1609. Since newspaper distribution was initially dependent on the available messenger and transportation services, it was

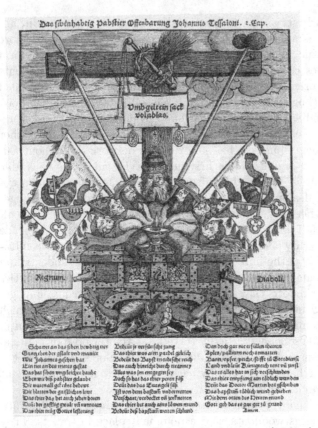

Fig. 2.9 Leaflet protesting the sale of indulgences (16th c.), from [194].

only available weekly. It is important to note that the beginnings of many newspapers ran parallel to the coffee house culture starting up at that time. This culture was rooted in the first European coffee house in 1847 Venice. Not only were coffee houses places where a cup of coffee could be enjoyed, but they were also havens for reading and discussion. Merchants did their business here, while intellectuals gathered to question old structures and superstitions For the just emerging editorial staff, coffee houses served as places to meet and exchange news.

On July 1, 1650, the first German-language daily newspaper was published and, simultaneously, the first daily newspaper worldwide in Leipzig. The six issues per week were edited by *Timotheus Ritzsch* (1614–1678) and the newspaper was entitled "*Neu-einlauffende Nachricht von Kriegs- und Welt-Händeln,*"(the latest news on actions in the world and in warfare). By the end of the seventeenth century there were already 170 daily newspapers in Germany alone. At first the daily newspaper was a marginal phenomenon. Before the nineteenth century its most interesting function was to provide the

Fig. 2.10 The title page of one of the first newspapers (*Relation aller Fürnemmen und gedenckwürdigen Historien*), 1609.

city's calender of events, as in the "*Daily Courant*," which began its London publication in 1702.

The Thirty Years' War (1618–1648) threw Germany back economically and led England and France to establish themselves as pioneer countries of the press. The first magazines originated there. Initially, they were only targeted at scholars but later concentrated on specific subject areas and topics, such as those of interest to women. Huge print runs (up to 300,000) were reached with calendars, which remain up to today an important and low-risk source of income for many printing houses. The publication of the printed book reached ever-greater proportions. At the end of the sixteenth century, books in print had reached over 200 million copies. The mass press was born in the nineteenth century, buoyed by the further technical development of the printing press. The so-called rapid press was invented in 1812, the rotary press in 1845 and the modern Linotype typesetting machine in 1884. At the same time, the general public became more and more interested in getting information from the realms of politics and society. The state advertising monopoly was abolished and the sale of advertising provided a new, important source of income. As a consequence, the newspaper itself could be sold more cheaply, which in turn expanded distribution. The rate of literacy in Germany experienced parallel growth. At only 10%, in 1750, literacy rose to over 88% in 1871, and consequently the newspaper became interesting for a much larger audience. Press censorship relaxed in Germany and in 1848 the Paulskirchenverfassung (Paulskirche Constitution) legally established freedom of the press. There were approximately 3,500 newspapers in Germany at the end of the nineteenth century. Considered the oldest public mass medium, the press was the subject of intense cultural-critical debate, just as every new mass medium initially. The first criticism to be leveled in book form was not long in coming. In "Diskurs über den Gebrauch und Missbrauch von Nachrichten, die man Newe Zeitung nennt" (Discourse about the Use and Abuse of News that is Named the New Newspaper), published in Jena in 1679, a campaign was leveled against the "newspaper reading addiction." The pastime was characterized as a "vain, unnecessary, untimely and work disruptive" pursuit.

2.5 Telecommunication Systems and Electricity

2.5.1 Optical Telegraphy

Smoke and fire signals are considered the beginning of optical telecommunication. Used in antiquity, they could bridge a greater distance more easily than was possible with relay messengers. The technology of optical signal transmission by means of relay stations had already found widespread use in ancient Greece. In his tragedy "Agamemnon", the poet *Aeschylus* (525–456 BC) reported that the Greek commander sent news of the fall of Troy (1184 BC) to his wife by way of a fire signal message. The relay spanned 9 stations on the way to the 555 km distant Argos. From Greek historian *Thucydides* (460–399 BC) comes the first description detailing the use of previously arranged fire signals in the Peloponnesian War 431–404 BC. Whereas smoke signals do not allow freely formulated messages another type of messaging that did was described by the Greek historian *Polybius* (200–120 BC). He reported about the invention of torch telegraphy in 450 BC, which allowed messages to be formed using individual letters of the alphabet. Two telegraphers stood behind a large plate and positioned the torches corresponding to letters at specific places right or left next to the plate. The Romans set up signal towers and watch towers along their empire's border (e.g., along the Limes Germanicus from the Rhine to the Danube). From these points they could communicate with each other via fire signals. The Roman writer *Vegetius Renatus* (400 AD) described how movable beams were set on high towers to signal previously arranged messages based on the varying position of the beams. As the Roman Empire declined, optical telegraphy initially lost its importance, but, especially during the times of war in the Middle Ages, it was later rediscovered in all its variations. Optical telegraphy first achieved dramatic improvement in modern history.

Prompted by the beginning Industrial Revolution as well as the profound social changes taking place in Europe in the wake of the French Revolution, the heyday of optical telegraphy broke out at the end of the eighteenth century. The **telescope**, invented in 1608 by Dutch eyeglass maker *Jan Lipperhey* (ca. 1570–1618) played a decisive role in multiplying the optical range of human perception. Englishman *Robert Hooke* (1635–1703) presented his ideas for the transmission of "thoughts over great distances" to the Royal Society in London in 1684. Hooke is also considered the inventor of the "string telephone," which however is purported to go back to the tenth century to Chinese philosopher *Kung-Foo Whing*. Hooke's telecommunication idea involved transferring individual letters, by way of rope hoists, onto large engraved boards that were to be set up on a mast system near London. Using a relay chain of similar installations it was then planned to "telegraph" all the way to Paris. The technical implementation of Hooke's idea however proved ahead of its time.

French physicist *Claude Chappe* (1763–1805) was the first to succeed in inventing a practical application – amidst the turmoil of the French Revolution. Chappe's invention was a signal transmission system with swiveling signal arms called a **semaphore** or an optical shutter telegraph and telescopes. The invention was based on the idea of deaf physicist *Guillaume Amontons* (1663–1705). In 1695, Amontons fastened and successively exchanged large pieces of cloth adorned with huge letters onto the ends of the long circular blades of a windmill in Belleville. Those in distant Meudon near Paris were able to read the letters with a telescope. British politician, inventor and writer, *Richard Lovell Edgeworth* (1744–1817) had already developed an optical telegraph in 1767 that was operated "privately" between New Market and London. It was not until 30 years later, after Claude Chappe had already successfully presented and introduced his telegraph system in France, that Edgeworth offered his telegraph to the British Admiralty.

Claude Chappe presented his telegraph for the first time to the Legislative Assembly in March 1792. The invention consisted of a five meter high mast with a two-arm cross beam and swiveling beams fastened on both its ends. The Assembly immediately decided to build one of the first 70 km long test lines between Pelletier St. Fargau and St. Martin de Thetre. After a series of successful trials, in which Chappe could prove that his apparatus was sufficiently robust and simple to operate, the first regular telegraph line could be set up in 1794 between Paris and Lille. One letter of the alphabet could be sent the length of the test line – which was 270 km long and with 22 station houses – within 2 minutes. Impressed by this speed, and the potential for military utilization, it was quickly decided to expand the telegraph system throughout France. Chappe was given permission to use any tower or church steeple desired for his telegraph line and granted the authority to remove any obstacle in the way. *Napoleon Bonaparte* (1769–1821) used the system and transported a mobile version of it with him on his campaigns. In this way he was able to coordinate troop formation and logistics over greater distances more successfully than any other army.

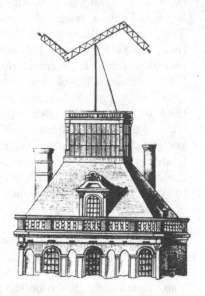

Fig. 2.11 A Chappe semaphore telegraph at the Louvre in Paris.

A disadvantage of the semaphore was that the signal poles could be seen by everyone and unauthorized people and spies could also read the military messages. This problem was resolved using encryption techniques. A country-wide star-formed network emanating from Paris existed until 1845. It connected the capital city with all other important cities in France. Depending on the terrain and visibility, the semaphores were located at intervals of nine to twelve kilometers so that the signals from the neighboring station could be unmistakably recognized. The two "telegraphists", who worked at each station, read the signals of one of the two neighboring stations and passed it on to the next station. Despite its advantages, the implementation possibilities of the optical telegraph were very limited. While one signal could be transmitted over a great distance very quickly – in 1834 a signal needed only 15 minutes for the 600 km long stretch between Berlin and Koblenz – the transmission of a complete text took a long time. The capacity of the described telegraph line was limited to two telegrams per day. On top of that, poor weather conditions were responsible for irregular and unreliable operations. These shortcomings, as well as the advent of the electric telegraph, led to giving up the last optical telegraph line in France in 1853.

2.5.2 Electric Telegraphy

The research and exploitation of electricity at the beginning of the eighteenth century had far-reaching consequences for the further development of tele-communications. Until that time the phenomenon of electricity was often viewed as a curiosity or discounted as a parlor trick. The Greek philosopher *Thales von Milet* (ca. 640–546 BC) had already recognized the magnetic effect of static electricity. He observed how a piece of amber attracted feathers when it was rubbed with a cloth. The Greek word for amber, *electron,* has been used since this time to describe the effects of electricity. Archaeological findings indicate that electricity was already being used to galvanize gilded metals in antiquity. But there was still a long way to go before electricity could be practically utilized.

Only in 1730 was the British physicist *Stephen Gray* (1666–1736) able to prove that electricity could propagate along a wire. The vision of electrical message transmission was born. With the help of conductive materials, greater distances were soon being bridged. An early form of the modern battery, the 1745 Leyden jar, was developed by Dutch physicist *Petrus van Musschenbroek* (1692–1761) Musschenbroek's invention allowed the possibility of storing electricity. In a letter published in Scots Magazine in 1753 and signed "C. M.", the writer proposed for the first time an apparatus for the electrical transmission of messages consisting of wires that corresponded to the twenty six of the letters of the alphabet[2]

However, a truly reliable and continuous supply of electricity was still missing for a practical implementation of this new means of electric communication. First in 1800 the Italian physicist *Alessandro Volta* (1745–1827), developed the first constant source of electricity, which was named the voltaic pile in his honor. Even with this source of electricity it took another twenty years before the Danish chemist *Christian Oerstedt* (1777–1851) discovered the effects of electromagnetism. This led to the development of the first **electromagnetic needle telegraph** by French scientist *André Marie Ampère* (1775–1836) in 1820. Yet even before this time in 1804 (some sources say it was already in 1795) Spanish physician and natural scientist *Francisco Salva y Campillo* (1751–1828) had constructed an **electrolyte telegraph** that used twenty-six separate transmission lines. At the end of each line was a glass tube in which a surge of power caused the fluid inside to form gas bubbles that rose to the surface. German anatomist and physiologist *Samuel Thomas von Sömmering* (1755–1830) was successful in improving the range of this technique in 1809. Nevertheless this type of electric telegraphy proved of little interest as recognition of the transmitted sign was a tedious and unreliable process.

The first truly significant practical device was invented by *Carl Friedrich Gauss* (1777–1855) and *Willhelm Weber* (1804–1891) in 1833. This was the

---

[2] The true identity of the author could never be conclusively discovered. There is evidence it was the Scotch surgeon Charles Morrison who lived in Greenock.

pointer telegraph, based on the use of just two wires and introducing a binary code system for the letters of the alphabet. In that same year they succeeded in carrying out the first telegraphic message transmission: from the physics building near St. Paul's church in the town center of Göttingen to the observatory. The inventive spirit of the times was reflected in the novel array of possibilities following in the wake of the pointer telegraph. But it was only the **writing telegraph,** presented in 1837 by *Samuel Morse,* (1791–1872), which achieved the breakthrough that led to worldwide dissemination. With his assistant *Alfred Vail* (1807–1859), Morse developed a successful alphabet code in 1840. The power of Morse's invention lay in its ingenious simplicity. It was improved even further in 1845 with the introduction of the Morse keys, which were named after the inventor, who was also an accomplished portrait painter. According to legend, just at the time Morse was working on a portrait of Portrait General Lafayette in Washington his wife became seriously ill and died. The news of her illness took seven days to reach him and as a result he never saw her alive again. In his time of mourning it was said that the idea first occurred to him of trying to break the time barrier by means of modern technology – in other words transporting messages using electricity. This would ensure that a person would never again be unable to contact a loved one in an emergency. It is, however, more probable that the idea took root when he was studying in Paris in 1829. At that time Morse became fascinated with Claude Chappe's optical telegraph, which he had seen often on his frequent trips to the Louvre. Twenty years before that time, Chappe had ordered his semaphore be placed on the Louvre's roof (see Fig. 2.11).

Besides the captivating simplicity of his invention, Morse's telegraph was impressive due to its high transmission power and weather-independent reliability.

The first 64 km long experimental line between Baltimore and Washington became the starting point for the soon rampant "telegraph fever." On May 1844 it was ceremoniously opened with the transmission of the Biblical quote: "*What Hath God Wrought!*" By 1845 there were already more than 1400 telegraph lines spanning the U.S. Because the U.S. government rejected the purchase of Morse' patent – it was of the opinion that such an undertaking could not earn a profit – the expansion of the telegraph network in the United States was financed by private operators. The first telegraph line in Europe began operation between Bremen and Bremerhaven on January 1, 1847. Quickly, telegraph networks spread out along the new railway lines.

The lion's share of the telegraphed news was initially related to the trading, shipping, stock market and the newspaper industries. The advantages it offered to these sectors soon became indispensable. Messages became commodities with an extremely short shelf life. The first news agencies that opened, e.g., the Associated Press in New York (1848) or Reuters in London (1851), owe their existence to the success of telegraphy. Morse's system was continually being improved upon and was soon passed up by a directly readable telegraph – the so-called *ticker*. This invention by music professor

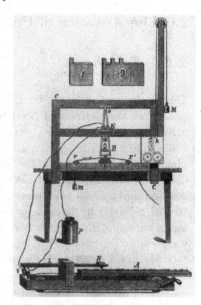

Fig. 2.12 Samuel F. B. Morse's first telegraph, from [246].

David Hughes (1831–1900) had a transmission speed of 150 characters per minute. All major telegraph lines began to use it starting in 1873. Optical telegraphy, barely a few years into operation, was being overrun by technical innovations whose possibilities met the increasing communication needs of a society formed by the Industrial Revolution. The gains in transmission capacity and speed, as well as the opening of telegraphy to individuals and private message traffic, ensured massive expansion.

Especially in terms of range, electric telegraphy opened up completely new dimensions. The first cable between England and the continent was laid in 1851 and with it the boundary created by the sea was essentially conquered. The U.S. businessman *Cyrus W. Fields* (1819–1892) succeeded in laying the first sea cable between Europe and North America in 1858. However, it could only be operated a few weeks before finally being abandoned as unusable. It was not until 1866 – and a further number of costly failures – that a reliable telegraph connection could be set up across the Atlantic between Newfoundland and Ireland. It didn't take long after that until the telegraph network had spread out throughout the whole world.

2.6 The Advance of Personal Telecommunications

2.6.1 Telephone

Telegraphy was only used for private communication in exceptional situations. Yet the desire and need to use the new form of communication for private purposes increased, particularly at the end of the nineteenth century. Coded data transmission was only carried out in one direction in telegraphic technology . But now the idea arose of transporting speech over greater distances with the help of electricity, thus opening up the possibility for a genuine dialogue to take place. A prerequisite was the realization that the **sound** received by human ears is nothing more then the periodic rise and fall in changing air pressure – in other words it takes the form of a wave. The wave character of sound was already recognized in antiquity. Roman architect *Marcus Vitruvius Pollio* (first c. BC) compared the expansion of sound to the waves of water. This knowledge was lost in the Middle Ages and it was only the physicist *Isaac Newton* (1643–1727) who was first able to establish a connection between the speed of sound and air pressure based on the wave theory he developed.

Physics teacher *Phillip Reis* (1834–1874) constructed one of the first "apparatus for the reproduction of all types of sounds,"which was modeled on the human ear. He succeeded in conducting a first public test in 1861 to electrically transmit – more or less successfully – a French horn solo with the apparatus he had developed. In contrast to Reis, whose sound transmission was based on the interruption of an electrical circuit by the vibration of a membrane, the U.S. physiologist, *Alexander Graham Bell* (1848–1922) used the electromagnetic induction discovered by *Michael Faraday* (1791–1867) to transmit speech.

"*Mr. Watson – come here – I want to see you*", is the historical phrase that comprised the first telephone call in Bell's Boston home on March 19, 1876. Watson heeded Bell's request – in other words the **telephone** – had worked. Thomas A. Watson, Graham Bell's technically gifted assistant, has this phone call to thank for his fame today. It also shows the shift in research from one scientist working alone to scientists working in research groups to advance technical innovations by way of teamwork. Bell's telephone was demonstrated for the first time on June 25, 1876 as part of the centennial celebration of America's independence in Philadelphia. After further improvements, the final, and thereby simplest, version of Bell's phone was ready in May 1877. In this case, the transmitter and the receiver were one, which meant that to make a telephone call Bell's device had to be held interchangeably to the mouth to speak and to the ear to hear.

At the same time as Graham Bell, *Elisha Gray* (1835–1901) turned in a patent for a telephones he had invented to the Washington Patent Office. A legal battle of eleven years ensured until the Supreme Court finally deter-

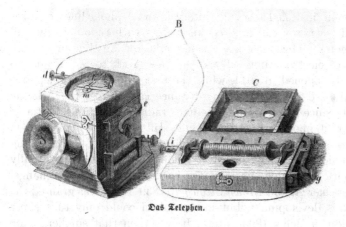

Das Telephon.

Fig. 2.13 The Phillip Reis telephone (1863).

mined Graham Bell to be the telephone's inventor.It is believed that Bell filed his patent application approximately two hours before Gray did. The *Bell Telephone Association,* founded to implement Bell's patents, used the authorization granted by the patent law ruthlessly and suppressed all other productions of telephones with its monopoly. The *American Telephone and Telegraph Company* (AT&T) eventually emerged from this company as the largest private telephone company in the world.

Just a year after Bell's invention, the first telephone network went into operation. It had just five connections and it was owned solely by bankers. Initially, the telephone had the same purpose as the telegraph, with the advantage of much greater speed and more extensive performance. As early as 1910 one fourth of all private households in the U.S. had a telephone connection. This number grew to 40% by 1925. The telephone no longer played only a significant role in business but became more and more important in inner-family communication and social life.

There were many problems that had to be solved before the telephone network would see worldwide expansion. For a long time, for example, there were unresolved issues concerning signal attenuation on longer telephone lines. While in telegraphy essentially a "digital binary" signal was transmitted, in analog telephone conversations it was necessary to transmit a complete frequency spectrum of signals. The degree of an electrical signal's attenuation on a cable depends on the signal's frequency. This means that different frequencies are attenuated in different degrees and the more the cable length increases the greater the distortion of the original signal becomes. American electrical engineer, *Michael Idvorsky Puppin* (1858–1935) developed the self-induction coil in 1899. Bestowed with the name of its inventor, the coil improves the transmission performance of telephone lines.

Pupin induction coils, installed in regular intervals on telephone lines, enabled long-distance calls over several hundred kilometers with economically still viable cable diameters. The range restriction could first be eliminated with the introduction of electron tubes. Thus, the New York to San Francisco connection could be opened in 1914, while the first transatlantic telephone cable was not finalized until 1956. Long-distance calls across the Atlantic had been possible since 1927 via intermediate radio connections. Initially, the small number of phone subscribers could still be easily managed via plug-in connectors run by the fabled "switchboard operator". The growing number of telephone subscribers, however, made it necessary to eventually change to automatic switching centers – the so-called automatic exchange. In 1889, the undertaker *Almon Brown Strowger* (1839–1902) was granted the first patent for this development, but his invention could only take effect with the expiration of Bell's 1893 patent. It was then that smaller, more flexible telephone companies arrived on the scene and gave new impetus to the market. The first completely automatic telephone exchange in the world began operation in La Porte, Illinois in 1892. In 1896, Strowger's company invented the first rotary-dial telephone.

2.6.2 From the Phonograph to the Gramophone

Around the same time as the advent of the telephone, devices for the permanent recording and conservation of sound and speech were being developed. *Thomas A. Edison* (1847–1931) set up his famous research laboratory in Menlo Park in 1876. Together with fifteen colleagues, he worked on the problems of telegraphy and telephony. In 1877, he developed the carbon microphone which considerably improved the transmission quality of the telephone and came up with the basis for constructing the **phonograph**, a device for recording sound. Three days before December 6, 1877, when Edison played the nursery rhyme "*Mary had a little lamb*" on his phonograph, a sealed envelope was opened at the Paris Academy of Science with the plans of Frenchman *Charles Cros* (1842–1888). Cros described his voice recording and playback machine, the „Pa(r)leophon," which he had already submitted on April 30 of that same year. But Cros lacked the financial means to patent his invention. Edison's phonograph, or "speaking machine" basically consisted of a tinfoil-wrapped metal cylinder that was turned with a hand crank. Recording and playback were separate. A horn directed the sound to a recording diaphragm that was caused to vibrate. With the help of a steel needle, the vibrations were scratched as spiral-shaped elevated and recessed grooves on the cylinder. If the cylinder was played again at the same speed with the needle, the recorded sound moved the diaphragm via the needle and the recorded vibrations became audible again through the horn. Copies of recordings could not be made as each cylinder could only be spoken on (= recorded) once. The sound of the recording was tinny and flat, but improved considerably after 1888 when Edison replaced the tinfoil cylinder with a wax cylinder.

Fig. 2.14 Edison with an early phonograph in 1878.

In the beginning, the phonograph was solely intended as a dictating machine for business use. Edison even tried to position his phonograph as the first telephone answering machine – without success. Due to the complex processing necessary to obtain a relatively high degree of accuracy in self-recording, and of the electric motor needed to power it, the Edison phonograph was very expensive initially. The phonograph only achieved widespread use when less expensive devices with a spring drive came on the market. The major disadvantage of the phonograph was primarily the absence of a practical method for copying the recorded cylinders.

Emil Berliner, (1851–1929), an American electrical engineer of German descent, presented the first music playing device in 1887. He called it the the **gramophone**. The gramophone was different than the phonograph from the start since it was intended purely as an entertainment medium. Because of its simple construction it could be offered much more cheaply than the phonograph. This device was only for playing and not for recording, but the Edison cylinders, which were difficult to produce on a large scale, gave way to the much easier to manufacture record. Upon entering the private market, the gramophone established itself quickly and the record became a mass product. In the years before World War I, record companies were making incredible dividends of up to 70 percent. There were already over one hundred record ("labels") by 1907. This including one dedicated to Emil Berliner's legendary dog Nipper, who was pictured famously in front of the horn of a gramophone listening to "his masters voice." Edison ended the production of cylinder phonographs in 1913 and changed to the record business.

2.6.3 Photography

Much earlier in history the development of photography had already begun with the attempt to capture a real image. As early as 900, Arab scholars had used the **pinhole camera** as an astronomical instrument for observing the solar and lunar eclipses. The principle of this invention had been discovered in antiquity and outlined by *Aristotle* (384–322 BC). The pinhole camera was described by Arab physicist and mathematician *Ibn Al-Haitham* (965–1040). In the sixteenth century this invention was fitted with a lens and developed further into the **camera obscura** (=[Lat.]dark room). The camera obscura is nothing more then a box that was blackened on the inside. On its transparent back wall (the focusing screen) an image outside of the camera, seen from a hole or a converging lens on the front of the box, is produced. The image is reduced in size, upside down and reversed. The Thüringian Jesuit priest and natural scientist *Athanasius Kircher* (1601–1680) was the first to come up with the idea of installing a lens in the camera obscura. At night, with the aid of candles, he would project pictures on the paper windows of the house across from his. He amused and terrified viewers by projecting frighting devils or enormous flies on the wall. Such images led to the use of the name magic lantern – or laterna magica – in popular vernacular.

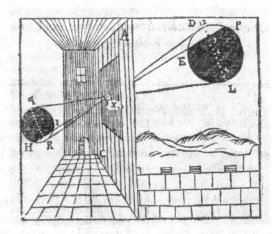

Fig. 2.15 The principle of the camera obscura (1646), from [135].

The camera obscura was also used as a tool by artists to make their drawings as life-like as possible up through the nineteenth century. *Antonio Canaletto* (1697–1768), famous for his magnificent cityscapes, worked out initial sketches of the view of a city using a portable camera obscura. But what was still missing in photography was a way to make a lasting image on the screen.

By the seventeenth century it was known that numerous substances, such as silver compounds, change their color or become black when exposed to the sunlight. In Halle on the Saale River in 1727, the German physician *Heinrich Schulze* (1687–1744) discovered that this phenomenon was not caused by the sun's heat but by light energy. Schulze successfully produced the first – albeit non-permanent – photographic images.

An article written *Thomas Wedgewood* (1771–1805) appeared in London in 1802 providing a complete description of the most important ideas of photographic technology. Fifteen years later, the French officer and scholar *Nicéphore Niepce* (1765–1833) was successful in the first practical application of these ideas and developed lasting photographs using a method he had invented called **heliography**, The celebrated Paris theater designer *Louis Jacques Mandé Daguerre* (1787–1851), a highly ambitious businessman, became his partner, carrying on Niepce's work after his death. Daguerre developed a technique that was subsequently named after him: the **daguerreotype**. With this technique an exact reproduction of the scene was created using silver iodine plates. However, the image could not be duplicated and therefore remained an original. He asked the famous French scientist *Francois Dominique Arago* (1786–1853), to present his invention at the Paris Academy of Science in 1839. Because Daguerre's background was non-academic he was not taken seriously in scientific circles. Arago succeeded in justifying the new process as a scientific method and motivated the French government to buy the process from Daguerre for a considerable sum of money. Daguerre had already ordered a patent application for the procedure in London five days earlier.

The first positive-negative process to allow the reproduction of unlimited prints was invented in 1839 by Englishman *William Fox Talbot* (1800–1877) and called the **calotype**. Talbot had the ingenious idea of creating a negative image from which any number of positive prints could be made, rather than making just a single positive image as had been done previously. To do this he pressed an already exposed paper together with one that was unexposed under a glass plate and placed them in the sunlight. The dark objects appeared on the second sheet and – in contrast to previous methods – as a non-reversed image. This image, which is still produced today in a similar manner, is known as a contact print. In the years that followed, the market for photography expanded rapidly. Besides the artistic abilities required, craftsmanship skills were also necessary. Photographers had to produce their photo material themselves, which stood in the way of even greater dissemination of the medium.

With the further development of photographic technology it became possible to reduce the exposure time needed. While with Niépce's method several hours were necessary, Daguerre was already able to reduce this time to minutes. The English sculptor *Frederick Scott Archer* (1813–1857) developed a wet process based on collodion plates in 1851. Exposure time could be decreased to just a few seconds, which made the daguerreotype obsolete. Collodion is a viscous emulsion composed of nitrocellulose in alcohol and ether. It was commonly used in medicine to close open wounds. Archer's collodium plate had to be prepared at the photo location directly prior to being exposed and put into the camera while it was still wet (thus the name of the procedure). English physician *Richard Leach Maddox* (1816–1902) improved the technique even further. In 1871, he replaced Archer's collodion with a gelatin mixture containing bromide silver as a photosensitive layer. The bromide silver paper prepared this way enabled reprints to be produced from negatives in seconds. It is still the basis for the process used today. In contrast to Archer's collodion plates, the gelatin coated plates did not need to be processed immediately, but could be stored for months at a time before their actual exposure.

The breakthrough of photography for the general public was initiated by the American *George Eastman* (1854–1932). Eastman, a former savings bank employee, brought to the market a flexible and easy to handle roll film in 1888. This film was part of a complete infrastructure ranging from the camera to the development and enlargement service, all of which was incorporated under the name he invented: "Kodak." Eastman's "Kodak box" camera was sold already loaded with film and cost 25 U.S. dollars. After the hundred film images had been photographed, the camera was sent to the Kodak plant. The pictures were then developed and camera returned with a new film – all in just a few days. By separating the actual photography process from the chemical film development process it suddenly became possible to be an amateur photographer without any special training or prior knowledge. With his slogan, "You press the button, we do the rest," Eastman paved the way to mass market photography.

The path from analog film to the digital image was a short one. It began between 1960 and 1970 when ideas were being generated during the U.S. space program about how to get still images and moving video images from groups of discrete sensor elements. The breakthrough in the development of **digital photography** came in 1973 with a CCD image sensor (Charge-Coupled Device), developed by the Fairchild company. With this high-resolution sensor, light pulses could be transformed into electrical signals. *Steven Sasson* (*1950), developmental engineer at Eastman Kodak, constructed the first prototype of a digital camera in 1975 using this technology. The black and white photographs could be saved on an incorporated tape cartridge. The camera's resolution was just 10,000 pixels (0.01 mega pixels). Weighing nearly 4 kg, the camera required 23 seconds to take one picture. The first reasonably priced digital camera appeared on the retail market at the end of 1990s, sparking a huge interest in digital photography. Digital camera technology has now almost completely replaced its analog predecessor.

2.7 Wireless Telecommunications – Radio and Television

2.7.1 Wireless Telegraphy

In terms of their historical origin – the telegraph – the development of both wireless telegraphy and the radio are closely connected to telephone technology. A number of radio pioneers were fundamental in laying the groundwork for wireless technology. They include Michael Faraday, *James Clerk Maxwell* (1831–1879), *Heinrich Hertz* (1857–1895) and *Eduard Branly* (1846–1940). Two other great figures stand out in light of their work at the end of the nineteenth century, which paved the way for wireless communication: the Russian naval architect *Alexander Stephanowitsch Popov* (1858–1906) and the Italian engineer and physicist *Guglielmo Marconi* (1874–1934).

Maxwell was the first to postulate the existence of electromagnetic waves that originate when electric and magnetic fields rapidly change their strength. He created the theoretical basis for a new way to communicate over virtually boundless distances. Maxwell's **radio technology** theory, as described in his essay published in 1873, "*A Dynamical Theory of the Electromagnetic Field,*" was completely unknown until that time. In his laboratory in Karlsruhe, Hertz succeeded in producing evidence of Maxwell's wave theory in 1885. Hertz proved that electromagnetic waves do in fact have all of the characteristics of physical waves and only differ in their frequencies. He did not however yet see a practical use for his discovery. The next step in developing the radio receiver was undertaken by French physicist Branly in 1890. Branley was able to convert electromagnetic waves into electrical impulses. He discovered that metal shavings, which are normally poor conductors, align themselves into coherent – unidirectional and contiguous – bundles under the influence of electromagnetic waves. On the basis of this discovery, he developed the first radio tube in the world known as the *coherer*.

Popov presented a complete receiver for electromagnetic waves in 1895. Because an adequate transmission device was still lacking, Popov constructed a thunderstorm detector on the basis of Branly's coherer. It could receive the electromagnetic waves in the atmosphere caused by lightning discharges. The next year at the University of St. Petersburg he succeeded in sending wireless signals over a distance of 250 meters with the help of a transmitting device he had constructed. That same year Popov was also able to prove that wide area signal transmission is possible over a distance of more than 30 kilometers. He did this by means of his specially developed balloon antenna.

One of the first areas of application for this new **wireless telegraphy** was in marine radio. Marconi's first experiments were designed for this area. Marconi received a patent in 1896 for his work, combining the technology of Popov (antenna, relay and bell), Hertz (high frequency generator) and Branly (coherer). This was the foundation of his ongoing work in increasing the remote effect of radio signals. Up to that time electromagnetic waves had been generated using a spark gap. German physicist and radio pioneer *Karl Ferdinand Braun* (1850–1918) used an oscillating circuit, which he coupled directly with an antenna. By way of this 1898 patented "coupled" transmitter it was possible to direct radio waves in a certain direction and achieve greater range.

Fig. 2.16 Portrait of the radio pioneer Guglielmo Marconi (1874–1937).

On December 12, 1901 Marconi carried out the first wireless transmission across the Atlantic between England and Newfoundland. The first commercial, transatlantic wireless telegraphy service was then set up in 1907. The military's demand for the written documentation of a message was an important reason why the new technology was only able to catch on slowly. Nevertheless, the new wireless technology was used by the army and the navy on opposing sides in World War I. With the sinking of the Titanic in the night from April 14 to April 15, 1912, the new wireless technology was suddenly seen in a different light. It had become a medium to enable coordinated rescue operations on the high seas. The most advanced ship in the world had gone down, but even as it was sinking the new technology had made it possible to maintain a connection with the mainland. The sinking of the Titanic had far-reaching consequences. Only a few months later at the Third International Radiotelegraphic Convention in London – the so-called Titanic conference – it was decided that all owners would have to equip their ships with wireless technology. Additionally, the international distress frequency and establishment of the "SOS"-emergency signal were declared.

The introduction of the three-electrode vacuum tube with metal mesh, known as the **triode**, was invented in 1908 by the American *Lee De Forest* (1873–1961) and the Austrian *Robert von Lieben* (1878–1913). This led to a breakthough in amplifier technology, which until now had been based on the Branly coherer. From this point on, until the advent of the transistor in 1947, triode tubes became the foundation of wireless technology.

2.7.2 Radio

The first radio broadcast in history happened on December 25, 1906. Radio operators on ships off the coast of Newfoundland were undoubtedly astonished to suddenly hear a voice – between the beeps of the Morse code – read the Christmas story from the Gospel of Luke, followed by a violin rendition of "Silent Night". *Reginald Fessenden* (1866–1932), a Canadian engineer and inventor, can be credited with this first experimental transmission. Fessenden and his assistant had already been able to carry out the first broadcast of a voice in 1900 with the help of the modulation process he had developed.

The idea of establishing a "broadcast medium for everyone" and developing it as a viable financial commodity can be attributed to *David Sarnoff* (1891–1971), one of Marconi's radio technicians and later the deputy director of the American Marconi Company. Sarnoff achieved fame as the radio operator who received the signal of the sinking Titanic at Nantucket Island in Massachusetts. For a continuous seventy-two hours thereafter he received and forwarded the names of those who had been saved. Sarnoff had already contacted Marconi in 1916 with his idea of a "radio music box." He visualized it as a household consumer article such as the piano or phonograph. Initially dismissed as a crazy idea, Sarnoff's vision was seen as having little chance of success in the face of the ongoing patent war between various wireless pioneers. But he presented his plan once again in 1920 in the light of its financial promise, and this time he was successful. The **radio** was born. Given the prevailing laws of warfare, the American government controlled all patents. This situation resulted in the formation of an pan-American radio company: the Radio Corporation of America (RCA). Subsequently, RCA became the largest manufacturer of radios worldwide.

The first commercial radio station to regularly broadcast was the American station KDKA. It received its license in October 1920 and then began transmission on November 2, 1920 in Pittsburgh. KDKA used the medium wave range and broadcast entertainment and informational programs. This first radio station was born out of the activities of an early radio operator, former navy officer and employee of the telegraph company Westinghouse, *Frank Conrad,* (1874–1941). Between 1918 and 1919, Conrad began playing phonograph records and piano compositions on the radio from his garage, at first, only for testing purposes. He requested that neighboring amateur radio operators give him feedback on the quality of transmission. His "ether concerts," alway broadcast Friday nights, soon turned into a popular recreational activity. Conrad began working on a broadcast station. The first public radio transmission was a live broadcast of the American presidential election results. Within just a few months numerous other stations and companies in a range of branches began the autonomous transmission of shows and programs for promotional purposes.

At the same time in Germany a public broadcasting system was also developing. On November 19, 1919, radio pioneer *Hans Bredow* (1879–1959) showed the function of entertainment broadcasting during a public demonstration. It was Bredow who first coined the German term for radio broadcasting: "Rundfunk." A decisive event took place in the development of the medium with the so-called "*Funkerspuk*" (radio operator ghost). Following the example of the revolutionaries in Russia, on November 9, 1918 workers took over the headquarters of the German Press News Service and erroneously announced the victory of the radical revolution in Germany. As a result, the first control laws went into effect to prevent abuse of the new medium. The German Empire adopted the right of sovereignty in 1919. This meant that the establishment and operation of transmission and receiving equipment was subject to authorization. From 1922, the reception of radio broadcasts was forbidden for private citizens. Although this law was revoked the following year, an obligatory fee was enacted. The birth of German radio is considered October 29, 1923, the date that the first radio entertainment show was broadcast from the Vox-Haus in Berlin-Tiergarten, near Potsdamer Platz in Berlin.

Radio broadcasting quickly became a mass medium with politicians also recognizing the immense potential of wireless communication. The abuse of broadcasting for manipulative propaganda took place at the latest in 1933 with the German National Socialists much promoted "Volksempfänger" – the so-called people's wireless. The first inexpensive Volksempfänger, the famous VE301 (the number 301 signified the day that the National Socialists had seized power in Germany), was produced in the millions. Two of its features were that it could not be attached as an asset in the case of financial debts nor could it receive foreign broadcasts.

On December 23, 1957, the Americans *John Bardeen* (1908–1991), *Walter House Brattain* (1902–1987) and *William Shockley* (1910–1989) presented the first **transistor** at Bell Laboratories/New York. As a group they were awarded the Nobel Prize for their invention in 1956. For demonstration purposes they removed all vacuum tubes from a conventional tube radio and replaced them with transistors. This marked the birth of the transistor radio. The Bell Telephone company, which laid out tremendous personnel costs for the upkeep of their telephone network, had offered the challenge of developing a more reliable and durable switch than the error-prone vacuum tube. After countless trials, the team led by Shockley was able to develop the first transistor from semiconducting materials as a switching element. No one at that time could guess what the impact of this discovery would be and its importance in all areas of electronics. Because Bell laboratories had to release the patent in return for payment of license fees, many producers were able to share in a further utilization of the transistor from the beginning. The U.S. company Texas Instruments put the first commercial transistor radio on the market in 1954. The transistor allowed the construction of lighter and more mobile devices, which was a crucial advantage for radio manufacturers. Transistor radios achieved dramatic widespread success.

2.7.3 Film and Cinema

The film or moving picture created by optical or mechanical means did not originate using images from the real world but with man-made sketches and pictures. The underlying principle relies on the phenomenon of retinal inertia, which was already described by *Ptolemy of Alexandria* (85–165 AD) in the second century. A visual image remains on the retina of the human eye for approx. 1/16 second before it disappears. This phenomenon, only first rediscovered in the nineteenth century, led to the development of the first mechanical apparatus for viewing moving images. Viewed in rapid succession, a sequence of stroboscope pictures gives the illusion of movement. Founded on developments such as French physiologist *Étienne Jules Marey's* (1830–1904), "photographic gun" (1882), Thomas A. Edison turned in a patent in 1889 for the **cinematographer**. This was followed in 1894 by the cinematoscope, a projection device for the new medium. Both apparatus were based on the same principle. A celluloid film strip was mechanically transported past a lens and could thereby be illuminated and viewed. A definite disadvantage of the cinematoscope was that only one person at a time could use it. Because Edison underestimated the importance of film, he did not make any further efforts to develop the cinematoscope as a projection device.

This was first accomplished by the brothers *Louis Jean Lumière* (1864–1948) and *Auguste Lumière* (1862–1954) with their fully developed cinematographic process in 1895. On December 28, 1895 the team introduced their first film to a large, paying audience at the Grand Cafè on Boulevard des Capucines in Paris. The event heralded the beginning of the cinema era. It should be noted that two months before the success of the Lumière brothers, the two German showmen *Max* and *Emil Skladanowsky* (1863–1939 and 1859–1945) had shown their first film to an astounded audience at the Berlin Wintergarten vaudeville. They used a projector of their own invention called a bioscope. As factory owners, the Lumière brothers had the necessary capital and contact to the industry as well as their own "cinématographe," which functioned as a film camera, copier and film projector all in one. They were thus able to support their invention's success in the years ahead. The Lumières lent and sold their apparatus to showmen who presented short films, first at county fairs and then later in their role as traveling cinema operators. As the recognition and popularity of films grew, the first local cinemas sprung up. In Germany they were given the name "kintop" and in the U.S. "nickelodeon."

To attract visitors, these cinemas relied on a continuous supply of new films. The Lumières saw film purely as an expansion or complement to photography and limited themselves to documenting actual experiences. The French theater owner *Georges Mèliés* was the first film producer to recognize the narrative (story-telling) potential of moving pictures. The birth of the film industry is recognized as taking place in 1896 when *Mèliés* started to make films exclusively presenting staged narratives.

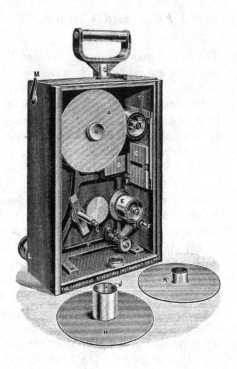

Fig. 2.17 1917 Cinema-tograph, from [46].

As soon as film came into being an attempt was made to combine it with the Edison phonograph, yet the necessary synchronization of both media presented a significant problem that had yet to be solved. In scenes with dialogue, irregularities in synchronization were perceived immediately. A way still had to be found to capture image and sound in one medium. At the same time, cinema films were never truly silent. From the beginning, live music accompanied films in movie theaters. Usually pianists called "tappeurs" performed this task. However, at film premieres or in large theaters, orchestras might even be used to carry out accompaniment. A practical procedure to make the "talkies" possible first came along with implementation of the so-called photo-electric effect. This effect allowed the conductivity of certain substances to change their properties in different lighting conditions. With this optical sound recording process, a soundtrack can be stored synchronous with the image on the optical film carrier medium. In 1922, the Polish engineer *Jòzef Tykociński-Tykociner* (1877–1969) developed the first technical implementation of this optical sound recording process in the U.S. Independent of Tykocinski-Tykociner's invention, the German engineer *Hans Vogt* (1890–1979) also developed an optical sound process, and on September 17, 1922 presented the first short optical sound film to the public in the Berlin movie theater Alhambra on Kurfürstendamm.The talkies were not immediately successful in Germany. The sound film patent was purchased by *William Fox* (1879–1952) in the U.S. who would make the talking picture into a worldwide success. On October 6, 1927 the "The Jazz Singer," with Al Jolson in the leading role, premiered. The film, produced by Warner Brothers, was the first full-length talkie and a fitting beginning to herald the new era in film making. Now there are digital optical tracks, such as the Dolby Stereo SR Digital, the most often used digital sound procedure today. Here, in contrast to the analog optical sound process, the sound is not copied onto the movie in analog form, but rather as digital information. This information is collected by a photo cell and subsequently converted into audio signals via a decoder. Digital optical tracks allow a higher dynamic range and thus a better sound quality, more channels for improved spatial imaging of sound and increased noise reduction.

2.7.4 Television

Just as with film, television uses the phenomena of retinal inertia. Television, the electromagnetic transmission of moving pictures, is founded on the principle of the resolution of a mosaic image, consisting of a series of lines and points. When instantaneously reassembled, the original image appears. Retina inertia is exploited in television viewing in the sense that it is possible to recognize a whole picture when each individual image frame is displayed. Based on the systematic scanning of a scene for obtaining signals, engineer *Paul Nipkow* (1860–1940) developed a scanning disk. The disk, with a series of holes spiraling toward the center, rotates as it picks up a part of the image. Nipkow obtained a patent for his invention in 1884. On the transmitter side, the scene to be recorded is scanned line by line with the help of the Nipkow disk. Thereby, the spatial juxtaposition of the individual image points i.e., their brightness value, is converted, with the help of light sensitive selenuium cells, into a temporally aligned coexistence of different voltage levels. The same principal is applied on the receiving side and the image is reassembled. The invention was called the "electrical telescope". Nipkow's patent, which had already expired in 1885 due to a lack of funds, served as the foundation for the work of numerous other television pioneers. The word "television" came into use in France and the U.S. after the turn of the century, whereas the German word "fernsehen" first came into being around 1890.

With the advent of the cathode radio tube, invented by Karl Ferdinand Braun in 1897 and named after him, it became possible to develop the first electro-mechanical television in the world. This was first done by the German physicist *Max Dieckmann Rosing* (1882–1960) and the Russian physicist *Boris Iwanowitsch Rosing* (1869–1933) and intended for use as a playback device. The first public telecast did not take place until 1925, when it was then broadcast – nearly simultaneously – in three countries at once: in Germany by *August Karolus* (1893–1972), in Great Britain by *John Logie Baird* (1888–1946) and in the U.S. by *Charles Francis Jenkins* (1867–1934). The first era of the electromechanical television ended in 1928/1929. At this time there were already 60-line scanning instruments available and the first "regularly scheduled" television shows were being aired in the U.S.

The first completely electronic television camera, the iconoscope, was patented in 1923 by *Vladimir K. Zworykin* (1889–1982), who is considered the father of modern television. The first electronic picture tube – the kinoscope – followed in 1929. Initially, Zworykin could only broadcast a simple cross with his method. Thus the company where he worked, the Westinghouse Electric Corporation in Pittsburgh, showed little interest in his new invention. Armed with a new version in 1929, Zworykin succeeded in convincing radio pioneer David Sarnoff about the promise of his invention. Sarnoff hired Zworykin as the director of electronic research at RCA. Zworykin received the patent for his completely electronic television system based on the iconoscope and the kinoscope in 1939.

The first regular television program started in Germany in 1935, but it would only be in operation for half a year. It was based on a 180-line method. The British Broadcasting Corporation (BBC), founded in 1922, was already operating a high-resolution 405-line television service between 1936–1939. This is generally considered to be the first modern television service in the world. The BBC television service was based on a system developed by *Isaac Shoenberg* (1880–1963). It was a further development of Zworykin's method using microwaves for signal transmission. BBC retained the Schoenberg system (405 lines, 25 images per second) until 1962. In 1953, the American NTSC color television process (NTSC=National Television System Committee) was released. While the American company CBS had already presented a color television system in 1940, it still had a long war to go. The American public made a slower than expected transition from the black and white to the color receiver. The NTSC sytem had been developed too quickly to ensure a truly optimal coloration. Consequently, NTSC was soon dubbed "Never The Same Color." The NTSC color television system was finally able to prevail over the black and white television because of its compatibility properties. Color television broadcasts could be viewed with a black and white receiver without a loss of clarity, and black and white television broadcasts could be seen via color television receivers as well as black and white receivers.

The SECAM ([Fr.] *Séquence á Mémoire*) norm followed in France in 1957. In 1963, based on the experience with NTSC and SECAM, *Walter Bruch*

Table 2.2 Milestones in the History of Communication Media (2)

1184 BC	News of the fall of Troy is telegraphed to Greece via torch signals
150 BC	First description of retinal inertia
1608	Invention of the telescope in Holland
1684	Robert Hooke's "On Showing a Way How to Communicate One's Mind at Great Distances"
1690	Guillaume Amonton's first experiment with the semaphore
1730	Stephen Gray shows that electricity propagates along a wire
1745	Electricity can be stored for the first time by means of the Leyden jar
1794	Start of the first regular optical telegraph line between Paris and Lille
1809	Samuel Thomas Sömmerring improves the electrolyte telegraph
1816	Nicèphore Niepce develops photography
1819	Christian Oerstedt discovers electromagnetism
1820	Andrè Marie Ampére's invents the electromagnetic needle telegraph
1831	Michael Faraday discovers electromagnetic induction
1833	Carl Friedrich Gauss and Wilhelm Weber develop the pointer telegraph
1838	Samuel Morse's writing telegraph heralds the breakthrough for the telegraph
1840	Introduction of the Morse alphabet
1845	Star-shaped optical telegraph network established throughout France
1851	First undersea telegraph cable laid between England and the Continent
1856	Laying of the first Transatlantic cable
1860	James Maxwell develops a unified theory for electricity and magnetism
1877	Alexander Graham Bell and Elisha Gray develop the telephone
1877	Thomas A. Edison demonstrates the first phonograph
1886	Heinrich Hertz discovers electromagnetic waves
1888	George Eastman develops photography for the general public
1889	Almon B. Strowger invents the automatic telephone exchange
1889	Thomas A. Edison's cinematography heralds the dawning of a new age
1893	The first automatic exchanges for telephone calls are set up in the U.S.
1893	Louis und Auguste Lumière present a public viewing of the first film
1896	Alexander Popow succeeds in making the first wireless message transmission
1901	Gugliemo Marconi carries out the first wireless communication across the Atlantic
1919	Hans Bredow propagates the notion of "radio for the people"
1924	August Karolus succeeds in transmitting the inaugural television picture
1927	"The Jazz Singer,"the first talking movie, is released in cinemas
1935	First regular television program service in Berlin is set up
1935	First tape recorder with electromagnetic recording from AEG
1962	Premier of direct television transmission via satellite between U.S. and Europe
1973	Earliest digital image sensor (CCD) for digital cameras
1982	Phillips and Sony introduce the digital audio compact disc (CD)
1995	Introduction of the digital versatile disc (DVD) as a storage medium
2002	Specification of the Blu-ray Disc and the HD DVD
2008	Terrestrial analog television is replaced in Germany by the digital version DVB

(1908–1990) developed PAL (*Phase Alternation Line*) color television broadcast technology in Germany. And in 1983, the first high definition television
technology was introduced in Japan (High Definition TeleVision). A more
detailed look is presented in section 4.6.1.

2.7.5 Analog and Digital Recording Methods

The possibility of recording image and sound content on the basis of an
electromagnetic process can be traced back to the nineteenth century. The
first magnetic recording technologies, for example from *Paul Janet* (1863–
1937) in 1887, proposed magnetic sound recording on steel wire. *Kurt Stille's*
(1873–1957) dictaphone, "Dailygraph,"made a recording time of two hours
possible via its extremely thin 4400 meter long wire. The great breakthrough
came however with magnetic tape. In 1928 a magnet tape method based
on paper was patented by *Fritz Pfleumer* (1897–1945). The AEG and BASF
companies subsequently replaced the paper with plastic-based magnetic tape .
The first **tape recorder** in the world, the "Magnetophon K1," was presented
to the public at the Berliner Funkausstellung (Broadcasting Exhibition). Used
at first only in the professional arena, tape recording technology witnessed a
worldwide boom in the wake of a complete loss of German patent ownership
following World War II. The first device for private use was put on the market
in 1947 by the the American company Brush Development Co. In 1956, the
first technologically feasible method for magnetically recording wide-band
television signals was presented in 1956. *Charles P. Ginsburg* (1920–1992),
an engineer at the Ampex company, introduced a new frequency modulation
method for picture signals.
The replacement of analog storage media, and thus the introduction of digital storage and reproduction technology, had its origin in wide-area telephone
transmission via a wireless connection. *Alec A. Reeves* (1902–1971) developed the pulse code modulation method (PCM)in 1938. A series of individual
impulses were transmitted in rapid succession with a constant amplitude.
The discrete signals to be transmitted can be represented with the help of a
binary code. Because the stored information is not dependent on the pulse
amplitude, i.e., signal noise does not change the coded information, PCM
signals are virtually disturbance free, compared to the standard modulation procedurePCM audio recorders were first used at the end of the sixties.
Phillips and Sony introduced the digital audio **compact disc** (CD-DA) to
the public in 1979. This disk-shaped storage medium has a radius of 11.5
centimeters (coincidentally the same size as Emil Berliner's first record!) and
offered (initially) a storage space of seventy-four minutes or 650 MB. A CD
is a 1.2 thick polycarbonate disk coated with a vaporized layer of aluminum.
Digital information is pressed inside before the disc is sealed with a lacquer
coating. In contrast to the spiral grooves of the analog audio record, the in-

formation on the CD is represented on microscopically small, long recesses called ("pits"). These recesses are scanned by a 780 nanometer laser beam and then converted back into acoustic signals by the electronics of the player. The running track from the inside to the outside has a recordable spiral of nearly six kilometers (with a width of 0.6 μm). The transition from the pit to the higher area around it, called the "land", or from the land to the pit, represent a logical one. A transition from pit to pit or land to land represents a logical zero.

A long battle ensured over the establishment of a unified standard and methods of copyright protection. Once agreement had been reached the first Digital Versatile Disc (DVD) was born in 1995. In comparison to a CD it offered multiple memory (up to 17GB by using multiple optical layers and both sides of the DVD). It was initially used for the digital storage of compressed video data. At the same time, demand increased for even greater storage capacity such as was necessary for recording the high resolution television standard **HDTV** (High Definition TeleVision). At the beginning, there were two competing standards in this area: the Blu-ray disc and the leading HD DVD (High Density DVD), developed by Toshiba. The **Blu-ray Disc**, whose name comes from the violet-blue short-wavelength laser beam employed in the scanning process, has a higher storage capacity, at 25GB (single layer) up to 50GB (dual layer), than does the HD DVD, with its 15GB or 30GB storage capacity. The Blue-ray Disc was able to gain a firm foothold on the market in February 2008 with Toshiba's announcement to cease further development and production of the HD DVD.

2.8 The Computer as a Universal Personal Communication Manager

Today the computer is often viewed as the "key medium" of the future, having already surpassed television in this role. It is often overlooked that viewed from the perspective of its historical development the computer was actually not intended as a medium specialized in the functions of recording, storing, transmitting and reproducing information. Developments in the past twenty-five years have allowed the computer the capabilities of processing analog, acoustic or optical information But first with the advent of the Internet and WWW did the computer come to the forefront as a medium offering the integrative transport of multimedia information.

The computer's origin as an instrument for performing automatic calculation goes back to antiquity. Calculating instruments made of wood, metal or stone – the so-called **abacus** – were prevalent as early as the third century BC in Greece and Rome. The size of a postcard, they were easy to transport and widely used. Our word "calculation" stems from the name for the stones of the abacus – *claviculi* or *calculi*. These stones were moved on the board by the counting master, the *calculator*, to carry out the four basic types of arithmetic.In China the use of a calculating instrument much like the abacus – the suan-pan – can even be traced back to the first century BC. To be able to carry out complicated multiplication more easily, the Scottish mathematician *John Napier* (1550–1617) invented the first slide rule in 1617. It was a simple multiplication table of movable rods that was based on the logarithms and decimal point that Napier had introduced in 1614.

Fig. 2.18 The personified arithmetic (Arithmetica) with Pythagoras (left) and Boethius (right), as they carry on a contest of calculation using the abacus and modern Arabic numerals (1504).

Even before this time, *Leonardo da Vinci* had designed the first mechanical clock with a pendulum in 1494. Two hundred years would still pass before a successfully working pendulum clock was to be constructed. At the same time, the precision engineering necessary to create the clock became the basis for the first mechanical calculator. Work on designing a complex calculating machine was done in the seventeenth century mainly by *Willhelm Schickard* (1592–1635), *Blaise Pascal* (1623–1662) and *Gottfried Wilhelm Leibniz* (1646–1716). Schickard constructed the first **gear-driven calculating machine** in 1623 to help reduce the tedious calculation his friend, the astronomer *Johannes Kepler* (1571–1630), had to carry out in determining the position of the planets. Unfortunately, Kepler never had a chance to implement the machine as it was destroyed by a fire still in its semi-finished state. Schickard's machine could perform the four basic arithmetic operations, whereby it was necessary to rely on the manual assistance of calculating rods in figuring subproducts. There was a six-digit decimal display. His invention was subsequently forgotten, and in 1642 French mathematician Blaise Pascal reinvented the gear-driven calculating machine. For centuries Pascal was considered the inventor of the mechanical adding machine. The nineteen-year old Pascal developed his adding machine to help his father, a royal tax official, with his work. Both basic arithmetic types – addition and subtraction – could be performed with the machine and it was built over fifty times with just a few sold. One of the first **mechanical calculating machines**, which also allowed direct multiplication based on repeated addition, was constructed by German mathematician Gottfried Wilhelm Leibniz.

In order to perform multiplication with larger numbers it is necessary to store the multiplicand, in contrast to a simple adding machine. The entry register must also be movable parallel to the result register so that correct addition can be performed with multiple positions. To do this Leibniz used the so-called stepped drum, an arrangement of axially parallel ribbed teeth of graduated length. Depending on the position of a second movable gear, as the stepped drum turned it was rotated from zero up to nine teeth. In his lifetime Leibniz was never ever to solve the problem of the ten transfer across multiple positions. His machine was first perfected in 1894 with the advance of precision mechanics. Leibniz developed the binary number and arithmetic system in 1679, which was to become the foundation for the construction of the modern computer.

The **punched card** first appeared as an important element for the storage and calculation of information when *Joseph Marie Jacquard* (1752–1834) perfected his early programmable pattern loom in 1805. Jacquard first separated the software – the control program in the form of punched cards or strips – from the hardware – the machine itself, which worked according to instructions punched into the cards. Depending on the punched card or program, the machine was capable of producing a fabric with a predetermined pattern and colors. Via the punched card, Jacquard designed the basic architecture of all data-processing machines and computers binary systems in mechanical engineering that is still relevant today. Where the needle met a hole in the punched card that had a one one a change took place. The state remained unchanged – a zero – when the needle touched the pasteboard.

The punched card was first used in a mechanical calculating machine in 1822 – *Charles Babbage's* (1791–1871) "**difference engine.**" As a professor of mathematics, Babbage noticed that the creation of mathematical tables was often based solely on the simple "mechanical" repetition of certain steps. However, errors in calculation very often resulted. His subsequent research was thus based on the mechanical transformation of mathematical problems and their solution. His steam-driven and locomotive-size difference engine, presented in 1822, was designed to solve differential equations and to print out the results immediately. After Babbage had worked for ten years on this machine he had the idea of designing a freely programmable calculating machine capable of performing any given calculations. He called it the "**analytical engine.**" Conceptually, it exhibited all the qualities of a modern computer:

a number memory for fifty-digit decimal numbers to be implemented with the help of 50,000 individual gear wheels, an arithmetic unit and a control unit for the entire program operation, including calculating operation and data transport. Babbage's assistant, *Augusta Ada King, Countess of Lovelace* (1815–1842), daughter of English poet Lord Byron, contributed significantly to the design of the machine. As one of the few people who was in able to assess the possibilities of the analytical engine, she developed the first program routines with such advanced concepts as branching logic, program loops and jump instructions, which made possible the cyclical operation of computational instructions. Babbage's conception of mechanized computing was ahead of its time. He was however thwarted by precision mechanics that were not yet advanced enough for the manufacture of such a complex machine. It was not until 1989 and 1991 that a fully functional reproduction of Babbage's Difference Engine could be made by the London Science Museum.

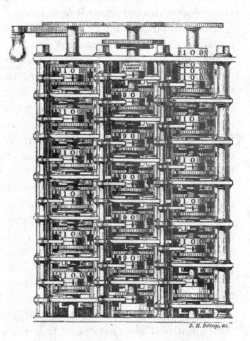

Fig. 2.19 Conceptual sketches for Charles Babbage' Difference Engine (1833).

Like Babbage, the American inventor *Hermann Hollerith* (1860–1929) also used punched cards and, with the help of the first functional data processing system, supported efforts to carry out the American census. Analyzing the previous U.S. census without any mechanical means had been a huge undertaking and lasted nearly seven years. With the population boom and increase in the number of questions, the authorities feared that the time needed for a new census could even stretch to ten years. It was clear that they had to find a solution. Hollerith received the patent for a **punched card tabula-**

ting machine in 1890. In contrast to Babbage's machine, it used punched cards to store data rather than to control the calculation process. Hollerith's punched card was a highly flexible storage medium, which together with an electro-mechanical reader anticipated the possibilities of today's data processing: database setup, counting, sorting and searches based on specific criteria. Using Hollerith's machine it was possible to complete the evaluation of the 11th U.S. population census in a period of only six weeks instead of the ten years that had been originally projected.

The first operational, **program-controlled computing machine** was constructed in 1937 by *Konrad Zuse* (1910–1995). The fully automatic "Z1", was based on the principles of the binary calculation introduced by *George Boole* (1815–1864). In 1941, on orders of the Reich Ministry of Aviation, Zuse built one of the first electromechanical computers, the "Z3."It used logical switching elements based on electromechanical relays [261]. Besides Zuse there were a number of other scientists who worked on the realization of freely programmable computing machines at the end of the 1930s. The American mathematician *Howard H. Aiken* (1900–1973) began constructing a mainframe computer at Harvard University in 1939. The "Harvard Mark I,"was completed in 1944. In addition to punch-card assemblies, it was consisted of electromechanical relays and tubes. The war effort and new possibilities of secret military wireless communication, for example the German cipher machine "Enigma," for the encryption of alphanumerical information, or the prediction of missile trajectories, encouraged the development of automatic computing systems. England began construction of a computing system under the alias "Colossus."It became operational in 1943 and was used for decrypting secret radio messages transmitted by the German Wehrmacht.

The first **fully-electronic, general-purpose** computer, based entirely on electron tubes, was invented in 1945 at the University of Pennsylvania. It was constructed by *John P. Eckert* (1919–1995), *John W. Mauchly* (1907–1980), *Herman H. Goldstine* (1913–2004) and *John von Neumann* (1903–1957). It was given the name "**ENIAC**" (Electronic Numerical Integrator and Calculator). The ENIAC contained 18,000 electron tubes, an unbelievable number for that time, and required an output of 160 kilowatts of electrical energy for operation. Unlike its predecessors, "Colossus" and "Mark I," the "ENIAC" was a fully programmable computer. It was capable of a computational performance that was up to 1,000 times faster than its predecessor due to its entirely electronic construction, Upon completion of the "UNIVAC I" in 1951, the Sperry Corporation began mass production of the standard, general purpose computer.

The invention of the transistor in 1947 by Americans *John Bardeen* (1908–1991), *Walter House Brattain* (1902–1987) and *William Shockley* (1910–1989), at Bell Laboratories in New York, changed the development of the computer to a large degree. The extremely complex tube construction, which involved a high degree of maintenance, entered a whole new phase by way of the smaller and more reliable **transistor** as a switching element. Based

The Five Generations of the Modern Computer

First Generation (1945 – 1956)
The development of the modern computer started at the beginning of World War II. It was based on the efforts of individual governments in the hope of gaining a strategic advantage. The machine commands and work instructions implemented in computers of this first generation were especially designed for the specific purpose of the computer. Every computer had a different set of instructions (machine code), which was binary coded in different ways. This made programming a costly and time-consuming endeavor. Basic technology in computers of the first generation were: vacuum tubes, punch cards, and magnetic drum memory storage.

Second Generation (1956 – 1963)
The 1947 transistor revolutionized the design and development of the computer. Computers constructed on the basis of a transistor were more reliable, more energy efficient and smaller than their tube predecessors. With the second generation of the computer, programming languages, such as COBOL or FORTRAN made their debut. Programming turned out to be much easier now than with cryptic machine code. Computers allowed only so-called batch processing, i.e., the jobs to be processed could only be done individually, one after another. With its cost significantly lowered, the computer was gaining a foothold in the business world. Punch cards continued to be used for input and output but now magnetic tape was used as well.

Third Generation (1964 – 1971)
While transistors had clear advantages over vacuum tube technology, the surplus heat they produced was often so great that it damaged the computer. In the next step of miniaturization and with the introduction of integrated switching circuits, a much larger number of switching elements could be built in a much smaller space and implemented in a more energy efficient way. As a result the computer became more powerful, smaller and also cheaper. Operating systems were simultaneously developed that allowed a multiprogram operation. In this way, different jobs could be processed at the same time using the computer's resources.

Fourth Generation (1971 – present)
Since the development of the first microprocessor, miniaturization has continued to advance rapidly. The high integration (VLSI – Very Large Scale Integration) at the beginning of the 80s, and the subsequent ULSI (Ultra Large Scale Integration), allow for the possibility of millions of transistors on a single integrated switching circuit. Due to the steady drop in prices computers entered private households in the form of the PC. The easy to use graphical interface makes it possible for even a layperson to operate a computer. Internet and local networks enter the computer world.

Fifth Generation (present –)
The end of the 80s saw the fifth generation of computers developed further in terms of artificial intelligence as well as the arrival of the super computer. This development is characterized by a parallelization of computation in multi-processor systems combined with speech recognition and natural language understanding.

Fig. 2.20   The five generations of the modern computer.

Fig. 2.21 ENIAC – the first completely electronic digital, universal computer.

on Bell Telephone Laboratories' 1955 first transistor computer "TRADIC," the transistor came to the forefront along with the IBM development of the magnetic disk memory in 1956. For the first time, the complicated programming of the computer – which until had been carried out customized in the binary code machine language in correspondence with the architecture of the individual computer – could be replaced with a programming language on a higher level of abstraction. For example, the commercially-oriented COBOL (Common Business Oriented Language) or the scientific FORTRAN (Formula Translator).

Already in the 1950s, the tendency toward a gradual reduction in the use of transistors was evident. In 1958, *Jack S. Kilby* (1923–2005) succeeded in inventing a circuit consisting of several components at Texas Instruments. These were resistors, transistors and capacitors on a crystal germanium plate serving as an integrated carrier. The **integrated circuit** (chip) was born. The steady decrease in switching elements led to the emergence of a new computer size at the beginning of the 1960s, the so-called **minicomputer**. The first minicomputer, equipped with a smaller switching element, was the "PDP-1" from the Digital Equipment company. It came on the market in 1960 and for the first time at a cost less than a million dollars. The "PDP-1" was not a universal computer, but limited to tasks of process control. At the same time, the new minicomputers with their specialized areas of work resulted in an unprecedented boost in automation in the 60s and 70s. Integrated circuits were produced industrially for the first time on a large scale starting in 1961. The next step in reducing switching elements took place in 1970 with the development of the **microprocessor**. For the first time, all of the components of a universal computer – the arithmetic logic unit, the control unit, the data bus, and the various registers – could be accommodated on a single chip – the Intel 4004. Nevertheless, until 1976 microprocessors were still used only as components of minicomputers and in process control.

Table 2.3 Historical Development of the Computer

30,000 BC	Use of primitive numerals
3,000 BC	First abstract numerical concepts in Mesopotamia based on the sexagesimal system
3rd c. BC	Use of the abacus by the Greeks
circa 500	Introduction of the Arabic decimal numbering system
1494	Leonardo da Vinci constructs the first pendulum clock
1617	John Napier develops a slide rule
1623	Willhelm Schickard constructs the first mechanical calculator for addition and subtraction
1642	Blaise Pascal constructs a mechanical calculator for addition and subtraction
1675	Gottfried W. Leibniz constructs a mechanical calculator for all four basic mathematical operations
1679	Gottfried W. Leibniz introduces the binary numerical system
1805	Joseph Marie Jacquard invents a punched card to control the operation of mechanical looms
1822	Charles Babbage constructs the differential engine, a mechanical calculator for solving differential equations
1832	Charles Babagge designs the analytical engine, the first freely programmable mechanical computer; Babbage's assistant, Ada Augusta King develops the first computer programs
1890	Herman Hollerith develops a punch card counting machine for the US census
1937	Konrad Zuse constructs the Z1, the first program-controlled and actually deployable mechanical computer
1941	Zuse constructs the Z3, the first electromechanical and freely programmable computer
1943	In England the mainframe computer Colossus is built to be used for deciphering German secret wireless transmission
1944	The first American mainframe computer, Harvard Mark I, is completed
1945	Work on ENIAC, the first fully electronic computer, is finished at the University of Pennsylvania
1947	Invention of the transistor
1951	First series computer is built – UNIVAC from Sperry
1955	First computer based on transistors is built – TRADIC from Bell Labs
1956	IBM develops magnetic disk storage
1958	Jack S. Kilby develops the integrated circuit
1960	The first minicomputer is born – the DEC PDP-1
1969	Launch of the ARPANET, predecessor of the Internet
1971	First microprocessor, the Intel 4004, comes on the market
1977	Market entry of the first personal computer – the Apple II
1981	IBM introduces the first IBM PC
1984	Apple introduces Macintosh, the first user-friendly computer

The idea of making the microprocessor the heart of a universal computer was not born in a big computer company but came to fruition among students. This group of young people included *Steve Jobs* (1955–2011) and *Stephen Wozniak* (*1950), who founded the Apple company in 1976. A few years later they succeeded in developing the first successful **personal computer**: the „Apple II.“ IBM introduced its first personal computer (PC) to the market in 1981. It was targeted for offices, schools and home use. The new computer age had dawned. Every year more powerful and ever-smaller microprocessors appeared on the market, offered at constantly lower prices. The PC was equipped with graphic and acoustic output capabilities. Introduction of the Apple Macintosh window-based graphic user interface in 1984 provided the user with easier operation and the PC finally took off in the mass market. Bill Gates (*1955) founded the Microsoft company in 1975 with Paul Allen. The company's success was based on its deployment of the operating system MS-DOS for the IBM PC. It became market leader in the 1990s with the graphic operating system Microsoft Windows and the office software Microsoft Office. New unfathomable possibilities were opened up for the PC as a universal communication medium with the introduction of local networks and public access to the Internet. Equipped with a user-friendly interface – the browser – everyone was now able to use the Internet, or more precisely the World Wide Web. It is a mean of communication that makes it possible to exchange information in every imaginable form whether text, voice, music, graphic or video – thus, a virtual multimedia exchange.

2.9 The Inseparable Story of the Internet and the Web

2.9.1 The ARPANET – how it all began ...

The beginning of the Internet stretches back to the time of the Cold War. The idea of a packet-switched communication service was conceived to ensure a resilient and reliable command and communication connection – even capable of withstanding an atomic attack. Capable of bridging the most different computer networks, this service was called the ARPANET. It was named after its sponsor the American government authority ARPA. Different American universities were involved from the onset in the basic research. Launched in 1969, ARPANET was soon split up into a subnetwork, one area used purely for military purposes and another area used for civilian scientific communication. The civilian section developed rapidly, especially after the National Science Foundation (NSF) began supporting its own high speed network between American universities and research institutions (NSFNET). As a result, the original ARPANET gradually lost its importance and was finally deactivated in 1989.

The idea of packet switching is a cornerstone of Internet technology. It would be hard to imagine secure communication in an uncertain, error-prone network without it. This method of network communication was already developed at the beginning of the 1960s by Paul Baran at the American RAND Corporation, Donald Davies at the British National Physical Laboratory (NLP) and Leonard Kleinrock at Massachusetts Institute of Technology (MIT).

At a meeting of the ARPA research directors in the spring of 1967, the **Information Processing Techniques Office** (IPTO or only IPT), under the direction of Joseph C. R. Licklider and Lawrence Roberts, first put the topic of how to bridge heterogeneous networks on the table. The connection of non-compatible computer networks suddenly became the order of the day. Already in October 1967 the first specifications were being discussed for **Interface Message Processors** (IMP). These dedicated minicomputers, similar to the currently used Internet routers, were to be installed upstream via telephone connection to be coupled to computers. The decision to use standardized connection nodes for the coupling of proprietary hardware to a communication subnet (cf. Fig. 2.22) simplified the development of the necessary network protocols. It was thus possible that the software development for communication between IMPs and the proprietary computers to be left up to each communication partner. In the 1960s and 70s it was also not necessary to grapple with the problem of comptuers not implementing a standardized architecture. Neither the operating system architecture nor the hardware used had common interfaces. Thus for every communication connection between two computers a dedicated interface needed to be developed. Based on the use of a communication subnet in which communication itself depends on the specially provided computers only a special interface would need to be created between the host computer and the communication computer in each case . Accordingly, the number of newly created interfaces grew linearly with the number of different computer architectures and was therefore much more efficient business-wise.

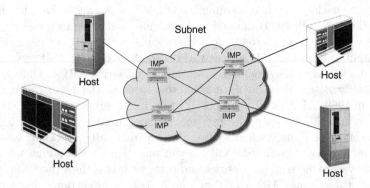

Fig. 2.22 ARPANET – network model with communication subnet.

It was then possible at the end of 1968 to lay down the final specifications of the IMPs based on the work of the **Stanford Research Institutes** (SRI). The respective host computer communicated with the upstream IMPs via a bit-serial high speed interface in order to connect with the communication subnetwork.. The design of the IMP, based on proposals by Larry Roberts, was implemented by the company Firma Bolt, Beranek & Newman (BBN) using Honeywell DDP-516 minicomputers. The IMPs themselves communicated with each other via modems. The modems were connected via permanently switched telephone lines and could thus cache data packets as well as forward them (store-and-forward packet switching). The first four network nodes of the ARPANET to be connected were based at university research institutes. These were the universities of Los Angeles (UCLA, Sigma-7), Santa Barbara (UCSB, IBM-360/75), Stanford (SRI, SDS-940) and Utah (DEC PDP-10). On October 29, 1969 the long awaited day had finally arrived. The first four IMPs were successfully connected with each other and also with their host computers. Despite the network node at UCLA crashing when the letter G of LOGIN was entered on the first login attempt, the age of the Internet had clearly begun.

In March 1970, the new ARPANET's expansion first reached the East Coast of the U.S. By April 1971 there were already twenty-three hosts connected with each other via fifteen nodes. The first "prominent" application of the new network was a software for the transfer of text messages from the first email program, developed in 1971 by Ray Tomlinson of BBN. In January 1973, the number of computers in the ARPANET had grown to thirty-five nodes. With the addition of computers in England and Norway, in mid-1973, the first international nodes were added. In that same year the first application for file transfer – the File Transfer Protocol (FTP) – was implemented. Starting in 1975 the network nodes located outside of the U.S. were connected via satellite link. The number of computers in the net grew from 111 connected host computers in 1977 to over 500 hosts in 1983. One of the first successful public demonstrations of internetworking took place in November 1977. Via a special gateway computer, the ARPANET was interconnected with one of the first wireless data networks, the Packet Radio Network, and a satellite network, the Atlantic Packet Satellite Network. 1983 was turning point year in ARPANET history. The communication software of all connected computer systems was changed from the old **Network Control Protocol** (NCP) to the communication protocol suite **TCP/IP**, developed in 1973 under the direction of Vinton Cerf (Stanford University) and Robert Kahn (DARPA). The changeover to the TCP/IP protocol, initiated by the **Department of Defense,** was necessary because the possibilities to ensure communication across heterogeneous networks with the NCP were limited. This changeover proved to be crucial for the worldwide expansion of this network of networks. A decisive factor in the development of an **internet** – a network association made up of networks with different communication architectures – was to find the answer to one important question. How can the communication between computers at the endpoints of networks with different technologies be carried out without the computers themselves being involved in what happens along the path between each other? The ARPANET was split into a military (MIL-

NET) and a civilian user area in 1983. Administratively and operationally there were now two different networks, but because they were linked by gateways the user was oblivious to this separation. The ARPANET had grown to become an Internet. More and more independent local networks were being connected to the Internet so that in the first half of the 1980s the Internet resembled a star. The ARPANET was at the center of different networks grouped around this focal point. However, this picture changed at the end of the 1980s. At the beginning of the 1980s the ARPANET-integrated CSNET (Computer Science Network) from the American **National Science Foundation** (NSF) had been linking more and more American universities. It finally became possible for its successor, the NSFNET, to connect all universities via a specially designed high speed backbone, thus giving every college student the chance to become an Internet user. The NSFNET quickly developed into the actual backbone of the Internet. One reason for this was its high-speed transmission lines – more than twenty-five times faster than the old ARPANET. Besides its scientific use, a commercial use also became established via the NSFNET. This had been strictly forbidden in the original ARPANET.

At the beginning of the 1990s, the number of networked computers in the NSFNET far exceeded those in the ARPANET. DARPA management – in the meantime the ARPA had been renamed the **Defense Advanced Research Project Agency** – made a crucial decision in August 1989. Having been determined that the ARPANET had outlived its purpose, it was shut down on the occasion of its twentieth anniversary. The NSFNET and the regional networks that emerged from it were to become the new, central backbone of the Internet as we know it today.

2.9.2 The Internet Goes Public

There are two primary reasons for the Internet's triumph as a mass communication medium. First, the opening of the new medium for the general public and the provision of a simple user interface – the WWW browser. Laypeople were also empowered with the ability to easily use the medium of the Internet and the services it offered, such as WWW or email. The date of the Internet's birth is often set at the same time as the changeover from the until then valid network protocol of the ARPANET – NCP – to the new **protocol family TCP/IP**. The three basic protocols of the TCP/IP protocol family are: IP (Internet Protocol), TCP (Transmission Control Protocol) and ICMP (Internet Control Message Protocol). These had already been established and published as Internet standards in 1981 in the form of RFCs (Request for Comments). By using the TCP/IP protocol family the interconnection of different network technologies in a simple and efficient way was possible for the first time.

Table 2.4 From the ARPANET to the Internet – An Overview (1957 – 1989)

1957	Launch of the first Soviet satellite Sputnik and founding of the ARPA
1960	Paul Baran, Donald Davies and Leonard Kleinrock produce their first works on packet switching
1962	The IPTO is launched as a department of the ARPA
1965	The ARPA sponsors groundbreaking research at American universities
1967	First meeting of ARPA managers on the subject of ARPANET
1968	Specification of the IMP communication computer concluded
29.10.1969	The first four nodes of the ARPANET are interconnected
1970	ALOHANET, the first wireless computer network connecting the main Hawaiian islands, begins operation
1971	Ray Tomlinson sends the first email
1972	ARPA is renamed the Defense Advanced Research Projects Agency (DARPA); Larry Roberts organizes the first public ARPANET demonstration
1973	The ARPANET contains 35 nodes; Vinton Cerf and Robert Kahn develop the TCP protocol; Robert Metcalfe develops ideas for Ethernet technology (LAN)
1973	The FTP file transfer program is implemented
1975	Launch of the satellite network connection: Hawaii, the U.S. Mainland, London via Intelsat 1
1975	ARPA hands over operation of the ARPANET to the DCA
1977	First public demonstration of internetworking
1978	The standardization organization ISO adopts the OSI communication layer model
1983	Splitting of the ARPANET into one section for civilian purposes and another for military use (MILNET); conversion of the entire ARPANET to TCP/IP
1984	The supercomputer program of the National Science Foundation (NSF) includes construction and maintenance of a high-speed network (NSFNET, 56kbps backbone)
1986	NSFNET begins operation
1988	First Internet worm attacks the net; 10% of the 60,000 hosts at that time are affected
1989	150,000 hosts are connected on the Internet; the decision is made to close the old ARPANET

The new technology was quickly accepted by the scientific community as it allowed the scientific communication process to become greatly simplified and accelerated. Interestingly, the ongoing development and refinement of the Internet constantly received new inspiration from the gaming instincts of its participants. The first weekly "net meetings", were already taking place between 1973 and 1975. Participants from a variety of linked research institutes organized "virtual" meetings to play "STAR TREK", , a distributed computer game based on the television series with the same name. The development and spread of the operating system **UNIX** also played an instrumental role in the expansion of TCP/IP and in contributing to the popularity of the Internet. This was particularly true with the development of the free operating system BSD-UNIX at the University of California in Berkeley. From the very beginning it was ARPA's aim to make the Internet as attractive as possible for university researchers and scientists. A great number of computer science institutes at American universities used UNIX as their computer operating system, in particular BSD-UNIX. On one hand ARPA supported BBN in their rapid implementation of the TCP/IP protocol and on the other hand Berkeley, in order that the TCP/IP protocols would be adopted in their operating system distribution. In this way it was possible for the ARPA to reach over 90% of the computer science departments at American universities. The first computer science departments were namely just being established at this time and in the process of buying their computers and connecting them to a local network. The new communication protocols therefore arrived at the right place, at the right time.

Internet Design Principles

In 1974, Vinton Cerf and Robert Kahn publish architectural principles known as **Open Network Architecture** These principles remain the foundation of today's Internet:

Minimalism and autonomy: A network should be able to work in autonomously. No internal modifications should be necessary in order to link to other networks.

Best possible service: Crosslinked networks are designed to offer the best possible service from one terminal to another. So that reliable communication can be guaranteed, corrupted or lost messages are retransmitted by the sender.

Stateless switching computer: The switching computer in crosslinked networks should not store or process information on the state of an existing network.

Decentralized control: There should be no global control over individual crosslinked networks. Organization is carried out in a decentralized manner.

Further reading:

Cerf, V., Kahn, R.: A Protocol for Packet Network Interconnection, in IEEE Transactions on Computing, vol. COM-22, pp. 637–648 (1974)

Fig. 2.23 Internet design principles from V. Cerf and R. Kahn.

While the original ARPANET was shut down in 1989, the NSFNET network association, created by civilian funding, was technologically superior as a backbone and had a considerably higher bandwidth. The number of computers connected to the Internet had risen to over 150,000 in 1989. When on the evening of November 2, 1988 the first **Internet worm**, a self-replicating program, paralyzed a fabled 10% of the 60,000 computers connected to the Internet it was a public sensation. Directly affected were the VAX and SUN-3 computers. The widely used Berkeley BSD-UNIX operating systems ran on various versions of these computers, which were then used as a base for attacking other computers. Within a few hours the program had spread across the entire U.S. Thousands of computers were put out of commission due to system overload caused by the high level of activity. In the meantime, the significance of data networks such as the Internet for public life has greatly increased. It is a growing dependency that makes such attacks a serious threat to public life. In an extreme case scenario an entire country and its economy can be thrown into information chaos In response to this early attack, the **Computer Emergency Response Team** (CERT) was set up by the U.S. Department of Defense, its headquarters at the Carnegie Mellon University in Pittsburgh. The role of the CERT is to establish the strongest possible expertise in cyber security, to identify weaknesses of previous Internet installations and applications, as well as to to give recommendations, which should be followed by the users and operators of the Internet. Security incidents are reported to the CERT, with attempts made to clarify them and to take the necessary precautions to prevent such incidents from occurring in the future or bringing those responsible to justice. CERT is however purely a research institute without any police or government authority and may not tax legal action against a threat or its cause.

2.9.3 The WWW Revolutionizes the Internet

The World Wide Web (WWW) and its easy to use interface, the browser, finally helped the Internet to achieve its legendary success and worldwide dissemination. The fact that the browser, as an integrative interface, is able to combine access to many different types of Internet services, such as email or file transfer, simplified the use of this new medium to such an extent that it could expand to become a major mass communication medium.

The basis of the World Wide Web is the networking of separate documents via what are called **hyperlinks**. A hyperlink is nothing more than the explicit reference to another document in the web or to another location within the same document. As long as text-based documents are involved, one speaks of interlinked **hypertext** documents. The underlying idea of the referencing to another text or to another text document is not an invention of the computer age. The Jewish laws of the Talmud, whose origin goes back to the first century of our calender system, contains such cross-references. Another prominent historical example of a hypertext document is the great French encyclopedia (*Encyclopèdie, ou dictionnaire raisonnè des sciences, des arts et des mètiers*), which was published by Jean le Rond d'Alembert (1717–1783) and Denis Diderot (1713–1784) between 1751 and 1766. The history of the electronic hypertext first began in the the twentieth century. In 1945, an article by Vannevar Bush (1890–1974) appeared in the magazine "Atlantic Monthly" entitled "As We May Think."Bush envisioned a device he called the **Memex**. Working by electromechanical means it was designed to link and set microfilm documents in relation to one another, to represent the knowledge of a person and serve as a memory aid [34]. Bush is regarded as a visionary and a harbinger of the World Wide Web.

While many experts do not recognize the Memex as a genuine hypertext system, with his article Bush influenced the work of WWW pioneers who followed him. As early as 1965 the terms "hypertext" and "hypermedia" were coined by Ted Nelson, who in 1968 contributed to work on the development of the **Hypertext Editing Systems** (HES) at Brown University in Providence, Rhode Island. Douglas Engelbart (1925–2013) developed the **NLS** (oNLine System) between 1962 and 1968. This was a hypertext system with, among other things, a window-based user interface and a mouse as an input device. Hypertext and hypermedia reached the personal computer in the 1980s with Apple's **HyperCard**.

In 1989 at the Swiss nuclear research institute CERN, Tim Berners-Lee drafted "*Information Management: A Proposal.*"He described a distributed hypertext-based document management system designed to manage the documentation and research data produced in massive amounts at CERN. The following year he received the green light to actually implement his idea on a NeXT computer system with Robert Cailliau. It was already possible to run the first WWW server in November 1990. Tim Berners-Lee called it **WorldWideWeb** and in March 1991 the first WWW browser followed.

Table 2.5 The History of the World Wide Web

1945	Vannevar Bush describes the first hypertext system, Memex
1965	Ted Nelson is the first to coin the word **Hypertext** at the ACM yearly conference
1968	Douglas Engelbart develops a hypertext-based prototype system NLS and invents the mouse as its input device
1980	Tim Berners-Lee writes a first notebook program (ENQUIRE) with hypertext links
1989	Tim Berners-Lee writes a first memorandum about his documentation management system at the nuclear research center CERN
1990	Together with Robert Cailliau, Tim Berners-Lee develops the first WWW server and WWW browser: the WorldWideWeb is born
1993	NCSA Mosaic, the first WWW browser with graphic user interface introduced
1994	Netscape is founded
1994	The World Wide Web Consortium (W3C) is founded
1995	Microsoft debuts its operating system Windows95 together with the Internet Explorer as WWW browser
1998	Netscape is sold as AOL, the browser war comes to an end
2004	Dale Daugherty and Tim O'Reilly coin the term Web 2.0 and speak of a rebirth of the WWW

A few months later in September 1991, the American physicist Paul Kunz from Stanford Linear Acceleration Center (SLAC) visited CERN and was introduced to the WWW. Excited about the idea, he took a copy of the program back with him to the U.S. and in December 1992 the first WWW server entered the network at SLAC. The new server can be attributed to the personal initiative of university members. While in 1992 there were just twenty-six WWW servers, at the beginning of 1993 the number of world-wide operated WWW servers had doubled to almost fifty. The development of the first WWW browser with a graphical user interface – co-authored by Marc Andreesen for the X Window System – finally made it possible for the non-specialist to use the WWW from the end of 1993 on. This was even more the case after the NCSA released versions for IBM PCs and for Apple's Macintosh. The number of WWW servers rose to 500 by the end of 1993, with the WWW responsible for approximately 1% of the worldwide Internet data traffic.

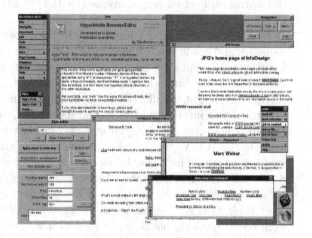

Fig. 2.24 WorldWideWeb – the first web browser for the WWW.

1994 was to become the year of the WWW. The first International World Wide Web Conference was held in May 1994 at CERN. Many more had actually registered than the 400 researchers and developers who were in attendance – there was simply not enough space to accommodate everyone interested in the WWW. Reports about the WWW reached the attention of the media and in October a second conference was announced in the U.S. It was attended by 1,300 people. Due to the widespread dissemination of the Mosaic browser, developed for the Netscape Navigator, and its market competitor the Microsoft Internet Explorer, included in every Microsoft operating system sold since 1995, the World Wide Web experienced unbridled popularity. If the growth rate of linked computers had been doubling yearly until this time, it now doubled every three months. The WWW spread like a wild fire around the world, finding its way into offices and homes.

Based on the Internet and its regulatory institutions, Tim Berners-Lee saw the necessity of an independent body regulating the development and growth of the WWW. Furthermore, standards should only be defined by an independent body and not solely by the industry to prevent the formation of monopolies. Thus, together with Michael Dertouzos, the director of the Laboratory of Computer Science at MIT, Berners-Lee started raising resources for the creation of a **World Wide Web Consortium** (**W3C**). The W3C was laun-

Table 2.6 The WWW – how it all began

First WWW server in the world:
nxoc01.cern.ch
First WWW page in the world:
http://nxoc01.cern.ch/hypertext/WWW/TheProject.html

ched in 1994 with the support of MIT, the Institute National de Recherche en Informatique et en Automatique (INRIA) in Europe, the DARPA and the European Commission. It set its goal as monitoring the further development of WWW protocols and supporting the interoperability of the WWW. As economy and trade discovered the WWW and its myriad of possibilities, **E-Commerce** became a recognized concept starting in 1995. The first shopping systems were set up and companies such as **Amazon.com** or **Google.com** emerged overnight to quickly become trading giants on the stock market. The registration of Internet addresses and names became a paid service, with large companies often spending large sums of money for legal protection of their name in the WWW. A virtual hype was created and took the entire business world by storm. The "New Economy" became a way to describe the euphorically celebrated new Internet-based economic model. The so-called Silicon Valley in the U.S. saw the birth of **dot-coms**; businesses so named because of their WWW address **.com** suffix. Most of the time these companies were based on a simple business idea of a web-based service. Supported by venture capital and investors, they were built up within just a few months before being bought out by a larger competitor and – if successful – earning astronomical profits However, in most cases the earnings these companies had projected never materialized. The consumer remained hesitant about online shopping – at least as long as no unified and secure transaction mechanism was available. Suddenly in the middle of 2000 the market collapsed and, at the same time, the "dot-com bubble" burst. In keeping with the old stock market adage, after the exuberant hype a long descent followed, before a real market assessment could – slowly – be made.

2.9.4 Web 2.0 and the Semantic Web – The Future of the WWW

Although the second decade of the WWW is coming to a close, there is no end in sight to the development of the WWW. The WWW is continuing its further development with the possibilities provided by new access devices. Already at the end of the 1990s the first attempts were made toward developing WWW accessibility on mobile devices and cell phones. This va-

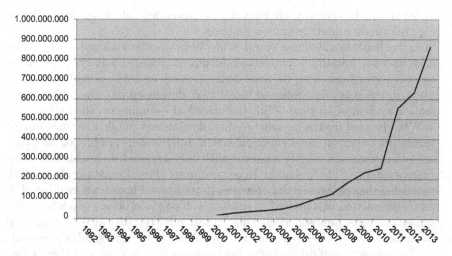

Fig. 2.25 Growth of the World Wide Web.

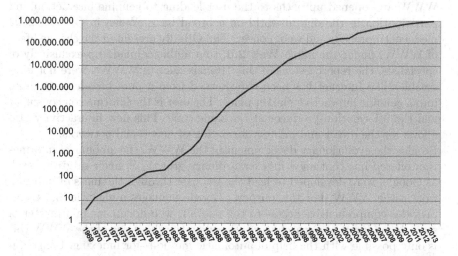

Fig. 2.26 Number of Internet-connected hosts.

riation of WWW data traffic could only find gradual success, due in part to the poor quality of the respective mobile user interface. Mobile devices as such offer a relatively small display for the WWW contents. Tight limitations were also set on mobile WWW traffic due to narrow bandwidths and weak display technology. Today however advanced miniaturization and fast mobile networks of the third generation allow nearly comparable operation in the mobile area. Additionally, satellite tracking systems (Global Positioning System, GPS) make possible geographical coverage of the respective browser location and in this way offer special, location-dependent services, such as e.g., information and navigation systems.

Since its birth in 1990, the World Wide Web has also changed dramatically content-wise. Initially, a networked document management system connected via hyperlinks, with its availability limited to only a small number of users, in the years that followed the WWW developed into the largest information system of all time. With the arrival of e-commerce, the focus of the WWW changed from a personal communication and publication medium for specialists to one of mass communication. Information production and consumption remained strictly separate, with only a specialist capable of putting contents online. The public at large consumed the information offer, which paralleled that of commercial providers in traditional broadcast medium. The user's interaction was limited to reading web pages, ordering goods and consumer products online and clicking banner ads. But the WWW continued to change. New technology was developed and it became suddenly possible for laypeople to publish information contents in a simple way themselves. Blogs, chatrooms, file sharing, tagging systems and wikis have conquered the WWW and opened up paths to the user leading to genuine interaction and participation in the digital world on a broad basis. When in October 2004 media entrepreneur and web pioneer, Tim OReilly presented the changed face of WWW, under the name **Web 2.0**, to a audience made up exclusively of specialists, the repercussions of this "Renaissance of WWW" were not foreseeable. The Internet has been transformed from a pure broadcast medium into a genuine interactive market place. The user is the information consumer and the information producer at the same time. This new interactivity also allows for the direct and indirect formation of new social networks.

Besides the evolutionary development of the WWW, the amount of information offered has continued its extraordinary growth. **Search engines**, such as Google, were developed to lead the the user through the mass of information in the WWW. For this purpose, Google manages a gigantic index that provides comprehensive access to the relevant web document in a matter of seconds, on input of a search word. Based on the sheer size of the WWW this is only possible with the help of automatic methods for indexing. Using statistical methods, all items within a web document are evaluated and brought into ranked order in terms of a specific subject heading. The amount of returned search results is no longer comprehensible for the user. For example, the search item "Web 2.0" alone produces more than 74 million results (as of 10/2008). However, the result list only contains documents in which this term appears literally. In this way, paraphrases and synonyms cannot be found. Just as a document containing the search item does not necessarily address it as its focal point. Based on the problematic interpretation alone, it is not possible for the completeness and accuracy of search results to even come close to natural language.

To do this it would be necessary to systematically supplement the web document with the relevant meaningful data (so-called **metadata**). Such a web document supplemented with metadata would contain along with each of the relevant terms in the document, a reference to one of the concepts described by the term. Besides containing any document relevant to this term, this type of a web document, supplemented with metadata, would need to have a reference to a descriptive concept that the term included. These conceptual descriptions – so called **ontologies** or knowledge representations – can be stored in a machine-readable standardized form and evaluated additionally by a search engine in order to raise the hit number of the search results. The WWW Consortium (W3C), the entity responsible for the WWW standardization, has already created the necessary foundation in the form of ontology descriptive languages such as RDF, RDFS, OWL, and SPARQL. Semantically annotated websites make it for possible autonomously acting agents to collect targeted information. The system then automatically makes decisions as defined by its client and initiates transactions via the web. This semantic network (**Semantic Web**) represents the next step in the evolution of the WWW and it is about to become a reality.

2.10 Glossary

Alphabet: The ordered sequence of letters (phonetic symbols) in a language; from [Lat.]*alphabetum*, [Gk.]*alphabetos*, the first two letters of the Greek alphabet: alpha (α) and beta (β). Beginning in the third century BC, the word designated the summary of all Greek letters. The word "alphabetum" was used for the first time in Latin by the early Christian poet Tertullian (ca. 160–220 AD). German script is based on the Latin alphabet, which evolved from a branch of the Phoenician alphabet. The German alphabet consists of twenty-six capital (majuscule) and small letters (minuscule), as well as letter combinations with umlauts and accented characters.

Analog: (*ana logum*=[Gk.] in the right proportion), Term for technology methods in which continuous, i.e., infinitely variable, physical qualities are used.

ARPANET (Advanced Research Projects Agency Net): The first packet switching data network and precursor of the Internet, it was launched by DARPA, a research initiative of the U.S. Department of Defense. The first network node (Interface Message Processor, IMP) was ready for implementation on August 30, 1969 and the ARPANET began operation on December 1969 with 4 IMPs in Stanford, Santa Barbara, Los Angeles and Utah. In its heyday it included several satellite links, among them from the west to the east coast of the U.S., to Hawaii, Great Britain, Norway, Korea and Germany. The ARPANET ceased operation in July 1990.

Block book: Multiple separate printed pages bound into a small book, whereby the texts and pictures of each page are printed from a woodcut.

Colophon: ([Gk.]= target, end point) Information about the printer, the place and date of printing, found at the end of a document or, as the case may be, information about the copyist of a manuscript.

Communication: Communication is understood as the process of a one-way or reciprocal transmission; the sending and receiving of information by people or technical systems.

Digital: (*digitus*=[lat.] Finger), Designation for technology/processes that use only discrete, variable, i.e., stepped, mathematical sizes. The foundation of digital technology is the binary number system that contains just two states: "true" and "untrue" or the numerical values "1" and "0". The binary numerical values are designated **bits** (**binary digits**) and represent the smallest possible unit of information.

Flyer: Politically or commercially motivated, event-focused, one page broadsheets. Originally flyers served less as a source of inciting political agitation and more as an actual trade article. Offered by barkers and traveling merchants, their author was usually anonymous.

Grammar: Description of the structure and rules of language as a part of linguistics (morphological and syntactic regularities of a natural language). In comparison to language and writing development, the fixed rule system of grammar as a basis for defining language use was a late development historically speaking (from the fifth century BC). In the realm of philology, grammar is viewed as a tool in language analysis for capturing the historical development of a language.

Homonym: Words that have the same pronunciation but designate different things or have a different meaning, e.g., „change" (as a noun and a verb).

Ideogram: Symbols or combinations of symbols that are used for the identification of non-object items, such as activities, abstract concepts, or feelings. The meaning of ideograms must first be learned and is based on the fixed formal system of each culture.

Illumination: Artistic highlighting and pictorial decoration of initials (sentence and chapter beginning) on a manuscript or an early printed work. Further decorative items (often vines) were sometimes added to an illumination. Depending on the importance of a paragraph, between two and ten lines were kept free for the design of an initial.

Imprimatur: ([Lat.]=it may be printed) Ecclesiastical permission to print a work. Papal bull by Pope Innocent VIII (1432–1492) and Pope Alexander VI (1430–1503) served to institutionalize the first censorship. Before a book was printed ecclesiastical permission was required.

Incunabula: ("in the cradle") Early printed matter that was produced between 1450 and 1500. The name derives from the Latin word for "diaper." The most famous among the incunabula works is the forty-two line, magnificent Gutenberg Bible. Of the original 185 copies only 48 have survived – some of them only partially.

Internet: The Internet is the world's largest computer network consisting of many networks connected to each other as well as individual resources. Among the most important benefits of the Internet – one speaks of "services"– are electronic mail (email), hypermedia documents (WWW), file transfer (FTP) and discussion forums (Usenet/newsgroups). The global network has attained its popularity mainly due to the introduction of the World Wide Web (WWW), which is often equated with the Internet, but is in fact just one of the many services the Internet offers.

Language: Linguistics defines language as the sound-based form of communication by humans. It is a method, not rooted in instinct, for the transfer of thoughts, feelings and wishes by means of a system of freely created symbols.

Medium: Manifestation of the transport channel for message transmission between a sender and a receiver.

Onomatopoeia: Words that describe a concept by way of sound transcription or imitation e.g., „bark".

Pamphlet: Although non-periodical, pamphlets are considered the forerunners of today's newspapers. Unlike flyers, they usually consisted of pages that were printed on both sides.

Parchment: Parchment is a writing material made of animal skin that was already known in antiquity. Parchment preparation involves curing animal skins with lye and cleaning them to remove flesh and hair. The skins are then stretched onto frames to dry.

Petroglyphs: Drawings by prehistoric, nomadic hunters that are carved in, or painted on, stone.

Photo effect: The photo effect (also photoelectric effect, Hallwachs effect, or light electric effect) describes the release of electrons from a metal surface when it is struck by electromagnetic radiation, in particular that created by light. The photo effect is the foundation of light-sensitive sensors, such as the CCD senors in digital photography.

Picotogram: Symbols that are used for the description of objects, people or animals, e.g., as information signs or traffic signs. Pictograms are considered an early stage in the development of writing.

Pulse Code Modulation (PCM):   Method of analog-digital conversion, based on the sampling of an analog signal, which is followed by the discretization of the obtained sample value. **Sampling** disassembles the continuous time course of a signal into discrete, separate time points, thus capturing the current value of an analog signal in each discrete point in time (sampling time). These exact sampling values are subsequently rounded to binary coding in predefined quantization intervals.

Relief printing: Considered the oldest method of printing technology, whereby ink is applied directly to the raised portions of a printing block and transferred with pressure directly onto the material to be printed. In a mirror-image print, the non-printed areas must be cut deeper on the block before printing.

Retinal inertia: The concept whereby a visually perceived image remains on the retina of the human eye for approx. 1/16 of a second before disappearing. Described in antiquity by Ptolemy of Alexandria (85–165 AD), retinal inertia forms the basis for the technology behind film and television. When individual frames are displayed quickly enough one after another – in a sequence of fifteen frames per second – an impression of continuous movement is achieved

Semantic Web: The Semantic Web describes an expansion of the existing World Wide Web. In the Semantic Web every piece of information receives a well-defined and machine-readable meaning that enables programs acting autonomously to interpret the information contents and, based on this, to make decisions. The concept of the Semantic Web is rooted in a proposal by WWW founder Tim Berners-Lee.

Semantics: Semantics designates that area of linguistics dealing with the theory of meaning. The focus is on the sense and importance of language and linguistic signs. The focus is on the question of how the sense and meaning of complex concepts is derived from simpler concepts. Semantics relies on the rules of syntax.

Sign: Designation for "something" which stands for something else ("signifier"). The relation between a signifier and and what is signified is always a direct one. The relationship of the signs to each other and how they can be combined together to form new terms is defined by syntax.

Synonym: Phonetically different words used to describe the same object, or which have the same meaning, e.g., "charwoman" and „cleaning lady."

Web 2.0:   Web 2.0 describes a "seemingly" new generation of web-based services, geared in a special way to the non-specialist and characterized by their simple possibility of participating and interacting in the WWW. Typical examples of these services are wikis, blogs, photo and video sharing sites or portals.

Woodcut: A variation of relief printing using paper as the printing medium. After a picture is drawn on the wooden block, the non-printed areas are deepened while the remaining raised portions are colored and then printed onto damp sheets of paper. These are laid over the inked wooden block and pressure is applied with a cloth roll. Because the ink often often seeps through paper, printing is usually done only on one side of the sheet. A woodcut printing pattern could be used several hundred times.

World Wide Web: Term for the "worldwide data network" (also WWW, 3W, W3, Web). The WWW refers to the youngest and at the same time most successful service on the Internet, characterized to a certain degree by its user-friendliness and multimedia elements. WWW actually denotes a technology capable of implementing a distributed, Internet-based hypermedia document model. Internet and the World Wide Web (WWW) are often erroneously used as synonyms. The WWW is just one of the special services transmitted by the HTTP protocol.

WWW server: Process on a computer with the functionality of answering enquiries from the browser via the WWW. From a technical point of view, a WWW server can be operated on every computer connected to the the Internet.

Chapter 3
Communication Fundamentals in Computer Networks

"If everyone only spoke when they had something to say
people would very soon lose the use of language."
– William Shakespeare (1564 - 1616)

Digital communication – that is to say, the transmission of digital messages and goods – needs computer networks. But how does information travel from one computer to another in the form of digital data? How can an email be delivered correctly? How is it possible that the right network participant can be found among all of those communicating on the global Internet – and that a million times over? This chapter introduces the basics of computer communication and helps us to understand how these technical procedures take place in a computer network such as the Internet. We learn how these multiple components interact together. The various subproblems that need to be solved before successful and efficient data transfer can take place in a computer network are bundled hierarchically. This is done with the help of a so-called layer model. The subsolutions are combined into one functioning whole. The principle of packet switching provides a successful approach to solving the problem of communication. It allows the efficient and secure communication of many communication participants via an error-free and simultaneously shared transmission medium. Communication is ensured by way of error detection and error correction procedures. These are what make reliable communication possible in the first place.

3.1 Basic Terms and Concepts

3.1.1 Communication and Data Transfer

Communication (*communicare* = [Lat.] impart, share, make common) is the exchange, provision, transmission and reception of **information**. In the case of digital communication, this means digital data between two or more communication partners. The basic components of every form of communication, whether it be an everyday conversation or the digital exchange between computers, are made up of the transmitted information itself, its sender and

C. Meinel and H. Sack, *Digital Communication*, X.media.publishing,
DOI: 10.1007/978-3-642-54331-9_3, © Springer-Verlag Berlin Heidelberg 2014

receiver, as well as the medium over which the information is transferred. This is called the **communication medium** (see also Chap. 1.2 "Digital Communication and Its Foundation"). For example, sound waves are the communication medium for our daily conversation. Spoken information is exchanged via sound waves, aided by acoustic signals. Other media is possible as well, such as radio waves or electric signals. The following conditions must be fulfilled so that communication can take place:

1. The information must be presented in a suitable system of signs for communication (e.g., sounds, text, binary coding, etc.),
2. It must be possible to transform these signs into physical signals (e.g., sound waves, electrical impulses, radio waves, etc.) , and
3. The receiver needs to be able to read the signals received and through this interpretation to understand the meaning contained in the message.

Besides this, it should be possible to recognize mistakes that might have occurred during message transmission and, as the case may be, to correct them.

When the communication partners involved are computer-based, one speaks of **data transmission**. Data transmission is defined as the exchange of units of information (**data**) between two or more physically separate computers that make up the information. Communication is conducted over the appropriate communication media – so-called data connections. The interconnected computers form a **computer network** or, in short, a **net**. The system of transmission lines is the **transmission network** or **network**. The computers involved in the transfer must follow the fixed rules – called a **communication protocol** – to the smallest detail. This means being able to send or receive the data so that the other computer can correctly interpret and process it. The principle of the data transmission system is defined in DIN 44302 [67]: every **data transmission system** is made up of (at least) two data stations (hosts), which are linked to each other via a transmission line – generally in one communication direction. Each participant connected by a computer to a transmission network needs to have two components. The first is the **data circuit transmission equipment** (DCE), which is normally directly connected to the (usually) public transmission line. It communicates with the second computing unit, the **data terminal equipment** (DTE). The DCE converts the data to be sent into electrical signals, or, as the case may be, the received electrical signals back into (usually binary coded) data (see Fig. 3.1). There is a standardized **interface** between the DTE and the DCE. Its function is established in DIN 66020 and DIN 66021 [68, 69]. This interface ensures that devices from different manufacturers are also able to communicate with each other. The tasks of the DTE and DCE in regards to transmission depend on the respective transmission method. A **transmission line** is understood as the connection between two data stations via a channel. Coded information is sent over the channel as electric or optical signals in the form of electromagnetic waves.

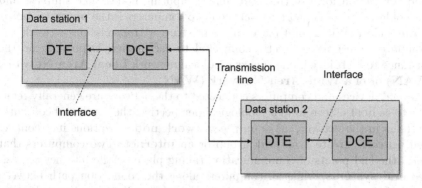

Fig. 3.1 Data transmission model based on DIN 44302.

The task of the **data terminal equipment (DTE)** is to send (data source = origin of the data) and to receive (data sink = destination of the data) data. A DTE contains one or more of the following components:

- input processing unit,
- output processing unit,
- arithmetic logical unit (ALU),
- control unit and
- memory.

The **data circuit transmission equipment (DCE)** is responsible for the following tasks:

- transformation of the sent data into signals suitable for the transmission medium and then transformation of the received signals into understandable data for the DTE (signal conversion),
- establishing and dismantling data connections,
- generating and maintaining a constant sending and receiving clock between the involved DCEs and
- detection and correction of transmission errors.

Examples of data circuit transmission equipment are, for example, a modem to connect to the telephone network or a transceiver for connection to an Ethernet network. Thus, DCEs are components of the actual communication subsystem.

If in a transmission network the DCEs are directly connected with each other via lines – without additional components being switched between them – one speaks of a **direct connection**. Otherwise, we refer to an **indirect connection**. Computers can be connected in a variety of arrangements in data transmission. Thereby, it is possible to classify the various networks according to their spatial extent and their **topology**, i.e., the distribution and connection form of the individual computing nodes. The simplest and also oldest type of networking between two computers is the **point-to-point connection**. When multiple computers share a transmission network the computers are only indirectly connected to each other. Depending on the distance to be bridged, one speaks of a local network **Local Area Network (LAN)** or of a **Wide Area Network (WAN)**.

The end devices and computers connected to the network are generally referred to as **hosts**. Seen from a topological perspective, the connected computer systems in the network make up the **network nodes**. Various interconnected networks create a network group or an **internet**. Two computers that form the end points of communication taking place on the internet are called **end systems**, while all computers along the connection path between both of the end systems are referred to as **intermediate systems**. If these intermediate systems are integrated into multiple communication links and connected directly to other intermediate systems in the internet, they must determine via what communication link the information is to be forwarded. This decision-making action is called **routing** and the intermediate systems that make this decision are known as **exchanges**, **switching computers** or **routers**. The fundamental concepts of network technology are shown in Fig. 3.2.

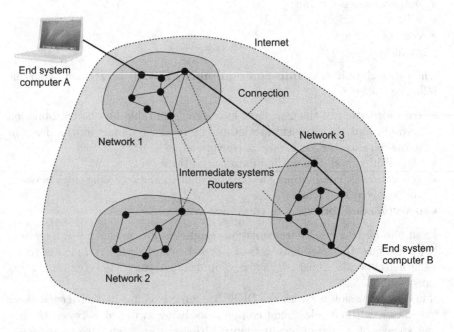

Fig. 3.2 Basic network concepts.

Different relationships or modes of transport between the end systems in a computer network can be distinguished. Depending on whether information is sent to one, several or to all network end systems, a distinction is made-between **unicast, multicast** or **broadcast** (see Fig. 3.3). Unicast data

Transport modes

The mode of transport indicates how many of the devices connected to the network, or network group, receive information from the sender. The main groups are:

- **Unicast**:
  A sender transmits information to a single receiver (point-to-point transmission). Examples for a unicast transmission are a telephone conversation or a private email.
- **Multicast**:
  A sender transmits information to a group of receivers (point-to-group transmission). Examples for a multicast transmission are a multi-party conference call or an email message sent via a mailing list.
- **Broadcast**:
  A transmitter sends a message to all receivers in a network (point-to-all transmission) An example of broadcast transmission is classic mass media such as newspaper, radio and television.

Fig. 3.3 Modes of transport in communication networks.

transport is the standard communication form between two end systems in a computer network. Multicast data transport is implemented, for example, when multimedia data streams are sent to multiple end systems addresses simultaneously to reduce network load. Information exchanged between intermediate systems to control network communication is also sent multicast. Broadcast data transport is seldom used in computer networks as it creates a considerable load on the available resources. The **mode of operation** in message transmission indicates in which direction information is to be exchanged between two end systems. A further distinction is made between different types. In **simplex operation** information is sent unidirectionally, i.e., in one direction, while in **duplex operation** a bi-directional information exchange is possible with two end systems exchanging in both directions. There are two variations of duplex operation: **half-duplex**, in which information can be exchanged between the two end systems in both directions only sequentially, i.e., alternatively exchanged in succession, and **full duplex**, in which exchange is possible in both directions at the same time (see Fig. 3.4).

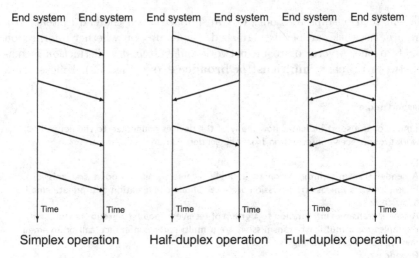

Simplex operation   Half-duplex operation   Full-duplex operation

Fig. 3.4 Types of operational modes in computer network communication.

3.1.2 Classification of Communication Systems

Computer communication systems can be classified according to different criteria. The following characteristics are essential regarding the practical implementation of computer networks:

- spatial extent of the network,
- type of computer networking (direct or indirect networking),
- particular application characteristics for which the network is designed,
- degree of homogeneity of the components involved,
- targeted user groups (public or non-public access),
- transmission capacity (bandwidth) of the network (narrowband vs. broadband),
- technical transmission concept of the network (broadcast network or point-to-point connection) and
- network operator type (private or public).

Depending on the distance between the computers or processors to be networked, different technologies are necessary. The technology implemented must be suitable for the distance to be bridged as well as in fulfilling the requirements posed in each case. Table 3.1 gives an overview of the possibilities of interconnecting multiple end systems. These are ordered based on spatial distance. At the top position are multiprocessor systems, parallel computers and computer clusters – that is, processors connected by very fast and short system buses

Those communication systems known as networks in the true sense of the word are first found on the next level of the order of magnitude.

Table 3.1 A classification of computer networks based on their spatial extent

Distance	Location	Example
0.1 m	Circuit board	Multiprocessor system
1 m	System	Multiprocessor cluster
10 m	Room	Personal Area Network
100 m	Building	Local Area Network
1 km	Campus	
10 km	City	Metropolitan Area Network
100 km	Country	Wide Area Network
1,000 km	Continent	
10,000 km	Planet	Internet

Personal Area Networks (PAN)

A personal area network is usually set up between small devices such as PDAs (Personal Digital Assistants) or mobile telephones, whose peripherals can be set up or dismantled ad hoc. PANs only extend a few meters spatially and bridge the working environment of a user at the workplace. Different wired technologies are used as transmission techniques, for example USB (Universal Serial Bus) or FireWire, as well as wireless technologies such as IrDA (Infrared Data Association) or Bluetooth. Bluetooth-based PANs are also known as piconets and wireless PANs (WPAN). PANs can be used both for the networking of small devices between each other as well as for the connection to a larger network (uplink).

Local Area Networks (LAN)

The local area network range extends from individual rooms, to entire floors and multiple building complexes, whereby it is rare that more than one individual piece of property is networked via a LAN technology. The scope of LANs encompasses a maximum of several kilometers and its main implementation is the networking of personal computers and their periphery in organizations, companies and home. Wired LAN technologies, such as Ethernet or Token Ring, are distinguished from wireless, mostly radio-based LANs – so-called wireless LANs (WLANs). LANs are mostly implemented as so-called broadcast networks, i.e., all connected end systems use the same communication hardware and are able to receive every message sent over it. In order to enable efficient communication between individual end devices, different procedures of static or dynamic channel allocation are used. LANs are often privately owned and their use is not governed by regulations.

Metropolitan Area Networks (MAN)

A metropolitan area network (MAN) is a broadband, communication network usually based on fiberglass technology. Its primary implementation is to link the most important office centers of one large city with another. Many cable television networks are also organized as MANs. A MAN can extend up to

100 km. Seen from a technical point of view, MAN technologies are usually not distinguishable from wide area networks (WAN technologies), the next higher category.

Wide Area Networks (WAN)

Remote networks and wide area networks extend over a large geographic area (e.g., country or continent) and serve the extended networking of end systems and individual LANs. While the end systems connected in a WAN are mostly privately-owned, the wide area network itself is normally operated publicly or by telecommunications company. In contrast to local networks, the number of end devices connected to a WAN is unlimited. The networking of multiple, different networks is known as an **internet** or as a **global area network (GAN)**.

A further criterion for the classification of computer networks is the type of computer networking within the communication system. Here a distinction is made between **direct** and **indirect networking**. If the computers, or more precisely data terminal equipment (DTEs), are directly connected to each other without independent routing computers being switched to organize the forwarding of data, one refers to a direct interconnection. If, in contrast, switching computers are involved in the forwarding of data one refers to an indirect connection. Independent switching computers are often not necessary in a LAN.

Computer networks and distributed systems

Distributed systems and computer networks have many **common characteristics** (see points 1-3), however they **differ** considerably in the software used and the transparency of the services provided (points 4-5):

- Similarities:

    1. An association of a multiple number of physically and logically different components whose tasks can be assigned dynamically.
    2. Individual components are spatially distributed.
    3. Individual components work autonomously but cooperatively.

- Differences:

    4. The services provided by the system components appear transparent in distributed systems and cannot be assigned by the user to a specific individual component.
    5. The computer network is controlled by a network operating system that coordinates the necessary processing steps of a user order.

Fig. 3.5 Computer networks and distributed systems.

Strictly hierarchically organized systems in which a series of dependent data stations – **slaves** – are regulated by a control system – a **master** – are not computer networks in the true sense of the word. Likewise, **distributed systems** are distinguished from computer networks. A distributed system appears as a homogeneous system to users, purposely concealing where and how the processing load is carried out. The user has the impression of working in one single system and not on a composite made up of individual processing units. Direct allocation of resources and access to the system periphery are not visible for the user. On the other hand, in a computer network the allocation of resources is dependent on the coordination of the user and not on the parent operating system.

Computer networks can also be subdivided according to their **application characteristics**. One speaks of **function sharing** when computers are connected in a network for special applications or when computers with special peripheral equipment or specific databases are connected. **Load sharing** occurs when a load distribution takes place between the individual connected components. When the network contains specific data repositories that are found distributed over different systems in the network, the term **data network** is used. If the main purpose of the network is the exchange of messages, this is referred to as **message sharing**. Whereas the term **safety network** is used if additional redundancy is provided in a network that can take over the function of one or more system components in the event of their failure. The **type** of interconnected computers is a further distinguishing criterion. A network is called **homogeneous** if all computers are of the same type, otherwise it is considered a **heterogeneous** network. Networks can be available for different kinds of user groups. Some computer networks are available via **public access**. In this case they can be accessed by everyone. There are also security-critical networks whose access is **nonpublic**. These networks are only available to a limited user circle, such as the network of of banks, the police or military. A further difference between networks can be identified that is based on **connection type**. Individual participants connect to a network based on need via a **dial-up connection** or they are permanently connected to the network via a **leased line**. Principally, **private networks** are distinguished from **public networks**. Among private networks are all of those whose network infrastructure, i.e., cabling, network hardware and software belongs to a company or a private owner. The vast majority of local networks (LANs) located on private property and connected to the computers of the owner are private networks . Large companies are also in a position to run their own wide area networks (WANs) linking various locations. The company can determine itself, within given limitations, the network structure, placement in the network and network addresses. A private company is however only able to execute its own cabling when it can be laid on its private property. For wide area networks, line sections must often be rented from public network operators, for example from a large operator such as German Telekom. A WAN that is partially operated via rented lines is nevertheless still considered private if the tenant has exclusive rights of use. Tenants themselves are then responsible for the operation and management of this network. A network that functions as a private network but is based on the infrastructure of the Internet is known as a **virtual private network** (**VPN**).

Conversely, a **public network** is a network that can be compared to the traditional telephone network. Anyone who wants to connect a computer to a public network pays a network operator for permission to use the network. However, the available network infrastructure must be shared with many other users and the tenant does not have exclusive rights of use as in the case of private networks. So that public networks can be profitably operated they must be made as attractive as possible for users. They are generally designed as wide area networks so as to be available for a great a number of users in a wide variety of places. The terms "private" and "public" therefore do not apply to ownership but to the availability of the services offered. Naturally, the communication via a public channel can be of a private nature. Because two computers connected via a public network are able to exchange data in encrypted form no third party user is able to gain knowledge of it. Although several public networks allow the communication of whole user groups (**multicasting**), it is as a rule not possible to communicate with all participants of the public network at the same time (**broadcasting**). In a private network the respective network owner (or tenant) is responsible for ensuring the operation and security measures. The individual owner monitors the connection of new computers to the private network, and sets access and communication restrictions to ensure compliance with its own safety standards. This is a complicated task that needs to be designed and implemented by qualified specialists. This is particularly the case when a company wishes to keep up with the current state of the art in technology. Replacement, or updates of the existing network infrastructure, which are often necessary, does not only involve huge costs but also a great effort in planning, implementation, training and operation.

From a financial point of view, the use of public networks is therefore often a better choice economically. The greater flexibility and less effort involved in implementing the most modern network technology is combined with much lower costs – in comparison to private networks. The network operator divides the costs among many customers. At the same time, the shared use of public networks also harbors dangers and security risks. The private computers connected to a public network must be protected from the unauthorized access of the rest of the network participants.

3.2 Computer Networks and Packet Switching

The principle of **packet switching** is a basic concept of the Internet. A message that is to be sent is disassembled into individual data packets of fixed, predetermined length at the sender. Independent of each other, these packets are sent separately through the labyrinth of the Internet. So that the packets are also able to find their way through different types of networks to the receiver there must be exchanges on the Internet. These are the so-called **packet**

switches or **routers**. Their task is to forward each of the individual packets to the next stop of a neighboring sequence exchange. The data packets reach their goal on completely different paths in this way. So that they do indeed arrive where they should and can be reassembled into a meaningful message again, every single packet must receive additional information for the journey. With the help of this additional information it is also possible to recognize transmission errors if they occur and even to be able to correct them. Without the technique of packet switching, modern high-speed communication networks would be unimaginable. Only in this way is it possible for a network to be used at the same time by many participants and the available capacity equally shared in a way that is both economical and efficient.

3.2.1 Classic Point-to-Point Connections

The first computer networks were based on the principle of the **point-to-point connection**. This was implemented, for example, via leased lines. Each one of the two communicating end systems has its own separate connection (cable, line, radio link), which means both terminals are permanently connected and can use the communication medium solely for their data exchange. It is also an advantage that only the two communication partners need to agree on a common communication protocol. Implementation of the communication software is thus simplified considerably: no consideration need be given to potentially different data formats, data sizes or error detection mechanisms. However, if more than two computers are linked to each other a point-to-point connection is a different matter. While theoretically simple to implement via an individual direct connection for all potential computer pairs, the required cabling effort quickly reaches its limits in practical application. If an attempt is made to link n computers with each other via a point-to-point connection, one needs nearly $n \cdot n = n^2$ connections to carry this out (see Fig. 3.6).

Point-to-point connections are only used today in special cases, e.g., for wide area networks that are coupled by a radio link.

3.2.2 Circuit-Switched Networks

Traditionally, data and telecommunications networks have been circuit-switched. In **circuit-switched networks**, also called **switching networks**, the communication partners have a fixed connection available. It is set up over a series of switching locations. The setup of a fixed link that must then be maintained for the entire duration of communication is prerequisite (see Fig. 3.7). While the connection is being established there is an initial waiting

Point-to-Point Connections

n=4   n=5

Number of computers	Number of connections
4	6
5	10
6	15
7	21
10	45
100	4,950
1,000	499,500

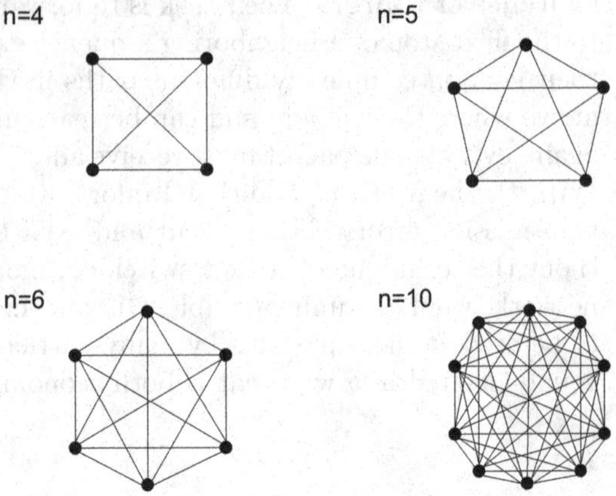

n=6   n=10

If n hosts are linked together using point-to-point connections, the following number of connections are needed:

$$\sum_{i=1}^{n-1} i = \frac{n^2 - n}{2}$$

Fig. 3.6 Point-to-point connections.

period before actual communication can begin. Once established, an active connection cannot be interrupted by other communication participants. Communication with multiple partners requires the setup of separate connections in each case. This is so all participants will have the same sending and receiving capacity. When setting up a connection, it can however happen that all channels to the desired communication partner are occupied. This can result from the momentary workload or from a lack of switching capacity. Failures at switching locations can also make the establishment of connections impossible and prevent communication from taking place. A circuit-switched network offers the communication partners a fixed data transmission rate at all times. **Delay** on a network transmission path is always uniform and remains minimal. It generally corresponds to the propagation velocity of the electromagnetic signal (approx. 5 ms per 100 km). At the same time, the establishment of this type of connection is usually very time-intensive. The costs are always proportional to the connection duration. Costs also accrue during breaks in the communication, even when no data is being sent. If one of the exchanges involved fails, the connection is lost and communication ends. In the worst case scenario it can happen that after the failure of just one exchange, entire subnets of the whole network become separated and inaccessible.

The maximum amount of data that can be transmitted per unit of time over a specific transmission medium is referred to as **bandwidth**. The bandwidth of a connection is always limited by the weakest section of the route through the network. An important example of a circuit-switched network is an analog **telephone network**. The connection to the desired party is established via the automated exchanges of the telephone network by dialing a number. After the participant on the opposite end has picked up the receiver, the connection remains active until the receiver is hung up. In a telephone network, speech is transmitted between the sender and the receiver with a more or less constant bandwidth

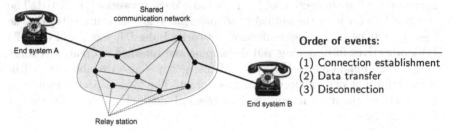

Fig. 3.7 Switching network.

3.2.3 From Circuit Switching to Packet Switching

The importance of computers for military and business use grew dramatically at the beginning of the sixties. The first so-called time-sharing systems – meaning computers that allow interactive work – came on the market. The idea of linking computers over wide areas to allow interactive work between users in different geographic locations was literally in the air. The data traffic generated by such networked-functioning computers is not steady in comparision to the normal telephone call, but occurs in varying clusters of activity – so-called **bursts**. Bursts occur as intervals of maximum activity on which follow intervals of inactivity, e.g., the length of time necessary for local calculation or the preparation time needed for a response. How can a fail-safe data flow be ensured in computer communications, also when exchanges do not work with absolute reliability or can even fail completely? If the failure of an exchange is recognized, then despite the fact that a new route can be established through the network it is not clear to the communication partners how much of the message contents has gotten lost in between. Just to be on the safe side, the transmission needs to be repeated. But then it could be that a connection channel is occupied. The other network participants are then forced to wait as long as is necessary before it becomes free again – a scenario that is far from an equal allocation of resources. The issue of how to structure large, fail-safe and fair-working data networks was the subject of scientific investigation at the end of the fifties. *Leonard Kleinrock* (*1934), a PhD student at Massachusetts Institute of Technology (MIT) published his thesis entitled *"Information Flow in Large Networks"* in 1962. His focus was on just this problem. As a solution he presented the principle of **packet switching** [136]. Also working on this problem independent of Kleinrock were *Donald Davies* (1924 – 2000) of the British National Physical Laboratory, who coined the term "packet switching," and *Paul Baran* (1926 – 2011), who worked at RAND Corporation, another of ARPA's contract partners. Baran took up the idea of packet switching and developed it into a fundamental principle for the connection of large, fail-safe data networks [11, 12, 61]. The way was free (at least theoretically) to make inherently insecure networks the basis for fail-safe data communication networks. Indeed, it was one of the ARPA's objectives in designing and developing the Internet to create networks with a high reliability and – in case of emergency – also the ability to withstand failure at one or more exchanges intact. The idea of packet switching is considered the most important fundamental idea behind the development of the Internet.

3.2.4 The Principle of Packet Switching

Packet switching is based on the principle of the disassembling the message to be sent into individual **data packets**, also simply called packets. After disassembly **(fragmentation)**, the packets can be transported over the communication network individually and independent of one another. The route taken by the individual packets is not fixed from the outset. The sender only determines the path to the next exchange, similar to the mail service for parcels. On the receiver's side the data packets are subsequently reassembled back into the original message **(defragmentation**, see Fig. 3.8).

Special **routing algorithms** serve to find the best path through the network. On their path through the network, packets can able to avoid any congestion and interference occurring at the exchanges. Although their way might be longer, they can reach their target faster than packets traveling on a shorter but blocked path. In addition, the entire network can also be utilized. The size of sent packets must be restricted for various reasons. Accordingly, a connection is never occupied for a long time and as a result all potential senders have equal and fair access to the network. Indeed it is the principle of packet switching that first allows truly interactive connections to be achieved at all. This is because the lines between the individual exchanges are only occupied for milliseconds and no user can block a connection for a long time as happens in circuit-switched networks.

In packet switching it is necessary that it be possible for data packets to be buffered for as long as is necessary at the network exchange. Every packet switch has its own intermediate storage (input buffer and output buffer) for its incoming and outgoing data lines. If an incoming packet is to be forwarded

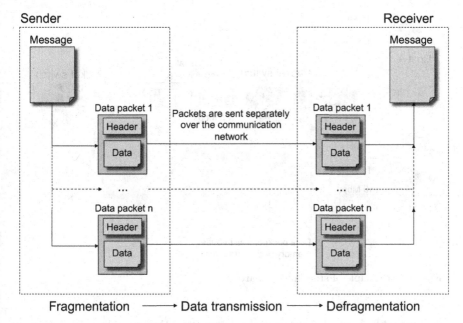

Fig. 3.8 Principles of fragmentation and defragmentation.

via an output that is momentarily occupied with sending another packet, the packet is buffered in the output buffer until the output is free again. This type of exchange is thus called **store-and-forward** (see Fig. 3.9). The latency that occurs is variable and depends on the network load. If a data packet cannot be accepted or forwarded because the input or output buffer is full packet loss occurs. Either the incoming packet or a packet from the output buffer is discarded. The order in which the packets are sent from the output buffer corresponds to their arrival. Because packets can arrive from different inputs arbitrarily, i.e., in random order, this bundling of different inputs to one output queue at the packet switch is referred to as **statistical multiplexing** or as **asynchronous multiplexing**. The procedure contrasts to regular **time division multiplexing (TDM)**, in which alternately each participant receives an equally large time slot.

Message switching is a special kind of memory switching. Messages are not disassembled as in packet switching but sent in their entirety, i.e., in one single packet, through the network. Just as in circuit switching, no explicit connection is established in this type of message transfer. The entire message has to be buffered at the respective switching stations; this also determines to which exchange the message will be sent next. In the early days of telegraphy, telegrams were transmitted this way. In the sender's office, the message was stamped on a punched tape, read and then forwarded over the telegraph cable to the next telegraph station. There it was temporarily stored again on a punched tape. In contrast to packet switching, there is no fixed, prede-

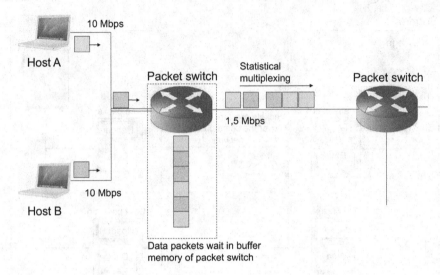

Fig. 3.9 Principle of store-and-forward.

termined block size for the sent data packets. Message switching is entirely unsuitable for data networks common today. This procedure would mean exchanges being blocked for a lengthy time or under certain circumstances their buffer not having enough storage space for even a single message (cf. Fig. 3.10).

3.2.5 Advantages of Packet Switching

The advantages of packet switching over circuit switching are clear:

- **High network utilization**
  Since the individual data packets in packet switching are usually very small, a high degree of network utilization can be reached. The waiting times for all other communication participants remains minimal

- **Fair resource allocation**
  The communication network is available to all participants equally. All connected devices can send data packets alternatively according to a pre-determined multiplex procedure.

- **Rapid error detection**
  If small data packets are always sent, transmission errors can be quickly detected and if possible corrected immediately. It's only necessary to retransmit the faulty packets and not the whole message.

- **High reliability**
  If one switching station fails, the whole message is not lost as in the case of

Packet switching vs. message switching

Why is packet switching the more efficient of the two procedures? The individual packet switches in the network can first forward a data packet when it has arrived completely. In the case of a smaller size data packet, the latency time is also correspondingly short. In message switching networks, the waiting time at each switching computer is proportional to the length of the message – theoretically speaking – with an unlimited length. This can be illustrated by way of a simple example.

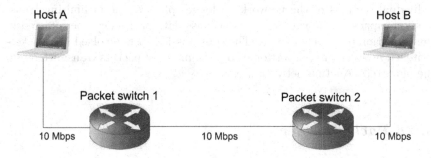

In our example network, a message with the length 80 MBit = 80,000 kBit is to be sent from host A to host B. The entire network has a bandwidth of 10 Mbps (megabits per second). In order to go from A to B, 2 packet switches have to be passed. In the case of a message-switched network, it is necessary to wait at the respective switching point as long as is necessary for the entire message to arrive. From computer A to the first switching computer that takes 80 Mb/10 Mbps = 8 seconds. This means that at least $3 \cdot 8 = 24$ seconds pass by before the whole message arrives at the destination computer. Let us now assume that the represented network is packet switched with a fixed packet size of 2 kBit = 2,000 bits. The message is then divided into 80,000 kBit/2 kBit = 40,000 packets. The 40,000 packets need the following transmission time. 2 kBit / 10 Mbps = 0,2 ms pass by before the first packet arrives at packet switch 1. Accordingly it takes only $40,000 \cdot 0.2 m = 8,000 ms = 8$ seconds until the last packet arrives at the first packet switch. Since the last packet must then be transmitted via a further packet switch to the end system host B, a total of $8 + 2 \cdot 0.0002 = 8.0004$ seconds pass by until the message has completely reached its target. In our example we can see that data transmission in the packet-switched network is three times faster than in the message-switched network. Data transfer in the packet-switching network proceeds for the most part **parallel** in a fashion similar to an assembly line, whereas data traffic in a message-switching network is carried out **sequentially**. In a message-switched network, the other switching computers must wait while one is receiving a message. In a packet-switched network all switching nodes transmit simultaneously.

Fig. 3.10 Comparison of packet switching and message switching.

circuit switching. In circuit switching it could be that a complete section of the network is no longer reachable if this situation occurs. Communication must start all over again with the establishment of a fixed connection path. In packet switching the rest of the network remains untouched and can continue to be used for communication. Data packets which are already. on the path are simply led along an alternative route that does not pass the failed exchange.

While circuit-switched networks with switching centers can be implemented without having their own intermediate storage, all forms of packet switching need buffers at every switching center. Packets must be temporarily stored for as long as is necessary until forwarding can be carried out. That's why the term **store-and-forward** is used for this technique. Buffering offers another very important advantage. In packet switching the transmission speed in the individual sections of the network no longer plays a role in limiting transmission capacity as a whole. This is because data packets can be buffered in the transition to slower sections. The transmission costs involved in a packet-switched network are proportional to the number of packets transmitted and therefore reflect actual network usage.

3.2.6 Packet header

So that the complete message in a packet switched network can reach its destination and be reassembled correctly again on the receiver side, all data packets must contain a range of additional information. This additional information is usually transmitted in a segment prefixing the package and is known as a **packet header**.

- **Address information**
  Packet headers contain address details about the sender and receiver so that the packet switches can determine over which path the packet needs to be forwarded.
- **Packet number**
  The individual data packets have to be numbered consecutively so they can be reassembled at the receiver and communicate the actual message sent.
- **Padding data**
  It is possible that the amount of data sent is smaller than the required packet size. In this case, the data packet must be supplemented with padding data, which must also be identified as such.
- **Error detection mechanisms**
  So that transmission errors can be recognized, extra error detection data must be added This does not only make it possible to identify errors but in some cases to also correct them (see Excursus 2).

3.2.7 Disadvantages of Packet Switching

It is precisely in the areas where packet switching differs from circuit switching that not only its advantages but also its disadvantages lie:

- **Overload (Congestion)**
  Because there are no dedicated, exclusive connections fixed in packet switching, it can happen that an exchange is not able to handle a sudden rush of incoming data packets, i.e., the available buffer overflows and as a result data packets are lost.

- **Complex communication protocol**
  Because data transmission in circuit switching is carried out in a completely transparent manner, it is irrelevant which communication protocol the sender and the receiver have agreed upon. Owing to this communication transparency the phone system, for example, is able to offer different services simultaneously. It is possible for language communication to be easily offered side by side with fax or data communication. In packet switching, by contrast, all communication partners must commit to a network based on a common network protocol. For example, the basic data packets and parameters for the communication process must be established such as bit rates and data fragmentation.

- **No quality of service guarantee**
  Another disadvantage of packet switching is that it is not possible to guarantee a constant bandwidth for transmission without taking extra steps. It is possible for the transmission rate to vary depending on utilization of the individual exchanges and it can be relatively large.

Besides delays caused by memory switching transmission, packets often face waiting time in the output buffer queue of the switching computer. Arriving packets must wait until all those packets that had already been lined up in the queue have been sent. These delay times are variable and depend on the particular utilization of the network.

Table 3.2 Comparison of packet switching and circuit switching

Property	Circuit switching	Packet switching
Fixed connection path	yes	no
Available bandwidth	constant	dynamically variable
Wasted bandwidth	yes	no
Store-and-forward transmission	no	yes
Each packet follows the same route	no	yes
Previous connection establishment	necessary	unnecessary
Congestion can occur	in connection establishment	anytime
Calculation procedure	per unit of time	per packet

Transmission time and total delay

How much time does a packet switched transmission need from one host to another? Let us assume that a data packet with a length of l bits is to be sent. Let us further suppose that there are exactly q switching computers between sender A and receiver B. These have a bandwidth of r bps and a dedicated connection does not need to be set up. Moreover, we shall assume that the waiting time in the queues of individual switching computers is relatively small. The time that a data packet needs from the starting computer A to the first switching computer is exactly l/r seconds. The packet is then forwarded exactly $q-1$ times and buffered so that the total delay time is $q \cdot (l/r)$. Practically-speaking, however, the connection paths between the individual computers have different bandwidths r_i, $1 \leq i \leq q$. Therefore, the total delay t_d is calculated as

$$t_d = \sum_{i=1}^{q} \frac{l}{r_i}.$$

Fig. 3.11 Transmission time in packet-switched networks.

3.2.8 Connectionless and Connection-Oriented Network Services

In principle, it is possible to make a distinction between **connectionless** and **connection-oriented** services in packet-switched networks. The previously discussed variations of packet-switched networks are considered connectionless network services, also called **datagram networks**. A data packet provided with additional information necessary for its correct transport through the network to the receiver is also known as a **datagram**. In contrast to connectionless datagram networks, in connection-oriented networks while messages are disassembled into separate data packets prior to transmission, a so-called **virtual connection**[1] (Virtual Circuit, VC) is set up at the same time. All packets are then transported between the two communication partners through the network via this virtual connection. Assignment of the individual, virtually switched connections is administered via the network exchanges. In the phase of connection establishment the connection state is fixed between the sender and the receiver at each exchange. This allows the connection to be uniquely identified. A potential mix-up in the sequence of the individual packets is therefore prevented. Sender and receiver exchange so-called "bit streams" (or byte streams) as messages over the datagram network on a higher level of abstraction, i.e., the virtual connection conceals the separation of the data packets in the individual data streams exchanged bet-

---

[1] A distinction is made here between virtual connections on the (hardware-near) network layer, such as ATM (Asynchronous Transfer Mode), frame relay or X.25 – the available switched virtual circuits or permanent virtual circuits and virtual connections on the overlying transport layer, such as with the Transmission Control Protocol (TCP), that is based on a datagram network and the virtual connection that is implemented purely by software. This will be discussed in greater detail in section 3.4.3.

ween communication partners. Because the allocation of available resources is stricter here than in conventional datagram networks a reaction to overload, line or node failure can be less flexibly addressed. Connection-oriented datagram networks are similar to circuit-switched networks because establishment and termination take place separate from actual user data transmission in both cases. While circuit-switched networks offer constant data transmission rates and latency times these normally vary in connection-oriented datagram networks.

3.2.9 Service Paradigms of Computer Networks

The organization and implementation of computer communication in a packet-switched data network is carried out in modular, individual layers, hierarchically structured in increasing degrees of abstraction. On the lower, hardware-close layers, the data packets are transmitted. The higher abstract layers in the hierarchy have protocols to implement the disassembly of the message into individual packets and to organize its transmission. Thus, details of the data transmission are kept from the user and provide him with a more comfortable and higher-quality service. A distinction in service is made between **connectionless service** and **connection-oriented service**.

3.2.9.1 Connectionless service

This category of network service can best be compared to the conventional postal network. Before a computer can send a message to another computer it must convert it into a predefined data packet format and include a receiver's and sender's address. This can best be compared to a written message put in an envelope on which the receiver's address is written. Just as a letter is brought to a mail collection point, the computer passes the completed data packet to the network for delivery. From there it is sent to the receiver. To keep administrative costs as low as possible, the connectionless service does not provide any guarantee that the packet actually arrives at the receiver or in what time frame. In contrast to connection-oriented service, no connection is made between the sender and the receiver; the individual data packets are transported independent of each other and without delay through the network. If the communication behavior is characterized by frequently changing addressees and short message lengths, connectionless service offers important advantages over connection-oriented service.

3.2.9.2 Connection-oriented service

We can compare the operation of a connection-oriented service with a standard, analog telephone network. Before the message exchange operation between two computers begins, a connection first has to be switched between them. This is similar to dialing a telephone number and triggering a connection to the dialed subscriber. As soon as the partner has recognized the communication wish and accepted it, a switched connection exists between them – much like picking up a ringing phone with the partner at the other end answering. The switched connection may then be used in a virtually exclusive manner for the communication to follow. When the communication comes to an end, the switched connection is terminated. A connection-oriented service always proceeds through three phases:

1. Connection establishment,
2. Data transmission and
3. Disconnection.

Connection-oriented services via packet-switched networks rely on the connectionless services available. In other words, the resource allocation of a fixed connection is in fact only a virtual one and displayed on a higher layer of the modularly organized communication schema. With connection-oriented services the user is provided an interface that allows exclusive use of the virtual connection. This interface shields the user from all processes running on a hierarchically lower layer of communication, such as structuring, addressing and transporting of individual data packets. Thus the user is offered comfortable communication access. Connection-oriented services via such a data connection must not run continuously. The connection can be temporarily interrupted and data traffic resumed again later. The connection remains active for the entire period until the point when one of the communication participants explicitly decides to end it (comparable to hanging up the phone). Network errors are noticed immediately in a connection-oriented service. If, for example, one of the exchanges along the switched virtual connection fails, the communication subscribers can react immediately. While a connectionless network service billing is usually based on the amount of transmitted data, in the case of connection-oriented services it is normally based on the duration of the existing connection. From a practical point of view, this calculation procedure is often less costly as well as being easier to carry out.

On the other hand, connection establishment in a connection-oriented communication takes a relatively long time. If just a short message needs to be exchanged, the time involved in setting up a connection can easily surpass the duration of the actual connection itself. But if the connection is to be sustained over a longer period it is an advantage that much less administrative and control information needs to be transported with the packets than would be the case with a connectionless service. Once the connection is established in a connection-oriented service, the data packets to be exchanged receive a network assigned connection identification (a so-called connection identifier). As a rule, this identifier is much shorter than the network address information that data packets need in a connectionless service. Use of a connection-oriented service pays off especially if connections are established to just a few communication partners and in each case over a longer period of time. It is possible to go even one step further and establish a **persistent connection** via a connection-oriented service. In the first computer networks, point-to-point links were used to set up a permanent connection via a dedicated physical connection (cable). However, today this can be done by setting up a dedicated, virtual information channel over a shared network. The configuration of these leased lines is stored in the non-volatile memory of the participating computers. This means it can be re-activated immediately if a power outage occurs. These type of permanent connections can be maintained for months or even years. They appear physically as point-to-point connections from the perspective of the connected computers. Persistent connections ensure a degree of availability that random connections do not. The connection is always ready and usable, i.e., a connected computer does not have to first wait for connection establishment with the receiver. Naturally this "connection fixing" also means a loss of flexibility. Dial-up connections are only then switched when they are really needed. The dial-up connection is dismantled the rest of the time, allowing the bandwidth to be available to other network subscribers.

3.2.10 Error Detection and Error Correction

To ensure reliable data transmission over a not always error-free transmission medium, mechanisms must be put in place to perform automatic detection and correction when transmission errors occur. The individual data packets are thus supplied with additional information to recognize errors. If errors occur they allow – at least up to a certain point – the reconstruction of the correct contents of a data packet. This extra information does not contribute anything to the actual contents of the information contained in the data packet. It is referred to as **redundancy**. For example, the sender calculates a **checksum** for the data packet to be sent and appends it to the packet. Once the packet has arrived at the receiver, the same procedure for checksum calculation is performed by the receiver (excluding the attached checksum). This calculated value is compared with the checksum value of the sent data packet. If both values match, the probability is high that the packet has been correctly transmitted. But if the values don't match it is an indication that the content has undergone changes during transmission. The receiver has the possibility to request the data packet again from the sender. In this case, the whole message does not need to be retransmitted but only the defective data packet. While it is true that data lines have become more reliable all the time, the widespread wireless communication technologies, e.g., **wireless LAN** (WLAN), have led to a huge increase in transmission errors stemming from noise or other disturbances. The receiver is then often not able to correctly reconstruct the received signals of the transmitted data packet. When errors do occur in wireless communication it happens – fortunately – in a cumulative manner in so-called **bursts** or bundles. If it were the case that errors only occurred in isolated individual bits, this would mean a constant error rate of, for example, 0.01% per bit for a package size of 10,000 bits. In this scenario nearly every single packet would be faulty and need to be retransmitted. But if errors occur in bursts of 100 on the average, then only one or two packets out of 100 are affected.

Table 3.3 Bit error probability.

Transmission medium	Bit error probability (Magnitude)
Radio	$10^{-1} - 10^{-3}$
Telephone line	10^{-5}
Digital data network	$10^{-6} - 10^{-7}$
LAN (coaxial cable)	10^{-9}
Fiberglass cable	10^{-12}

A measure for transmission errors is the so-called **bit error rate**. It is calculated from the ratio between the incorrectly transmitted bits and the total number of bits transmitted measured over a longer period of time. Table 3.3 shows an overview of the magnitude of the bit error rate in different transmission media. Methods of error detection and correction are often unable to accurately recognize all errors. Therefore, error correction procedures should work in such a way that the residual error probability is as small as possible. To be able to handle errors in the most efficient way, two fundamental (redundancy increasing) coding methods have been developed. These are **error-detection codes**, and a related **retransmission** in the case of recognized errors, or automatic error correction, via **error correcting codes** (for the basic concepts of coding, see also section 4.2.1).

Using error-correcting codes it is possible – when not too many errors occur at the same time – to draw conclusions based on the original output message (original code word). In comparison to error detection, a significantly higher effort is required for error correction. This procedure then becomes necessary when the effort required for retransmission of a sent message is excessive. Implementing an error-detecting code is sufficient if an efficient query is possible. A faulty data packet recognized as such can then be retransmitted. Which procedure is used in each case depends on the bit error rate of the transmission medium. For example, in the case of mobile data transmission the bit error rate can be very high. Accordingly, more complex error-correction procedures must be implemented. It could happen that after error detection the new transmission is found faulty again and stringent time restrictions prohibit a renewed transmission. A further factor is the data transmission rate of the transmission medium used. If it is high enough – as in the case of a high-speed fiberglass network – then the repeated transmission of an incorrectly transmitted data packet has no significant consequences and a simpler error-detection coding can be used.

Excursus 2 introduces the theoretical foundation of error-detecting and error-correction codes and gives examples of Hamming coding and checksum procedures.

Excursus 2: Error-Detecting and Error-Correcting Codes

Message and redundancy
Let us look at the structure of a random data packet – in this context it is also referred to as the **codeword**. The codeword (message) itself has a length of $n=m+r$ bits and consists of the payload to be transmitted (the communication) and extra bits that enable the detection of a transmission error (the redundancy).

Codeword:

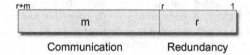

Hamming distance
Let's now look at two random binary code words of equal length. We see that it is easy to identify positions where the bits do not correspond. For example,

Codeword C_1 1000100010001000
Codeword C_2 1000000011000000

The two codewords differ in exactly three positions. The number of positions that differ between the two codewords a and b is referred to as the **Hamming distance** $H(a,b)$ (after *Richard W. Hamming*, 1915 – 1998) of the two codewords. The importance of the Hamming distance quickly becomes clear. If two codewords differ by n bits, then exactly n single bit errors can transform the one codeword into the other. In order to determine the Hamming distance of two given codewords, they are linked bit by bit with the logical XOR-Operator ($\oplus$-Operator, $0 \oplus 0 = 0$, $1 \oplus 1 = 0$, $0 \oplus 1 = 1 \oplus 0 = 1$) and sum up the number of ones in the result of this operation:

$$H(a, b) = \sum_{i=0}^{n-1} a_i \oplus b_i$$

In our example, there is a Hamming distance of $H(a,b)=3$:

```
        a 1000100010001000
        b 1000000011000000
 a ⊕ b 0000100001001000
```

Overall there can be 2^m different messages with the length m. Independent of which procedure is used to calculate redundancy, it is impossible for each of the 2^{r+m} theoretically possible codewords to occur. With the help of the algorithm that calculates redundancy, the list of all "valid" or "permissible" codewords can be created. The codeword pairs from the list of permitted codewords exhibiting the smallest Hamming distance define the Hamming distance of the code. This code' Hamming distance is then considered the measure for its **immunity to interference**.

To be able to recognize n-1 errors in a codeword, the implemented code must have at least a Hamming distance of n. In such a code it is not possible that n-1 single bit errors will result in the faulty codeword matching another permissible codeword. Also a code with a Hamming distance of n single bit errors, which affects fewer than (n-1)/2 bits, can be automatically corrected. This is done by simply searching for the closest permissible codeword to the received codeword.

Parity bit

The simplest example for an error detecting code is the addition of a **parity bit** to the end of a string of binary code. The parity bit corresponds to the parity of the 1-bit in the code word. If the number is even then the parity bit is equal to 0, otherwise it is equal to 1.

$$\text{Parity}(a) = \bigoplus_{i=0}^{n-1} a_i$$

For a=1000100010001000 e.g., the number of 1-bits is equal to 4, a – the parity is therefore even. a is added with the parity bit p=0, the code actually transmitted is a'=0100010001000100|0. A code with a single parity bit has the Hamming distance 2 and can be used to detect individually occurring bit errors – so-called **single bit errors**. Those codes in which the message remains unchanged as a block, with the check bits simply appended, are referred to as **systematic block codes**. If the bits of multiple code words are summarized together into a matrix, in addition to horizontally determined parity bits, (Longitudinal Redundancy Check, LRC) parity is also defined in columns (Vertical Redundancy Check, VRC).

LRC

1	1	1	0	0	1	0	0	0
0	0	0	1	1	0	1	1	0
0	1	1	0	0	1	0	0	1
1	0	1	1	0	1	0	1	1

VRC

0	0	1	0	1	1	1	0

With the simultaneous use of LRC and VRC, error correction can be carried out as long as per matrix line and column at least one bit has been corrupted.

How large must the redundancy R be chosen in order to make sure that every single bit error can be detected with a message of the length m? Considering a_i, a single one of the possible 2^m messages, after the addition a_iR_i with the redundancy R_i the length r all together there are n=m+r possibilities to create for a_iR_i permissible codewords with the Hamming distance 1. These unreliable codewords can be created by simply inverting one bit after the other into the codeword a_iR_i. In this way each of the 2^m messages n+1 has different bit patterns that could possibly arise from bit errors and which can only be assigned to it alone. The total number of possible bit patterns in our code is 2^n, therefore it must apply that

$$(n + 1)2^m \leq 2^n.$$

The code length n=r+m results in

$$(m + r + 1) \leq 2^r$$

as a lower limit for the number r of the bits required to detect all possible single bit errors.

Hamming code

The **Hamming code**, named after its inventor, Richard Hamming, is a code that follows this pattern and detects all individual bit errors. All bits of the codeword are numbered starting with 1. Bits numbered with a power of two (1,2,4,8,16, etc.) are implemented as **check bits**, while the remaining bits (3,5,6,7,9,10, etc.) are filled with the m bits of the message. Every check bit now stands for the parity of a number of individual bits. One bit can thus be included in different parity bits.

The data bit at position k, $1 \leq k \leq n$, is allocated to the check bits contained in the binary encoding of k. For example, if k=11, then $k=1+2+8=2^0+2^1+2^3$ and the k-th bit enters in the parity calculation of check bits 2^0, 2^1, and 2^3.

Codeword

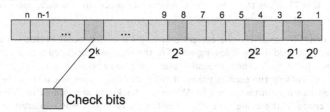

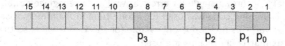

Check bits

For example, let us consider a Hamming code for transmitting codewords each made up of m=11 data bits and r=4 check bits. This code made up of n=15 bit long codewords is also known as 15/11 Hamming code.

The check bits are designated p_0 - p_3. Bits with c_1 - c_{15} are numbered. In accordance with the specified rule, check bits are generated as follows:

$$p_0 = c_3 \oplus c_5 \oplus c_7 \oplus c_9 \oplus c_{11} \oplus c_{13} \oplus c_{15}$$
$$p_1 = c_3 \oplus c_6 \oplus c_7 \oplus c_{10} \oplus c_{11} \oplus c_{14} \oplus c_{15}$$
$$p_2 = c_5 \oplus c_6 \oplus c_7 \oplus c_{12} \oplus c_{13} \oplus c_{14} \oplus c_{15}$$
$$p_3 = c_9 \oplus c_{10} \oplus c_{11} \oplus c_{12} \oplus c_{13} \oplus c_{14} \oplus c_{15}$$

To illustrate the interaction of individual check bits (position 1, 2, 4 and 8), they are shown in tabular form.

Pos	15	14	13	12	11	10	9	8	7	6	5	4	3	2	1	Parity
p_0	x		x		x		x		x		x		x		x	0
p_1	x	x			x	x			x	x			x	x		0
p_2	x	x	x	x					x	x	x	x				0
p_3	x	x	x	x	x	x	x									0

All check bits are made up out of 7 coefficients each. If the parity is calculated via a p_i check bit with its associated coefficient it must always be even. Therefore, $p_i \oplus c_{i1} \oplus \ldots \oplus c_{i1}$ $=0$ (see last column of the table). For example, let us assume that the following bit sequence is to be transmitted: 00010111001. Together with the calculated check bit p_0 - p_3 the codeword 000101111000111 results. Let us further assume that during data transmission an error has occurred in position 7, and that c_7 is inverted. This results in the incorrect code: 000101110000111 reaching the receiver. For checking and correction of the received codeword it can once again be viewed in the given tabular form:

Pos	15	14	13	12	11	10	9	8	7	6	5	4	3	2	1	Parity
C	0	0	0	1	0	1	1	1	0	0	0	0	1	1	1	
p_0	0		0		0		1		0		0		1		1	1 F
p_1	0	0			0	1			0	0			1	1		1–F
p_2	0	0	0	1					0	0	0	0				1–F
p_3	0	0	0	1	0	1	1	1								0–ok

The parity check for p_0 - p_2 results respectively in the incorrect value 1, only p_4 is calculated correctly. Carefully choosing the collocation of the check bits makes an exact localization of the individual bit error possible. Only the place c_7 as single bit error is capable of distorting calculation of the check bit p_0 - p_2. Adding the powers of the check bit index $(2^2+2^1+2^0 = 4+2+1 = 7)$, gives the results of the incorrect place. In this way, every bit error of the code can be detected and corrected.

An algorithm for checking the correction reception and possible correction of a Hamming code could proceed in the following way. For the received codeword a counter z is initialized with the value 0, $z=0$. Then, the calculation for every check bit p_i is repeated to determine whether it contains the correct parity. If the calculation does not match the set check bit, i is added to the counter, $z := z+i$. When all check bits are verified in this way and if the counter contains the value 0 ($z=0$), then the transmission was correct and the next data packet can be checked. But if the counter is unequal 0 ($z=k$, $k\neq0$) it is an indication that it contains the exact position of the incorrect inverted bit c_k. Via the coding scheme of the Hamming code, a Hamming distance of $\delta_{min}=3$ results as the minimum distance permissible between any two random code words. Therefore it is possible with the Hamming code to detect individually occurring single bit errors as well as to recognize double-occurring single bit errors. The Hamming code was used for a long time in main memory access routines of computers. However, this method is only viable for short codewords so that today different methods such as matrix checksums are used.

Checksum procedure

Another widely used practice for error detection is to identify **checksums**. Here, the characers representing the transmitted bit sequences are interpreted as numerical values and their sums calculated. This checksum is simply appended onto the transmitted data as a binary-coded number. Checksum procedures are used, for example, in the Internet protocol IP. The most well-known procedure is the so-called (**Cyclic Redundancy Check CRC**, also called **polynomial code**. The fundamental concept of the CRC procedure is representing the transmitted bits of the message as coefficient u_i, $0\leq i\leq m-1$, of a polynomial, which could be either 0 or 1. The payload bits of the message are interpreted as follows:

$$M(x) = u_{m-1}x^{m-1} + u_{m-2}x^{m-2} + \ldots + u_1x + u_0.$$

The polynomial $M(x)$ is of degree $m-1$. The message 11000101 has e.g., exactly 8 bits and generates the polynomial $M(x)=x^7+x^6+x^2+1$. The calculation rules for this polynomial correspond to the usual rules of calculation in a body of of characteristic 2 ($\mathbb{F}_2$). Addition and subtraction correspond to the XOR operation. The division is exactly the same method for binary numbers except that the subtraction is calculated again as XOR. The polynomial $M(x)$ is then divided by a **generator polynomial** $G(x)$, used both by the sender and the receiver and the resulting remainder constitutes the block checksum to be appended. The generator polynomial is of degree r, the first and the last bits must be equal to zero, $g_r, g_0 \neq 0$:

$$G(x) = g_r x^r + g_{r-1} x^{r-1} + \ldots + r_1 x + r_0.$$

Now r zero bits are appended to the message, which corresponds to the polynomial $x^r M(x)$. $x^r M(x)$ is divided by $G(x)$ using the calculation rules for finite fields. This results in a remainder polynomial $R(x)$, which is r-1 degree at the most. The coefficients of $R(x)$, $r_{r-1}, \ldots, r_0$, are appended to the message. Thus, the transmitted message corresponds to the polynomial $N(x) = x^r M(x) - R(x)$.

This polynomial is now divisible by $G(x)$. If $N(x)$ is transmitted without error, the receiver calculates $N(x)/G(x)$ and gets the remainder 0. It is clear that $N(x)$ is divisible in any case by

Message:	1101011011
Generator:	k= 4, G(x) = $x^4 + x^1 + 1$, (10011)
Multiply message with x^4 :	1101011011 0000

Determination of remainder:

```
11010110110000 : 10011
10011↓||||||||
 10011
 10011↓↓↓↓
 0000010110||
    10011↓↓
    0010100|
     10011↓
      001110   Remainder
```

Codeword for transmission:	1101011011 1110

Fig. 3.12 CRC checksum procedure.

$G(x)$, because for any division problem it holds true that if one subtracts the remainder from the dividend, the result of the subtraction is always divisible by the divisor. To now analyze the usefulness of the method let us assume that in the transmission of $N(x)$ there actually occurs a transmission error. Instead of the bit string $N(x)$, the receiver gets the incorrect message $N(x) + E(x)$. Each 1 bit in $E(x)$ corresponds to one single bit error, i.e., a place in $N(x)$, that was inverted by the transmission error. If $E(x)$ contains k 1 bits, then k single bit errors have occurred. In order to analyze the method's usefulness, we shall assume that a transmission error occurred in the transmission of $N(x)$. Instead of the bit string $N(x)$ the receiver gets the incorrect message $N(x) + E(x)$. Each 1 bit in $E(x)$ corresponds to a single bit error, therefore a position in $N(x)$ that was inverted due to a transmission error. If $E(x)$ contains k 1-bits, then k single bit errors have occurred. The receiver then divides the received message, extended by the checksum, by $G(x)$, i.e., $(N(x) + E(x))/G(x)$. As $N(x)/G(x) = 0$, the result is equal to $E(x)/G(x)$. Errors that occur at exactly the place where the generator polynomial $G(x)$ also contain 1 bit are ignored. However, all others are recognized. If a single bit error occurs then $E(x) = x^i$, whereby i indicates which bit of the message is incorrect. This can be detected when the generator polynomial is constructed in such a way as to contain at least 2 terms, so that $E(x)$ is never divisible by $G(x)$. All single-bit errors can thus be recognized when the generator polynomial contains at least two terms.

If two isolated single bit errors occur so that $E(x)=x^i+x^j$, $i>j$, then is $E(x)=x^j(x^{i-j}+1)$. If $G(x)$ is not divisible by x, then all such double errors can be detected if $G(x)$ is selected in such a way that x^k+1 is not divisible by $G(x)$, for $k\leq i-j$ (whereby i-j is limited due to the packet size). In [237] simple example polynomials are presented, such as $x^{15}+x^{14}+1$, which for no polynomial the form x^k+1 is shared for $k<32.768$. Also another interesting property of arithmetic based on F_2 can be used here: No polynomial of odd length, i.e., with an odd number of single terms, has $x+1$ as a divider. If we now simply include $x+1$ in the generator polynomial, it can additionally be ensured that all errors affecting an odd number of bits are detected. So-called burst errors start and end with a 1-bit. The region between the two delimiting bits can include 1-bits as well as 0-bits, the outer area only 0-bits. A polynomial code with r check bits can discover all burst errors with the length $\leq r$. A burst error with the length k, meaning $E(x)=x^i(x^{k-1}+\ldots+1)$ – whereby i designates the offset of the error – is detected when the expression $(x^{k-1}+\ldots+1)$ has a lower degree than $G(x)$ has, because the remainder can never be equal to 0.

Additionally, it must apply that x^0 is part of $G(x)$,so that the divisibility of the remaining part x_i of the polynomial is excluded. If the bundle length is equal to r+1, only exactly a zero results as division reminder if the burst error is equal to the generator polynomial $G(x)=E(x)$. In accordance with its definition, the burst error has on each of its two end points a 1-bit, the r-1 bits in between are optional. If we consider all possible bit combinations as equally likely, then the probability that an incorrect data packet is accepted as correct is $(\frac{1}{2})^{r-1}$. It can be shown that in the case of a bundle error with the length $\geq$ r+1, or in the case of multiple shorter bundle errors, the probability that an incorrect data packet being erroneously accepted as correct is $(\frac{1}{2})^r$.

The most common standard CRC polynomials are:

$$\begin{aligned}
\text{CRC-12} &= x^{12} + x^{11} + x^3 + x^2 + x + 1 \\
\text{CRC-16} &= x^{16} + x^{15} + x^2 + 1 \\
\text{CRC-CCITT} &= x^{16} + x^{12} + x^5 + 1 \\
\text{CRC-32} &= x^{32} + x^{26} + x^{23} + x^{22} + x^{16} + x^{12} + x^{11} + \\
&\quad + x^{10} + x^8 + x^7 + x^5 + x^4 + x^2 + x + 1
\end{aligned}$$

CRC-12 is used for the transmission of 6-bit characters and generates a 12-bit block test sequence. CRC-16 and CCRC-CCITT are both used for 8-bit transmissions and generate a 16-bit block test sequence. Applications requiring a higher transmission security can turn to CRC-32. It generates a 32-bit block test sequence. CRC-32 is used, for example, in standard transmission technology (Ethernet, FDDI, IEEE-802). With CRC-16, or CRC-CCITT, all single bit errors as well as all doubled single bit errors and all errors of odd length are detected. Moreover, 100% of all errors are detected that are shorter than 16 bits, 99.997 % of all 17-bit burst errors and 99.998% of all burst errors of 18 bit length or more. The CRC algorithm may seem relatively complex, it can however be implemented quite easily in hardware by means of a simple sliding register operation.

Error correction method
In codes for **error correction** a distinction is made between so-called **block codes** and **convolutional codes**. Just as in error detection, also here the payload data of redundant information is added. The quotient m/n is referred to as the code rate, whereby n=m+r. Commonly used values are 1/2, 3/4 and 7/8. With block codes the redundant information is calculated similarly as when parity bits are used, i.e., from blocks of the payload information

to be transmitted. In contrast, convolutional codes calculate the redundancy continuously from successive bit strings. The processing overhead for error-correcting codes is relatively high, with a correspondingly low code rate. This low code rate is responsible for the methods of error correction only being used where a retransmission is not practical. An important example are terrestrial radio systems (**GSM**: Global System for Mobile Communication). These are transmission systems subject to strict bandwidth limitation, e.g., radio traffic with interplanetary space probes (deep space communication) or digital storage media, or digital storage media such as memory (**RAM**: Random Access Memory) or mass storage devices such as the CD-ROM.

Further reading:

E. R. Berlekamp: Algebraic Coding Theory, Aegean Park Press, Laguna Hills, CA, USA (1984)

E. R. Berlekamp: Key Papers in the Development of Coding Theory (IEEE Press Selected Reprint Series), IEEE Press (1988)

J. Gibson [Hrsg.]: The Communications Handbook, CRC-Press, Boca Raton FL, USA (1996)

R. W. Hamming: Error Detecting and Error Correcting Codes, in Bell System Technical Journal, vol. 29, pp. 147-160 (1950)

V. Pless [Hrsg.]: Handbook of Coding Theory, Vol 1-2, Elsevier, Amsterdam (1998)

3.3 Performance Ratios of Computer Networks

The average user is likely to judge a network according to its speed – it is either a "fast" or a "slow" network. But because network technologies are changing so rapidly, the network considered "fast" today will already number among those that are "slow"tomorrow. So that an objective comparison of different network technologies is possible, hard quantitative metrics must be used to describe network performance rather than vague classifications. These measured values called **performance indicators** deliver a quantitative, qualified description of the concrete properties of communication networks. A distinction is made between **user-related services**, which are referred to as technology-independent, and **technology-related performance indicators**. At the same time, this distinction is not always consistent and cannot always be categorized. Therefore, technical performance indicators are normally grouped together and combined with those that are user-related.

3.3.1 User-Related Parameters

A compilation of user-related performance parameters is published by the ANSI (American National Standards Institute) as ANSI X3.102, based on a simple model (see Table 3.4). The ANSI model assumes a connection-oriented service and provides a rating for each of its three phases

- Connection establishment (network access),
- Data transmission and
- Disconnection.

An assessment is made of the following connection-oriented network service criteria evidenced in each phase:

- Speed
- Correctness – What are the chances that a (repairable) error will occur? – and
- Reliability – What are the chances that a (irreparable) error will occur that results in termination?

Table 3.4 User-related performance parameters according to ANSI X3.102

	Speed	Correctness	Reliability
Connection establishment	Duration of connection establishment	Probability of incorrect connection establishment Probability of total failure	Probability of denied connection
Data transmission	Transmission duration	Probability of error Probability of incorrect delivery Probability of denied transmission	Probability of data loss Probability of denied transmission
Connection establishment	Duration of connection establishment	Probability of denied transmission	Probability of denied connection setup

3.3.2 Qualitative Performance Criteria

Besides quantitative recordable performance parameters, communication networks are also characterized by properties described as qualitative. Although an exact measurement of these properties is not possible, they share the same level of importance as measurable quantitative performance criteria. Numbering among qualitative performance parameters are:

- **Availability**
  Specifies how much of the operation time of the communication network is actually available to users (expressed in percent) with the performance required by the service provider. The operation time is often given in 24 hours a day and 365 days a year.

- **Usability**
  An elusive parameter, whereby user satisfaction is measured by the network available from the service provider. Both ease of use and compliance with acceptable performance specifications are criteria in this group.

- **Compatibility**
  Indicates the extent to which the end devices of the user are compatible with the network interface from the service provider and can be operated without a great adaptation effort.

- **Security**
  Combination of multiple criteria defining the reliability of data transmission in a communication network, as well as in terms of intervention by unauthorized third parties.

- **Scalability**
  Expresses the extent to which a communication network can be operated, when actual use far exceeds what was laid down as the original operational parameters.

- **Manageability**
  This criterion indicates the extent of which the communication network is monitored, adapted to changing circumstances and regulated in the sense of control engineering. A network can only function satisfactorily if monitoring occurs on a continuous basis and if the necessary adjustments are made quickly.

Even in problematic situations it is necessary that a communication network still perform satisfactorily. The extent to which the network is resilient in emergency situations – without a loss of functionality – is referred to as **robustness**. A robust network can, e.g., compensate for failed connected computers with fast reconfiguration. After error resolution a robust network also has the capability of quickly returning to the initial state and then proceeding with normal operation. Following a total or partial failure, a network of this type is able to independently resume operation (self-stabilization).

3.3.3 Quality of Service

A central concept used in the measurement of network performance parameters is the so-called **Quality of Service (QoS)**. QoS describes the properties of a communication network in terms of the services rendered by a specific network service. As a rule, the following service quality attributes are applied

- **Performance** The two most important parameters for the quantitative assessment of the service provided in a communication network are:

  - **Throughput**:
    The throughput is understood as a guaranteed amount of data that

can be transmitted error-free per unit of time. The throughput is often given in bits per second – **bps**. The term throughput is often incorrectly used as a synonym for **bandwidth**. While bandwidth indicates the technically possible rate at which data can be transmitted in a network, throughput measures the amount of data actually transferred.

– **Delay**:
Delay refers to the maximum guaranteed length of time between the start of a data transfer and its conclusion. The delay is measured in seconds or in fractions of seconds and can vary greatly depending on the location of the communicating computers and the transmission technology used. Although, ultimately the user is only interested in the delay as a whole, the causes of delay can be identified at different points in the communication process (see Excursus 3.3.3).

• **Performance fluctuation** As a performance parameter, fluctuation describes all deviations from the maximum guaranteed performance:

– **Jitter**:
Jitter is a term used to express the fluctuation that takes places during delay. As a parameter for a communication network, jitter describes the maximum allowable fluctuation. These delays are unavoidable in packet-switching networks. At the same time they can have a major impact on the usability of the network. General distinctions are made between:

· **Asynchronous behavior**: The residence time of the packets at the sender and at the receiver in the network is completely uncertain. In certain cases it can reach any length. At the same time, in many communication processes this behavior is not a problem. For example, in the case of data exchange via email.

· **Synchronous behavior**: Although the length of the residence time of data packets in the communication network is still indeterminate and variable its upper limit is capped. This limit can be specified exactly in each case. Synchronous behavior is a minimum requirement for the transmission of voice and moving image (although frequently inadequate alone) .

· **Isochronous behavior**: Here, the length of residence is the same for all data packets in the network. A transfer of voice and moving image information is also possible in packet-switching networks isochronously.

– **Error rate**:
The term error rate expresses the probability of data loss during transmission and data corruption along the transmission path. An essential element of this definition is the **bit error rate**. This gives the number of corrupted bits transferred, in relation to the total number of transmitted bits. If the bit error rate of a transmission medium is too high

for a certain application, then error detection and error correction measures need to be implemented. For this purpose the user determines a viable **residual error probability**. This decides the complexity of the error recognition and correction procedures.

- **Guarantee**:
  All of the performance parameters promised by the service provider of a communication network can only be guaranteed up to a certain degree of probability. This characteristic is a measure of the reliability of the service provider's performance parameters.

- **Reliability**
  Besides the quantitative measurements of performance and fluctuation, the reliability of the connection supplied by the service provider is included in the level of service and defined by the following QoS parameters:

  - **Completeness**:
    The service parameter completeness ensures that all data packets sent reach their designated target at least once. However, information concerning the required time is not stipulated.

  - **Uniqueness**:
    If uniqueness is guaranteed for a data transmission then the user can be certain that the sent data reaches its designated goal one time. If uniqueness is not guaranteed and individual data packets reach their destination more than once, ambiguities can easily result due to errors along the transmission path.

  - **Order-preserving**:
    The user is assured that all sent data packets sent reach their destination in the same sequence in which they were transmitted by the sender.

- **Security**
  QoS parameters are grouped together under the attribute of security. They guarantee the integrity and authenticity of the transmitted data:

  - **Confidentiality**:
    With a guarantee of the confidentiality of data transmission no unauthorized third party is able to understand the contents of the communication between the sender and the receiver.

  - **Integrity**:
    This service parameter stands for a guarantee of the received data's integrity. This means, in particular, that no unauthorized third party can distort the data along the transmission path.

  - **Authenticity**:
    With this QoS parameter the user is assured that the received message is actually from the user indicated and not from an unauthorized third party who claims to be the sender of the message.

- **Liability:**
  The liability parameter provides evidence that a communication actually took place between the sender and the receiver. With this proof it is not possible for either sender or the receiver to the deny the occurrence of this communication.

- **Availability:**
  This QoS parameter indicates to what extent the service made available by the service provider can actually be used.

In order to make statements about the quality and commitment of specific QoS parameters so-called guarantee levels have been defined.

- **Best Effort**
  The specified values of the QoS parameters are adhered to as closely as possible. At the same time no binding guarantees are given.

- **Imperfect**
  All specified limits for the QoS parameters are adhered to "theoretically." The service provider cannot, however, provide definitive confirmations on all available components.

- **Predicted**
  All limits specified by the service provider QoS parameters are guaranteed, if the service provider's future utilization is not higher than in the past.

- **Statistical**
  All limits given for the QoS parameters specified by the service provider are only guaranteed with a certain degree of probability.

- **Deterministic**
  All specified limits for the QoS parameters laid out by the service provider are guaranteed as long as the service provider's hardware and software work without error.

Yet packet-switched networks can give no guarantee for the the QoS parameters throughput and delay. The promised performance is specified in the **Best Effort** quality level. In contrast, it is possible to provide a high guarantee for throughput and delay in a circuit-switched network. Excursus 3 provides a detailed explanation of various causes of delay in packet-switched networks.

Excursus 3: Delay in Packet-Switched Networks
Let us look at an end-to-end connection via a packet-switched network. Computer A sends a data packet to computer B. In its transfer through the network, the packet passes one or more switching computers (in Fig. 3.13 the routers C and D). The tasks of a switching computer can be seen, for example, in computer C. One of the connections from router C along the transmission path leads to the next switching computer – in this case to router D. This connection is upstream with its own queue at an output buffer. When a data packet reaches the switching computer C, the destination address is determined by the data in the packet header. In this way, the appropriate output connection is established. The data packet is now sent to router D via the output connection. It can only be forwarded via this

output if the connection is not blocked by other data packets. These would already be at the output buffer ahead of the data packet to be forwarded. In this case, the data packet must line up in the output buffer queue. Every computer the data packet passes causes delay. Reasons for this are:

- **Processing delay**
  Delay caused by the pre-processing of the involved computers,
- **Queueing delay**
  Delay due to waiting in the queue,
- **Transmission delay**
  Delay in the sending the packet by the transmitting computer and
- **Propagation delay**
  Delay caused by the runtime of the packet on the connection path.

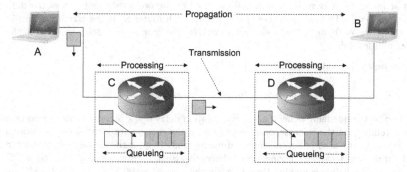

Fig. 3.13 Example configuration for delay times in the LAN.

Processing delay

The processing delay d_{proc} is the time that the switching computer needs for pre-processing, i.e., to read the data packet header and to determine where the packet is to be sent. Calculated into this time is also the time necessary for error correction, if need be. In case bit errors have occurred in the transfer to the switching computer they can be recognized with the help of error detection methods and corrected in an appropriate manner. Today the processing delay at switching computers is on the order of microseconds and less. After this pre-processing, the switching computer directs the data packet to the output queue in the direction of router D.

Queueing delay

Packet transmission in the network proceeds on a strictly first-come-first-served basis. A packet can only first be transferred when all the packets that arrived before it at the output connection have been transferred. This means that while the packet is waiting in the queue at the output connection to router D for its transfer, it undergoes a delay d_{queue}. The delay is proportional to the number of data packets that are already in the queue. There is considerable variation in queue delay time. If the queue is empty, then the delay time is zero. The number of packets that an incoming data packet could encounter in the queue, depends on the intensity of network traffic. Practically-speaking, router queueing delay varies, ranging from the area of microsecond to millisecond.

Transmission delay

If l designates the length of the data packet measured in bits and r the data transmission rate between router C and D measured in bit/second, then the transmission delay – also referred to as store-and-forward delay – is calculated simply as l/r. It defines the time required to deposit all of the packet's bit into the connection line. The transmission rate as such does not depend on the distance that the data packet has to bridge. It depends on how quickly the switching computer can transmit the data over the connection and also on the bandwidth of the connection. The transmission delay d_{trans} is in practical application in the microsecond range or less.

Propagation delay
If a data packet is sent on the connection between routers C and D it must follow the connection until router D is reached. The time between sending on the designated connection path and arrival at the receiver computer is referred to as propagation delay – d_{prop}. It is for the most part determined by the properties of the transmission medium (optical fiber, copper cable, radio waves, etc.) and at $2\text{-}3\cdot10^8$ m/s is close to the speed of light. The propagation delay is calculated from the distance b of the two switching computers divided by the propagation speed s, therefore b/s. When the last bit of the data packet has arrived at router D, it is stored temporarily with all of the previously sent bits of the data packet in router D. The entire process then repeats with router D as the starting point. In computer networks spanning large distances (WANs) the propagation delay d_{prop} is in the range of milliseconds.

The **total delay** d is calculated as

$$d = d_{proc} + d_{queue} + d_{trans} + d_{prop}.$$

In addition to the queueing delay d_{queue}, propagation delay d_{prop} plays the most important role. It extends from the microsecond range (e.g., if the routers are located in neighboring buildings) up to the area of several hundred milliseconds (e.g., if the routers are connected to each other via a satellite connection). There is also the transmission delay d_{trans}. It ranges from a negligible switching time (e.g., in the case of a 100 MBit Ethernet LAN) up to several hundred milliseconds (e.g., if data transmission is carried out via a slow 28 kbps modem).

Special attention must be paid to **queueing delay**. Unlike other delay times, queueing delay depends on the respective network load and therefore can vary considerably from data packet to data packet. For example, if 10 data packets reach the queue at the same time, while the first packet can be transmitted without delay the tenth packet has to wait until all other nine packets have first been sent before its turn comes. **Statistical measures** are used to define the queueing delay. A definitive measure is the arrival time of the individual packets in the queue as well as how they are distributed. This means that the packets can arrive evenly distributed over time or cumulatively in so-called bursts . Let us look at the situation more closely: a stands for the average arrival rate of data packets at our queue, measured in packets per second; r is the transmission rate and l is the length of the data packet. The average arrival rate of the data is l·a bps. For the sake of simplicity, let us assume that the length of the queue is unlimited, i.e., no data packets can get lost. In this case, the ratio $I=\frac{l\cdot a}{r}$ the **intensity** of the data volume. If I>1 then the average arrival rate of data is higher than the transmission rate of the connected line, i.e., the queue extends into infinity. It is therefore necessary that I>1 always apply.

Let us consider $I \leq 1$ in greater detail. The waiting time is determined according to how the data packets arrive in the queue. If the data packets arrive at the queue in periodic intervals, i.e., a packet arrives every l/r second, then there is no queue delay. However, if the data packets arrive in bursts, as is evident in practical application, then a significant queueing delay can occur. Let us suppose that n packets arrive simultaneously in a constant interval of (l/r)·n seconds. The first packet can be sent immediately – its waiting time is $d_{queue_1} = 0$. The second packet must wait $d_{queue_2} = l/r$ seconds, while the last packet with

$d_{queue_n} = (n-1)\cdot(l/r)$ seconds is subject to the longest waiting time. In reality the arrival of the data packets is a **random process**. The distance between the individual packets is not constant but a time span of random length. The intensity of data I no longer suffices for a complete and realistic description of the statistical distribution of the waiting time. More sophisticated mathematical methods are necessary for its definition. The data intensity can however at least contribute to an intuitive understanding for queueing delay.

If the intensity is near zero, then the delay is negligible. If the intensity is close to one, time intervals occur in which the arrival rate exceeds the transmission rate and the data packets must wait in the queue. If the intensity continues to be near one, then the queueing delay grows rapidly. Just a small percentage increase can lead to a tremendous rise in the queuing delay.

Packet loss

Up to now we have followed the simple assumption of the availability of unlimited queues. In practical application this situation is naturally a different one as the queueing capacity is always limited. Thus, the queue cannot extend to infinity when data intensity approaches unity. If an incoming packet finds that the queue is filled, and there is no further memory available, then the switching computer cannot accept the data packet, i.e., the packet is ignored and consequently lost. This represents the loss of a packet for the end system: the packet was sent but never reached its destination. With a rise in data intensity, the number of packets that are lost increases. Therefore, the performance of a network computer is quantified by the probability of packet loss occurring, in addition to information concerning the average delay time.

Further reading:

D. Bertsekas, R. Gallagher: Data Networks, 2nd Ed., Prentice Hall, Englewood Cliffs, NJ, USA (1991)

J. N. Daigle: Queueing Theory for Telecommunications, Addison-Wesley, Reading MA, USA (1991)

L. Kleinrock: Queueing Systems, Vol1, John Wiley, New York, NY, USA (1975)

U. Black: Emerging Communications Technologies, 2nd Ed., Prentice Hall, Upper Saddle River, MA, USA (1997)

Table 3.5 Required minimum rates for different applications.

Application	Required data rate
E-Mail transmission	0.3 – 9.6 kbps
Mobil telephony (GSM)	9.6 kbps
Digital voice transmission	64 kbps
Audio signal (compressed)	64 – 256 kbps
Audio signals (uncompressed)	1.4 Mbps
Video signals (compressed)	0.768 – 1.4 Mbps
Video signals (uncompressed)	2 – 10 Mbps
Video signals (high quality, e.g., telemedicine)	50 Mbps
Video signals (HDTV uncompressed)	2 Gbps

Performance Characteristics of Communication Networks

- **Bandwidth**
  Depending on the physical characteristics of a transmission medium, the bandwidth in telecommunication and communication engineering specifies a frequency range in which a signal, or data transmission, is even possible. The bandwidth is determined by a maximum frequency, indicated in Hertz (Hz) at which a reconstructible data transmission can take place. In everyday usage, the bandwidth is often confused with the amount of data that can be sent via a transmission medium per second.

- **Data rate**
  Depending on the signal coding used for data transmission, the available bandwidth of a transmission medium is limited and only a certain data transmission performance (data rate) can be achieved. The data rate is measured in bits per second (bps).

- **Throughput**
  Refers to the actual amount of data transferred per time unit in a partial section of the network. Throughput takes any delay that occur into consideration, e.g., the propagation time of a signal on a physical line.

- **Runtime**
  The runtime describes the time interval needed by a signal to travel across a transmission path. The runtime depends on the signal propagation speed of the respective transmission medium. If there are intermediate systems between the sender and the receiver, this leads to propagation delay. In the intermediate system, the propagation delay is determined by the processing power of the intermediate system and the waiting time in the output buffer.

- **Response time**
  The sending of a message usually initiates an answer from the receiver in bidirectional data connections. The answer is calculated from the time span between the sending of the first bit of a message until the receipt of the last bit of the answer. The minimum guaranteed answer time in a network corresponds to the so-called **round trip time**. It is determined by the maximum distance to be bridged (or the slowest connection).

- **Delay-throughput product**
  If this property is applied solely to the hardware, it is often given as delay-bandwidth product. This product measures the volume of data that can be found in the network at any given time. In a network with throughput T and delay D, at any given time a maximum of $T \times D$ bits is found in transit.

Fig. 3.14 Line parameters of communication networks.

3.4 Communication Protocols

The hardware of a network is made up of components whose tasks consists of transmitting bits from one computer to another. If one wanted to organize computer communication at this level alone, it would be comparable to programming a computer in a rudimentary machine language, i.e., with just zeros and ones. Doing things this way, it would be impossible to manage the effort and complexity of the tasks involved. Just as in computer programming, complex software systems have been created for the control and use of computer networks. With their assistance, we are able to operate and utilize computer networks on a higher level of abstraction. The user, as well as most of the application programs communicating over the network, exchanging data and offering services, come into contact with this network software. Only in rare instances do they have direct contract with the network hardware concealed underneath.

3.4.1 Protocol Families

It is necessary in communication – and not only in digital communication – that all communicating parties agree on a fixed set of rules for message exchange. This applies both to the language used as well as to the rules of conduct which enable efficient communication to even take place at all. These rules are summed up in technical language with the term **communication protocol** or simply **protocol**. A communication protocol establishes the format of the messages to be exchanged by the communication partners and specifies all the actions necessary to transmit them. In the case of communication in computer networks, the software that implements the network protocol at a computer is called **protocol software**. Instead of supplying immense, highly complex and universal network protocols to govern the tasks of network communication, the principle known as "divide et impera" (divide and conquer) is carried out. The whole problem is thus split up into a large number of individually manageable sub-problems. Problem-specific (sub)protocols provide a solution in each case. This method of disassembly into individual sub-problems makes sense, especially considering how many different complications can occur in computer communication that need to be solved (see Fig. 3.15).

The various sub-problems are handled by special protocols. Working together they must all mesh seamlessly. This is the second problem to be solved, the complexity of which is not to be underestimated. To ensure this interplay, the development of the network protocol software is viewed as a comprehensive task, the solution provided by the **protocol suite** or protocol family. All of the individual protocols interact efficiently with one another and in this way solve the overall problem of network communication. Some of the most popular, in part already historical, protocol families are summarized in Table 3.6. While the different protocol suites share many similar concepts, they were developed, for the most part, independent of each other and are therefore not compatible. Nevertheless, it is possible for computers in the same network to use different protocol families simultaneously. They can also all use the same physical network interface without it resulting in interference.

Sources of Error in Communication Networks

When many computers communicate with each other over a shared communication network, numerous problems can arise. These all have to be handled by the network protocol software. Just a few examples of these problems are:

- **Hardware failure**
  A host computer or an intermediate system, such as a router, can fail because of a defect in the hardware or because the operating system has crashed. A network connection could also break down. The protocol software needs to detect these errors and, after a restart of the faulty system, ensure smooth operation of the communication again.

- **Network congestion**
  Even if network hardware functions error-free, the capacity of a network is still limited by the performance ability of its system components. **Congestion** can result if data traffic becomes too great. In the most extreme case, all traffic in the network comes to a standstill. The protocol software must be able to detect traffic jam situations and make a detour around the affected areas of the network until the overload can be resolved again.

- **Packet delay and packet loss**
  Individual data packets may be affected by extreme delay due to the waiting time at switching systems. They might even get lost. Protocol software needs to handle these types of delays and data loss.

- **Data Corruption**
  Data sent over the network is subjected to physical sources of disturbance along the transmission path such as interference or electromagnetic radiation. Just as when there is a malfunction of the involved hardware, these disturbances can result in the transported data being altered to such an extent that it is no longer usable. It is necessary that protocol software be able to detect these kinds of errors and take the appropriate corrective action.

- **Duplicated data packets and mixed up sequence**
  In a packet-switched network, the data packets transported over potentially different routes are independent of each other. Along the way, data packets can easily lose their original sequence or individual packets can be duplicated by the switching systems The protocol software must have mechanisms available to detect and filter out duplicated data packets. It must also be possible to restore the original order of the data packets.

Fig. 3.15 Some complications that can occur in network communication.

Table 3.6 Examples of protocol families.

Manufacturer	Protocol family
Novell Corporation	Netware
Banyan Systems Corporation	VINES
Apple Computer Corporation	AppleTalk
Digital Equipment Corporation	DECNET
IBM	SNA
many	TCP/IP

3.4.2 Layer model

To support protocol designers in their work, tools and models have been developed that minutely break down the entire process of network communication and arrange it hierarchically. Clear interfaces are established between the separate hierarchical levels. This enables the largely independent development and improvement of each of the network protocols settled on the layers and makes them as simple as possible. The most well-known of these models is the **protocol stack** (layering model) (see Fig. 3.17). Here the entire network communication process is broken down into individual layers organized one on top of the other. Every layer addresses a specific sub-problem of the network communication and with each layer a new level of abstraction is added to the communication. Ideally, the designer constructs a protocol family – the so-called **protocol stack** – from these layers where each protocol addresses the task presented at a specific layer. A message is transmitted from the application program of one computer to the application program of another computer. The message is passed from top to bottom via the various protocol layers on the source computer and processed one part after the other on the way. It is then physically transported via the transmission medium. Subsequently, at the destination computer the same protocol layers are run through in the reverse order and the message transferred to the application (see Fig. 3.16).

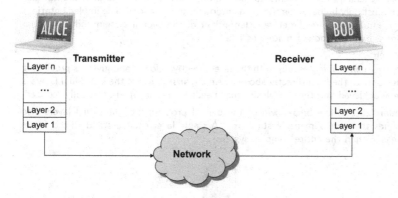

Fig. 3.16 Data transfer via a protocol stack.

In the layer model, each layer is responsible for solving a certain part of the tasks in network communication. For this purpose, at the sending computer is added the necessary command and control information at every single layer of the protocol stack for solving the particular task. (see Fig. 3.18). At the receiving computer, this extra information is read by the corresponding layer of the protocol software and processed further so that the transmitted data can be delivered correctly at the end.

General Aspects of the Layer Model

Layer models play an important role in communication technology as well as in other areas of computer technology. The **shell model** is a modified form consisting of individual shells rather than hierarchical layers one on top of the other.

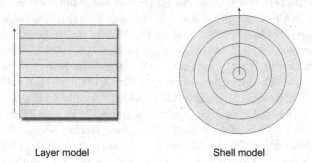

Layer model   Shell model

The following reasons justify the use of a layer model:

- **Divide and Conquer (divide et impera)**
  Based on this strategy, a complex problem is divided into individual sub-problems. Each problem, considered alone, is easier to handle and solve. It is often this approach that even allows the whole problem to be solved in the first place.

- **Independence**
  The individual layers cooperate, with each layer only using the interface specification of its immediate predecessor. With fixed, predetermined interface specifications, the internal structure of one layer is irrelevant for the other layers. This makes it possible to easily exchange the implementations on one layer for improved implementations. These must only be based on the same interface specifications. The implementations at individual layers are therefore **independent** of the overall system and a **modular** (building block) structure made possible.

- **Shielding**
  Each layer communicates only with the layer directly below it and gives its processing output only to the layer directly above it. An **encapsulation** of the individual layers is thereby achieved and the complexity that needs to be managed drastically reduced.

- **Standardization** The breakdown of the overall problem into individual layers also simplifies the development of standards. A single layer can be standardized faster and easier than the entire complex system.

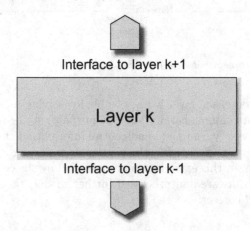

Interface to layer k+1

Layer k

Interface to layer k-1

Fig. 3.17 General aspects of the layer model.

Based on the layer model of network communication, the protocol software of a specific layer k at the destination computer must receive exactly the message that was transmitted by the protocol software of layer k at the sending computer. Every change or adjustment applied to the data to be transmitted by the protocol of a certain layer has to be completely reversed at the receiver. If layer k adds an additional command and control header to the sent data, then layer k at the receiving computer must remove it again. When data encryption takes place at layer k on the receiver's side, the encrypted data at layer k must then be decrypted again (see Fig. 3.18 and Fig. 3.19).

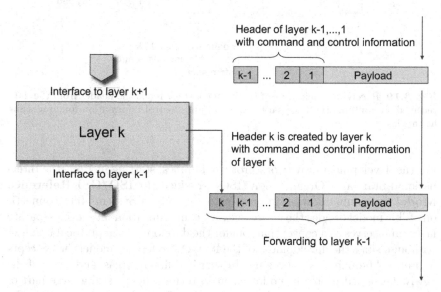

Fig. 3.18 Sending: Each layer of the protocol stack adds to the data to be forwarded its own header with command and control information.

Actual communication is always carried out in a vertical direction in the protocol stack. When data is sent, each protocol layer adds its own command and control information. Most of the time this information is then prefixed to the layer above as a header – one speaks of the data packet as being "encapsulated." The protocol software at the receiver's side, or in an intermediate system, receives the necessary command and control information from this additional data to ensure that the forwarded data is transmitted correctly and reliably. At the individual protocol layers it appears as if the protocol software is directly communicating on both sides – between the sender and receiver. But in fact the data is forwarded vertically through the protocol stack. This seemingly direct communication at the individual layers is referred to as **virtual communication**.

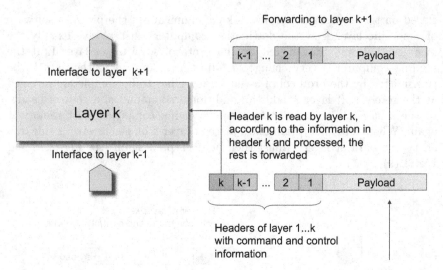

Fig. 3.19 Receiving: each layer of the protocol stack reads the header from the data received. It contains the necessary command and control information for processing at this layer.

For the development of network protocol families, starting in 1977, the International Standards Organization (ISO) provided the **ISO/OSI Reference Model** for communication in open networks (Open Systems Interconnection). This model divides the entire network communication into seven separate layers and serves as a conceptual tool for the development of protocol families. Although since the development of the ISO/OSI reference model the concepts of protocol families have developed further in different areas, and many of the newly developed protocols no longer fit into this scheme, still a large part of the terminology has been retained until today. This is particularly true in the case of the names and the numbering of the individual layers. The ISO/OSI reference model standardization process was completed in 1983. In practical terms, the Internet protocol-based **TCP/IP Reference Model** had already established itself by this time – and this before an implementation of the ISO/OSI standard even existed.

Excursus 4: The ISO/OSI Layer Model

The ISO/OSI Layer Model

The ISO/OSI reference model, developed at the beginning in 1977 by the International Standards Organization, divided the basic tasks of network communication into seven hierarchical layers, built one on top of each other (see Fig. 3.20). While it no longer plays a critical role today practically speaking, the model is often used in textbooks to show the individual network communication tasks and sub-problems and to demonstrate their interaction. The standardization initiative of ISO, begun in 1982, was designated **Open Systems Interconnect** (OSI). It was intended to create a single network protocol standard. Network protocols existing before the ISO/OSI initiative were for the most part a proprietary nature developed for the network devices of the individual manufacturer. Among the pre-ISO/OSI network protocol standards, which were incompatible with respect to each other, were : IBM SNA, AppleTalk, Novell Netware and DECnet. While standardization efforts for ISO/OSI were still ongoing, the protocol suite underlying the Internet – TCP/IP became more and more important in heterogeneous network made up of components from different manufacturers. Even before the final standardization of ISO/OSI could be carried out, TCP/IP was able to establish itself on a broad base. In the ISO/OSI model, the lowest layer corresponds to the actual network hardware (physical layer). The constituent layers comprise the respective firmware and software used on this network hardware. The highest layer – layer seven – is the application layer. It provides an interface between the communication system and the various applications wishing to use the communication system for their own purposes. Layers 1-4 are generally known as the **transport system**, and layers 5-7, which provide the increasingly general functionalities of the communication process, are called the **application system**. Although they share the same names, these layers should not be confused with the actual application programs themselves. These programs are located outside of the layer model.

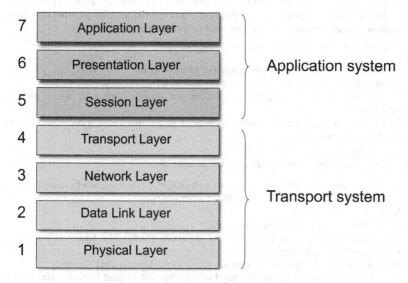

Fig. 3.20 The individual layers of the ISO/OSI Reference Model.

The individual layers of the ISO/OSI reference model handle the following tasks:

- **Layer 1: Physical Layer**
  The physical layer defines the physical and technical qualities of the transmission medium (transmission channel). In particular, the relationships between the network hardware and the physical transmission medium are regulated. This includes the layout and allocation of connections with their optical/electrical parameters, cable specification, amplification elements, network adapters, the transmission method used, etc.

  Among the most important task at the physical layer are:

  – Connection establishment and termination to a transmission medium and

- Modulation, i.e., the conversion of binary data (bit streams) into (electrical, optical or radio) signals that can be transmitted over a communication channel.

Important protocol standards at this layer are e.g.,

- ITU-T V.24, V.34, V.35
- ITU-T X.21 and X.21bis
- T1, E1
- SONET, SDH (Synchronous Data Hierarchy), DSL (Digital Subscriber Line)
- EIA/TIA RS-232-C
- IEEE 802.11 PHY

- **Layer 2: Data Link Layer**
  In contrast to the physical layer, which mainly focuses on regulating the communication between a single network component and the transmission medium, the data link layer is always concerned with the interaction of multiple (i.e., at least two) network components. The data link layer ensures that along a point-to-point connection, in spite of occasional errors that may occur at the physical layer, reliable transmission can take place. This point-to-point connection can thereby be implemented as a direct connection or as a broadcast procedure via a **diffusion network**, such as in Ethernet or WLAN. In a diffusion network all computers connected can receive the transmitted data via all other connected computers without the necessity of any kind of intermediate system.

  Among the tasks carried out at the data link layer are:

  - Organizing data into logical units referred to as **frames**,
  - Transmitting frames between network components,
  - Bit stuffing, i.e., completing frames that are not entirely filled with special padding data, and
  - The reliable transmission of frames by way of simple error detection methods such as checksum calculation.

  Among the most well-known protocols at this layer are:

  - BSC (Bit Synchronous Communication) and DDCMP (Digital Data Communications Message Protocol), PPP (Point-to-Point Protocol)
  - IEEE 802.3 (Ethernet)
  - HDLC (High Level Data Link Protocol)
  - X.25 LAPB (Link Access Procedure for Balanced Mode) and LAPD (Link Access Procedure for D-Channels)
  - IEEE 802.11 MAC (Medium Access Control)/LLC (Logical Link Control)
  - ATM (Asynchronous Transfer Mode), FDDI (Fiber Distributed Data Interface), Frame Relay

- **Layer 3: Network Layer**
  The network layer provides the functional and procedural means to enable the transfer of data sequences of variable lengths (**data packets**) from a sender to a receiver via one or more networks.

  The tasks of the network layer include:

  - Assigning addresses to end and intermediate systems,
  - The targeted forwarding of data packets from one end of the network to the other (routing) and subsequently,
  - Linking individual networks (internetworking),
  - Fragmenting and reassembling data packets, since different network are determined by different transport parameters, and

- Forwarding error and status messages regarding the successful delivery of data packets.

Among the most important protocol standard at this layer are:

- ITU-T X.25 PLP (Packet Layer Protocol)
- ISO/IEC 8208, ISO/IEC 8878
- Novell IPX (Internetwork Packet Exchange)
- IP (Internet Protocol)

- **Layer 4: Transport Layer**
  The transport layer provides transparent data transfer between end users. It also provides a reliable transport service to the upper layers. The transport layer defines the details necessary for a reliable and secure data transmission. This ensures that a sequence of data packets travels from the sender to the receiver in a form that is error-free, complete and sequentially correct. Also at the transport layer, the imaging of network addresses into logical names occurs. The transport layer therefore provides an end-to-end connection for the end systems involved. Because it hides the details of the intervening network infrastructure, it is considered **transparent**. The protocols at this layer are among the most complex in network communication.

  Among the most important protocol standards on layer 4 are:

  - ISO/IEC 8072 (Transport Service Definition)
  - ISO/IEC 8073 (Connection Oriented Transport Protocol)
  - ITU-T T.80 (Network-Independent Basic Transport Service for Telematic Services)
  - TCP (Transmission Control Protocol), UDP (User Datagram Protocol), RTP (Real-time Transport Protocol)

- **Layer 5: Session Layer**
  Also referred to as the layer of communication control, the session layer regulates the dialogue between two computer connected through the network.

  The main tasks of the session layer include:

  - Establishment, management and termination of connections between local and remote applications,
  - Control of full-duplex, half-duplex or simplex data transport, and
  - Establishment of security mechanisms, such as authentication via a password method.

  Important protocol standards at this layer are:

  - SAP (Session Announcement Protocol), SIP (Session Initiation Protocol)
  - NetBIOS (Network Basic Input/Output System)
  - ISO 8326 (Basic Connection Oriented Session Service Definition)
  - ISO 8327 (Basic Connection Oriented Session Protocol Definition)
  - ITU-T T.62 (Control Procedures for Teletex and Group 4 Facsimile Services)

- **Layer 6: Presentation Layer**
  The presentation layer creates a context between two entities (applications) of the overlying application layer. The two applications can then use different syntax (e.g., data formats and coding) and semantics. The presentation layer is thus responsible for correctly interpreting the transmitted data. The respective local data coding is converted into a special, uniform transfer coding for the presentation layer. At the receiver it is then transformed back into locally valid coding. Further tasks at this layer are: data compression and encryption.

  Among the most important protocol standards of the presentation layer are:

- ISO 8322 (Connection Oriented Session Service Definition)
- ISO 8323 (Connection Oriented Session Protocol Definition)
- ITU-T T.73 (Document Interchange Protocol for Telematic Services), ITU-T X.409 (Presentation Syntax and Notation)
- MIME (Multipurpose Internet Mail Extension), XDR (External Data Representation)
- SSL (Secure Socket Layer), TLS (Transport Layer Security)

- **Layer 7: Application Layer**
  The application layer provides an interface for application programs wishing to use the network for their specific purpose. The application programs themselves do not belong to this layer – they just use its services. The application layer provides easily manageable service primitives. These hide all of the network internal details from the user or application programmer, thus allowing simple use of the communication system. Among the most important functions of the application layer are:

  - Identifying the communication partner,
  - Determining the availability of resources and
  - Synchronizing communication.

  The following protocol standards are among the most important on this layer:

  - ISO 8571 (FTAM, File Transfer, Access and Management)
  - ISO 8831 (JTM, Job Transfer and Manipulation)
  - ISO 9040 und 9041 (VT, Virtual Terminal Protocol)
  - ISO 10021 (MOTIS, Message Oriented Text Interchange System)
  - FTP (File Transfer Protocol), SMTP (Simple Mail Transfer Protocol), HTTP (Hypertext Transfer Protocol), etc.
  - ITU-T X.400 (Data Communication for Message Handling Systems). ITU-T X.500 (Electronic Directory Services)

Further reading:

U. Black: OSI – A Model for Computer Communications Standards, Upper Saddle River, NJ, USA (1991)

H. Zimmermann: OSI Reference Model – The ISO Model of Architecture for Open Systems Interconnection, in IEEE Transactions on Communications, vol. 28, no. 4, pp. 425–432 (1980)

3.4.3 The Internet and the TCP/IP Layer Model

Today the global and ubiquitous Internet connects computers, telephones, consumer electronics and, soon, the household appliances and goods we need everyday. The Internet continues to enter more and more areas of our life. So that all of the different devices are able to communicate efficiently and without disturbing one another, the communication protocols implemented need to follow one common, basic scheme. This foundation is today's TCP/IP reference model. It defines the individual layers of Internet communication based on tasks, degrees of abstraction, complexity and respective range of functions. The means and manner in which these specifications are implemented are not stipulated by the model. In this way, the TCP/IP reference model has been formed by practical application and defines today, as in the foreseeable future, a solid base for all digital communication tasks. The **TCP/IP reference model** stands in clear contrast to the ISO/OSI reference model (see Excursus 4). It does not effectively exist in its own right, but is derived from the protocols used in the Internet. Conversely, the ISO/OSI protocol was theoretically planned and approved before the protocols that the individual layer functions of the ISO/OSI reference model implement were designed. Most of the ISO/OSI-conform protocol implementations are rarely used today. Instead, the protocols that resulted from their practical application in the TCP/IP reference model dominate the Internet. The most important protocol family today – the **TCP/IP** protocol suite – is thus not based on the specifications of a standardization committee but on the requirements and experiences of the developing Internet. The ISO/OSI reference model can be adapted to a point where it can also define the TCP/IP protocol stack, however both are based on completely different principles. Because of the far-reaching significance achieved by the Internet – and correspondingly the TCP/IP protocol suit – it is useful to take a closer look at the TCP/IP protocol stack, also referred to as the **TCP/IP Reference Model**.

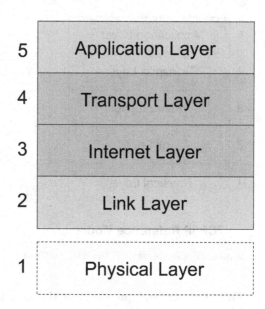

Fig. 3.21 The TCP/IP Reference Model consists of four layers (2-5); together with the network hardware layer (1) the model is referred to as the hybrid TCP/IP reference model.

The first description of the TCP/IP reference model (RFC 1122) dates back to 1974, even before the first specification of the ISO/OSI model was created. In principle, the TCP/IP protocol family is subdivided into four separate layers. These layers are organized based on the core protocols TCP and IP (see Fig. 3.21). It should be noted that descriptions of the TCP/IP reference model can also be found that define five separate layers. Here, a communication hardware descriptive layer (hardware/physical layer) is included with the original four layers that make up the model. The names of the individual layers given in Fig. 3.21 are those used in RFC 1122 and also the ones used in this book. Layer 2 of the TCP/IP reference model, the link layer, is also often referred to as the data link layer, network access layer or host-to-network layer and corresponds to the first two layers of the ISO/OSI reference model (physical layer and data link layer). Layer 3 of the TCP/IP reference model is known as the internet layer or the network layer and corresponds to layer 3 of the ISO/OSI reference model (the network layer). Layer 4 of the TCP/IP reference model, the transport layer, is also known as the host-to-host layer and corresponds to layer 4 of the ISO/OSI reference model (transport layer). Layer 5 of the TCP/IP reference model, the application layer, corresponds to layers 5-7 of the ISO/OSI reference model (the session layer, the presentation layer and the application layer; see Fig. 3.22).

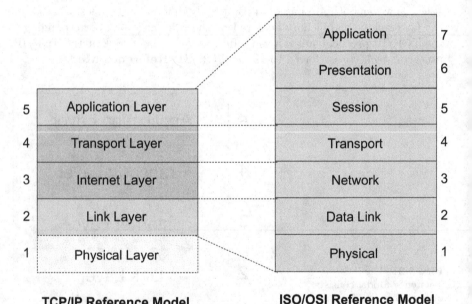

TCP/IP Reference Model   **ISO/OSI Reference Model**

Fig. 3.22 Comparison of the TCP/IP and the ISO/OSI reference models.

The functions and protocols of the individual layers are described in the following paragraphs. A detailed presentation of the TCP/IP reference model layers and their protocols is presented in Volume 2 of this trilogy, "Internetworking."

The Link Layer

The link layer of the TCP/IP reference model combines the first two layers of the ISO/ISO reference model – the physical layer and the data link layer, whereby the link layer does not contain the aspects of the physical layer that are part of the ISO/OSI reference model. The main task of the link layer involves the secure transmission of individual data packets between two adjacent end systems. Bit sequences are grouped together into fixed units (data packets) and provided with the extra information necessary for transmission, e.g., checksums for simple error detection. The adjacent end systems can either be directly connected to each other by a transmission medium or connected via a so-called bus (diffusion network). This bus connects several end systems with each other directly, i.e, without the use of intermediate systems. A distinction is made at this layer between **secured** and **unsecured services**. In unsecured service, data packets that are recognized as defective are eliminated. The request for retransmission first takes place at a higher layer of the protocol stack. A secure service, in contrast, accepts the request for retransmission itself. In local area networks (LANs), layer 2 of the TCP/IP reference model is normally divided into two more sub-layers:

- **Media Access Control (MAC)**
  This sub-layer controls access to the transmission system, which is shared by (many) other computer systems. Because of the competitive nature of the communication medium, protocol mechanisms must be provided to allow fair and efficient access to all participants.

- **Logical Link Control (LLC)**
  This sub-layer regulates the so-called data link layer of the LAN. Some of the tasks performed here are:

  - Flow control (to avoid overload at the receiver),
  - Error handling (error detection and error correction),
  - Transmission control (link management; orderly and error-free transmission) and
  - Data packet synchronization (assuring that the beginning and the end of a data packet are detectable).

  Additionally, the LLC sub-layer ensures so-called multi-protocol capability – the ability to use different communication protocols simultaneously.

Besides the important, practically-oriented protocols at layer 2 of the TCP/IP reference model, there are also standard LAN protocols. These have been standardized by IEEE, in accordance with the **IEEE 802** LAN standard. They include technologies such as Ethernet, Token Ring or FDDI. Other protocols at layer 2 of the TCP/IP protocol family are:

- ARP und RARP (Address Resolution Protocol and Reverse Address Resolution Protocol),

- SLIP (Serial Line Interface Protocol) and
- PPP (Point to Point Protocol).

The Internet Layer

Just as the network layer of the ISO/OSI reference model, the main task of the internet layer of the TCP/IP reference model is to enable data communication between two end systems at different ends of the communication network. For this purpose, an addressing scheme must be used that is valid across the borders of individual physical networks. The data packets to be sent must each be provided with the addresses of the sender and the receiver so they can be delivered correctly. As communication is carried out across one or more independently operating networks, computers at the connections and intermediate systems must be capable of correctly forwarding data packets along the chosen communication path (routing). The central protocol of layer 3 is the **Internet Protocol (IP)**.

IP offers unreliable and data packet-oriented end-to-end message transmission. It is responsible for fragmentation and defragmentation of the so-called **IP datagrams**. It has protocol mechanisms for relaying messages across intermediate systems to the designated receiver. IP is an unreliable protocol because it does not have mechanisms for dealing with data loss. A detailed treatment of IP can be found in Volume 2 of our trilogy,"Internetworking." The **ICMP** protocol (Internet Control Message Protocol) is also located on layer 3. Its sphere of responsibilities includes reporting errors that might occur during an IP transmission. ICMP is a protocol that is structured directly on IP. It can also be used to request system information concerning other end systems. There are other protocols on layer 3 of the TCP/IP protocol stack as well, for example:

- IGMP (Internet Group Management Protocol), used for managing (multicast) groups of end systems in a TCP/IP network.
- RSVP (Resource Reservation Protocol), used in requesting and reserving resources for implementing IP to transfer data streams
- ST 2+ (Internet Stream Protocol, Version 2), a connection-oriented protocol for transporting real-time data via IP that requires a guaranteed quality of service,
- OSPF (Open Shortest Path First), a routing protocol used primarily in Internet routers,
- BGP (Border Gateway Protocol), a routing protocol for so-called autonomous systems.

The Transport Layer

The transport layer corresponds roughly to the layer of the same name in the ISO/OSI reference model. Its primary task is to establish a communication link between two application programs that are located on different computers in the network. A flow control is carried out on the transport layer. This ensures that overload situations are avoided as much as possible. It safeguards against the transmitted data arriving at the receiver with an error, besides ensuring that the correct order is maintained (sequence numbered). There also exists an acknowledgement mechanism by which the receiver can confirm correctly sent data packets or re-request defective ones. Unlike the internet layer, the transport layer is not under jurisdiction of the network operator but instead offers the user, or user program of the respective end system, the possibility to deal with data transmission problems that are not taken care of at the internet layer. Ways to deal with such problems include bridging internet layer failures as well as following up on the delivery of data packets that have gotten lost at the internet layer. The transport layer is capable of transporting packets of any length (streams). A long message is divided into segments; these segments are transmitted separately and then reassembled at the receiver. The **TCP (Transport Control Protocol)** is a core element of the Internet protocol architecture and the most widely used protocol at layer 4 of the TCP/IP protocol stack. It implements a reliable, bidirectional data exchange between two end systems. A detailed description of the TCP protocol is presented in volume 2 of this trilogy, "Internetworking."

In addition to TCP, there is also the **UDP protocol (Universal Datagram Protocol)**. This is the second most popular protocol of the transport layer. It transmits independent data units – so-called datagrams – between application programs that run on different computers in the network. The transmission is unreliable and thus it offers no mechanisms for the recognition or correction of errors, e.g., data loss, the multiplication of datagrams or sequence changes – conditions that can occur at any time. The datagrams recognized as defective are discarded by UDP without ever reaching the receiver. In contrast to TCP, UDP is characterized by a lower complexity, which is subsequently reflected in an increased data throughput. However, this is paid for with a drastic loss of reliability and security. Other well-known protocols at the transport layer are:

- VMTP (Versatile Message Transaction Protocol), a transaction-oriented communication protocol,
- NETBLT (Network Block Transfer Protocol), a uni-directional, connection-oriented, reliable transport service. It has been optimized for high throughput with large amounts of data,
- MTP (Multicast Transport Protocol), a reliable transport service for multi-cast groups,
- RDP (Reliable Data Protocol), a bidirectional, connection-oriented, point-to-point transport service. It is especially designed for applications that

are able to handle sequence changes in the transmitted data packets independently, or at least to tolerate them,

- RIP (Routing Information Protocol), an internal routing protocol designed for smaller networks,
- SSL (Secure Socket Layer), a protocol mechanism for secure data transfer in the WWW,
- TLS (Transport Layer Security), successor of the Secure Socket Layer (SSL), a protocol for secure data transfer in the WWW.

The Application Layer

The functionality of the application layer in the TCP/IP protocol stack essentially summarizes the top three layers of the ISO/OSI reference model. This layer basically serves as the interface for the actual application programs that want to communicate via the network. The applications themselves are located outside of this layer and the TCP/IP reference model. The services offered at the application layer have a high level of abstraction. This means that it is possible to shield the user, or communicating application, from the communication details regulated on the lower protocol layers for the most part. The application layer of the TCP/IP protocol family includes the following protocols:

- TELNET, allows the creation of an interactive session at a remote computer,
- FTP (File Transfer Protocol), is used to transfer files between two computers connected over a TCP/IP network.
- SMTP (Simple Mail Transfer Protocol), a simply structured protocol for the transmission of electronic mail in the Internet. Today, as a rule, ESMPT (Extended SMTP) is used since it allows a transparent message transmission of different formats.
- HTTP (Hypertext Transport Protocol), protocol for data transfer in the World Wide Web,
- RPC (Remote Procedure Call), is used for the operation call by application programs located at a remote computer,
- DNS (Domain Name Service), directory service that supplies mapping between end system names (strings) and IP addresses,
- PGP (Pretty Good Privacy), encryption mechanism for electronic mail and its authentication,
- SNMP (Simple Network Management Protocol), protocol for the monitoring, managing and controlling of networks,
- RTP (Realtime Transport Protocol), protocol for real-time transmission (streaming) of multimedia data streams.

The protocols of the application layer of the TCP/IP reference model are described in detail in volume 2 of the trilogy, "Internetworking."

3.4.4 Protocol Functions

If we look at the individual protocols located at each layer, it becomes clear that protocols at different layers frequently offer the same functionality. These shared functionalities are called **protocol functions** or **protocol mechanisms**. The arrangement of the individual protocol functions at each layer proceeds with the help of concrete protocol implementations that correspond to the reference framework and level of abstraction at each layer. The protocol functions can be divided into the following basic categories:

- **Basic protocol functions**
  These includes all functions that regulate data traffic as a basic task of network communication:

  - **Data transfer:**
    It is possible to define **priority data traffic** in data transmission. This means that "important" data may be specified and given priority, in contrast to "regular" data. Priority data can even overtake ordinary data that has been sent. If a data packet is correctly received it is possible to establish a special **acknowledgement procedure** to signal successful data transfer. Acknowledgements can apply to single data packets or to several data packets (piggy back acknowledgement).

  - **Connection management:**
    Besides the data transfer itself, the establishment and termination of a data connection is one of the fundamental tasks of network communication. The protocol mechanism used must be capable of reacting appropriately to successful or unsuccessful connection requests. Data that is transmitted via a switched connection needs to be delivered in the correct order. The protocol mechanism must therefore be capable of handling late, lost or duplicated data packets. Consecutive **sequence numbers** are thus assigned to data packets. Additional fallback and recovery mechanisms are also provided. In the event of an unintentional break in communication (disconnect), these mechanisms return communication to a normal state.

- **Error handling**
  Included in the category of error handling are all mechanisms that serve to detect and correct all transmission errors that may occur:

  - **Error detection:**
    Different checksum procedures or parity bits can be implemented in error detection. User data is supplemented with redundant information that can be completely reconstructed from the message transmitted. Using comparison as a basis, it is possible to detect errors that have occurred.

- **Retransmission**:
  If a data packet is identified as defective, it can be requested again from the sender. This can be done by way of a special acknowledgement procedure.

- **Time monitoring**:
  If the time a data packet needs through the network exceeds a specified, maximum limit, it is considered "lost" and subsequently retransmitted (**timeout**). Determining this time period is extremely important in terms of efficiency and network performance.

- **Error correction**:
  By providing the information to be transmitted with sufficient redundancy, it is possible to ensure an automatic correction of transmission error. The need to request a new data packet from the sender to replace a defective one can thus be avoided.

- **Length adjustment**
  Due to technical and organizational constraints, the length of data packets is always limited. However, the message to be transmitted is often longer than the predetermined data format allows. When this happens, the message must be broken down before transfer into size-appropriate, separate parts or packets (**fragmentation**). Once having arrived at the receiver, the data packets fragments are then assembled again into the original message (**defragmentation**). At the same time, it is also possible that messages are shorter than the prescribed data packet length. In this case, the data packets are then expanded with so-called padding bits (**bit stuffing**).

- **System performance adjustment**
  The computing systems involved in data transmission must be able to adjust to the momentary network load. Protocol mechanisms influence the internal processing in the intermediate systems. They regulate the data flow and help to prevent overload.

  - **Flow control**:
    Data flow usually operates via a window mechanism. This mechanism serves to protect the data receiver from becoming overwhelmed by a possible overload. Therefore, the receiver indicates to the sender a maximum number of packets that it is can send without getting an acknowledgement.

  - **Congestion control**:
    The protocol mechanisms provided for this purpose also use a window mechanism that protects the respective receiver from getting swamped by incoming data packets. Based on the current network load, the receiver indicates how many unacknowledged data packets can be sent to it.

- **Rate control:**
  Before the actual start of data transmission (e.g., during connection establishment) the sender and the receiver can agree on a maximum data transfer rate. This rate corresponds to the amount of transmitted data per unit of time.

- **Transmission adjustment**
  Different performance capabilities can show up in the end and intermediate devices connected to the network. This in turn is reflected in fluctuating transmission performance. Special protocol mechanisms must be provided to balance out these differences.

  - **Multiplexing:**
    If a connection channel has a significantly higher transmission capacity than the individual connected computing systems, then connections to multiple computing systems can be mapped to one connection with a high transmission capacity. The linked systems are then served interchangeably.

  - **Inverse multiplexing:**
    In the opposite case if, for example, a computing system connected to the network has a higher transmission capacity than the available data connection, via the inverse multiplexing mechanism, the connection to the computing system can be mapped simultaneously as multiple data connections.

- **User-based protocol mechanisms**
  Protocol mechanisms in which the user can determine data transmission qualities are also important. These qualities include the establishment of service parameters or the granting of rights.

  - **Connection classes:**
    Network services can deliver their performance in different quality levels – so-called service classes. Protocol mechanisms must be provided to the user during connection establishment so that it is possible to fix the desired service class in each case.

  - **Rights management:**
    The use of certain system services or special data connections can be user-related or time-limited. Protocol mechanisms are needed to authorize specified users access to the limited network resources.

  - **Quality of service management:**
    When establishing a connection, the initiator of the intended communication can express the wish for certain quality of service parameters, e.g., a specific minimum throughput. The wish must be expressed to the intended communication partner, who can accept it entirely or partially.

3.5 Glossary

Bandwidth: The bandwidth of a communication path in a network is a physical quantity that is measured in Hertz (1 Hz=1/s). In the analog domain, the bandwidth indicates the frequency range in which electrical signals are transmitted with an amplitude decrease of up to 3 dB. The greater the bandwidth, the more information can theoretically be transmitted in a unit of time. Although the term bandwidth is often used to mean the transmission of digital signals, in this case actually the **transmission rate** is meant. There is, however, a direct relationship between the bandwidth and the transmission rate. In data transmission the attainable transmission speed is directly dependent on the bandwidth of the network. The maximum bandwidth utilization for binary signals is 2 bits per Hertz of bandwidth.

Broadcast: A broadcast transmission is the simultaneous transmission from one point to all participants. Classic broadcast applications are radio and television.

Checksum procedure: Checksums are often used in communication protocols for error detection. The sender calculates a checksum for the message to be sent and appends it to the message. Once arriving at the receiver, the same procedure is used on the received message (excluding the appended checksum) and a checksum is made. This calculated value is then compared to the checksum value appended by the sender. If both values match, it can be assumed with a large degree of certainty that the message has been transmitted correctly. Generally in a checksum procedure, the transferred bit string is interpreted as numerical values grouped into individual blocks and their sum calculated. This checksum is simply appended onto the data to be transmitted as a binary coded number. Checksum procedures are used, for example, in the IP protocol. The best known procedure is the so-called **Cyclic Redundancy Check** (CRC, also referred to as **polynomial code**).

Circuit switching: A method of message exchange via a network. An exclusive, fixed connection is set up between the communicating end devices at the beginning of the message exchange. The connection exists for the entire duration of communication. Telephone networks, for example, work according to this principle.

Code: A code is a mathematical relation that maps each character of a character string (protoype set) to a character or a string of a different character set (image set). Codes serve the representation and encryption of messages in technical systems as well as the detection and correction of errors.

Communication medium: Physical carrier used to transport communication signals between the transmitter and the receiver. For example, in direct verbal communication the sound of air is the carrier medium of the communication.

Communication protocol: A communication protocol (also called simply a protocol) is a collection of rules and regulations that fix the data format of the messages to be transmitted, as well as determining all the mechanisms and procedures for its transmission. It contains agreements regarding the establishment and disconnection of a connection between the communication partners and the manner of the data transmission.

Computer network: A computer network (or simply, **network**) is a communication network of autonomous computing systems connected to a single data transmission network. Each system is equipped with its own memory, own storage, own periphery and own computing capability. As all participants are linked together, the host systems of each subscriber has the possibility of contact with any of the network nodes.

Congestion: With its means of operation (transmission media, router and other intermediate system) a network can handle a certain load (communication, data transmission). However, if the load created reaches 100% of the available capacity, an overload (congestion) occurs. The network must respond properly in order not to lose data and to avoid the breakdown of communication.

Data rate: The data rate (or transmission speed) is a measure of the speed at which data, in the form of bits per time unit, can be transferred via a transmission medium. This speed is given in bit/s or with the prefixes k (kilo=10^3), M (mega=10^6), G (giga=10^9) or T (tera=10^{12}). In bit-serial binary transmission it is equal to the **step rate**. Conversely, in character bit-parallel transmission the data rate of transmission is greater than the step rate. This is because with every step, multiple bits can be sent at the same time. In English technical publications, the transmission rate is specified in bps (bits per second). According to DIN 44302, the transmission speed is the product of the step rate and number of bits transmitted per step.

Data Transmission: Data transport from one computing system to another is called data transmission.

Delay: Parameter that indicates the maximum guaranteed length of time between the beginning of a data transmission and its conclusion. The delay is measured in seconds or fractions of a second and can, depending on the location of the computers communicating with each other, vary strongly. Although the end user is only interested in the total delay, at different places in the communication process different causes can occur, such as **processing delay queueing delay transmission delay** and **propagation delay**.

Diffusion network: In a diffusion network, the sender's signal is received directly by all of the computers connected in the network, taking into account the respective propagation delay. Every receiver must therefore determine itself whether the message is intended for it and whether to accept and processes it or not.

Error-detecting code: A code that is provided with redundancy and the capability to detect transmission errors. Simple examples for forms of error-detecting codes are appended **parity bits** or **checksum procedures**.

Error-correcting code: A code that is capable of not only detecting transmission errors but also, to a certain degree, of correcting them.

Error rate: The ratio of the defective information transmitted to the information transmitted as a whole is referred to as the rate of error. The **bit error rate** is, in particular, a measure for the error rate in the data network. It is calculated based on the relation between the defective bits transmitted and the total number of bits transmitted measured over a longer period of time.

Flow control: In a communication network, flow control prevents a faster sender from swamping a slower receiver with transmitted data and thus causing congestion. The receiver usually has a buffer memory where the arriving data packets can be stored until they are processed. To prevent an overflow of the intermediate storage, special protocol mechanisms must be provided. These allow the receiver to decide how long the sender has to wait until the receiving computer's storage buffer has been processed.

Fragmentation/defragmentation: The length of the data packet that a communication protocol sends below the application layer is always limited by technical restrictions. If the length of a message to be sent is longer than the prescribed data length, the message is broken up into separate sub-messages (fragments), which adhere to the prescribed length restrictions. So that the individual fragments can be correctly reassembled (defragmented) into the form of the original message at the receiver following transmission, they must be provided with **sequence numbers**. This is necessary because the transmission order cannot always be guaranteed in networks.

Hamming distance: In comparing two different code words of equal length, the Hamming distance of both code words is the number of positions at which the corresponding bits are different.

Interface: An imaginary or real technically fixed transition at the boundary between two similar units (hardware or software), or between a system and its environment (external interface) with a set of precisely defined rules and procedures. In communication systems, interfaces are responsible for the transfer of data or signals (e.g., as described in DIN 44300).

Jitter: Term to describe the fluctuation of data transmission delay time in communication networks. This effect is unavoidable in packet-switched networks as the paths of individual data packets through the network are determined independent of each other. Because of this, the intermediate systems employed are utilized to different degrees.

Layer model: Complex problems can be modeled and solved when it is possible to disassemble them into hierarchically layered sub-problems. In this way, the level of abstraction increases from layer to layer. This means that a higher layer in the layer model is shielded from the problem details handled at one of the lower layers. Layer models play an important role in communication technology, but also in other areas of computer science. Such models correspond to the modified representation of the **shell model**. Instead of consisting of layers arranged hierarchically one on top of each other it is made up of individual shells.

Message switching: A method of network communication in which the individual exchanges temporarily store the complete contents of a message before it is passed on. The sender only needs to known the path to the next exchange, which in turn sends the message it has received in the same way to the next exchange.

Multicast: A multicast transmission takes the form of a broadcast to a limited circle of participants. It is a simultaneous transfer from a single point to a dedicated subset of all network participants.

Network: A term for the group of several communication devices, the associated linking transmission medium and the intermediate systems necessary for operation of the network between systems. If the communication end devices are computers, one speaks of a computer network. Principally, networks can be separated into **private networks**, which are found in the private sector, and **public networks**, which are operated by a carrier and offered for public use.

Packet header: In a packet-switched network, the communication protocols used require that the transmitted information be fragmented into individual data packets. In order to be sure that the data packets are correctly transmitted, reach the designated receivers, and can be reassembled there into the original information again, data packets are preceded by command and control information in a so-called data packet header.

Packet switching: The main method of communication in digital networks. The message is disassembled into separate data packets of a fixed length and the packets are sent separately and independent of each other via intermediate exchanges to the receiver. A distinction is made between **connection oriented** and **connectionless** packet switching networks (**datagram networks**). A virtual connection is established in the network before the beginning of actual data transmission in connection-oriented packet switching networks. There is no fixed connection path chosen in advance in connectionless packet switching networks and the data packets are each transmitted independent of each other and possibly even via different paths.

Point-to-point connection: The simplest form of a computer network architecture. Every computer in a point-to-point network is directly connected with every other computer in the network. The individual connections can be used exclusively by each of the communication partners involved and in this way allows for a high degree of communication efficiency. Point-to-point networking requires considerable effort (the square of the number of computers involved), therefore the networks are either very small or implemented in individual, dedicated wide area connections to the application.

Protocol stack: The various subproblems of network communication are each addressed by specially designed protocols in order to solve the overall problem of network communication. In order to ensure the necessary interplay, developing the network protocol software must be viewed as a comprehensive task to be solved in its entirety. A **family of protocols** (protocol suites) must be developed in each case to solve the sub-tasks and to integrate efficiently with each other. The entire problem of network communication can be well represented using a **layer model**. Because the individual protocols of the families are each assigned to a specific layer, the term **protocol stack** is used. The most well-known protocol stacks are the TCP/IP protocol suite of the Internet and the ISO/OSI layer model. The latter often serves as a textbook example.

Quality of Service (QoS):   Quantifies the performance of a service that is offered by a communication system. QoS describes the quality of service attributes: performance fluctuation, reliability and security. These are each specified via their own, quantifiable quality of service parameters.

Redundancy: The redundancy of a message does not contain the actual message itself. This redundant portion can often be an aid to understanding the contents of the message when the message has been transmitted in defective form.

Remote data transfer: If the computing systems between which a data transfer takes place are more than one kilometer apart, the term remote data transfer is used. This distance is however not fixed. The procedures used in remote data transmission distinguish themselves considerably from those used in data transmission systems with less distance between them.

Routing: In a WAN there are often several intermediate systems along the path between the sender and the receiver. These systems are responsible for forwarding the transmitted data to the respective receiver. The determination of the correct path between the sender and the receiver is referred to as routing. The dedicated routers thereby receive a transmitted data packet, evaluate its address information and forward it on to the next intermediate system on the path to the receiver, or to the receiver directly as the case may be.

Security: In network technology there are different security objectives summed up under the term security (quality of service parameters). These define the degree of integrity and authenticity of the transferred data. Among the most important security objectives are: **confidentiality** (no unauthorized third party is capable of understanding the data communication between the sender and the receiver), **integrity** (incorruptibility of the received data), **authenticity** (guarantee of the identity of the communication partner), **liability** (legally binding proof of that a communication was carried out) and **availability** (guarantee that a service offer is actually available).

Topology: A computer network's topology refers to the geometric order of the individual computing nodes within the network. Widespread computer network topologies are the **bus topology**, **ring topology** and **star topology**.

Throughput: A measure for the performance of a communication system. The total data is measured within a certain time span that is processed or transmitted. Throughput is calculated from the ratio of correctly transmitted data bits and the sum of all the transmitted bit based on a specified span of time. It is expressed, for example, in bit/s or data packet/s.

Virtual connection: Packet-switched networks can implement connectionless and connection-oriented services. In order to implement a connection-oriented service, a virtual connection is established between both communication partners. This means that all of the data to be transmitted is transported through the network along this virtual connection. Message exchange between sender and receiver is carried out over so-called "bit streams" (there are also byte streams). The disassembly of the exchanged data streams is concealed from the communication partner in data packets.

Virtual Private Network (VPN):   Software, technically-realized linking of computers in a public network to a virtual network that demonstrates the properties of a secure, private network. Network management and network security are the exclusive responsibility of the "private" operator. External, non-authorized computers are not able to access the VPN.

Chapter 4
Multimedia Data and Its Encoding

"The new world"
- From the heraldic motto of Christopher Columbus
(1446 – 1506)

The rapid development of digital communication technology in the areas of diversity and performance is ongoing – with no end in sight. The trend toward the integration of classic media continues. Verbal communication and data transmission have now become inseparable in modern mobile networks. The debut of digital technology has made it no longer necessary to distinguish between different types of media, such as text, graphic, audio or video. Encoded and in digital form, they all take the same shape of an extremely long series of zeros and ones and can be transferred indiscriminately via the same medium. In order to convert this stream of 0s and 1s back to its original media expression, methods and procedures of encoding and decoding are necessary. This task is taken on by powerful computers, which in the future will appear less in the form of a standard monitor and keyboard and more as an integrated system component of nearly all everyday devices. Today the computer is the window to the digital world and functions as an integrative communication medium. It allows multimedia data communication via the standard interface of the World Wide Web (WWW) with its simple and intuitive user interface – the browser. In the following chapters, we will take a closer look at the encoding of multimedia data. We will also examine the data formats developed for its transmission through the digital network and in the WWW. The most important media formats for audio, image and video data will be our focus.

4.1 Media Variety and Multimedia – A Question of Format

The computer was not originally designed as a communication medium. The punched cards first used for input and output would have been much too cumbersome. A long time passed before the computer was developed to the point where the medium of general information such as text or images, could be printed as output or displayed on a monitor. Already very early in the computer's development, telex or text printers were used as output media, before the introduction of plotters or graphic-capable screens. These could output digitally calculated images. It is only in the last 20 years that capabilities of displaying high-resolution graphics in true color, moving images and animation with real-time video output have evolved, as well as the ability to reproduce and produce sound – up through artificial voice synthesis. With the additional development of computer networks and the Internet the computer has become the universal communication medium we know today, The constantly growing capabilities of the computer combined with a continuous decrease in manufacturing costs has turned the computer into a consumer product for the mass market. The computer has found a place in nearly every household. Our lives today could simply not function without it. *Vannevar Bush* (1890 – 1974) was one of the pioneers of computer development. In 1945 Bush was Director of the Office of Scientific Research and Development, an institute of the U.S. government responsible for all military research programs, among them the coordination of the Manhattan Project for the development of the atomic bomb. Bush's vision of the computer as a universal communication medium took concrete form in his **Memex** system [34], which we have looked at previously. Bush envisioned the Memex (Memory Extender) as an electromechanical apparatus for the storage of books, personal records and communication. It offered fast, flexible and goal-oriented access to all data and its shared links. Today's hypermedia systems expand on this idea, allowing access to a number of different media types and formats, for example text, image, audio or video information. These various media formats are described as **multimedia**.

All types of media that are to be processed by a computer must first be digitally (binary) encoded. A distinction is made between the following traditional expressions of computer displayable media types:

- **Text**
  To encode alpha-numeric information – that is, encoding the displayed information by means of characters and letters of different alphabets - many different procedures exist. For example, ASCII, the 7 bit standard, which dates back to the days of the telegraph, or the 32-bit Unicode, which can be used to encode nearly all alphabets in the world. Closely related to the nature of the code is the required memory space. Many codes are redundant in order to ensure a certain degree of security in the face of transmission errors.

- **Graphics**
  Based on the complexity of the displayed visual information, different procedures are used for encoding image information. The range extends from simple procedures for monochromatic images to those for so-called true color display.

- **Monochrome**: Only one color is used here. The image to be displayed is created by coloring (or not coloring) the individual pixels with this color. The implemented encoding methods are kept quite simple and based on the encoding procedures for universal binary data.

- **Limited color palette**: Information graphics, symbols and pictograms often contain only a few colors. To enable a space-efficient representation of this information, encoding is carried out with a predetermined color palette, or a predetermined color intensity. This method has however limited use in encoding photographs with their nearly unlimited color variety.

- **True color**: Photographs depicting reality often have millions of color values. At the same time, these color values are usually not random (i.e., randomly arranged) but appear in the form of so-called color gradients. These can also be encoded in a space-efficient way. A distinction is made between lossy and lossless coding.

- **Audio**
  In the playback of acoustic information, such as speech or music, the dimension of time plays a critical role. The encoded data must be reproduced in real time, otherwise the value of the information, such as speech intelligibility, will be lost for the user. Besides complex, lossless encoding, there exists a number of lossy procedures. These methods are based on so-called psychoacoustic models. The frequencies and sound signals that cannot be detected by the human ear are filtered out and not saved.

- **Video and animation**
  Just as in the playback of acoustic information, the suitability for reproduction in real-time is also of importance in encoding video and animation sequences. To be able to encode an image sequence in a space-efficient way, often only the differential image sequence is saved. This means that just the changes in successive images are saved. It is also possible that only predictions are made about the sequence of images and accordingly just the difference between the predicted image and the actual image is encoded. The better the prediction, the less this difference is and the smaller the memory is needed.

Different media forms have specific characteristics. Special consideration must be paid to the characteristics of the data formats used in encoding. Principally, a distinction is made between two variations of multimedia data [226]:

- **Time-independent media**
  Text and graphics are members of this media group consisting of a sequence of elements without a relevant time component. This group is often referred to as **discrete media**. While representation and processing should be done as quickly as possible it is not subject to time restraints.

- **Time-dependent media**
  Acoustic information or video images are essentially characterized by their change over a span of time. The information to be displayed is not just a result of the information content alone but first revealed completely in its chronological execution over a span of time. This media group also includes tactile and sensory information, which will not be examined in greater detail here. The presentation of such media is time-critical and its correct reproduction dependent on time factors.

Media encoding requires the implementation of procedures especially designed for the medium in question. Space efficiency and ease of manipulation are the basic requirements for encoding. Different data formats have been developed for each medium addressing certain requirements and the desired quality of output. Their suitability varies as far as the ability to display and manipulate the media content. In their development, storage space efficiency and ease of handling the algorithms of manipulation often vie for dominance. Incidentally, the more compact a data format is, the more difficult the processing of the information proves to be.

If data is also transferred between the communication systems, transmission reliability in combination with error detection of the transmitted data also plays an important role. Data exchange between communication systems proceeds over a communication channel that is normally subject to disturbances of varying degrees. These can result in errors in the transmitted data (see also Fig. 1.3). These errors can be detected through the skillful use of encoding redundancy and possibly even corrected.

4.2 Information and Encoding

4.2.1 Information and Entropy

Before we take a closer look at data encoding and compression, we need to first tackle the notion of **information**. Just what exactly is information? In everyday terms, "information" is understood as a specific knowledge that is important and valid to the situation at hand. Messages and news in all their various embodiments contain information. Information is communicated in the form of a message. If the message is understood by the receiver it will be the starting point for changes in the receiving system. Things get more difficult if we want to grasp the meaning of information in a scientific sense. Questions arise that can no longer be satisfactorily answered with everyday definitions. How can information be quantified or, in other words, measured? How much information is in a message? When does a message contain too much or too little information? When can a message be shortened without information getting lost? The information theoretician *Claude E. Shannon*

(1916 – 2001) occupied himself with these questions in the context of his mathematical information theory (see also Chap. 1.2).

In mathematical information theory, the definition of information applies to the probabilities of certain sequences of elements occurring (news items, events) from a predetermined amount of elements. Based on this approach it was possible for Shannon to define information as a calculable measure for the probability of future events as they occurred in a technical system. In Shannon's sense, information refers to the measure of uncertainty that is eliminated e.g., through notification or clarification. The elements or events are seen as the **characters** generated from a selection process based on a predetermined character set (**alphabet**). The greater the information content of an element, the more unsure its occurrence will be, i.e, the less frequently it occurs [217, 219].

Basic concepts from information and encoding theory

A **message** can be understood as a series of characters from an alphabet that are transmitted by a sender (source) to a receiver (sink). The message string cannot be finite but needs to be countable so that the individual characters of the message can be numbered with natural numbers based on a mapping function and thus clearly identified.

(Permissible) messages are constructed according to specific, predefined rules (**syntax**). Through their subsequent transfer to processing, messages are given a meaning (**semantics**).

An **alphabet** consists of a countable set of characters. It defines the character set from which a message is constructed. The quantity of all messages that can be formed with the characters of an alphabet is referred to as the **message space**.

An **encoding** is the mapping of character strings from one message space into another. In computer science, the encoding of messages as a series of bits is of particular importance, i.e, message space via the alphabet $\{0, 1\}$ (**binary encoding**).

A **code word** is a sequence of code elements (signs) of the destination message space, which has been assigned to a message from the source message space.

Redundancy denotes that part of a message which conveys no information within the communication process. The redundant portion of the message ensures that the message will still be understood if it has been received incorrectly.

Fig. 4.1 Basic concepts of information and encoding theory.

More specifically, a sequence of elements from an alphabet is called a **character string**. Character strings transferred from a sender to a receiver in a communication procedure are referred to as the transmitted **message**. The objective of communication is to exchange information. Information is thus encoded in the form of character strings as a message The character string of a message is usually constructed based on specific rules (**syntax**). Through the processing of the message at the receiver, the message receives a particular meaning (**semantics**). This meaning, derived from the current situation (context), results in a change of status at the receiver. The most important basic concepts of the information and encoding theory are summarized in

Fig. 4.1. The length of the message, which is encoded and transmitted with the information, depends on the respectively used encoding rules, i.e. based on the code chosen. The more efficient the code, the shorter the message. Now the information content of a message is measurable as the length of the shortest possible encoding (see Fig. 4.2).

Information Content and Entropy

The establishment of a message's information content is attributed to *Ralph Hartley* (1888 – 1970). It was expanded by Claude E. Shannon who consistently applied this method in the information theory founded by him. Information – according to Shannon – is nothing more than uncertainty eliminated. If one succeeds in determining the measure of this uncertainty as an equivalent expression of the information contents, an approach to the quantitative definition of information can be achieved. Let us consider a set $X = \{x_1, x_2, \ldots, x_n\}$ of events, whereby the event x_i with the probability $0 \leq p(x_i) \leq 1$ für i=1, 2...,n occurs. This event can, for example, be the selection of a certain character from a previous alphabet, therefore, e.g, the selection of a letter from the Latin alphabet. The reciprocal $1/p(x_i)$ then represents a measure for the uncertainty of the occurrence of the event x_i. The greater the probability of the occurrence of a character, the larger $p(x_i)$, the smaller the uncertainty of its occurrence. If the event x_i occurs with certainty, i.e. $p(x_i)=1$, there is then no longer uncertainty as to whether the event has taken place or not, i.e., the uncertainty of an event or its information content is zero. In order to make this condition possible, it is necessary to construct the logarithm (base 2) via the reciprocal $1/p(x_i)$. The information content H_i of the event x_i, occurring with a probability of $0 \leq p(x_i) \leq 1$, is therefore

$$H_i = \log_2 \frac{1}{p(x_i)} = -\log_2 p(x_i).$$

The term H_i is both a measure of uncertainty that existed prior to the occurrence of x_i, as well as a measurement for the information that was also achieved after the occurrence of x_i. The information content of a message results from the information content of each character in the message multiplied by its frequency. If N is a message that consists of a message string of a given alphabet $X = \{x_1, x_2, \ldots, x_n\}$ and its relative frequency within the message N is $0 \leq p(x_i) \leq 1$. If $|N|$ denotes the length of message N, then the information content of message N is

$$H(N) = |N| \cdot \sum_{i=1}^{n} p_i \cdot (-\log_2(p_i)).$$

The unit of measure for the information contents of a message is a **bit**, which denotes a *binary digit*, in Shannon's sense as a *Basic Indissoluble Information Unit* – the smallest unit of information. The average information content of a message is also referred to as **entropy** – an analogy to entropy in thermodynamics and statistical mechanics.

Further reading:

Hartley, R. V.: Transmission of Information, Bell Syst. Tech. Journal, vol. 7, pp. 535–563 (1928)

Shannon, C. E.: A Mathematical Theory of Communication, The Bell System Technical Journal vol. 27, pp. 379–423, 623–656 (1948)

Fig. **4.2** Information content and entropy.

4.2.2 Redundancy – Necessary or Superfluous?

Based on the information content of a message, as defined in the previous chapter, it is possible to derive a lower bound for the length of every encoding of this message. Not all encodings are equally efficient – the same information may be encoded in messages of different lengths. Encodings whose message lengths exceed the theoretical lower bound described by Shannon therefore include parts which themselves do not contribute to the information content of the encoded message. These parts of the message are called **redundancy**. Redundant message portions are distinguishable in that they can be removed from the message without altering the information content. The removal of redundant portions of a message is known as message **compression**. We can look at the English language, for example, and immediately identify there a considerable amount of redundancy. If a few letters are removed from a word like "S‗nta Cl‗us"and the missing letters replaced by "‗" the word "Santa Claus" can nevertheless still be easily recognized by an English native speaker. But if still more letters are removed (without violating the uniqueness of the word or the Shannon limit) the readability of the word clearly suffers, e.g., "S‗ta C‗‗us". Redundancy clearly has a purpose in language. It is also use in case of incomplete message delivery or transmission error, so that in spite of a faulty transfer the original message can still be reconstructed and understood. The quality of redundancy is not only found in our verbal communication but also applied in digital data communication. Transmission errors can be detected using redundancy together with error detection codes. These type of errors can then be remedied using error-correcting codes.

A further important characteristic of redundancy has already become clear in the example above: redundant messages are (for us human) easier (=more efficient) to read and understand. In addition to error tolerance, message processing is also simplified. However, these advantage are paid for by the much larger amount of data that must be transmitted or stored for a message with redundant parts. If and in what form redundant message encoding should be carried out is determined by the respective application. In the case of a data transmission via an insecure and defective transmission medium, an error-tolerant encoding is an advantage. But with an optimal use of the existing storage or available transmission capacity, redundancy is avoided in order to encode the message as space-efficiently as possible. Thanks to Shannon's definition of the information contents of a message, there is also a lower limit to determine to what extent a message can be compressed without the loss of information. A further compression is then only possible when information-bearing parts of a message are deliberately omitted. In contrast to lossless compression, the procedures in which information is lost is referred to as lossy compression. Lossy compression is used e.g., in the compression of audio, image or video data. In such cases, weaknesses in the human system of perception can be exploited. It is then possible to dispense with those parts of information that are perceived poorly or not at all by humans.

4.3 Text – Data Formats and Compression

4.3.1 Text Encoding

Coding methods were developed early on for the transmission of text-based messages. Depending on its use, coding can require varying degrees of storage space. If coding is only used to preserve a message, it is then designed to be as space-saving as possible. If, however, other criteria are in the forefront, such as secure transmission or encryption for security reasons, the code used often contains redundant information, which does not contribute to the information content of the message in the true sense of the word. The most common form of displaying a message for transmission – whether it be in direct communication or with the receiver getting a time-delayed message – is a transfer in written form. In our western culture a spelling alphabet is used. Strings of letters are formed, which already contain some redundancy. For example, if one reads the series of letters in the English word "*ecember*", the receiver, who is at the same time an English speaker, is sure that it is the name for the the last month of the year – "December." To transmit messages that are written in an alphabet font with a modern means of communication, a suitable form of coding must be found for the communication medium. One historical example of letter transmission was the code that was devised to express individual letters via the positioning of the signal arm of a semaphore (or "wing telegraph"). The Morse alphabet, developed for simple, electrical or wireless communication, is another example. The character by character encoding of an alphabet is called **encryption**. As a rule, this coding must be reversible – the reverse encoding known as decoding or decryption. Examples for a simple encryption are the international phonetic alphabet (Table 4.1) or Braille script (Fig. 4.3), named after its inventor *Louis Braille* (1809 – 1852).

Table 4.1 The International Phonetic Alphabet

Alpha	Bravo	Charlie	Delta	Echo
Foxtrott	Golf	Hotel	India	Juliette
Kilo	Lima	Mika	November	Oscar
Papa	Quebec	Romeo	Sierra	Tango
Uniform	Victor	Whiskey	X-Ray	Yankee
Zulu				

Braille is an example of a code that is based on the binary character set $\{0, 1\}$, with every character represented by a 3×2 matrix of binary characters. The **Morse code** also uses a binary representation for the individual letters. The length of the code for one character depends on the average frequency of its occurrence (see Fig. 4.4).

Louis Braille and the Braille Writing System

Louis Braille (1809 – 1852) lost his eyesight in an accident as a child. He refused to to accept that his only access to literature would be when it was read to him and sought early in life to develop a form of writing that would make it possible for the blind to read and write.

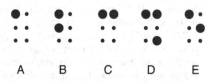

In 1821, he published his easy to learn writing system called Braille. It had been developed from a complex "night writing" system designed for the military by artillery captain *Charles Barbier* (1767 – 1841). Commissioned by Napoleon, Barbier had invented night writing to make it possible for soldiers to communicate with each other without sound or light. However, because of its overly complicated system of dots and syllables the system writing turned out to be unsuitable for military use. Louis Braille simplified this writing by replacing the syllables with letters and reducing the number of dots per symbol from twelve to six. A letter could be easily felt with the tip of the finger, making it unnecessary to move the finger, which made rapid reading possible. Each letter of the writing system developed by Braille consists of six dots arranged in a 3x2 matrix. The encoding of the letters was done by raising certain points in the matrix so they could be felt with the fingertip.

Fig. 4.3 Louis Braille and the Braille writing system.

The first telegraph at the beginning of the 20th century still used the Morse code to transmit letters. But decoding proved to be much easier if every letter was encoded with a binary code word of a constant length. Those codes whose code words are of a constant length are called **block codes**. Frequently used characters are encoded in a block code with a code word of the same length as those code words with rarely used characters. Therefore a certain amount of redundancy is to be expected. This disadvantage is made up for by the simpler mechanical handling of the decoding. The Morse code was soon replaced by the **Baudot code**, a code developed by *Emile Baudot* (1845 – 1903) in 1880. With its 5 bits per character, it can encode two different character sets with altogether over 60 different characters. It became famous as the **International Telegraph Code No.1** (ITC-1, IA-1, CCITT-1). In addition to the 26 letters of the alphabet and the 10 digits, the Baudot code also contains control characters. These serve in formatting the font or in controlling the telegraph [15]. It is only possible to display $2^5 = 32$ characters with 5 bits – which is insufficient when it come to encoding the alphabet and the ten numerical digits. The situation was remedied with a partial double occupancy of the code words. In order to still ensure unique assignment it is possible to switch between the letter and the digit mode by means of special control characters. In 1900 another 5-bit telegraph code was introduced: the so-called **Murray code**. It later became recognized as the **International Telegraph Code No.2** (ITC-2, IA-2, CCITT-2) and is often mistakenly referred to as the Baudot code.

An important step in coding was achieved with the 7-bit telegraphic code, standardized in 1963 by the ANSI (American National Standards Institute) as **ASCII-Code (American Standard Code for Information Inter-**

Morse Code and Entropy

Samuel F. B. Morse and Alfred Vail began developing their electrical "writing" telegraph in 1836. The telegraph was based on the principle discovered by Hans Christian Oerstedt (1777 – 1851) in 1821 called electromagnetism – messages are encoded via changing currents, which control an electromagnet on the receiver's side. However, with the technology available at that time it was not possible to print the text that had been received. This led to both inventors finding an alternative method of text encoding. Aided by the electromagnetism of the Morse telegraph, impressions could be raised on a paper strip that was constantly moved by the mechanism of a clockwork under the electromagnet. Morse and Vail used a form of binary encoding, i.e., all text characters were encoded in a series of two basic characters. The two basic characters – a "dot" and a "dash" – were short and long raised impressions marked on a running paper tape. To achieve the most efficient encoding of the transmitted text messages, Morse and Vail implemented their observation that specific letters came up more frequently in the (English) language than others. The obvious conclusion was to select a shorter encoding for frequently used characters and a longer one for letters that are used seldom. For example, "E" – the most frequently used letter in English, is represented by only one basic character, a "dot." On the other hand, the rarely used "Q" is represented by a four character string: "dash dash dot dash." Numbers are shown with a five characters encoding and punctuation with a six character encoding. Word bord(

A	B	C	D	E	F	G	H	I	J	K	L	M
.-	-...	-.-.	-..	.	..-.	--.	....	..	.---	-.-	.-..	--

N	O	P	Q	R	S	T	U	V	W	X	Y	Z
-.	---	.--.	--.-	.-.	...	-	..-	...-	.--	-..-	-.--	--..

The selected encoding reflects how often the letters are used and are therefore chosen relative to the **entropy** of the encoded character. For this reason, this variation of encoding is also known as **entropy** or **statistical encoding**.

Fig. 4.4 Morse code and entropy.

change). It is still used up to today as the standard form for representing text information in computers. From the early developmental phase of the first commercial computer systems until the end of the fifties there was no standard character encoding for computers. The computers sold by IBM in 1960 used nine different letter codes alone. But as the idea of networking became more and more a reality there was a huge increase in the demand for a standard letter encoding. In 1961 *Robert Bemer* (1920 – 2004), an IBM employee, proposed ASCII encoding to the ANSI as the standard. It was adopted in 1963. The 7-bit SCII code also became an international standard in 1974, the **ISO I-646**.

However, it took another eighteen years for ASCII to actually be recognized as a general standard. This was due to IBM's newly introduced computer architecture System/360. Still independent and separate from the standardization process of ASCII, it used its own coding called **EBCDIC (Extended Binary Coded Decimals Interchange Code)**. For reasons of compati-

Fig. 4.5 Extract from the 7 bit ASCII code.

Binary	000	001	010	011	100	101	110	111
0000				0	@	P	'	p
0001			!	1	A	Q	a	q
0010			"	2	B	R	b	r
0011			#	3	C	S	c	s
0100			$	4	D	T	d	t
0101			%	5	E	U	e	u
0110			&	6	F	V	f	v
0111				7	G	W	g	w
1000			(	8	H	X	h	x
1001			)	9	I	Y	i	y
1010			*	:	J	Z	j	z
1011			+	;	K	[	k	{
1100			,	<	L	\	l	|
1101			-	=	M	]	m	}
1110			.	>	N		n	~
1111			/	?	O	_	o	

bility, the succeeding generations of IBM System/360 continued to use the EBCDIC encoding. EBCDIC is an 8-bit encoding, an expansion of the 6-bit BCD used previously by IBM. Successive characters in the alphabet were not necessarily provided with consecutive codes since this type of encoding was still being influenced by Hollerith's punched cards. There are different variations of EBCDIC that are incompatible with each other. Most of the time, the American variation uses the same characters as the ASCII code, yet some special characters are not included in the respective other code. IBM designed a total of 57 different, national EBCDIC codes, each containing country-specific special characters and letters. It was not until 1981 that IBM changed to the ASCII code, while in the process of developing its first personal computer.

Also the 7bits of the original ASCII encoding proved insufficient in representing all of the international character sets with their associated special characters. By adding an eighth bit some manufacturers introduced their own proprietary encoding to allow for a display of diverse special characters. But a unified standard for different international characters based on an 8 bit ASCII encoding could first be achieved with **ISO/IEC 8859** encoding. With the ISO/IEC 8859-x standard, the first 7 bits are assigned the original encoding of the 7-bit ASCII. This ensures compatibility with the previous encoding. Various national extensions of the ASCII codes are implemented via the 8th bit. Altogether there are some 15 different national standards for the 8-bit ASCII code, ISO/IEC 8859-1 through ISO/IEC 8859-16, whereby ISO/IEC 8859-12, for characters of the Indian Devanagari language, was dropped in 1997. ISO/IEC 8859-1 (Latin 1) includes special national special characters for the regions of Western Europe, America, Australia and Africa, ISO/IEC

8859-2 (Latin 2) supplements the basic characters of the 7-bit ASCII codes with other Central European special characters. ISO/IEC 8859-5 contains Cyrillic, ISO/IEC 8859-6 Arabic and ISO/IEC 8859-8 Hebrew special characters. Hebrew like Arabic has a reversed textual direction from European writing systems. For this reason, two special characters with zero width were adopted at the positions 253, or 254 respectively. These characters change the text direction from left to right or from right to left.

With Asian sets of characters such as Chinese, and its more than 10,000 ideographic characters, or Korean or Indian an 8-bit encoding is not sufficient to represent all of the characters. Moreover, the concept of what constitutes a character or letter as a "basic" unit for the encoding of a text is not the same in all languages and writing systems. In some languages, individual characters can consist of a further series of individual characters. These have a different meaning when in a group and can also change their external form when they are combined.

The Korean Hangul writing system combines symbols that in Korean each stand for an individual sound and in quadratic blocks each represent an individual syllable. Depending on the user as well as on the intended application individual symbols as well as syllable blocks can be represented as "characters." In Indian systems of writing every character that stands for a consonant hides an inherent vowel, which in different ways is either eliminated or replaced when individual characters are combined together into blocks. Also here, independent of user or application, individual consonants and vowels or entire consonant vowel blocks can be seen as "characters." Therefore it was necessary to develop an encoding system that could fulfill the challenges of different international writing systems in an appropriate way. The **Unicode** was designed to ensure that such a standard of encoding could be implemented for nearly all existing alphabets. Unicode encoding was introduced in 1991 and with the norm **ISO/IEC 10646 ISO/IEC 10646** and adopted as the international standard **Universal Character Set** (UCS). The nonprofit Unicode Consortium, founded in 1991, was responsible for the Unicode industry standard.

Unicode first used 16 bits for encoding multilingual characters. This was later expanded to 21 bits[1] and also included codes for Indian, Chinese, Japanese and Korean characters for which a huge supply of 2^{21} characters were available. This was to ensure that Unicode encoding in fact fulfilled the desired requirements of universality (i.e,. for every existing writing system there should be an encoding possibility) and extensibility. In addition to national alphabets of a variety of countries, additional typographic symbols and special national characters are also included.

---

[1] In the UTF-32 transformation, 21-bit Unicode characters are encoded with a full 32 bits.

Excursus 5: The Unicode Standard

The Unicode standard assigns a number(**code point**) and a name to each character, instead of the usual glyph.[2] It represents each individual character in an abstract manner, while the visual representation of the character is left up to the text-displaying software, e.g., the web browser. This makes sense since the graphical representation of the character may vary greatly depending on the font type chosen. Characters can be assigned to several different code points since the same characters often belongs to different writing systems.

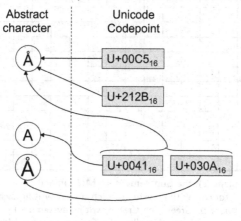

In Unicode, a code point defines a specific character. However, it is entirely possible that a character is used in different writing systems. Structure and organization of the Unicode arranges individual writing systems within each contiguous block of codes. Some characters are assigned several code points. It is also possible for one character to be composed of several basic characters that exist separately.

Organization of Unicode Encoding

In Unicode encoding, the first 256 characters of the Unicode are assigned characters of the ISO/IEC 8859-1 code to ensure a compatibility between the old 8-bit ASCII encoding and Unicode. Unicode characters are usually displayed in the form U+xxxxxxxx, whereby xxxxxxxx stands for a code point in hexadecimal format. Leading zeros can be omitted. The code space provided in Unicode is divided into individual planes. Each of them contains 2^{16}=65.536 code points. Of these planes, currently 17 are available for use (as a result the character space, encodable by means of Unicode, is limited to $17 \cdot 2^{16}$=1.114.112 characters), with only planes 0–1 and 14–16 in use.

Plane	Title	from	to
0	Basic Multilingual Plane (BMP)	U+0000$_{16}$	U+FFFF$_{16}$
1	Supplementary Multilingual Plane (SMP)	U+10000$_{16}$	U+1FFFF$_{16}$
2	Supplementary Ideographic Plane (SIP)	U+20000$_{16}$	U+2FFFF$_{16}$
14	Supplementary Special-purpose Plane (SSP)	U+E0000$_{16}$	U+EFFFF$_{16}$
15	Supplementary Private Use Area-A	U+F0000$_{16}$	U+FFFFF$_{16}$
16	Supplementary Private Use Area-B	U+100000$_{16}$	U+10FFFF$_{16}$

---

[2] In typography, a character signifies the abstract idea of a letter, whereas a glyph is its concrete, graphic display.

The first level – plane 0 with the code points 0 – 65.535 – is called the **Basic Multilingual Plane** (BMP) and includes almost all spoken languages.

Area with general scripts

Symbols

Unified CJK Han

Not used

Hangul

UTF-16 Surrogate and private use

The second level (plane 1), the **Supplementary Multilingual Plane** (SMP), contains rarely used and mostly historical writing systems, such as the writing system of the Old Italian language, or a precursor to Greek, the Cretan writing systems – Linear A and Linear B.

The next level or plane (plane 2), called the **Supplementary Ideographic Plane** (SIP), contains additional, rarely used, ideographic characters from the "CJK" group of Chinese, Japanese and Korean characters that are not classified in the BMP. Level 14, the **Supplementary Special-purpose Plane** (SSP), contains additional command and control characters that were not assigned on the BMP. Planes 15 and 16 accommodate privately used characters.

Within the planes, code points that belong together are grouped into blocks. Principally a Unicode block contains a complete writing system. However, a certain degree of fragmentation may be observed. In many cases new characters were later added to an already completed block and then had to be accommodated elsewhere.

Unicode UTF Transformations

Unicode codepoints can be encoded in different ways via so-called „**Unicode Transformation Formats**" (UTF). As the writing systems most often used are located within plane 0, omitting lead zeros in encoding for reasons of efficiency seems an obvious choice. The various UTF Transformations (UTF-7, UTF-8, UTF-16 or UTF-32) were developed to enable the efficient encoding of Unicode code points.

UTF-8 is the most well-known variety and implements an encoding of variable length from 1–4 bytes (based on the UTF-8 procedure, strings of up to 7 bytes long can be theoretically generated, however because of the limitation of Unicode code space, the maximum length allowance is 4 bytes). The first 128 bits of the Unicode, encompassing the characters of the 7-bit ASCII code, are only represented by one byte. The byte order of every UTF-8 encoded character starts with a preamble that encodes the length of the byte order. To ensure maximum compatibility with ASCII encoding, the 128 characters of the 7-bit ASCII code are assigned the preamble "0." If a UTF-8 encoded character consists of several bytes, the start byte always begins with a "1" and every succeeding byte with the preamble "10". With multi-byte characters, the quantity of of 1-bits in the preamble of the start bytes, gives the byte length of the entire UTF-8 encoded character. The resulting encoding scheme is therefore:

1 byte 0xxxxxxx	(7 bit)
2 bytes 110xxxxx 10xxxxxx	(11 bit)
3 bytes 1110xxxx 10xxxxxx 10xxxxxx	(16 bit)
4 bytes 1111xxxx 10xxxxxx 10xxxxxx 10xxxxxx	(21 bit)

The shortest possible encoding variation is chosen for the UTF8-encoding of a code point. The Unicode code point is always entered in the encoding scheme right-justified. The following examples illustrate the principle of UTF-8 encoding:

Character	Codepoint	Unicode binary	UTF-8
y	$U+0079_{16}$	00000000 01111001	**0**1111001
ä	$U+00E4_{16}$	00000000 11100100	**110**00011 **10**100100
€	$U+20AC_{16}$	00100000 10101100	**1110**0010 **10**000010 **10**101100

For all scripts based on the Latin alphabet, UTF-8 is the most space-saving method for the mapping of Unicode characters. A further variation is **UTF-16** encoding, which allocates every Unicode code point a 2 – 4-byte long bit sequence. UTF-16 is especially designed for the encoding of BMP characters. It is superior to UTF-8 encoding for texts in Chinese, Japanese or Hindi. Whereas these BMP characters are encoded in a 3-byte long bit sequence with UTF-8, a corresponding UTF-16 encoding is comprised of just 2 bytes. **UTF-32**, in contrast, assigns every Unicode codepoint a bit sequence with a constant length of 4 bytes. It therefore represents the simplest of all encoding variations as the Unicode code point can be directly translated into a 32-bit binary number. However, in regards to the characters from the BMP, UTF-32 is quite inefficient. Further encoding variations exist. Of these, the **UTF-7** encoding should be mentioned here. It was originally intended for use in communication protocols based on a 7-bit transmission standard, for example for the SMTP protocol for emails. However in email communication Base64 encoding of the MIME standard finally prevailed over UTF-7.

Further reading:

The Unicode Consortium: The Unicode Standard, Version 5.0, Addison-Wesley Professional, 5th ed. (2006)

Unicode has also been introduced in the WWW. In RFC 2070, the WWW language HTML was prepared for Unicode support. RFC 2077 also recommends the support of ISO 10646 for all new Internet protocols.

4.3.2 Text Compression

The available bandwidth of the implemented communication medium limits the amount of data transmitted. Methods were therefore developed early on to minimize the redundancy contained in a message and to use the available bandwidth as efficiently as possible. The techniques that came to be used for this purpose are called **compression** (compaction). They are commonly employed on text files or multimedia data. These methods prove to be especially advantageous if, e.g., certain characters or strings of characters appear more often than others in text files, or if graphics contain large, contiguous and homogeneous fields or extensive repetitions of the same pattern. The space savings of the different compression methods vary, depending on the characteristics of the file to be compressed. For text files 20% to 50% are a typical values for space saving, while savings of 50% up to 90% can be achieved with graphics files. However, with file types consisting largely of random bit patterns little can be achieved with these methods of compression.

In principle, several different types of compression can be distinguished. These are generally valid and do not depend on the type of medium to be compressed.

- **Logical vs. physical compression**
  Semantic, or logical, compression, is achieved by continuous substitution, i.e., replacing one alphanumeric or binary symbol with another, for example, if the term "United States of America" is replaced with "USA." Semantic compression can only be used on data that is above the abstraction levels of alphanumeric characters. It is based solely on information is contained in the data to be compressed. Compression algorithms encode the information to be displayed in such a manner that there is minimum redundancy. Syntactic or physical compression can be implemented on the given data without the information contained in the data being used. One coding is simply exchanged for another that is more compact. The compressed data can be mechanically decoded again into the output data, however the correspondence between the output data and compressed data is generally not obvious. The following methods presented belong to the group of syntactic compression methods.

- **Symmetric vs. asymmetric compression**
  In symmetrical compression, encoding algorithms and decoding algorithms have approximately the same computational complexity. It's a different case with asymmetric compression methods. Here, the computational complexity of both algorithms is clearly different. Asymmetrical compression methods are useful if a complex encoding is carried out only one time during compression, while decoding must be performed every time the compressed data is accessed and, accordingly much more often.

- **Adaptive vs. semi-adaptive vs. non-adaptive compression**
  Many methods, such as **Huffman encoding**, are used exclusively for the compression of certain media formats and thus use format-specific information. This information is maintained in so-called dictionaries. Non-adaptive methods use a static dictionary with predetermined patterns known to occur frequently in the information to be compressed. Thus, a non-adaptive compression procedure for the English language could contain a dictionary with predefined character chains for the words "and, or, the", because these words occur frequently in English. Adaptive compression methods, e.g.,

the LZW method, build their own dictionaries, with its own commonly found patterns for each application. These dictionaries are not based on predefined, application-specific patterns. Semi-adaptive compression methods present a mixture of both forms. These methods usually work in two separate steps. First, a dictionary of the data to be compressed is established, then the actual encoding itself follows in a second step.

- **Lossless vs. lossy compression**
  In lossless procedures the encoding and decoding of the data to be compressed is performed in such a way that the original data remains unchanged after completion of the process. The information in the compressed data is fully preserved. The maximum achievable compression rate is prescribed by the Shannon information complexity. Lossless compression methods are essential for text and program files. On the other hand, lossy compression methods, attempt to achieve a higher compression rate by sacrificing parts of the information to be compressed, considered less important for the use intended. For example, in audio compression lossy procedures dispense with sounds and sound sequences that cannot be perceived by the human ear. With the help of heuristic methods, lossy compression procedures for image data determine how maximum compression can be achieved with a minimum loss of the existing visual information.

Excursus 6: A Simple Data Compression Procedure

Run Length Encoding (RLE)
The simplest type of redundancy in a text file are long sequences of repeated characters. For example, the simple character sequence:

AAAADEBBHHHHHCAAABCCCC

This character string can be encoded in a more compact way. Every sequence of repeated characters is replaced with a one-time entry of the character and the number of its repetitions. The above sequence of characters would thus be encoded like this:

4ADEBB5HC3AB4C

This form of encoding is known as **Run Length Encoding** (RLE). Run length encoding is not feasible for a single character or for two identical letters because at least two characters are necessary for encoding. Very high compression rates can be achieved when long sequences of the same character occur.

When encoding binary data, for example, as is the case in various media formats, a refined version of this method is used. It exploits the fact that the data is made up of only the binary values 0 and 1. It depends only on the change of these values, while storage of the actual 0 and 1 values themselves can be omitted. This method works efficiently when long sequences of 0 or 1 values occur. It is possible to save encoding space if the number of characters in a sequence need less space than the number of bits that are necessary to represent the length of this sequence as binary number. No run length procedure works efficiently if the length of the repetitions is too short. RLE is also implemented in the post-compression process, when lossy compression is used for image and audio data.

Variable length encoding

This encoding method of compression is especially well-suited for text files. The idea is to deviate from the conventional procedures based on encoding all characters with a code of a fixed, prescribed length. Instead, characters that often occur in the text often are assigned shorter code words than characters that only appear rarely. For example, let us assume that the character sequence:

ABRAKADABRA

is to be encoded with a standard encoding that uses a 5-bit code for every letter of the alphabet, e.g., the i-th letter of the alphabet is simply assigned the binary representation of i. This results in the following bit sequence:

00001 00010 10010 00001 01101 00001 00100 00001 00010 10010 00001

For decoding, 5 bits each are read and, based on the encoding instructions, converted into the appropriate letters. The letter **A** is encoded with a five-digit bit sequence just as the letter **K**, which occurs only once in the encrypted text. Space saving can be achieved if frequently used letters are encrypted with fewer bits so as to minimize the total number of bits used for the string. The specified string sequence can be encrypted in the following way. First, the letters to be encoded are arranged according to the frequency of their occurrence. The top two letters are encoded with a bit sequence of the length 1. The following letters are encoded with for as long as possible with 2 bits each, subsequently with 3 bits each and so on. i.e., **A** can be encoded with **0**, **B** with **1**, **R** with **01**, **K** with **10** and **D** with **11**:

0 1 01 0 10 0 11 0 1 01 0

With this encoding, the addition of limiters (the spaces in the example) is also necessary between the separate letters to be encoded. If this is not done, ambiguous interpretations of the code words are possible. Ambiguities can be avoided if attention is paid that no code starts with the bit sequence of another code. Such codes are also referred to as **prefix codes**. The condition for generating the prefix code – the **Shannon-Fano code** – is named after its inventors Claude E. Shannon and *Robert M. Fano* (*1917). For example, we can encrypt **A** with **11**, **B** with **00**, **R** with **10**, **K** with **010** and **D** with **011**:

110010110101101111001011

The original 55-bit comprehensive standard coding could therefore be reduced to only 24 bits by encoding with variable length encoding. Prefix-free encoding can be represented with the help of a binary tree whose leaves are assigned the letters to be encoded. Starting from the root it is possible to obtain the code word assigned to a letter based on the path to this letter. If the path branches left to an inner node, bit **0** is added to the code, if it branches to the right then bit **1** is added (see Fig. 4.6). On the basis of a tree diagram simple encodings can be achieved that meet the Shannon-Fano condition – with none of the bit strings used the prefix of another codeword.

Huffman Coding

The question can also be raised of the best way to obtain the most efficient variable length code. An appropriate answer is found in **Huffman coding**. The procedure, published in 1952, is named after its developer *David A. Huffman* (1925 – 1999). The optimal encoding for a text file can be represented by a binary tree whose inner nodes always have two successors, i.e., if the amount of A represents all letters to be encoded, then as an optimal prefix code for A the tree has exactly $|A|$ leaf nodes and $|A|-1$ inner nodes. If we consider a tree T, which corresponds to a predetermined prefix code, then the number of bits for the encoding of a predetermined file can be easily calculated. f(c) denotes the frequency with which a character c of the given alphabet A is found in our file. $d_{T(c)}$ denotes the depth of the leaf node for the character c in the binary tree T, which incidentally corresponds to the length of the code word for c. The number of necessary n bits B(T) to encode a file result in

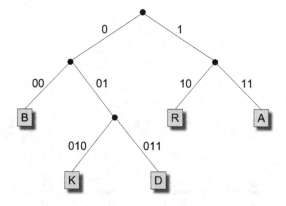

Fig. 4.6 Prefix coding in a binary tree representation.

$$B(T) = \sum_{c \in A} f(c) d_T(c).$$

The procedure developed by Huffman for the construction of an optimal prefix code works in the so-called bottom-up manner, i.e. it begins from below with a number of $|A|$ (unrelated) leaf nodes and leads to a a range of $|A|$-1 merger operations to construct a result tree. Besides bearing the letters $c \in A$, the leaf nodes also represent its frequency $f(c)$ within the encoded file. Next, the two nodes c_1 and c_2, which contain the smallest frequency data are selected. A new node c_{neu} is generated, which is marked with the sum from the two frequencies $f(c_{neu}) = f(c_1) + f(c_2)$ and connected to the two nodes selected as its successor. The nodes c_1 and c_2 are taken out of the amount A, while the new node c_{neu} is added to it. By proceeding in the same way, increasingly large subtrees are generated and number of the nodes in A becomes smaller and smaller. At the end all of the nodes are connected into one single tree. Nodes with a lower frequency are then the farthest away from the root node, i.e., they are also allocated the longest used code word, while codes with greater frequency are near the root nodes and have accordingly short code words. A tree generated in this way is a direct result of the Huffman code (see Fig. 4.7).

With the help of induction it can be shown that in fact the Huffmann method generates an optimal prefix code.

Further reading

Huffman, D. A.: A Method for the Construction of Minimum-Redundancy Codes, in Proc. of the IRE, 40(9), pp. 1098-1101 (1952)

Cormen, T. H., Leiserson, C. E., Rivest, R. L.: Introduction to Algorithms, MIT Press, Cambridge MA, USA (1996)

4.4 Graphics – Data Formats and Compression

Graphics represented and processed in a computer are traditionally prepared in the form of vector graphics or bitmap graphics (also referred to as raster graphics). With **vector graphics**, lines, polygons or curves are defined by the specification of key points. A program reconstructs the geometric figure to be displayed from these key points. Additionally, the key points have specific

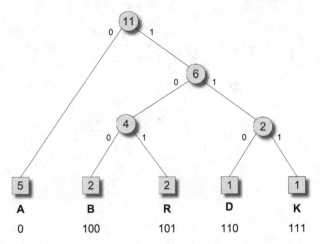

Fig. 4.7 Huffman coding represented by a binary tree.

attribute information, such as color or line thickness. The suitable program, aided by an output device, reconstructs the image to be displayed from these basic graphic elements. In a historical context, vector graphics were developed together with **plotters** – a graphic output device for computers. Plotters print by moving one or more pens across a drawing surface based on given coordinate values. An advantage of vector graphics is that the image to be represented may be scaled as desired without any quality-reduction effects. **Bitmap graphics** consist of a set of numeric values, color and brightness information of individual pixels or whole picture elements. Encoding such an image means that it has to be put into the form of a grid and spatially discretized (screened), with each pixel assigned a color or brightness value. Historically, bitmap or raster graphics were associated with the development of the **cathode ray tube** (CRT) as a graphical output device. In order to display an image made up of pixels on this type of a screen the pixels are illuminated in a certain color and brightness. Raster graphics are suitable for displaying more complex images such as photographs, which cannot be created with vector graphics.

One of the disadvantages of bitmap graphics, as compared to vector graphics, is the relatively high memory consumption that normally occurs. Because bitmap graphics usually consist of a limited number of pixels, two-dimensional geometric forms can only be approximated. It is also possible that the so-called „alias effect" can occur, i.e., rounded lines are approximated with step-like pixel sequences. In addition, information gets lost in geometric transformation, e.g., in an enlargement (scaling) or rotation of an image section. It can happen that so-called "artifacts" appear, i.e., through the transformation of the pixels color tones can be created which were previously not there, reducing the quality of the transformed image. Although vector graphics are also used today in the WWW, in this chapter we will limit ourselves to the most important data formats from the area of bitmap graphics.

In the efficient storage of graphic data, the following properties must be taken into account when characterizing a graph:

- **Picture Resolution**
  The picture resolution is determined by the number of pixels along the x axis and the y axis.

- **Color Depth**
  The color depth determines the number of colors a pixel has. It is given as logarithm $\log(c)$ of the actual number of possible colors c (e.g., color depth 8 corresponds to $2^8 = 256$ colors), i.e., the number of bits that are necessary to describe or specify a color uniquely. Starting at 24 bits we speak of a display of true color. Modern image processing systems even allow a 32 bit or 48 bit deep color representation.

- **Palette Size**
  Some graphics systems limit the number of available bits for specifying colors. From the outset, there is a fixed color palette with a reduced number of colors from which the image can be made. The palette colors are selected in such a way that they come as close as possible to the original colors of the image to be coded.

- **Picture Resolution (Density)**
  The picture resolution is given as the density of the individual pixels per length unit. The common unit of measure is adopted from the American system: **dpi** (dots per inch), in other words, the number of pixels per 2.54 cm. Image resolution for computer screens is about 100 dpi and more, with resolutions greater than 300 dpi normal in the area of printing. The higher the picture resolution chosen, the more detailed the display of the image, but at the same time the more storage space is needed

- **Aspect Ratio**
  The aspect ratio of an image describes the relation of the image length to the image width. It also distinguishes the aspect ratio of a single pixel (pixel aspect ratio), which also affects the aspect ratio of the total image and how it is perceived.

In a bitmap graphic, in the simplest case, the individual pixels are stored next to each other in a line and the lines sequentially in rows. Based on the depth of color to be displayed, a varying degree of storage space is needed for each pixel. While in a monochromatic image a single bit is sufficient for a single pixel, in a so-called true color display at least 24 bits are required per pixel.

Color itself is not a property of the physical world, but rather a sensory perception. The perception of color enables us to distinguish between two featureless surfaces of equal brightness. In the way it is perceived by humans, color is nothing more than light made up of multiple wavelengths.

The white light that we know is simply light made up of different frequencies whose wave lengths are in the realm of human perception at between approximately 380 nm and 780 nm (1 nm = 10^{-9}m). Ideally, colored light is generated from a radiating black body (black-body radiation). Depending on the temperature of the radiating body, the spectral composition of light differs. Therefore, different light sources are assigned **color temperatures** that correspond to the temperature of an ideal black body radiating a corresponding light spectrum. The color temperature of a standard 60 watt light bulb is 2,200° Kelvin, while the color temperature of sunlight is about 5,500° Kelvin. Low color temperatures appear to us reddish and warm while higher color temperature are perceived as bluish and cold.

Color first comes into being when white light is broken down into individual components of fixed or a similar frequency. Color is also created when, in the process of being reflected or scattered on a white light surface, certain frequencies receive preference while others are suppressed, absorbed or filtered through colored, transparent bodies. In the first case, colored light from a body (sun, light bulb) is radiated. This color is therefore also referred to as **light color**. In the second variation, color generated through reflection, absorption, scattering or filtering is called **body color**. The human eye can however, only perceive a limited number of colors in each case. At the same time, up to 10,000 colors can be distinguished simultaneously. All in all, the human eye is capable of perceiving up to 7 million different color valences, with approximately 500 different levels of brightness and about 200 different shades of color. However, this depends in each case on different parameters, e.g., background illumination and the size of the field of brightness. With optimal conditions, the value of the perceived level of brightness can increases up to 1,000. The maximum sensitivity of the human eye is dependent on the wave length and the light intensity. In daylight, the maximum sensitivity is 554 nm and with the adaption of the eyes to night conditions shifts to 513 nm. There are different mathematical **color models** for the display of color on a computer. A systematic arrangement of color had already been done by Aristotle , who ordered colors on a palette between black and white. Many scientists and artists have attempted to achieve a systematization of color throughout the centuries. The color systems developed all have the goal of arranging colors in a way that they can be described by a geometric arrangement or provide a guidelines for the mixing of new colors.

A fundamental distinction is made between additive and subtractive color models. In an **additive** color model, colors are mixed with the base color black to create new colors. The more colors are added, the more the color mixture tends toward white. Each of the colors are self-illuminating in an additive color model. A typical example of this is the raster image of a television or computer screen. The image is made up of many small dots, thus the three primary colors of the luminous red, green and blue pixels are "added" together. At a sufficient distance to one another, the adjacent red, green and blue pixels are seen by the eye as mixed and correspondingly create the perception of color. A **subtractive color model** works in the opposite way. Fundamentally speaking, individual colors are subtracted from the base color white to create new colors. The more colors are removed, the more the color mixture tends toward black. Viewed in another way, black in a subtractive color model represents the complete absorption of the light of the color pigment. Subtractive color models are based on reflection and absorption. The colors we perceive result from the reflection of light from an external light source, such as the printed colors on a piece of paper. In a color model, colors may be subdivided into **primary colors, secondary colors** and **tertiary colors**, according to the degree of the mixing of the primary colors involved. The basic colors of the color model are the primary colors. If two primary colors are mixed together in equal parts the results is a secondary color. The secondary color yellow is created by mixing the primary colors red and green in the additive RGB color model. If a primary color and a secondary color are mixed together, the result is a tertiary color. The most common color models – the RGB color model, the CMY(K) color model, the HUV color model and the YUV color model – are introduced in detail in Excursus 7.

Excursus 7: What is Color? – Color and Color Systems

The ability to classify natural colors in a system and the study of such systems goes back to ancient times. Already *Aristotle* (384 – 322 BC) presents an arrangement of colors in his work entitled *"De sensu et sensato"* (about the senses). He orders colors in a strand from black to white and assigns them to the time of day. In the Middle Ages the very existence of color was debated by scholars. The Persian doctor and physicist, *Avicenna* (980 – 1037) argued about whether colors were present in the dark. Without light, colors lacked "verum esse" – their very existence. His opponent, *Alhazen* (and Ibn al-Haitham, 965 – 1040) countered with the argument that colors were still present when it was dark even though they were no longer visible to the eye. During the Middle Ages in Europe, philosopher *Roger Bacon* (1214 – 1294) addressed the question explaining that light and color only appear in combination with each other: *"Lux ... non venit sine colore"*.

Many scientists and artists have since then tried to arrange colors into a color system based on specific and different objectives. While physicists see no more than the different wave lengths of light in color, a painter sees the mixture of color on the palette in terms of physiology and the affect color has on people. The purpose of a color system is to arrange colors in such a way that a guide to color mixing can be obtained from this geometry.

The knowledge that colors are nothing more than components of white light was achieved through experiments made with a **glass prism**. This insight was documented for the first time by Bohemian physicist *Marcus Marci* (1595 – 1667) in 1648 in his writings *"Thaumantias liber de arcu caelesti"* (1648) and *"Dissertatio de natura iridis"* (1650). Colors with different wave lengths are broken at different angles on a prism (**chromatic Aberration**). The colors produced by a prism cannot be further split up. Building on this theory, the English physicist *Isaac Newton* experimented with prisms and in 1672 published his results. This later became the basis for his opus, *"Opticks, or A treatise of the reflections, refractions, inflections and colours of light"* (1704). It was Newton who coined the famous phrase: *"The rays are not coloured."* A different impression of color was instead created – one dependent on the frequency of perceived light. Long-wavelength light corresponds to the color red, while short-wavelength light correspond to the color purple. In between are the spectral colors: orange, yellow, green and blue (in that order). Light is referred to as **monochromatic light**, if it has only a single wavelength. Newton bent the expanse of generated spectral colors into a circle subdivided into seven sectors – red, orange, yellow, green, cyan blue, ultramarine and violet blue. In the middle of this **color circle** he put white as the one color made up of all the others. He refrained from arranging colors according to their degree of brightness, i.e., from light to dark, as had been usual up to that time. In a further step, Newton placed purple (magenta) between its bordering colors in the natural spectrum – red and violet. Purple, which results from a mixture of red and violet, does not occur in the spectral decomposition of white light.

But the concept behind Newton's color theory was slow to gain interest. One hundred years later, the poet, scientist and art theorist, *Johann Wolfgang von Goethe* (1749 – 1832) disputed Newton's color circle. Newton suspected that light was composed of corpuscles, that is, small particles of different sizes. In contrast to Newton, Goethe tried to show in his *color theory*, which he incidentally considered the most important work he had written, that white light is not "assembled" and that colors result from an interchange of light and dark. Goethe explained the color separation in a prism due to an"overlapping" of light and dark, which results in a yellow and a blue border. Depending on the respective portion of light and dark, these borders become mixed as green or red – thereby creating the spectral colors. Goethe's color theory does not focus on physical color separation, but rather on the "sensory and moral effects" of color. His observations and methods regarding the effect of color are considered the beginning of modern color psychology. Goethe discovered the phenomenon of subjective color and basic principles of color vision, such as the afterimage effect and simultaneous contrast.

In 1802, English doctor and physicist *Thomas Young* (1773 – 1829) postulated his **trichromatic theory** (three-color vision). Young proposed that the human retina is only capable of perceiving three different base colors (based on different types of receptors). Young's trichromatic theory gained credibility in 1855 when a statistical analysis of color blindness was presented for the first time. It was shown that the recorded observations could only be explained if the assumption was made that one or two receptor types had failed in the people affected.

Then in 1859 the Scottish physician *James Clerk Maxwell* showed that in fact all colors in the spectrum could be created through a mixture of three components, provided that added together these components produced white – i.e., are located far away enough from each other in the spectrum (e.g. red, green and blue). He represented the corresponding combinations within a triangle whose corners were marked by the three primary spectral colors: red, green and blue. Each compound color was thereby in the focal point of the line that connected the primary colors to be combined. With his "theory of color vision" Maxwell was responsible for the origin and start of modern, quantitative color measurement (colorimetry).

The first person to bring attention to the difference between additive and subtractive color mixing was the German physicist *Hermann von Helmholtz* (1821 – 1894). In his handbook "Handbook on Physiological Optics" (1867), he presented the **Helmholtz coordinates**. These coordinates, named after him, were: brightness, hue and saturation. Helmholtz developed Young's trichromatic theory further in 1850 into what is known today as the Young-Helmholtz theory.

The color system presented by American painter *Albert Henri Munsell* (1858 – 1918) also met with great success. In his 1915 **color atlas** colors were categorized in relation to how they were visually perceived. He grouped all colors in three dimensions around an axis extending from black to white luminance (value). It was done in such a way as that opposite color shades (hue) mix to gray. The saturation of the respective color (chroma) is represented by the distance of the color to the central axis. He also considered the different degrees of brightness of pure spectral colors; for example that the spectral color yellow appears subjectively brighter than the spectral colors blue or red

A first truly objective assessment of color was made possible by the **Color Standard Table**, which was established by the International Commission on Illumination (Commission Internationale d'Eclairage, CIE) in 1931. The Color Standard Table was determined with the help of subjective test persons. Test subjects were required to mix the three primary colors of monochromatic light until a prescribed spectral color was achieved. A numerical value resulted for each primary color. Each given color could be described unambiguously with the three determined numerical values. Through suitable transformation and scaling these three coordinates could be mapped in a two-dimensional coordinate system. Because of the fundamental condition $x + y + z = 1$ the z-share ($z = 1 - x - y$) can be determined easily.

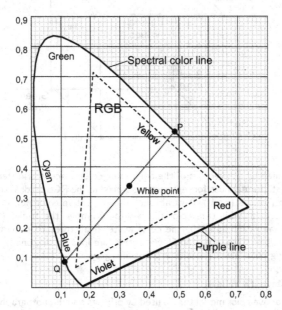

Within this coordinate system all of the colors perceived by those with normal vision lie within a horseshoe-formation whose upper border is delineated by a pure **spectral color**. The lower border is formed by the so-called **purple line** – an imaginary demarcation line between the two ends of the spectral line. The purple line does not contain any spectral colors, but only colors that can be obtained by mixing two spectral colors. The **white point** is on the inside. Proceeding from this white point, all colors perceived as the same shade can be read on one line from points P and Q on the edge of the spectral colors. On this line opposite points P and Q are **complementary colors**. The RGB color model defines the colors in the CIE Color Standard Table formed in the triangle of the primary colors red, green and blue.

The German Industrial Standard DIN 5033 defines color as "the sensation of a part of the visual field which the eye perceives as having no structure and by which this part can be distinguished from another structureless and adjoining region when viewed with just one motionless eye."

RGB Color Model (Red-Green-Blue)

RGB represents today the most widely used color model for graphic formats. It is an additive color mixing system in which respectively changing shares of the primary colors red (R, wavelength $\lambda = 700$ nm), green (G, $\lambda = 546,1$ nm) or blue (B, $\lambda = 435,8$ nm) are additively mixed to the initial black to generate new colors. G and B are lines of the mercury spectrum, while R represents the long-wavelength end of the visible light. These three components may be regarded as linear-independent vectors spanning a three-dimensional color space. This space is illustrated by the RGB color cube.

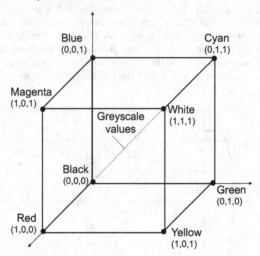

The plane spanned by the vertices of the color cube color space is also rferred to as **Gamut** The graphics data formats use for representing a pixel in the RGB color system a color triplet of the numerical values (r,g,b). It establishes the respective color portions of the primary colors in pixels. In a 24bit true color display, for example, the triplet (0,0,0) represents the color black and (255,255,255) the color white. If all three RGB parts have the same numerical value, therefore, e.g., (66,66,66) – they are located diagonally in the RGB cube and the resulting color always results in a specific gray.

CMY (Cyan-Magenta-Yellow)

CMY is a subtractive color model that is used by printers and in photography and is based on a white surface. Almost all devices using the principle of applying color pigments to a white surface use the CMY method. If the primary surface is illuminated then each of the three primary colors used absorbs proportionally the incident light of the complementary color assigned to it: **cyan** (a greenish blue) absorbs red, **magenta** (a light violet red) absorbs green and **yellow** absorbs blue. By increasing the yellow value e.g., the portion of blue perceptible in the image lessens. If all color portions are absorbed by the incident light through a mixture of all colors, then black results.

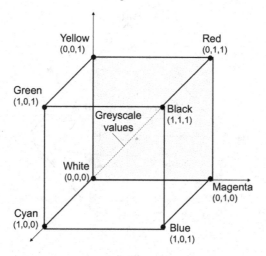

Since, practically speaking, no perfect black can be achieved through mixing the three primary colors, the extended CMYK has prevailed. K stands for the *key color*, black. The term "key" is used instead of "black" to avoid misunderstandings concerning the letter "b," which is used for "blue." The letter "k" stands for the "key plate" used in offset printing. This is the black printing plate on whose baselines the three colored printing plates are aligned with the primary colors. In the CMYK color model, back does not serve in coloring but rather in darkening the three primary colors. CMY colors are specified as numeric triplet (CMYK colors as quadruples). Thus, in a 24-bit true color system, the CMY triplet (255,255,255) represents the color black and (0,0,0) the color white. But in many color mixing systems often only percentages are given for the proportion of the primary colors used. These are between 0% and 100%.

HSV Color Model (Hue-Saturation-Value)

The HSV color system represents a color systems where in the creation of new colors color properties vary rahter than being mixed. Thereby, **hue** determines the color tone in the literal sense, such as red, , orange, blue, etc. The specification of the hue appears as a color angle on the color wheel (e.g., 0° = red, 120° = green, 240° = blue). **Saturation** specifies the amount of the white in the selected hue. A completely saturated hue, i.e., saturation 100%, contains no white and appears as a pure hue. But if, for example, red is chosen and a saturation of 50%, the resulting color is pink. Finally, **value** indicates the degree of self-luminosity of a hue, i.e., how much light the hue emits. A hue with a high self-luminosity appears light, while a hue with low self-luminosity appears dark.

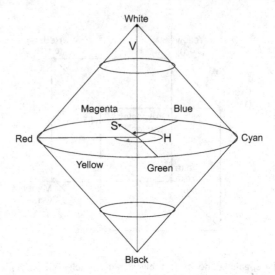

HSV closely resembles the color mixing system used by painters to achieve various degrees of color by mixing white, black or gray with a pure hue. There are a number of other, very similar, color models that change a color (hue) through the variation of two other properties. For example:

- **HSL** – Hue, Saturation, and Lightness (relative brightness),
- **HSI** – Hue, Saturation, and Intensity (light intensity),
- **HSB** – Hue, Saturation, and Brightness (absolute brightness).

Although there is a clear separation between brightness and color in this family of color systems, they have gained only minimal significance in graphic encoding and graphic compression. One reason for this is their discontinuity in the realm of color display. The color values of the angle 0° and 359° have an almost identical hue, yet their representation as a numerical value is vastly different. If, for example, both colors are to be mixed in a lossless compression, the result would be a color on the opposite side of the color wheel ((0+359)/2≈180), and the display would be strongly distorted.

YUV Color Model (Y-Signal, U-Signal, and V-Signal)

The YUV color model belongs to a family of color models distinguished from other models in its separation of image brightness from color difference. With a simple transformation the RGB components of a color image can be easily converted into its corresponding YUV counterpart. Historically, YUV color models are closely connected with the development of color television. In the transition from the black and white television to the color television it was necessary for reasons of compatibility to find a way to make it possible to continue to use the old black and white receivers as well as to allow the additional transfer of color television's color components. The brightness (luminance) (Y components) were therefore, separated from the color components (chrominance) (U and V components). The human eye has varying degrees of sensitivity in regards to brightness and color resolution. Therefore, separating the components enabled a simultaneous adjustment of the resolution of the components to human perception.

The conversion from the RGB to the YUV color model is carried out via:

$$(Y, U, V) = (R, G, B) \cdot \begin{pmatrix} 0,299 & -0,168736 & 0,5 \\ 0,587 & -0,331264 & -0,418688 \\ 0,114 & 0,5 & -0,081312 \end{pmatrix}$$

Within the family of these color models there are three basic models:

- **YUV** – This model is used in the PAL television standard.
- **YIQ** – This model is used in the competing NTSC color television system mainly in North America and Japan. The only difference to the YUV model is a shift in the chrominance by $33°$.
- **YCbCr** – This model was derived from the YUV model especially for digital television. It distinguishes itself from the YUV model through a scaling of the individual components and an offset for chrominance.

Further reading:

Falk, D., Brill, D., Stork, D.: Seeing the Light: Optics in Nature, Photography, Color, Vision and Holography, John Wiley & Sons, New York, USA (1986)

4.4.1 Variants of Run Length Encoding for Graphics Data

Image or graphics data is normally compressed in a sequential process. To do this, the 2-dimensional image is disassembled into a 1-dimensional data stream consisting of the color information contained in the individual pixels. This process can be carried out line by line from top left to bottom right (X-axis encoding), column by column in the same order (Y-axis encoding) or even diagonally in an alternating direction (zig-zag encoding). **Run length encoding** (RLE, see Excursus 6) for graphic files are as a rule lossless. In essence, the procedure corresponds to the previously presented method for text files. Irrespective of the chosen color model, the color values of the individual pixels are indicated by several numerical values. These numerical values can take the form of a binary number and thus be presented in a continuous form as a single, long bit string. The connected groups of zeros and ones can be summarized as discussed previously. The longer the connected groups, the higher the degree of compression. A contiguous group of identical bits can only be summarized in logarithmic space, based on the original storage size. This type of encoding is known as **bit-level run length encoding**. In contrast, **byte-level run length encoding** considers the identical byte values of image information to encode and does not take into account individual bits or bit groups. The most common methods are those which encode the contiguous groups of identical bytes into a 2-byte packet, whereby the first byte indicates the number of repetitions and the second byte the relevant byte value.

On a higher level of abstraction the so-called **pixel-level run length encoding** begins. It is implemented if two or more bytes are used to store the color values of a pixel. Special tricks are used to further increase the efficiency of this method. If a complete line in an image file repeats, it is then sufficient to mark this repetition by using a special, reserved codeword. A considerable amount of space can be saved this way.

4.4.2 LZW Method

One of the most used compression methods for graphics data is the so-called LZW method, named after its three creators *Abraham Lempel, Jakob Zif* and *Terry Welch*. In 1977 Lempel and Zif developed the first representatives of the LZ substitution compression method – **LZ77**. It was especially well suited for the compression of text files or for archiving [259]. LZ77 is contained in may popular archiving programs such as **compress**, **pkzip** or **arj**. The method developed the following year called **LZ78** is, in contrast, particularly suitable for the compression of binary data, e.g., Bitmaps. Terry Welch, who at this time worked for the Unisys, modified the LZ78 compressor in 1984. This modification adapted the compression for application in high-speed disk controllers and resulted in the LZW algorithm used today [251].

The LZW algorithm is suitable for any type of data and works very quickly in encoding as well as decoding because, among other things, execution of the floating point operation is omitted.

LZW is a dictionary-based compression algorithm, which is based on encoding a dictionary (Data Dictionary, Translation Table) from the character string (8-bit binary words) of an uncompressed data stream. The occurring data patterns (substrings) from a data stream are then assigned to the individual dictionary entries. New code words are generated iteratively for data patterns that do not not appear in the dictionary and are saved in the dictionary. If these data patterns appear again, they are replaced with their assigned codewords from the dictionary. Since they have a shorter length than the original data patterns, a compression takes place (see Fig. 4.8).

LZW Algorithm – Basic Sequence

- Read characters from the input stream and accumulate them to a string S, as long as S is found as a dictionary entry.
- As soon as a character x is read, for which the string Sx no longer belongs to the dictionary table, proceed with the following steps:

  – Add the string Sx to the dictionary table,
  – build a new string beginning with the character x.

- Repeat these steps until the end of the input stream has been reached.

Fig. 4.8 LZW compression algorithm.

The decoding of LZW compressed data is carried out in reverse steps. The advantage of the LZW algorithm is that the dictionary must not be also be

Example of a LZW Compression:

The following test string is to be compressed with the help of the LZW algorithm:

ABRAKADABRAABRAKADABRA.

The algorithm starts with a dictionary in which the first 256 entries consist of the respectively 1 byte long individual characters (00_{16} – FF_{16}). The following table illustrates the sequence of the LZW algorithm. The first column contains the still remaining to be compressed character string. The remaining string is read from the left as long as necessary until the last character string has been found for which there is already a dictionary entry. The found dictionary entry is displayed in the second column. The third column contains the output of the LZW algorithm, which was generated in the encoding of the found dictionary entry. The last column contains the new dictionary entry, generated when the next to be read character is added to the found dictionary entry. New dictionary entries consist of the character string to be coded and their encoding.

Remaining character string	Found entry	Output	New entry
ABRAKADABRAABRAKADABRA	A	A	AB <256>
BRAKADABRAABRAKADABRA	B	B	BR <257>
RAKADABRAABRAKADABRA	R	R	RA <258>
AKADABRAABRAKADABRA	A	A	AK <259>
KADABRAABRAKADABRA	K	K	KA <260>
ADABRAABRAKADABRA	A	A	AD <261>
DABRAABRAKADABRA	D	D	DA <262>
ABRAABRAKADABRA	AB <256>	<256>	ABR <263>
RAABRAKADABRA	RA <258>	<258>	RAA <264>
ABRAKADABRA	ABR <263>	<263>	ABRA <265>
AKADABRA	AK <259>	<259>	AKA <266>
ADABRA	AD <261>	<261>	ADA <267>
ABRA	ABRA <265>	<265>	-

After compression, we obtain the following code (column **output** read from top to bottom):

ABRAKAD<256><258><263><259><261><265>

While the original character string needs 172 bits (22 characters of each 8 bits long) of storage space, the LZW compressed character string needs only 156 bits (13 characters of each 12 bits long).

Fig. 4.9 An example of LZW compression.

stored with the compressed data and transmitted. It is implicitly contained in the compressed data and then reconstructed in the decoding process. The decompression algorithm reads a code word and translates it with the help of the dictionary back into the uncompressed original data. The LZW algorithm works with a dictionary size of 4K (4,096) bytes. In the dictionary, there is already at the start of the algorithm individual bytes each from 0 to 255, the entries 256 to 4,095 are filled at the run time of the algorithm and are intended for character strings that consist of two or more characters. New entries are generated as previously described; dictionary entries found are combined with a new character of the text to be compressed. With 4,096 entries in the dictionary, a 12-bit coding scheme ($2^{12}=4,096$) is involved. To save space, 1-byte long single characters are not coded as a dictionary reference (with a length of 12 bits). A special flag is used to distinguish between single characters and dictionary reference characters. Figure 4.9 and figure 4.10 each describe an example of compression and decompression with the LZW algorithm.

An Example of LZW Decompression:

When a LZW compressed file is decoded, the dictionary can gradually be reconstructed. This is because the output of the LZW algorithm always contains only dictionary entries that were already in the dictionary . In compression, each dictionary entry begins with the last character of the previously added dictionary entry. Conversely, the last character of a new dictionary entry, added to the dictionary in decompression, is at the same time the first output character in decoding. The following table illustrates the sequence of LWZ decompression. The first column contains the sequence of each of the code characters to be decoded. The second column shows the output of decompression and the third column contains the current dictionary entry added consisting of a character string and its associated code.

First character	Output	New entry
A	A	-
B	B	AB <256>
R	R	BR <257>
A	A	RA <258>
K	K	AK <259>
A	A	KA <260>
D	D	AD <261>
<256>	AB	DA <262>
<258>	RA	ABR <263>
<263>	ABR	RAA <264>
<259>	AK	ABRA <265>
<261>	AD	AKA <266>
<265>	ABRA	ADA <267>

The column **output** read from top to bottom gives the input string:

ABRAKADABRAABRAKADABRA.

Fig. 4.10 An example of LZW decompression.

The entire dictionary of an LZW compressed file can contain up to 4,096 entries. These can consist of character strings that are up to 4,096 bytes long. A new dictionary entry always has a prefix, which refers to an entry that is already in the dictionary, and a suffix. The suffix contains a character that serves solely to extend the found dictionary entry. The LZW algorithm for data compression was patented by the Unisys and IBM companies. Unisys requires the one-time payment of a license fee of all hardware developers who wish to use the LZW procedure in their products. The LZW procedure is implemented in the compression of graphics data in the formats **GIF** und **TIFF**. Table 4.2 gives a brief overview of the common graphics file formats and compression methods on which these are based.

Table 4.2 Some standard graphics file formats with compression, according to [162, 200].

BMP	Bitmap format, simplest graphics format that found great popularity as the standard format Windows BMP. Rare use in Internet because of weak compression and thus often very large files. BMP files can be uncompressed or encoded with simple RLE compression. The maximum dimensions of a BMP image file are (in theory) $2^{32} \times 2^{32}$ pixels, with color depth of up to 32 bits possible.
TIFF	TIFF (Tagged Image File Format) is typically used to transfer image files from one system to another. The image resolution is not restricted. TIFF supports a variety of color spaces and an 8-bit alpha channel. TIFF files can be uncompressed or encoded with the Huffman, LZW or RLE compression procedures. The maximum image dimensions limit TFF encoded image files to a length of 2^{32} bytes with a color depth of up to 32 bits.
GIF	(Graphic Interchange Format) Simple image data format with the possibility to store multiple images in a file. GIF files are encoded with the LZW compression procedure. The maximum dimensions of a GIF graphic file are 65.536 × 65.536 pixels at a color depth of 8 bits from a 24 bit color palette.
JPG	(Joint Photographic Expert Group, actually JFIF: JPEG-File Interchange Format) Image format with lossy compression. Achieves a better degree of compression for images with photographic characteristics than the above methods. In JPG files, the RLE compression procedure is used in combination with the Huffman compression or arithmetic compression. The maximum image dimension and color depth are dependent on the chosen compression parameters. The image dimension of the JPEG File Interchange Format (JFIF) is limited to 65,536 × 65,536 pixels with a maximum color depths of 24 bits.
PNG	(Portable Network Graphics) it supports images with a limited color palette besides supporting lossless compression. Among the special features of PNG are an 8-bit alpha channel, gamma correction, interlaced display and error detection. PNG files are encoded with the open "zlib" compression method. The maximum image dimension is not limited and color depths of up to 48 bits are possible.

4.4.3 GIF Format

The **Graphic Interchange Format (GIF)** was introduced in 1987 by the U.S. company Compuserve Incorporated. Because of its use of the LZW algorithm, this format was subject to copyright restrictions by the Unisys company until 2003/2004. Today the GIF image format can be freely used.

This image format achieved its widespread dissemination through the Internet. Fortunately, Compuserve allowed software use that took advantage of this graphic format. The software developer only had the obligation of formally recognizing the GIF data format copyright. A distinction is made between two GIF data formats: **GIF87a** and **GIF89a** – the latter the improved version of the older GIF87a. Every GIF file begins with a header and a so-called **Logical Screen Descriptor**, containing information about the images stored in the GIF files. After this normally comes a global color palette output and then the stored images in the GIF file, each of which can be re-initiated by a local color palette. The GIF file ends with a special terminating character (see Excursus 8).

Excursus 8: GIF – File Structure

The **header** (6 bytes) at the beginning of the GIF file uses a signature (3 bytes with the characters "GIF") to identify the file as a GIF file. This is followed by a version number (3 bytes with the characters "87a" or "89a").

The **logical screen descriptor** specifies how much space is necessary for the images stored in a GIF file. First the width (2 bytes) and the height (2 bytes) of the image file is given in number of pixels. For both measurements 2 bytes of storage space each is available, the maximum image size is limited to 2^{16}=65,536 pixels for each height and width. The subsequent byte provides information about the available color information. Bit 7 indicates whether a global color palette is used, bits 4–6 indicate the color resolution, bit 3 indicates whether the colors in the color palette are sorted according to their image frequency and bits 0–2 stand for the size of the global color palette. After this follows a byte that contains the color index of the background color of the image, and then comes a byte that stands for the aspect ratio of the stored image.

Up to 256=2^8 colors are indicated in the **global color palette**. These can be specified from 16.7 million (=2^{24}) possible colors. Every single color in the global color palette is composed of a 24-bit RGB-triple of the form (r,g,b). The global color palette indicates what colors make up the stored image is the GIF file.

A **local image descriptor** contains information about one of the images stored in the GIF file. At the beginning is an image separator (1 byte). It acts as an identifier to indicate the start of a new image. The next bytes give the position of the upper left corner of the image (in each case 2 bytes), followed by width and height of the image (also 2 bytes each). Then comes, as with the logical screen descriptor, one byte with details about the color information of the image. In contrast to the global color palette, it can also contain extra information about the displayed lines of the picture (interlace flag). If the interlace flag is set, the individual image lines are saved in the following order. For n image lines, the individual, consecutively numbered image lines from 0 to n-1 are listed in the order $0, \frac{n}{2}, \frac{n}{4}, \frac{3n}{4}, \frac{n}{8}, \frac{3n}{8}, \frac{5n}{8}, \frac{7n}{8}, \frac{n}{16}, \frac{3n}{16}, \ldots$ Although the interlace technique complicates the reading of the image content, it helps the user to recognize the image content after just a few rows have been transfered.

For each of the images contained in the GIF file follows its own optional **local color palette**. Just as the global color palette, it is coded. Afterwards comes the **image data**, compressed with the help of the LZW procedure.

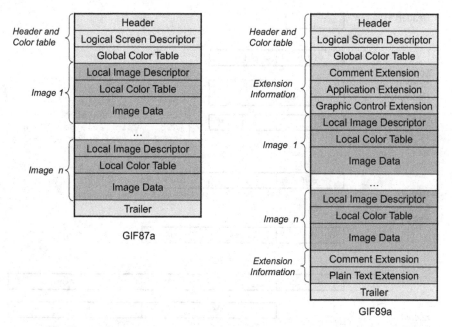

GIF87a

GIF89a

In the **GIF-89a** format, extra information about how to deal with the subsequent image data can be stored in a **graphic control extension** block . It contains, among other things, a transparency flag that indicates the color index to be displayed transparently in the next image, a control flag indicating the next user action to start in the following graphics sequence and a waiting period, indicating how long to wait between each frame.

In a **plain text extension**, the GIF-89a format offers the possibility of displaying additional alphanumerical information along with the stored image information. Besides overall size, position and dimensions of the individual letters to be displayed, this block contains the actual text information itself.

Additional information can be stored in an **application extension**. This information makes it possible for external application programs to carry out certain actions involving the read image data.

Other text data, which has been ignored in the actual image display, can be stored in a **comment extension**. It is possible here to store a 1 to 255 character-long text string, which is read by the user. The string allows for the addition of more comments about the stored image.

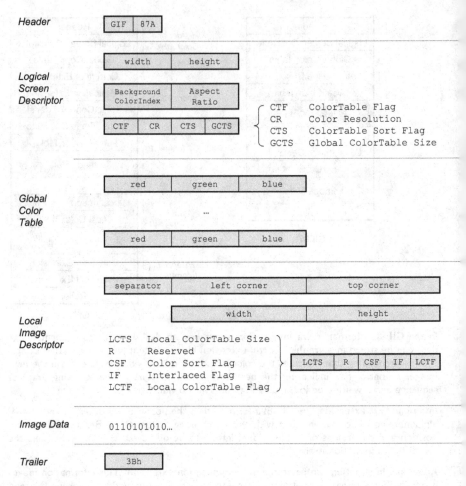

Header

Logical Screen Descriptor

CTF   ColorTable Flag
CR   Color Resolution
CTS   ColorTable Sort Flag
GCTS   Global ColorTable Size

Global Color Table

Local Image Descriptor

LCTS   Local ColorTable Size
R   Reserved
CSF   Color Sort Flag
IF   Interlaced Flag
LCTF   Local ColorTable Flag

Image Data   0110101010...

Trailer   3Bh

Further reading:

Murray, J. D., van Ryper, W.: Encyclopedia of Graphic File Formats, 2nd Edition, O'Reilly & Associates, Inc. Sebastopol CA, USA (1996)

While with the GIF data format there is an information loss due to the reduction of the color space, the actual compression itself works loss-free. The GIF data format was developed specifically by CompuServe for online application and offers the following features:

- A file can be stored in the **interlace method** , i.e., the order in which the separate image lines are displayed can be adjusted in such a way that during image transmission the actual content of the image can be recognized early on. This is extremely helpful for the online transfer of large image files via narrowband Internet connections. As the processing progresses the graphics represented become noticeably clearer and finer.

- Multiple images can be stored in a single file, coupled with the possibility of controlling the frame image sequence. With this option it is possible to store small animations in a graphics file.
- It is possible to define a transparent color (alpha channel), which can be used for achieving special effects on WWW pages.

A major disadvantage of the GIF format is the reduction of the color space to only 256 colors. For this reason, it has only limited use in the display of realistic image information, e.g., high-resolution photographs. To still be able to create an impression of realism with a limited color palette, the so-called **dithering** procedure may be used in image coding. This technique exploits the interaction of different, adjacent color pixels, whereby the absent colors appear present to the human system of perception (see Fig. 4.11). The GIF format is ideal for the storage of schematic and placative displays as well as for graphics with extreme contrasts. Although now considered technically outdated, it continues to be popular in the WWW, used in particular for advertising banners and small images (icons).

The Dithering Procedure

Dithering (*to dither*= vacillate) is a technique in computer graphics which creates the illusion of a higher depth of color in images with a low color depth. The absent colors in the image are closely modeled by a specific pixel order with the colors available. In this way, hard transitions between the colors are avoided. Seen from a certain distance the human eye perceives the dithering as a mix of the individual colors. The illustration here shows the effects of dithering with black and white pixels. Their sufficiently reduced arrangement appears to the viewer as a shade of gray. For dithering there is a multiple number of different algorithms that often operate with an error diffusion. Especially when working with a small color palette, it is possible that artifacts appear, which cause the image to have a coarse-gained pattern. For example, this book has been printed with just a single color (black). Subsequently, with a special screening process it is possible to give the impression that different degrees of gray were used in the display of graphics and photos.

Fig. 4.11 The dithering procedure.

4.4.4 PNG Format

The PNG graphics format (Portable Network Graphics) was developed in 1994 as a replacement for the older, and until 2004 still subject to patent regulations, GIF graphic format. In 1996 it achieved the status of official W3C recommendation and in 1997 it was standardized as RFC 2083 by IETF.

In 2003 the PNG specification 1.2 became the international ISO standard ISO/IEC 15948:2003. The compression of graphics data is lossless and it is carried out with a compression procedure that is public domain.

Similar to GIF, the PNG can process color palette-limited graphics data. Moreover, the color coding of individual channels is possible, with up to 16 bits per channel. This allows the display of grayscale images with up to $2^{16} = 65,536$ levels of brightness and color images with a color depth of 48 bits. Additionally, PNG may contain transparency information (alpha channel) in increments of up to 16 bits. Therefore, a seamless display of arbitrarily shaped images across a background is possible. PNG also offers the possibility of embedding color profile data, color and brightness correction (gamma correction) for the adjustment of graphics data in various output devices. But other than RGB and grayscale there are no alternative color spaces supported. For this reason, the PNG graphics format has never found widespread use in the professional field.

Before the actual graphics data compression, PNG allows a line by line pre-filtering of the data. Because adjacent pixels can barely be distinguished from one another in many images, it is an advantage to process only the value diffe-rence between neighboring pixels. Substantial differences are rare in "natural" images such as photographs and, if so, then only at the edges of the depicted objects. Long sequences of identical difference values are advantageous in da-ta compression. PNG distinguishes between difference formation variations, in which different neighboring pixels are included in the calculation. In de-coding, inverse filters are used on the stored difference values to reconstruct the original image data. Compression of the filtered image data proceeds with the public domain lossless **deflate** algorithm, which is also used in various file archive formats such as the **zip** of **gz**. The PNG graphics standard also has integrated checksum mechanisms that allow data transmission errors to be recognized early.

4.4.5 JPEG Format

The JPEG compression procedure for image and graphics files falls under the category of lossy compression techniques. Together with the GIF compression procedure, JPEG is one of the most popular methods of compressing image files today. JPEG stands for **Joint Photographic Expert Group**, a sub-group of the ISO, which standardized the procedure in 1990 in collaboration with CCITT as ISO 10918-1. As the name already indicates, JPEG involves a compression procedure that is particularly well suited for the compressi-on of "natural," e.g., photographic, depictions. The compression technology used is based on the de-correlation of image elements through the use of the **Discrete Cosine Transformation** (DCT) together with Huffman coding. For image files compressed with the JPEG method, the American company C-Cube developed a suitable data format, the **JPEG File Interchange Format** (JFIF). This format makes the exchange of JPEG encoded information possible between incompatible computer systems. Based on the JPEG compression technology for static images, a compression procedure was developed for animated image sequences: the MPEG compression procedure (**Motion JPEG**).

JPEG compression is an asymmetrical compression procedure, i.e., the encoding needs considerably more computational effort than the subsequent decoding. JPEG compression allows the storage of graphic files with a color depth of 24bits. The principle of the JPEG procedure is to save the color changes of the image to be displayed in the graphics files. While the human eye is particularly sensitive when it comes to changes in brightness, it is much less sensitive toward color changes (see Fig. 4.12). If the color changes in the JPEG encoded image deviate from the output image only to a minimal degree, the JPEG encoded image is perceived as nearly identical. Therefore, loss of image quality in the color range that results in JPEG compression is hardly recognized up up to a certain threshold of tolerance.

JPEG is therefore not only based on the reduction of redundancy in the image to be compressed (redundancy reduction), but also on the suppression of parts of images that are barely relevant or not relevant at all (irrelevance reduction) in human perception .

A distinction is made between different coding modes in the JPEG procedure:

- **Baseline mode**: Baseline mode is the name of the centerpiece of the JPEG coding process. It predetermines the minimal functionality and must be mastered by all JPEG implementations. Founded on DCT-based coding (Discrete Cosine Transformation), this mode allows processing of images with a color depth of 24 bits (8 bits per color component). Encoding proceeds block by block sequentially with Huffman coding allowed exclusively as entropy encoding.

- **Sequential mode**: The encoded image can be decoded in a single run – from the upper left downwards to the lower right. This mode is well suited to most applications. It delivers good compression rates and is the easiest to implement.

- **Progressive mode**: The image is encoded or decoded in several runs that build on each other. With every cycle, the image is displayed more and more sharply. Only a part of the DCT coefficient information is coded in each run. It is an ideal procedure for data communication. The receiver immediately gets a rough overview of the whole picture and can subsequently decide whether or not it is worthwhile to wait for the complete transmission.

- **Hierarchical mode**: The image is initially saved with low resolution and subsequently in full resolution. It is a special variation of the progressive mode with increasing spatial resolution. The smaller image (**thumbnail**)) can be decoded very quickly, which makes it particularly suitable as a **pre-**

Visual Perception in Humans

Human visual perception is primarily determined by the structure of the eye. Light passes through the pupil and lens onto the retina, where incident light energy is converted into nerve impulses. The pupil acts a shutter, its diameter (of 2 – 8 mm) changing according to the amount of incident light (adaption). The lens itself is flexible due to a special muscle (ciliary muscle) and can map objects at various distances on the retina (accommodation)). The accommodation capability is age-dependent.

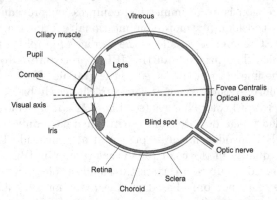

In the retina there are two different types of receptors. Light and color-sensitive **cones** that enable us to perceive color and detail (photopic vision). Numbering approximately 6 million, they are located in the central area of the retina (macula) and function in normal daytime brightness. While **rods**, are not capable of distinguishing color they are considerably more sensitive to light. They become active in low-light (scotopic vision). They number about 120 million per eye. No rods are located in the center of the retina itself (fovea). The light spectrum perceptible to the human eye extends from a wave length of 780 nm (red) to 390 nm (violet). Those rods responsible for the perception of brightness exhibit their greatest light sensitivity at wave lengths in the area of 500 nm (corresponds to the color green). Three types of cones are distinguished based on their maximum sensitivity. Each type of cone has different light-sensitive visual pigments (rhodopsin). Type A has a maximum at green (long-wavelength pigment, 558 nm), type B at yellow-red (medium-wavelength pigment, 531 nm) and type C at blue-violet (short-wavelength pigment, 419 nm). The light absorbed by the light receptors causes a change in the stimulation of the efferent nerves (approx. 1 million), which affects the visual cortex of the brain and is processed there as a perception of light and different colors. The retina with its different photo receptors also exhibits two distinct regions: the **fovea centralis**, the area with the greatest visual acuity located approximately in the center of the retina but not exactly on the optical axis. Only cones are located in this area, in fact their density is the highest here. The so-called **blind spot** (papilla) is also located here. This is the spot where the optic nerve, with its approximately 1.5 million nerve endings, leaves the retina. Accordingly, there are no visual cells here and incident light cannot be perceived. The ratio between the optical receptors and the optical nerves is about 80:1, i.e., the pre-processing of the visual information is already carried out here with a high compression factor.

Fig. 4.12 Visual perception in humans.

view. It might be used, for example, in image databases where a preview supports fast decision making.

- **Lossless mode:** This mode both encodes and decodes in lossless form, in contrast to other modes. This mode process is used in automatic image analysis. Because the information content of the original image is not subject to further reduction, the rate of compression is lower.

Excursus 9: JPEG – Compression and JPEG – File Format

The JPEG compression method, which is carried out in four steps, is shown schematically in Fig. 4.13.

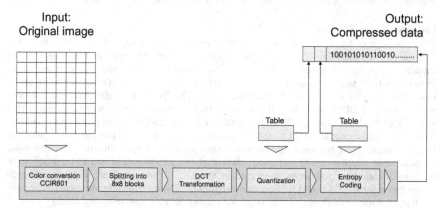

Fig. 4.13 JPEG processing steps.

Color conversion and sampling

In the first part of JPEG compression every color component (red, green, blue) is decomposed into the components: **luminance** (brightness) and **chrominance** (color information). Because the human eye is less sensitive in terms of chrominance, JPEG allows a higher information loss in this area.

While all of the color components of the RGB model bear brightness information, green influences the perception of brightness more strongly than blue or red [3]. With a procedure established in the norm **CCIR/ITU-R BT.601**, the RGB information is transformed into the components Y (equivalent to the brightness), C_b (equivalent to the blue component) and C_r (equivalent to the red components). This YC_bC_r color model is a special variation of the YUV color model.

$$\begin{pmatrix} +0.299 & +0.587 & +0.114 \\ +0.1687 & -0.3313 & +0.5 \\ +0.5 & -0.4187 & -0.081 \end{pmatrix} \cdot \begin{pmatrix} R \\ G \\ B \end{pmatrix} = \begin{pmatrix} Y \\ C_b \\ C_r \end{pmatrix}$$

---

[3] The maximum sensitivity of the brightness-sensitive rods in the retina of the human eye is 500 nm, the color green.

In the image separation process (**sampling**) the parts C_b and C_r are assigned a lower resolution than the Y components. A typical sampling rate gives the Y components, for example, four times higher resolution than the other two components. This means that the number of chrominance pixels are both horizontally as well as vertically reduced by the factor 2. Thus, four (r,g,b) pixels that originally occupy a memory of $4 \cdot 3$ byte $= 12$ bytes can be reduced to 4 (Y) $+ 1$ (C_b) $+ 1$ (C_r) $= 6$ bytes. The lower the sampling resolution, the higher the compression and the shorter total compression time is. The process is known as **downsampling** or **chroma subsampling**. JPEG allows the following downsampling variations:

- (4:4:4): no downsampling, luminance and chrominance values are recorded in the same resolution.
- (4:2:2): reduction by a factor of 2 in a horizontal direction.
- (4:2:0): reduction by a factor of 2 in a horizontal and vertical direction.

Depending on the downsampling variation, a reduction of between 33% and 50% of the memory requirements can be achieved without a noticeable loss of quality.

Discrete Cosine Transformation (DCT)

With the help of DCT, intensity data is transformed into frequency data, which indicates how quickly the intensity of the color and brightness information vary in the image. Image signals do not have a stationary character. This means that the spectral portions of an image vary from section to section. Thus the transformation is not calculated for the entire image but only for the individual image segments. The image is divided into image blocks of 8×8 pixels in JPEG encoding. If the image to be encoded cannot be broken down into exactly 8x8 pixel size blocks, it is necessary to supplement partially filled blocks with padding data. The padding data cannot simply be empty (=black or white) pixel as the subsequent DCT transformation and quantization would then produce visible artifacts. Attention must be paid when supplementing the image data that the padding data has as little influence as possible on the coefficients generated in the DCT transformation. Further on, each image component (Y,Cb,Cb) is processed separately. The individual components may have a different number of image blocks (e.g., for reasons of different sampling rates)

The data points in a 8×8 pixel size block start at the top left (0,0) and end in the lower right (7,7). The pixel (x,y) has the image information f(x,y). The DCT generates a new 8×8 block (u,v) via the transformation

$$F(u, v) = \frac{1}{4} C(u)C(v) \left[\sum_{x=0}^{7} \sum_{y=0}^{7} f(x, y) \cos \frac{(2x + 1)u\pi}{16} \cos \frac{(2y + 1)v\pi}{16} \right]$$

with
$$C(z) = \begin{cases} \frac{1}{\sqrt{2}} & \text{if } z = 0 \\ 1 & \text{otherwise.} \end{cases}$$

The inverse transformation in the decoding proceeds via the Inverse Discrete Cosine Transformation (IDCT)

$$f(x, y) = \left[\sum_{u=0}^{7} \sum_{v=0}^{7} \frac{1}{4} C(u)C(v)F(u, v) \cos \frac{(2x + 1)u\pi}{16} \cos \frac{(2y + 1)v\pi}{16} \right]$$

The DCT transformation can be implemented with a minimal calculation effort using the fast, discrete Fourier Transform (FFT). Via the DCT transformation, a time-discrete signal is transformed from the local into the frequency range. This means that the transformation of gray values results in 64 DCT coefficients. Instead of storing the intensity of the 64 individual pixels in a 8×8 pixel size block, every 8×8 block is displayed via a linear combination, shown in Fig. 4.14 (left), represented by 64 individual blocks on a DCT coefficient basis. In contrast to the discrete Fournier Transform, in the DCT transformation no complex number coefficients are displayed.

Because of the DCT transformation there results – as in the case of a Fournier transform – a frequency matrix indicating the frequency and amplitude distribution for the considered space. The 64 function values of the original matrix, dependent on the two spatial dimensions x and y, are transformed in their spectrum. The DCT performs a basis exchange on the basis of 64 orthogonal, discrete signals. Large, regularly colored spaces are therefore reflected as low frequency areas in the image and in fine detail in the high frequency areas. $F(0,0)$ expresses the average value (direct current) of 8×8-Matrix, $F(1,0)$ describes the proportion in which the image values change slowly (low frequencies) and $F(7,7)$ the proportion in which the image values change quickly in both directions (high frequencies). Sharp lines and abrupt color change are rare in a natural image. The largest share of the output signal is concentrated on the lower frequencies, many of the individual coeffciencies are therefore very small, i.e. nearly zero. The 64 DCT coefficients of a 8×8 pixel size block are divided into a direct current (DC), which is stored in $F(0,0)$, and 63 alternating currents (AC).

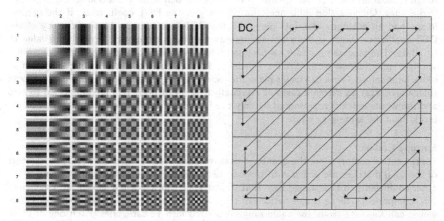

Fig. 4.14 Graphic representation of the 64 DCT coefficients (left) and zigzag coding (right) of the 8×8 image blocks.

The DCT transformation alone does not result in compression. On the contrary, the original image is only converted into another display format and the amount of data is often even increased (e.g., if work is carried out with real-valued coefficients while the original image of 8 bits per color channel is present). The transformation goal is information compression through the decorrelation of image components. While the components of the original image are displayed in terms of their respective amplitude, in the area of frequency they should be represented with the smallest shares of frequency as possible. The actual information loss in JPEG encoding first occurs in quantization. This is followed by entropy encoding (Huffman encoding or arithmetic coding); a technique that reduces the remaining redundancy and brings the image information into a more compact display form. In decoding the JPEG data, the implementation of inverse discrete cosine transformation allows a lossless transformation back into the original form

Quantization
Next, the coefficients of the 8×8 matrix are quantized , i.e., the values $F(u,v)$ are divided

by a value Q(u,v), derived from a quantization table determined by the JPEG committee, and rounded to the next whole number:

$$S(u, v) = \left\lfloor \frac{F(u, v)}{Q(u, v)} + 0.5 \right\rfloor .$$

The quantization table uses a finer quantization for coefficients with low frequencies and a rougher one for higher frequencies. High frequencies that already have a coefficient F(u,v) close to zero are quantified through this procedure to zero. The given quantization table can then be replaced by a personal one, which then has to be stored in the JPEG file (DQT-Marker in the JPEG Header). The quantization matrix is responsible for the quality as well as for the compression rate. A suitable decoding is carried out by a multiplication of S(u,v) with the corresponding coefficients from the quantization table Q(u,v). The original value, F(u,v), can however only be recovered approximately as an exact reconstruction is not possible. The neurophysiological properties of human vision are especially utilized in this method. A quantization matrix works optimally when it represents the corresponding local frequency in terms of the sensitivity of the human eye. The human eye is more sensitive to rough structures, therefore the quantization value for such frequencies is lower than for high frequencies. Quantization influences the accuracy of the DCT coefficients. If the original image had an accuracy of 8 bits per pixel, the DCT results in an 11-bit accuracy of the DCT coefficient, which is, for example, decreased through a quantization with the value 16 to 7 bits. The processing into 8×8 pixel large blocks proves to be disadvantageous with a stronger quantization of the DCT coefficients. It leads to discontinuities in the respective block boundaries. These can be visible in the reconstructed image and are known as **artifacts** (block artifacts). In extreme cases all AC coefficients F(1,0) – F(7,7) are quantified to zero and the whole block is represented by only the DC coefficients F(0,0), i.e., all pixels of the block have the same gray value.

Entropy Coding

For the actual compression, the quantized data is prepared as follows: The F(0,0) coefficients of the 8×8 matrices are coded with the help of a predicative procedure independent of the other coefficients. It is assumed here that the adjacent blocks have a similar DC coefficient (DC component). Since the deviations of the actual values to the corresponding predictive values can be quite large, the value range is divided into 12 categories. Each one of these is assigned a Huffman code word. It is up to the user to construct a Huffman code with which to achieve optimal compression results for the intended purpose. The code used is embedded in the generated JPEG file. The remaining blocks – from F(1,0) to F(7,7) are written in a zigzag arranged sequence (see Fig. 4.14, right), i.e., the coefficients with lower frequency come first and the higher frequency components typically quantized to zero follow at the end. This enables an efficient compression, whereby zero sequences are combined with the help of a run-length encoding. All nonzero AC components are divided into subcategories. For this, the distance of each coefficient to its non-zero predecessor is determined. This distance (the run length) can have a value of 0 < x < 15. As the run length (number of adjacent zeros) and the subsequent coefficient are correlated with each other, new codes are made from the combination of run length and category. The end of a 8×8 block is marked by an EOB code (End of Block), which is set behind the last nonzero coefficient of the zigzag sequence. In this way, succeeding zeros need not be coded. The compression is ultimately carried out by a modified **Huffman coding** or, more rarely, via an **arithmetic coding** (see Fig. 4.15). The arithmetic coding, more elaborate in terms of calculation, achieves a compression that is 5-15% more compact. However, its use is dependent on acquiring a license as the procedure was patented by IBM, AT&T and Mitsubishi. The new code words created from the combination of run length and category are assigned code words of entropy coding. They are followed by further bits that establish the actual coefficient value within the category. The number of available bits is determined by the category number. In table 4.3, the categories for the coding of DC coefficients (i.e., the difference between the actual DC values and the calculated predicted values) and AC coefficients are given.

Table 4.3 Categories for the coding of DC coefficients and AC coefficients.

Category	Difference DC -Value – Prediction	AC-Wert
0	0	
1	-1, 1	-1,1
2	-3, -2, 2, 3	-3, -2, 2, 3
3	-7,. . . ,-4, 4,. . . 7	-7,. . . ,-4, 4,. . . 7
4	-15,. . . ,-8, 8,. . . 15	-15,. . . ,-8, 8,. . . 15
5	-31,. . . ,-16, 16,. . . 31	-31,. . . ,-16, 16,. . . 31
6	-63,. . . ,-32, 32,. . . 63	-63,. . . ,-32, 32,. . . 63
7	-127,. . . ,-64, 64,. . . 127	-127,. . . ,-64, 64,. . . 127
8	-255,. . . ,-128, 128,. . . 255	-255,. . . ,-128, 128,. . . 255
9	-511,. . . ,-256, 256,. . . 511	-511,. . . ,-256, 256,. . . 511
10	-1023,. . . ,-512, 512,. . . 1023	-1023,. . . ,-512, 512,. . . 1023
11	-2047,. . . ,-1024, 1024,. . . 2047	

The **decoding** of a compressed JPEG image file is carried out in the reverse manner of compression, i.e.,

- Entropy-decoding
- Reverse sorting of the image data in the zigzag arrangement
- Re-quantization (inverse quantization)
- Inverse Discrete Cosine Transformation (IDCT)
- Reversal of the downsampling for the chrominance components of the image data
- Color space conversion of the YCbCr color space in the target color space.

Due to quantization and downsampling, information is lost in JPEG compression. For this reason, an exact reconstruction of the output data after decompression is not possible most of the time. Repeated encoding and decoding changes the image data, i.e., so-called **generation loss** occurs. This is comparable to the analog dubbing of audio data. Generation loss in the JPEG compression can be kept to a minimum if at every compression cycle the same quantization matrix is used and the block boundaries are identical.

JPEG – File structure
The file format for the storage of JPEG encoded image data is the JFIF format (**JPEG File Interchange Format**). The JPEG norm only specifies the compression process of the image data and not how the compressed data has to be saved in order to be exchanged between different computer programs. JFIF is just one of the several ways of saving JPEG data. Additionally, there is also the **Still Picture Interchange File Format** (SPIFF) and the **JPEG Network Graphics** proposed by the Joint Photographic Experts Group. But JFIF remains the most widespread variation. If reference is made to a "JPEG file" the file concerned is usually in the JFIF format. JFIF only implements some the possibilities offered by JPEG. For example, there are limitations regarding the color space and types of entropy encoding supported.

JFIF files contain the actual image data in the just described form together with information necessary for unpacking this data. The size of an image stored in a JFIF image file is limited to 65,536×65,536 pixels. The individual segments of the JFIF file are separated from each other by marking blocks (2 bytes, content 0xFF) (cf. Fig. 4.17) and can appear multiple times in a JFIF file. They include in particular:

- **Start of Image (SoI)**
  A marking (2 bytes, 0xFFD8) to indicate the beginning of the information associated with the image. As a rule it is at the beginning of the file.

- **End of Image (EoI)**
  Analogous to the SoI marking, EoI indicates the end of the image (2 bytes, 0xFFD9). EoI is normally at the end of the file and contains no further information.

- **Application (APP0)**
  An application marker (2 byte, 0xFFE0) follows directly after the SoI, succeeded by the 4 characters "JFIF." After this comes a version number, information about the size of the image and pixel density. Optionally, a small preview image, when available, follows with associated size information.

- **EXIF Data (APP1)**
  The EXIF segment is intended for receiving metadaten in the **Exchangeable Image File Format** (EXIF). This standard, introduced by the Japan Electronic and Information Technology Industries Association (JEITA), aids in the storage of metadata particularly for images taken by modern digital cameras. Exif data contains information about the type of camera used and technical data concerning the recordings, e.g. shutter speed, aperture and other camera settings.

- **Quantization Table (QT)**
  The quantization table starts with an introduction (2 bytes, 0xFFDB). Next come the 64 entries of the quantization table and information on their precision (8 or 16 bit precision).

- **Start of Frame i (SoFi)**
  Marker (2 bytes, 0xFFCi), which indicates the actual beginning of image i. Information follows next about the preciseness of the data, image dimensions as well as the components. The component data is made up of a component number, horizontal and vertical sampling factor and the number of the quantization table used. An arbitrary number of components can follow each other.

- **Define Huffman Table (DHT)**
  DHT describes a Huffman table and starts with the DHT marker (2 bytes, 0xFFC4). First comes an index for the Huffman table, next counter values and finally content. The counter values indicate how many codes appear in the table with a certain number of bits. The i-th counter value indicates the number of code words with the number of codewords with i bits.

- **Comment (COM)**
  The comment segment (2 bytes, 0xFFFE) is used to record textual annotations to the stored image data.

- **Start of Scan (SoS)**
  Following the SOS marker (2 bytes, 0xFFDA) the bit stream begins that represents the actual image data. Previously, the number of components as well as the number of the corresponding Huffman table are specified.

Further reading:

ISO/IEC 10918-1:1994: Information technology – Digital compression and coding of continuous tone still images: Requirements and guidelines. International Organization for Standardization, Geneva, Switzerland (1994)

ISO/IEC 10918-2:1995: Information technology – Digital compression and coding of continuous tone still images: Compliance testing. International Organization for Standardization, Geneva, Switzerland (1995)

Pennebaker, W. B., Mitchell, J. L.: JPEG Still Image Data Compression Standard. Kluwer Academic Publishers, Norwell, MA, USA (1992)

JPEG compression is a very powerful, lossy compression method for "natural" pictures. These are photographs or pictures of realistic scenes with smooth variations and color and brightness transitions. High compression is achieved through a reduction of the information content. It is a method that takes advantage of the properties of human vision, but is not well suited for graphics or drawings. The compression rates reached are typically at a ratio of 20 : 1 (in lossless mode at 2 : 1). If the compression factor is raised, i.e., the quantization matrix chosen in such a way that as many zero strings as possible are generated, then the appearance of **artifacts** increases. Artifacts are artificially generated pictorial elements whose existence and form are determined by the nature of the compression method. They are not part of the original image information. Fig. 4.18 shows JPEG artifacts in a enlarged section of an image. Lossy JPEG encoded files are optimized for the human viewer and are not usually suitable for mechanical analysis. This procedure is, for example, not readily applicable in medical image processing, since the information loss in the procedure could lead to a misdiagnosis.

The designated successor of the JPEG encoding method is **JPEG2000**. This encoding method was adopted as the international standard ISO-15444 by the ISO in 2001. Just as the older JPEG compression method, JPEG2000 was issued by the Joined Photographic Experts Group. Based on the **discrete wavelet transform**, the JPEG2000 file format allows up to 16-bit grayscale per color channel, i.e., a color depth of up to 48 bits. The name "wavelet," – "little wave" – fittingly describes the form of the basic function of this transformation. In contrast to discrete cosine transformation, the basic functions of wavelet transform in JPEG encoding are time-limited. A better time resolution is therefore more likely than in classic signal transformation. The limitation of the maximum picture size is omitted in JPEG2000 and it is possible to choose either lossless or lossy compression. Thus, JPEG2000 is also suitable for use in medical image processing. JPEG2000 compression is able to efficiently compress both continuous color transitions, such as those in natural images, as well as abrupt color transitions with hard contrasts. However, when strong contrasts are present, the images compressed with JPEG2000 have a tendency toward blurry artifacts and shadows. JPEG 2000 allows the definition of individual "regions of interest." Special interest image segments can be encoded and compressed in a higher quality than the rest of the image. Unlike simple JPEG compression, the continuous encoding and decoding in JPEG2000 does not lead to generation loss, i.e., the picture quality is retained. The image structure is carried out incrementally. This means that the display of an image in a low resolution can be calculated without a complica-

Arithmetic Coding

A further variation of entropy coding is **arithmetic coding**, which can also be used in the JPEG standard instead of the modified Huffman coding. Arithmetic coding uniquely maps a series of characters from an alphabet $A = \{a_1, a_2, \ldots, a_n\}$ to a real number. Individual characters are coded as frequency interval character strings with the help of ("nested") frequency intervals. For this purpose, a standard interval $[0, 1)$ is first established. This interval is subdivided into subintervals whose length corresponds in each case to the relative frequency $p(a_i)$ of a character a_i. The **encoding** of a string proceeds as follows:

1. Initialize the current interval with the arranged start interval.
2. Break down the current interval into subintervals and assign each subinterval a character a_i.
3. The subinterval corresponding to the next input character becomes the current interval.
4. Repeat steps 2 and 3 until all the characters of the input are processed or until the maximum depth of processing has been reached.
5. Enter an arbitrary number x from the current interval plus the number of encoded characters. x is normally chosen in such a way that x has as few significant decimal places as possible (i.e., it is "round") and can be represented with as few bits as possible.

Decoding proceeds according to the following scheme:

1. Initialize the current interval with the arranged interval.
2. Break down the current interval into subintervals, whereby each encodable character a_i is assigned to a subinterval. The size of the subintervals is determined by the relative frequency of the character. The sequence of the subintervals is established by agreement.
3. Find out which of these subintervals is the encoded number x and enter the character associated with this subinterval. This subinterval is now the current interval. If there are other characters to decode, repeat 2 with the new, current interval.

The method can be illustrated with a simple example. The character string **CBC** is to be encoded, whereby the individual characters are to have the following relative frequency:

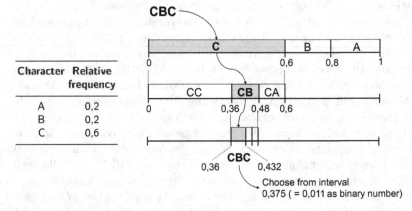

Character	Relative frequency
A	0,2
B	0,2
C	0,6

Fig. 4.15 The principle of arithmetic coding.

Arithmetic Coding (Part 2)

The number **0.375** may be decoded in the following way:

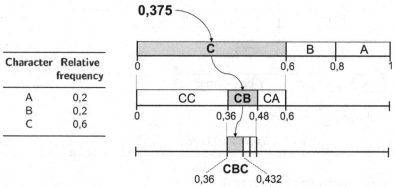

Arithmetic coding works, theoretically, with infinitely precise real numbers. However, because in actual implementation it is necessary to fall back on finite precise integer or floating-point numbers, the rounding up or down that is necessary ultimately leads to non-optimality. In practical terms, the less complicated Huffmann coding wins out over the complex arithmetic coding. The Q-Coder, developed and patented by IBM, represents an efficient implementation of arithmetic coding.

Further reading:

Witten, I. H., Neal, R. M., Cleary, J. G.: Arithmetic coding for data compression. Commun. ACM 30(6), pp. 520-540 (1987)

Moffat, A., Neal, R. M., Witten, I. H.: Arithmetic coding revisited. ACM Trans. Inf. Syst. 16(3), pp. 256-294 (1998)

Fig. 4.16 The principle of arithmetic coding (Part 2).

ted effort just by partial use of the original file. Moreover, the implemented encoding offers additional methods of error detection and correction. It allows step by step progressive image transmission depending on the given quality requirements, image resolution or individual components of the image. Random access to the data stream of the encoded image is also possible. ISO specifies the file extension .jp2 for the JPEG2000 file format. The new passports of the Federal Republic of Germany implement JPEG2000. Passport photos are saved in the JPEG2000 format with a picture size of 18 kbyte. JPEG 2000 is used in medical data, based on the DICOM standard, and for the long-term archiving of documents in large archives.

4.5 Audio – Data Formats and Compression

In contrast to the other types of media treated so far, the acoustic information in sound is not perceived with the aid of the eyes, but with the ears. Sound

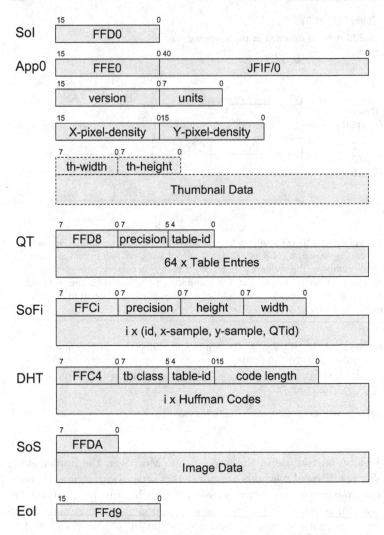

Fig. 4.17 JPEG file format – JPEG File Interchange Format.

is created by the spread of the smallest pressure and density fluctuations, caused by the oscillation (=regular, pendulum-like swinging movements) of bodies in an elastic medium (gases, liquids or solid bodies). The number of oscillations in one second is referred to as the oscillation frequency. Its measure – the frequency of oscillations per second – is described in **Hertz (Hz)**, named after the German physicist *Heinrich Hertz* (1857 – 1894). In 1884, Hertz proved the existence of electromagnetic waves for the first time experimentally, a theory that had been postulated by *James Clerk Maxwell*. Seen physically, sound is a wave (more precisely, a longitudal wave), which

Fig. 4.18 JPEG artifacts are disturbances caused by quantization in the JPEG compression process and are clearly visible at high compression rates.

propagates in the elastic medium of air. The frequency of a sound wave is the reciprocal of the duration of an oscillation ($f = 1/\Delta t$, see Fig. 4.19). The propagation speed of the sound – simply called the speed of sound – depends on factors that include the specific propagation medium. In the air, the speed of sound is 343 meters per second.

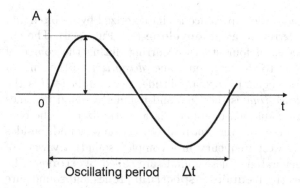

Fig. 4.19 Characteristics of a sound wave are volume (maximum amplitude, A) and pitch (frequency).

Noises are essentially characterized by their volume and pitch. The volume at which a sound is perceived corresponds to the amplitude. This is the acoustic vibration – strength of the change in air pressure as it reaches the ear. The pitch, on the other hand, is proportional to the frequency. The volume perception corresponds to the sound pressure, which is measured in Pascal (Pa), (1 Pa = 1 Newton/m^2), but mostly as a sound pressure level L_p, measured in decibels (dB). A sound pressure level of p_0=0dB corresponds to 20μPa the volume at which a sound of the frequency 1 kHz is still audible for people. This is also known as the **auditory threshold** . The perception of volume is the logarithm of the amplitude of the signal. This means that "doubled volume" corresponds to an increase in the amplitude by a factor of 10. The sound pressure level L_p indicates the magnitude of the relationships between two sound pressures p_1 and p_0. Therefore, the following applies:

$$L_p = 10 \cdot \log \left(\frac{p_1^2}{p_0} \right) dB.$$

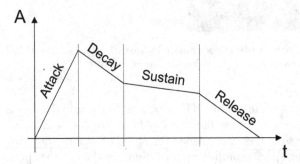

Fig. 4.20 The envelope of a sound shows its amplitude over time.

A sound as a subjective acoustic experience is characterized by its pitch and volume over time and referred to as an **envelope** (see Fig. 4.20). The envelope is identified in terms of four stages occurring during the course of time The *attack time* refers to the transient time, *decay time* is the time of subsiding after the attack begins to lose amplitude, the *sustain level* is the level maintained and *release time* is the time and manner a sound becomes inaudible. The synthetic production of sound via a synthesizer can be controlled over an envelope curve. In every natural generation of sound, besides the fundamental sound (lowest frequency in a complex sound) a variety of higher sounds are also generated. These sounds are called **overtones**. The sum of all overtones gives the **frequency spectrum**. Tones and sounds are analog signals (see Fig. 4.21), i.e., the signals themselves are both time and value continuous and therefore cannot initially be displayed on a computer directly. This requires a conversion to time and discrete value, i.e., digital signals (see Fig. 4.22).

The conversion from an analog output signal into a digital, computer-displayable signal proceeds in three steps:

1. Sampling,
2. Quantization (rounding) and
3. Coding.

Definition: Signal

A **signal** is defined as the "appearance of physical information." Signals can be described as:

- a mathematical function in a closed analytical form,
- a distribution law (e.g., for a stochastic signal in which the current value of the signal is not known but only its distribution function describing the global signal characteristics) or
- empirically, in the form of a series of measurements.

Most signals we encounter are described as a series of individual measuring points. Based on the number of variables the signal depends on, reference is made to a **one-dimensional signal**, such as all forms of acoustic signals that are only dependent on one variable, usually time, and **multiple signals**, such as two-dimensional image signals. Signals can only be stored as digital information in the computer. So that this is possible, there is a conversion of the original analog output information into a discrete display. This process is called **analog-to-digital conversion**

Fig. 4.21 Signals: A definition.

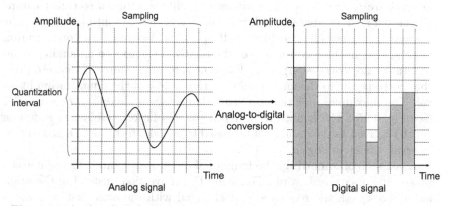

Fig. 4.22 Analog-digital conversion.

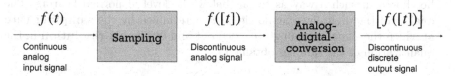

Fig. 4.23 Step-by-step process of digitalization.

4.5.1 Analog-to-Digital Conversion

Analog-to-digital conversion, also called AD conversion for short, begins with **sampling**. In the first step of digitalization, the continuous time profile of a signal is broken down into discrete points in time. For this, the current value of an analog signal is captured at a discrete time point (sampling time point) and thus may be subject to an analog-to-digital conversion. The sampling of a signal is usually periodic. So the course of the original sampled signal can be reconstructed without error, a minimum sampling frequency (sampling frequency) f_A, sampling rate, see Fig. 4.24) is necessary in a periodic sampling cycle. The sampling rate is measured in Hz and should be at least double the maximum frequency to be sampled. In practice, low-pass filters are used that limit the signal to be sampled to a maximum frequency f_{max}.

However, no perfect low-pass filters exist. With a low-pass filter there is always has a certain area of transition between complete signal transmission and complete signal attenuation. Therefore, in practical application a sampling frequency is used that is approximately 2.2 times the maximum frequency ($f_A \approx 2, 2 \cdot f_{max}$).

For the subsequent signal value discretization (**quantization**), the entire value area of the analog signal's amplitude is divided into a finite number n of intervals (quantization intervals), whose fixed, discrete amplitude value is assigned $q_0, \ldots, q_{n-1}$. As all sampling values that fall into a quantization interval are assigned the same discrete amplitude value, a so-called **quantization error** is created. At low signal levels (low amplitude) this can be perceived as a crackling or hissing. If $q_i - q_{i-1}$ designates the quantization interval size, in the reconversion of the digitized values into an analog signal (digital-analog conversion) an analog value is regained from the discrete value that corresponds to the analog value in the middle of the quantization interval. The maximum quantization error that arises is therefore $(q_1 - q_{i-1})/2$ (see Fig. 4.25). The quantization depth (bit resolution, resolution, sampling depth) is given as the number of bits used to encode the discrete quantization interval, therefore: $\log_2 n$.

In a last step of **encoding**, the individual quantization intervals are marked by specific binary codewords. Following DA conversion, instead of the original audio signal, the recovered digital signal with the quantization error is transmitted. In practice, this quantization error is barely noticeable as it can be chosen in such a way as to fall below the level of normal hearing. The quality of the digitalized audio signal is determined by the **sampling rate** at which the signal sampling is carried out and by the **bit resolution** in the quantization of the samples obtained.

Table 4.4 Common bit resolutions for audio digitalization.

Bit Resolution	Applications
8-bit	Games and multimedia software, telephone quality
16-bit	Compact Disk (CD) and Digital Audio Tape (DAT)
20-/24-bit	Professional studio systems

The described method of converting analog into discrete signals is also known as **waveform encoding** or **Pulse Code Modulation** (**PCM**). It was already developed and patented in 1938 by *Alec A. Reeves* (1902 – 1971). PCM

Sampling Theorem

based on Nyquist (1928), Whittaker (1929) Kotelnikow (1933), Raabe (1939) and Shannon (1949))

A signal function that only contains frequencies in a limited frequency band (band limited signal) whereby f_{max} is at the same time the highest signal frequency occurring. It is completely determined by its discrete amplitude value in the time interval

$$T_0 \leq \frac{1}{2 \cdot f_{max}}$$

This means that the sampling frequency f_A must be double the frequency of the signal to be sampled f_{max} (Nyquist criterion or Raabe's condition):

$$f_A \geq 2 \cdot f_{max}$$

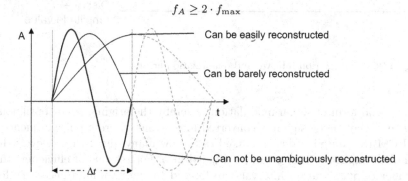

If the sampling rate chosen is too small (subsampling), the correct progression of the output signal can no longer be reconstructed. Disturbances occur taking the form of artifacts.

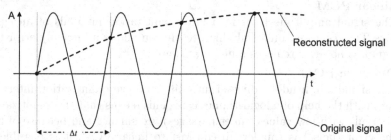

If a sampling frequency f_A is specified, the output signal should be limited by the use of a deep-pass filter at a maximum frequency f_{max}, which can still be correctly detected by the predetermined sampling.

Further reading:

Shannon, C. E.: Communication in the presence of noise. Proceedings of the IRE 37(1), pp. 10-21 (1949), Nachdruck in Proc. IEEE 86(2) (1998)

Unser, M.: Sampling-50 years after Shannon. Proceedings of the IEEE 88(4), pp. 569-587 (2000)

Fig. 4.24 Sampling theorem and sampling rate.

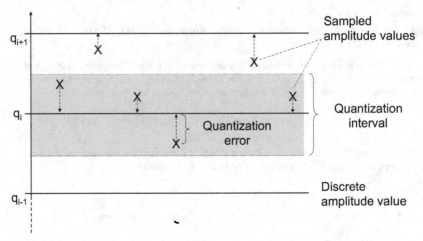

Fig. 4.25 Quantization interval and quantization error.

is a special form of signal modulation, whereby the original time-continuous course of the analog signal is converted into a time-discrete pulse sequence. In PCM the sampling depth is fixed as to how many quantization levels the sampled amplitude values can be divided into. For reasons of efficiency, the number of quantization intervals are limited to the minimum necessary for a qualitatively good transmission. In the technical realization of the PCM technique, the following procedures can be distinguished:

- **Linear PCM**
  The signal amplitude is divided into quantization intervals of an equal size. The resulting, uniformly high resolution allows a virtually error-free signal, it however requires a high data rate.

- **Dynamic PCM**
  The signal amplitude is divided into different size quantization intervals, e.g., with the help of a logarithmic scale. This means that the quantization intervals with low values (quiet passages) are smaller and because of this the error (noise) is smaller. In contrast to linear PCM, it is possible to work with a lower sampling depth (number of bits) to cover the same amplitude. Based on the type of encoding used, e.g. that from the CCITT standard for the audio coding of the telephony G.711, a distinction if made between a European variety (A-Law) and a variety used in the U.S and Japan – (μ-Law) (see Fig. 4.26). A-Law and μ-Law both use 256 quantization intervals (8 bits), whereby the subdivision of the quantization intervals corresponds to a low signal level with a resolution of 12 bits and a high signal level with a resolution of 6 bits. Logarithmic quantization functions have the advantage of better corresponding to human hearing. Large amplitudes occur less often in real signals and a larger quantization distortion is perceived as less disturbing.

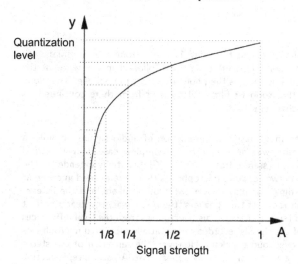

Fig. 4.26 Dynamic PCM with logarithmic quantization intervals.

- **Differential PCM (DPCM)**

  Since usually just small fluctuations occur between successive sampling values, the redundancy of the coding can be reduced if just the differential values of successive sampling values are coded. However, in fixed intervals, coded reference points must also be added, where in fact the true coding of the sampling value occurs. Serious quantization errors can occur in the case of rapid signal fluctuations. In an improved procedure, a predictive value is first stored for every sampling value (**predictive coding**). It is calculated from one or more previous values and only the difference between it and the value that actually appears is saved. Adaptive quantization of the resolution can also be adjusted, i.e., low resolution with strong fluctuation (loud) and high resolution with weak fluctuation (quiet) (**adaptive DPCM**). A distinction is made between **forward adaption**, in which the predicted audio parameters are estimated based on current values, and **backward adaption**, in which the prediction is based on several already past audio-based parameters.

The recovery of the original analog signal from the PCM sampling value proceeds via a **digital-analog conversion** and by applying a low pass filter to reduce the recovered analog signal on the previously limited frequency band. Audio CDs contain digitalized audio data in the PCM format. The digital encoding is normally carried out with two channels each for stereo playback with a sampling frequency of 44.100 Hz and a sampling depth of 16 bits.

From Mono to Dolby Surround

- **Mono**
  For monophonic audio playback, the recording is taken from a fixed point with only one audio track (channel). This principle soon followed in the wake of the first audio reproduction systems such as the phonograph or gramophone. The mono sound recording entered the world of film in 1927 and from there continued its development up to multi-channel sound.

- **Stereo**
  In an effort to achieve the most natural reproduction of audio signals possible, a multi-channel audio recording was necessary. In the simplest case, a two channel sound recording was sufficient (stereo, from *stereos*=[Gk.] spatially extended). The recording was carried out on two separate microphones that were located in different positions. When the recording was played over two loud speakers, and the listener positioned within a certain range of the speakers, the result was, the nearly perfect sensation of natural sound (stereo effect). This effect arises from the level differences and the time differences of the signals recorded over spatially separated microphones that is then played back over loud speakers. However, the sensation of the stereo effect in a limited space is restricted and usually appears flat. A natural reproduction of such a sound experience can therefore only be closely approximated. The first film to be released in the cinema with multiple channel sound was Walt Disney's "Fantasia"in 1941. The first stereo record appeared in 1958 and the first stereo UKW radio in 1961.

- **Multi-channel sound method**
  The development of multi-channel sound began in the cinema. As the cinema screen became ever wider in the 50s, in addition to the two stereo channels there were also central loudspeakers and surround loudspeakers with their own separate sound channels. The intention was to make it possible for the audience away from the screen middle to also localize dialog on the big screen. Since directional hearing in humans is strongest in middle and high frequencies, low frequency effects must not be replayed and divided over different channels. Low frequencies can be played centrally from any location, as they are sooner felt than heard. The American Dolby Laboratories developed the **Dolby 5.1** method providing six individual channels: left, center, right, surround left, surround right and an extra low frequency − compared to the other audio channels it only takes up about one tenth of the bandwidth.

Fig. 4.27 One and multi-channel audio signals.

4.5.2 Uncompressed Audio Formats

In the professional recording studio there are two important formats: S/P-DIF (Sony / Philips Digital Interconnect Format) and AES/EBU (Audio Engineering Society / European Broadcasting Union). They each work with a 20 bit or a 24 bit PCM sampling depth respectively. However, in the area of computer communications and the World Wide Web these formats do not play a significant role.

Many different audio data formats originated in the course of the development of personal computers. These were often tailored to the specific possibilities of the hardware used. The formats AU, SND, AIFF and WAVE are still common today. The **AU format**, Sun Microsystem's brainchild created for the UNIX world, is nearly identical to the **SND format** from NeXT. Both are distinguished by a very simple file structure. After a short header, the audio data is simply stored in sequentially coded form. Different types of encoding are possible, from 8 bit mono PCM sampling to 32 bit multi-channel PCM sampling, with sampling rates of 22.05 kHz to 44.1kHz, . If more than one channel is used, the data for the individual channels is alternately stored in a interleaving process. The **AIFF** format (**Audio Interchange File Format**) is a development of the Apple company, based on the EA/IFF85 standard for Interchange Format Files from the Electronic Arts company. Similar to the **WAVE format** (**Waveform Audio File Format**), developed together by Microsoft and IBM, the AIFF files consist of several independent sections called "chunks." An AIFF file contains at least one form chunk describing the size and the format of the file, a common chunk indicating the number of channels, the sample packets, the sampling rate and the word length of the sound data chunks. The sound data chunks themselves consist of individual sample packets containing the actual audio information. Besides these, there are also marker chunks, comment chunks and instrument chunks, which can be introduced to provide additional information in the audio file. Different types of chunks are listed in Table 4.5. An expansion of the AIFF format, **AIFF-C** was also introduced as a standard for loss-free audio coding. Its format follows the general structure of the AIFF format.

Table 4.5 Various AIFF Chunks

Form Chunk	Framework of the AIFF file, contains file size
Common Chunk	Describes the audio parameters used for coding, e.g., sampling rate, sampling depth, channels
Sound Data Chunk	Contains the actual sampling data
Marker Chunk	Marking of time points within the sampled values
Instrument Chunk	For generating digital instrument sounds
MIDI Chunk	Contains MIDI data
Application Specific Chunk	Arbitrary data
Associated Data Chunk	Additional information about the contained audio data
Comment Chunk	Commentary about the contained audio data
Text Chunk	Text information about the contained audio data

The WAVE file format is part of Windows **RIFF** (**Resource Interchange File Format**). This is a container data format, which can record audio data with different coding and compression variations. The significant difference to the AIFF standard lies in the coding and arrangement of the individual bytes (Intel standard). Although it is theoretically possible that a WAVE file can contain compressed audio data, the variation with uncompressed PCM coded audio data is the most common. Generally, a WAV file consists of a RIFF WAVE chunk, which identifies the file as a WAVE file. This is followed by a FORMAT chunk, which indicates the format of the individual sample blocks, the number of channels, the sampling rate and the block structure.

Then comes a DATA chunk, which contains a series of sample blocks with specific audio data in the chunk format. Since the field is limited to a file size of maximum 32 bits in length, a WAVE file can be maximum 6 GB (gigabytes) large. This corresponds to an uncompressed CD quality length of a little over 6 hours.

Additionally, CUE chunks and PLAYLIST chunks can be added to the file. These allow the definition of areas to be skipped or played multiple times. All chunks are oriented to word boundaries (16/32 bits) and may therefore need to be supplemented with padding bits. Analog to the AIFF/AIFF-C standard, the sampling data in the WAVE format is stored for a sampling time point, first for all channels, before the value of the next sampling time point follows (interleave format). The WAVE format can also be extended later to include new types of chunks. If a chunk type occurs in the playing of a WAVE file that is not known to the decoder then it is not decoded. Access to the back chunks of a WAVE file is carried out via the concatenation of the lengths of the preceding chunks. Therefore, knowledge of all previous chunks is necessary. This is why the WAVE format is not well suited for the real-time transmission of audio data files (streaming).

An audio data format that is somewhat of an exception is the so-called **MIDI** standard (**Musical Instrument Digital Interface**). The MIDI protocol, introduced in 1983, was originally developed for data exchange between electronic instruments called synthesizers, before being later standardized for data communication. In the MIDI format, audio data is not actually transmitted in the proper sense, but only the control signals for the synthesizer. The coding of sounds is carried out via an instrument-based display, containing the parameter specifications, e.g., the name of the instrument, the beginning and end of a note, base frequency, volume and much more. As the data rate of the control signal is very low, MIDI is well suited as an Internet music data format for instrumental music. For example, 10 minutes of music in MIDI coding need only 200 Kb. The general MIDI standard defines a sound library with 128 different instruments and allows the same sound to be set off via a specific control signal at each synthesizer. Real audio data can only be transferred via the MIDI sample Dump format.

4.5.3 Audio Compression

An efficient lossy compression of audio data is much more difficult to achieve than image compression, since errors and artifacts are perceived as causing considerably more disturbance. Depending on the application purpose, audio data can also be reduced in scope and sound without becoming unusable for a targeted application. This applies in particular to speech coding. Here, most of the time understandability is the central focus, compared to exact reproduction and optimal sound quality, unlike the compression of music. A

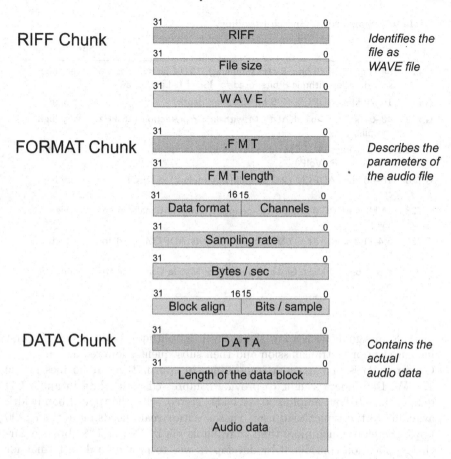

Fig. 4.28 The WAVE file format.

sufficiently good speech quality is based on the noise-free and undistorted playback of what was said. A sampling rate of less than 4 kHz is sufficient to reproduce a normal telephone quality. Numerous international standards have been established in terms of speech compression (see Table 4.6). Speech encoding that functions at a lower data transmission rate often needs a powerful computer for decoding.

The previously described PCM formats with nonlinear sampling already implement compression. With logarithmic sampling (see a-Law/μ-Law method), loud passages are sampled more coarsely than quiet ones – where small differences in the dynamic carry more weight. It is therefore possible with a lower sampling depth to get good results immediately, better than those that can be achieved in linear sampling with a greater sampling depth. The methods of a-Law and μ-Law in logarithmic encoding allow a reduction of the sampling depth from 13/14 bits to 8 bits. In order to achieve the minimum noise

Table 4.6 Standards in Speech Encoding.

Codec	Attribute	Speech quality
G.711	64 kbps PCM (8 bits, 8 kHz sampling), 13/14 bit samples are scaled on logarithmic 8 bits, used for ISDN μ-Law/a-Law	very high
G.721	16–72 kbps ADPCM (2-5 bit sampling depth)	high
G.722	48–64 kbps subband ADPCM with linear prediction (16 kHz sampling)	very high
G.723.1	5.3–6.3 kbps ADPCM (16 bits, 8 kHz sampling), used for voice-over IP (VoIP)	sufficient
G.726	16–40 kbps ADPCM (2-5 bits, 8kHz sampling) in DECT devices	very high
G.728	16 kbps ADPCM (backwards-adaptive, computationally intensive)	high
G.729	6.4-11.8 kbps, as G.723 but with 16 bits ADPCM, used for VoIP	high
GSM	z.B. 5.6–13.3 kbps, Global Standard for Mobile Communication	sufficient

possible in signals with a low signal level (amplitude), weak signals are first increased prior to transmission and then subsequently lowered again.

Compression is of particular importance in transmitting audio files in the WWW. Developers sought to provide compressed audio data in audio CD quality, i.e., 16 bit sampling at 44,1 kHz stereo, with the typical bandwidth available to the typical end user. Such a data stream needs more than 1400 kbps, therefore much more than is available via ISDN (64–128 kbps). A further application considered by developers was to provide a data format for use in audio databases that is accessible via the Internet.

The Fundamental Idea of Lossless Audio Compression

An efficient, lossless audio coding, i.e., a coding that allows the original signal from the compressed data to be exactly reconstructed, uses the principle of **adaptive difference coding** with **linear prediction**. A predictive value is determined for the current signal from past signal values, and only the difference to the actual signal is encoded. The objective is to obtain the lowest value possible for an efficient encoding. In the following step a **statistical coding** is used, e.g., Huffman coding step. It encodes frequently occurring signal values with short code words. This method makes it possible to achieve compression rates of approx. 1:2. Achieving even higher compressions rates is prevented by distortion or noise-like sounds in the audio signal.

Fig. 4.29 Lossless audio compression.

Lossless audio compression only allows compression rates of approx. 1:2 (see Fig. 4.29). This means that the starting point for an efficient audio data compression is a targeted reduction of the quality of the output data. The normal, i.e. lossless, compression is based on the principle of eliminating implicitly present redundancies. Complex reduction procedures relying on data reduction based on weakness in human perception can, in contrast, compress audio data up to one tenth of its original size without noticeable differences in quality. The principle of this perceptually adjusted data reduction is that every part of the audio signal that cannot be recognized by the human ear – so-called irrelevancies – are not coded at all, but filtered out even before the coding takes place.

Methods of Audio Compression

Three basic techniques are distinguished in the compression of audio information:

- **Predictive Coding**
  Knowledge about the previously sent or encoded signal is used to make a prediction about the signal to follow. The actual compression is made by only saving the difference between the signal and its prediction. This is smaller than the original signal and thus can be encoded more efficiently.

- **Spectral** or **Transform coding**
  Via the waveform of the signal a Fournier transformation is performed that transforms the signal in the frequency domain. Since the transformed representation of the signal changes more slowly, it is only necessary for a few samples to be transmitted. Transform encoders normally use a large number of sub-bands and view adjacent samples together in terms of frequency.

- **Sub-Band Coding**
  The available audio spectrum is divided into individual frequency bands. In encoding it is used to an advantage that almost all of the frequency bands have much less information (or less important information) than the loudest band. Consequently, in compression the important bands are given more space than the unimportant ones, which in some cases may even be left out completely. The elaborate work of selection as to how many bits are assigned to which sub-band, is done by the encoder based on a so-called **psycho-acoustic model**. In addition to the actual audio data, the information must also be transmitted via the bit distributor. Sub-band coding is often understood as a special type of transform coding.

Fig. 4.30 Methods of audio compression.

Seen conceptually, audio compression procedures carry out the same processing steps as the human ear. The signal is first broken down with respect to frequency. Based on anatomical conditions, the human ear can only perceive acoustic signals with a sound pressure of between 0 dB and 120 dB and with a frequency range of 20 Hz to 20,000 Hz. This is the so-called **auditory sensation area** (see Fig. 4.31). Acoustic signals outside of the human auditory sensation area must not be encoded (irrelevance reduction).

It is not necessary that all acoustic signals must be coded in the auditory sensation area. The reason for this is the phenomena of so-called **masking**, which is well known in everyday life. An acoustic signal that is very audible in a quiet environment cannot be recognized in a noisy environment. It is covered up. In order that an acoustic signal can be heard above simultaneous

The human ear

The human ear can only hear a sound wave within the frequency range that is perceptible for humans – between approx. 20 Hz and 20,000 Hz. Sound waves below this frequency range fall in the category of **infrasound**, which is directly adjacent to the frequency range know as **ultrasound**. The human ear reaches its highest level of sensitivity in the range between 2,000 Hz and up to 4,000 Hz.

The human ear is divided into three areas:

- The **external ear** is made up of the auricle, the external auditory canal and then finally the eardrum.
- On the inner side of the eardrum are the three small bones of the **middle ear** called the ossicles. These are named the hammer, anvil and stirrup. They transform the vibrations caused by air pressure to the eardrum membrane into a mechanical vibration. This is conducted further through the oval window to the
- **inner ear**. The oval window oscillates on an axis and in this way transfers the arriving vibration to the lymph fluid of the cochlea. The cochlea is divided into three compartments by two membranes. These membranes are filled with two different fluids. Between both of the fluids an electrochemical charge takes place, providing the stimulus for the forwarding and receiving of the necessary electrical energy. In the center of the cochlear runs the basilar membrane. This is where the organ of Corti is located. With its approx. 20,000 hair cells it picks up bio-electrical vibrations that are received by the auditory nerves and passed to the brain.

The inner ear performs a first frequency analysis of the perceived frequency range. The performance components of the spectrum are not evaluated by way of a linear frequency scale but each frequency range perceived with a different volume. The volume perception of an acoustic signal with a certain sound pressure level therefore depends on its frequency. A sound with a certain sound pressure level is perceived in varying degrees of loudness depending on its pitch. Plotting points of loudness on a frequency scale therefore does not result in a straight line but in a curve – the so-called isophone. The subjective perception of loudness is measured in the unit **phon**. The area between the **absolute threshold of hearing** and the **pain threshold** is known as the **auditory sensation area** or **listening area** (see Fig. 4.32). The absolute threshold of hearing in humans is at a sound pressure of approx. $p_0 = 20$ µPa and corresponds to the sound pressure level $L_{p_0} = 0$ dB. The pain threshold, in contrast, is about 130 dB. This corresponds to about three million times the sound pressure of the absolute threshold of hearing. The human ear is very sensitive and the inner ear can easily suffer irreversible damage when subjected to high sound pressure.

Fig. 4.31 The human ear.

ambient noise it must be correspondingly louder than in absolute silence. The required level of sound is called the **masking threshold**.

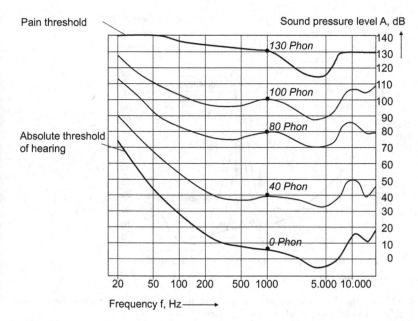

Pain threshold

Sound pressure level A, dB

Absolute threshold
of hearing

Frequency f, Hz⟶

Fig. 4.32 The listening area defines the range of human acoustic perception

Two types of masking are distinguished in **psychoacoustics**:

- **Simultaneous masking**
  A phenomenon whereby a signal with a low level (**masked signal**) is made
  inaudible by a concurrent strong signal (**masker**) if the frequencies of the
  masked signal and masker are located near to each other. The so-called
  auditory masking threshold indicates exactly the signal level at which a
  faint signal is just barely masked by the masker. All signals located below
  the masking threshold are inaudible to the human ear. Fig. 4.33 shows the
  shift in the masking threshold with simultaneous masking via a narrow-
  band noise at 1 kHz, with varied signal intensity.

- **Temporary occlusion**
  The occurrence of two nearly simultaneous acoustic events whereby the
  stronger signal can also mask the weaker one when it arrives shortly after
  (up to 200ms), or shortly before (up to 50 ms) the masker. Fig. 4.34 shows
  the path of a temporal signal masking .

Through simultaneous and temporal masking, signals do not have to be coded
that would in any case not be perceived by the human ear. The data rate of
the signal can therefore be lowered without a noticeable quality degradation
taking place.
Further important variables are the **Signal-to-Mask Ratio** (SMR), the
Signal-to-Noise Ratio (SNR) and the **Noise-to-Mask Ratio** (NMR).
SMR is the difference between the sound pressure of the masker and the

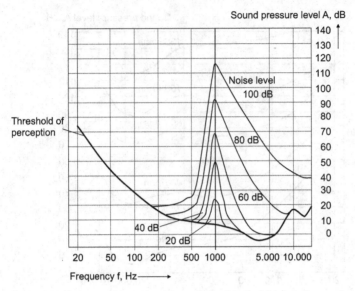

Fig. 4.33 Raising the auditory masking threshold in the case of narrow-band noise from 1 kHz with different levels of interference.

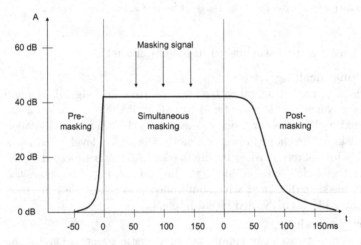

Fig. 4.34 Temporary occlusion.

masking threshold. SNR results from the relation between the masker and the quantization noise and NMR results from the difference between SMR and SNR. Audio compression methods are generally distinguishable by the techniques they use to calculate the masking threshold and by how much effort is invested in the signal process to perform the necessary calculations.

4.5.4 MPEG Audio Coding

MPEG stands for **Motion Picture Experts Group,** a committee that was originally involved in the coding and compression of video and audio data (see Fig. 4.35). The working results of this organization are usually standardized by the ISO and go by the name MPEG. The described audio coding procedures described do not stand alone but are part of the respective MPEG group standardized video compression procedure. This will be discussed later in greater detail.

MPEG – Moving Picture Experts Group

MPEG refers to a working group of the (International Standards Organization). The complete, formal designation of MPEG as a sub-organization of the ISO is: ISO/IEC JTC 1/SC 29/WG 11. Its task is to develop standards for the coded representation of audio and video data, including procedures for its compression and proccesion. The MPEG group held its first meeting in May 1988. Among its main developments have been the standards **MPEG-1** (ISO/IEC 11172) as basis for the Video Compact Disk (VCD) and the MP3 used in the Internet, **MPEG 2** (ISO/IEC 13818), implemented in the digital television area and the DVD and **MPEG-4** (ISO/IEC 14496) as a general multimedia standard, among other things for mobile communication devices of the next generation with low bit rates. Unlike MPEG-1, MPEG-2 and MPEG-4, which define different video compression procedures, the standards MPEG-7 and MPEG-21 define metadata, i.e., data that defines the content or important information for reproduction of the multimedia data contents.

MPEG-7 (ISO/IEC 15938) was adopted in 2002 and is a standard for XML-based meta data for the description and indexing of audio and video contents. The **MPEG-21** (ISO/IEC 21000) "Multimedia Framework," standardized in 2004, defines the complete infrastructure for the transmission and delivery of multimedia contents including copyright agreements. In 2004 and 2005, the standards **MPEG-A, MPEG-B, MPEG-C, MPEG-D** and **MPEG-E** were released for the definition of integrated solutions for system, video and audio technologies as well as multimedia middleware.

Fig. 4.35 The MPEG group and MPEG standards.

Besides the compression of audio data, there are a number of other goals that played a role in the development of the individual MPEG audio coding standards. For example: real-time encoders should be attainable at reasonable hardware costs as well as real-time decoders realizable in all common operating systems. In addition, it should be possible to navigate forwards or backward in the compressed data stream. Similarly, resistance to cascading encoding and decoding (generation loss) was necessary: no new artifacts should result when dubbing an audio file and carrying out the associated decoding and subsequent encoding processes.

The bit rate that should be transmitted with the signal in MPEG is taken as constant. This means that signals need not necessarily be displayed in the smallest possible space, but that the signal display can optimally utilize the given bandwidth. For example in the hardware implementation of a MPEG encoder, the configuration of the **filter banks** (including, e.g., the Fourier or cosine transformation, as well as information on the use of the psychoacoustic model) is firmly defined in the standard and does not depend on the signal to be encoded (see Fig. 4.36). Nevertheless, this approach does not guarantee optimal efficiency and quality from the onset.

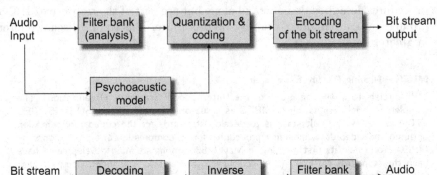

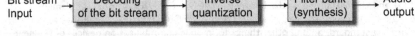

Fig. 4.36 Schematic flow of the MPEG audio encoding/decoding.

Previous information regarding the already coded signal is not taken into account in the encoding process, which would require too much of the encoder's memory.

Table 4.7 MPEG-1 audio encoding.

MPEG-1 Target bit rate	Use
Layer 1 192 kbps per channel	digital compact cassettes (DCC)
Layer 2 128 kbps per channel	digital radio (DAB), digital television (DVB) Audio to video CDs
Layer 3 variable bit rates 32-384 kbps	Internet, Audio-MP3

A basic distinction is made in the MPEG audio encoding procedure between **MPEG-1** and its extension **MPEG-2**, which allows the encoding of additional audio channels. The MPEG-1 specification for audio encoding is divided into so-called **layers**. This enables the compression of a stereo signal in sampling rates of

- 32 kHz (digital broadcasting),
- 44,1 kHz (CD audio quality) and
- 48 kHz (professional audio devices).

Encoders for each MPEG layers are backwards compatible, i.e., layer 1 is the basis that all encoders and decoders (also designated as **Codec**) must provide. Decoders for layer 2 must automatically be able to implement layer 1 data, but not vice versa. The well-known **MP3 files** are encoded according to the procedure established in MPEG-1 layer 3. A block diagram of the MP3 encoding and decoding process is given in Fig. 4.37. The complexity of the encoder and decoder increases with the number of the respective layer.

Excursus 10: MPEG-1 Audio Encoding

MPEG-1 Layer 1

In a first step – via the so-called polyphase filter bank – the input audio signal is divided into 32 equal-width **frequency sub-bands**, each is 750 Hz wide with a sampling rate of 48kHz. The filters used are relatively simple and have a good frequency and time resolution. The filter bank takes an input sample (sample value) and breaks it down into its spectral components, which are each distributed over 32 sub-bands. An MPEG layer 1 data packet includes 384 samples, whereby 12 samples are grouped into each of the 32 sub-bands. Based on the psychoacoustic model implemented, the encoder allocates the number of necessary bits to each sample group. For each sub-band, the suitable quantizer can be chosen out of 15 that are possible.

There is a disadvantage in this type of compression, because the human ear does not function in sub-bands of an equal width. The width of the sub-band grows exponentially with the frequency. The filter bank and synthesis are lossy here, which is however not audible. Additionally, so-called **aliasing effects** occur. This means that significant overlapping takes place in adjacent frequency bands in the MPEG layer 1 because the frequency bands are not sharply defined. Because of the overlapping, a tone on one frequency can appear simultaneously in two frequency bands. This is also noticeable in compression and takes the form of extra redundancy. Four different modes are defined in channel coding:

- **single channel coding** for the encoding of mono signals,
- **dual channel coding** for the encoding of two separate mono signals, e.g., bilingual audio,
- **stereo coding** for the encoding of a stereo signal, in which both stereo channels are however encoded separately, and
- **joint stereo coding** for encoding a stereo signal, in which the data irrelevancies and redundancies between the two channels are used for compression. A method is thereby used called "Intensity Stereo," in which only a mono signal is transmitted for high frequencies. It is then pushed back in the vicinity of the original stereo position by the decoder.

The quantization and the encoding that follows are implemented with a masking threshold determined by the psychoacoustic model used.

MPEG Layer	Compression
Layer 1	1:4
Layer 2	1:6 … 1:8
Layer 3	1:10 … 1:12

MPEG-1 Layer 2 – MP2

At the start of encoding there is an uncompressed audio signal sampled with a 48 kHz

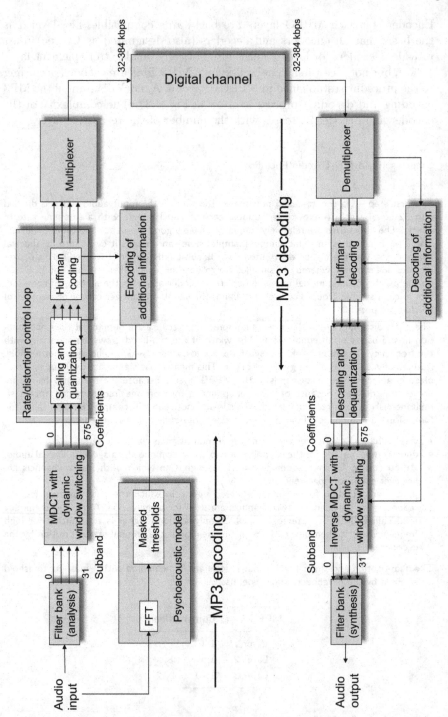

Fig. 4.37 Block diagram of the ISO/MPEG audio codec MP3.

sampling rate and quantized with a 16 bit sampling depth. MPEG-1 layer 2 – also known as MUSICAM (Masking pattern adapted Universal Subband Integrated Coding And Multiplexing) – encodes the data in larger groups and limits bit allocation in medium and high sub-bands, since they are not as important for auditory perception. In this way, bit allocation data, scaling factors and quantized samples can be saved in a more compact form. This extends the available space for the important audio data. An MPEG-1 layer 2 data packet contains 1,152 samples per channel and blocks of 3 each made up of 12 samples per subband (subframes). This results in an increased time resolution of the signal. Within a frame, the post-masking effect (temporal overlap) of human hearing can also be exploited.

MPEG-1 Layer 3 – MP3

MP3 is the most widely used compression option for audio data. Its development was begun in 1982 by the research group led by *Karlheinz Brandenburg* at the Fraunhofer Institut für Integrierte Schaltungen (IIS) in Erlangen, Germany. The research was carried out under the auspices of an EU project together with the University of Nuremberg and the companies AT&T, Bell Labs and Thomson. In 1992 it was adopted as ISO/IEC Standard 11172-3. For the general public, the MP3 data format became widely popular through music file-sharing platforms, such as Napster, and the popular portable devices called MP3 players. In fact, at the beginning of 1999 the most popular search term in the WWW was "MP3."

MP3 used an additional **Modified Discrete Cosine Transformation (MDCT)** on the output of the original filter bank, thereby bringing about a drastic rise in resolution from 32 to a maximum of 576 sub-bands. This even made it possible to reverse aliasing effects even those resulting from overlapping frequency sub-bands. In MP3 the sample sizes 18 and 6 were chosen for the MDCT. Because successive transformation windows have an overlap of 50% the window size that results is 36, or 12. The long block size (36 samples) allows a higher frequency resolution of stationary signals while the shorter (12 samples) ensures a better time resolution for transient signals. An exchange between the two block lengths is always initiated by a special control block.

Due to the lower time resolution and, consequently, increased time window in which the MDCT operates, the errors created through the quantization noise are also distributed in a larger time window. This increases the likelihood that they will actually be heard. In a signal where loud and quiet passages alternate in quick sequence , the distortion is not only found in loud segments – where it is barely heard – but also in quiet segments. These disturbances usually take the form of pre-echos, as the temporal masking before a signal is weaker – and therefore also shorter – than after it.

To handle these weaknesses, an attempt is made in MP3 to predict such situations in enough time via a suitably modified psychoacoustic model. Via a so-called **bit reservoir** it is possible to dynamically raise the resolution (number of quantization intervals) in these exceptional circumstances and thus lessen the quantization noise. The encoder can, in addition, switch to the smaller MDCT bock size, and in this way shorten the effective window length.

Among the improvements introduced in MP3 are:

- A compensation for the filter bank **aliasing effects**
- The **quantizer** potentiates the input to 3/4 in order to distribute the signal-to-noise ratio more evenly over the value range of the quantization interval.
- **Scaling factors** are summarized in MP3 in bands. One band includes multiple MDCT coefficients and has a width similar to that of the human ear. In this way, quantization noise is colored, similar to the contours of the masking threshold, and there are no more noise peak values.
- The MP3 encoder sorts the 576 coefficients (32 sub-bands × 18 MDCT coefficients) into a standardized order which ensures that the high values (with the low frequencies) are at the start and the minimal values at the end. For the high values at the beginning,

long code words are assigned to the Huffman coding that follows. While very short code words are assigned to the small values at the end. The coefficients are divided up into three regions for which a special, optimized Huffman table is used. It is possible that in part even multiple values are mapped onto one Huffman code.

- A **bit reservoir** is introduced, which can be used to increase the resolution. The encoder is only allowed to take bits from the reservoir that it had previously saved and stored there. The applied Huffman code uses short code words for the small quantization values that occur more frequently after the MDCT. If the bit sequence resulting from the Huffman coding exceeds the number of bits available, the size of the quantization interval can be expanded in this step. This results in an increased number of smaller quantization values, which can accordingly be coded shorter.
  The quantization noise is controlled for every frequency sub-band by way of a scaling factor. This means, if the noise exceeds the masking threshold and becomes perceptible, then the scaling factor of the affected sub-band is adjusted to reduce the quantization noise. To this end, it is however necessary to use finer quantization intervals whose encoding requires a higher bit resolution.

- The human ear is not able to directionally perceive very high and very low frequencies. With a technique called **Intensity Stereo**, certain frequencies in MP3 are only encoded monophone, with a minimal addition of directional information. This avoids a complete stereo encoding of the input signal. A further technique known as **Mid/Side-Stereo** is also used. If the two signals of the left (L) and right (R) channels are very similar, they are not encoded independently. Instead, only their difference (L-R) and their sum (L+R). This results in additional economization. From the original left and right channel stereo signal, results a signal from the middle and side channels. Therefore, allowing a more efficient transmission of a weakly produced stereo effect.

- The company Xing, RealNetworks expanded the MP3 standard to include the possibility of a **variable bit rate** (VBR). Since not all passages in a piece of music have the same degree of complexity, it can often be an advantage not to fix the data rate for the compression at the beginning, but rather adjust it to the complexity of the signal to be encoded. In this way it is often possible to achieve higher compression rates with an identical sound quality. The data rate is stored separately for each frame. Because this technique places high demands on the decoder used, it is not supported by many older versions.

Table 4.8 Typical compression rates achieved with MP3.

Quality	Bandwidth channel	Bit rate (kbps)	Compression
Telephone	2,5 kHz mono	8 kbps	96:1
Shortwave	4,5 kHz mono	16 kbps	48:1
Medium wave (AM)	7,5 kHz mono	32 kbps	24:1
UKW	11,0 kHz stereo	56 . . . 64 kbps	26 . . . 24:1
Near CD	15,0 kHz stereo	96 kbps	16:1
CD	> 15,0 kHz stereo	112 . . . 128 kbps	14 . . . 12:1

MP3 Audio quality

The targeted audio quality achieved by means of MP3 compression varies depending on the basic compression parameters used and the implementation of the encoder. In lossy MP3 compression, the choice of unsuitable basic parameters – such as the selection of a too low bit rate – result in disturbances and distortion in the form of artifacts. These type of artifacts are distinguished from those that normally occur in the analog world for example in broadcasting. Artifacts are dedicated error signals that change over time and across frequency and are not dependent on the harmonics of the audio signal. A distinction is made between

- distorted artifacts (but no harmonic distortion),
- noise artifacts (with noise affecting only a certain frequency range) and
- interference artifacts (interference in relation to the audio signal is very significant as the characteristics of the interference signal can change every 24 milliseconds).

If an encoder is not able to encode an audio signal with the available bit rate, there is a loss of signal bandwidth as typically high frequency components of the signal cannot be coded. In contrast to a steady bandwidth restriction, a bandwidth restriction caused by an excessively low bit rate is clearly noticeable as its spectrum can change (every 24 milliseconds) after every encoded data block.

Often so-called **pre-echos** occur, i.e., an interference signal is already generated before the audio signal, which caused the disturbance, is reproduced. This can be illustrated in the decoding process. The received bit stream is first decoded with its individual frequency bands. It is subjected to inverse quantization before the frequency bands are then recombined in a synthesis filter bank. The quantization error, caused by the encoder, could be regarded as an additional signal that is added to the existing frequency bands. The time duration of the quantization error corresponds to the length of the synthesis time window. For this reason, error in the reconstruction of the signal is distributed over the entire time window. If the music signal in the time window contains a sudden rise in amplitude, such in the clicking of castanets, the signal strength of the quantization error raises as well (normally artifacts with metallic rattling sounds are audible). If such a signal is in the analyze time window, its quantization error is distributed across the complete time window so that the error in reconstruction occurs even before its cause is audible. If the time duration of the pre-echo exceeds the temporal masking of the human ear, the pre-echo can be heard. A way of reducing audible pre-echos is the use of variable bit rates, or a local increase in the bit rate, in order to weaken the signal strength of the pre-echo. A further effect caused by an insufficient alignment between temporal resolution of the encoder and the time structure of the audio signal is seen most clearly in speech signals. This error, called **double speak** is mainly perceived when listening through headphones and appears as a second voice, overlapping the original one.

In the generation of an MP3 compressed audio file there must always be an appropriate compromise found between the acquired compression rate and the desired audio quality. Normally, a certain bit rate is fixed by the user. The lower the bit rate the less the audio quality. Some special audio files, such as those pieces with high and sudden dynamic variations or a high degree of incidental noise, prove difficult to compress. The quality achieved also depends on the encoder used in each case, as the MPEG specification allows a relatively free interpretation in the implementation of the standard. If the MP3 compressed signal can no longer be distinguished from an output signal, then the compression is called **transparent**. A sufficient transparency can be achieved in MP3 normally with bit rates of between 128 kbps and 192 kbps.

Further reading:

Dietz, M., Popp, H., Brandenburg, K., Friedrich, R.: Audio compression for network transmission. Journal of the Audio Engineering Society 44(1-2), pp. 58-72 (1996)

Painter, T., Spanias, A.: Perceptual coding of digital audio. Proc. of the IEEE 88(4), pp. 451-515 (2000)

Thom, D., Purnhagen, H., Pfeiffer, S.: MPEG-Audio Subgroup: MPEG Audio FAQ, ISO/IEC JTC1/SC29/WG11 Coding of Moving Pictures and Audio (1999)

Table 4.9 shows the ratio of the achieved file size with different, predetermined bit rates. As the bit rate increases, so does the quality of the audio data as well as the file size. From the figure it is also clear how many hours MP3 encoded audio data fill a 1 GB hard disk partition and how many pieces of music, each 4 minutes long, have room there.

Table 4.9 File size vs. bit rate in MP3 encoding

Bit rate	File size	Compression	Hours/GB	Pieces/GB
1,411 kbps (CD-Audio)	41,3 MB	None	1,7	25
80 kbps	2,3 MB	17,6:1	29,1	437
128 kbps	3,8 MB	11:1	18,2	273
160 kbps	4,7 MB	8,8:1	14,6	218
192 kbps	5,6 MB	7,3:1	12,1	182
256 kbps	7,5 MB	5,5:1	9,1	137
320 kbps	9,4 MB	4,4:1	7,3	109

Excursus 11: MP3 – File Structure

An MPEG file does not have a file header in the actual sense of the word, but only consists of a series of individual data blocks (frames) that each contains its own header as well as the saved audio information. For MPEG layer 1 and layer 2 these blocks are completely independent units. This means that an MPEG file can be removed from any location and still be played back correctly. The decoder plays the file from the first data block that is retrieved intact. In MP3, however, the individual data blocks are not always independent of each other. Due to the use of the byte reservoir the individual blocks are often dependent on one another, whereby a maximum of 9 data blocks are needed in order to reproduce a data block correctly. In order to obtain information about a MP3 file, it suffices to find a data block and read its header, as it can be assumed that this information applies in the same manner to the other data blocks. This is the case as long as the variable bit rate (VBR) is not being used, in this case the bit rate can be changed in each new data block. The structure of a MP3 file is shown schematically in Fig. 4.38.

- A **data block header** is 32 bits long and contains the following components:

  - The **synchronization word** takes the first 11 bits of the data block header and consists exclusively of bits that are set to the value '1,' to identify the beginning of a MP3 data block.
  - The **MPEG ID** consists of a 2 bit long string, with which the MPEG version of the data can be specified. The value 3, i.e., the bit string '11' designates MPEG version 1.

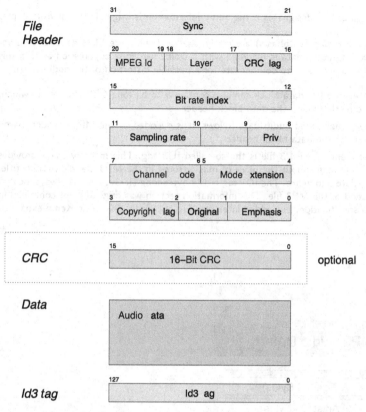

Fig. 4.38 MPEG-1 Layer 3 – MP3 file format.

- The next 2 bit long sequence identifies the corresponding MPEG **layer**. The string '01' denotes layer 3, '10' denotes layer 2 and '11' denotes layer 1.
- The following **CRC flag** indicates whether a CRC checksum is used (CRC flag='0') or not (CRC flag='1').
- The next 4 bits encode the **bit rate** used in the data blocks, with respect to the specific MPEG version used. For MPEG 1 layer 3 a bit rate of 128 kbps with, for example, the bit string '1001' is encoded.
- The **sampling rate** is encoded with the help of the two next bits, also based on the respective MPEG version. For MPEG 1 the bit string '00' denotes, for example, a sampling rate of 44100 Hz.
- The next bit (**padding**) indicates whether the data block is completely filled or not.
- The **private** bit is used only for informational purposes.
- The following 2 bits (**channel mode**) gives information regarding how many channels are coded and in what way. The bit sequence '00' stands for regular stereo, while the string '01' denotes the version *joint stereo*.
- The following 2 bits contain the information relevant to the audio signal only in the case of the *joint stereo* encoding. If both bits are set ('11'), the audio signal is coded with the *intensity stereo* and *mid-side-stereo* methods.
- The **copyright flag** designates copyright-protected audio information ('1' = with copyright).

– The **original flag** designates if the audio information is original ('1') or from copies ('0').
– The last two bits (**emphasis**) are rarely used and show the MP3 decoder whether the following audio data is recorded with a Dolby-like noise suppression and, in this case, if it is necessary to compensate for a possible distortion of the audio signal.

• Optionally, every MP3 data block can also contain a 16 bit long **CRC checksum**, which, if present, directly follows the data block header.

• Finally, the actual coded **audio data** follows. It is decoded by the MP3 decoder, based on the details in the data block header.

• The last element in a MP3 file is the so-called **ID3 tag**. This memory space provides storage for metadata about the piece of music stored in the MP3 file, e.g., artist, title, publication date and genre. The ID3 tag is 128 bytes long (ID3v1) and is always located at the the the end of the MP3 file. This information section was originally not contained in the MPEG specification, but added later (see Fig. 4.39). In 1996, Eric Kemp expanded

Fig. 4.39 MP3 ID3v1 tag with metadata.

MPEG-1 audio files with his program "Studio 3." He did this by adding a small 128 byte area to the end that contained information about the audio file: the ID3 tag (Version 1.0, ID3v1.0). With this version – that always starts with the string TAG – there are default fields for title, artist, album, year, commentary, as well as a field where a musical genre can be indicated from out of 80 predetermined genres (Winamp expanded this genre list to 148 entries). The ID3 tag was purposely placed at the end of the data block to ensure compatibility with other decoders. The rigid structure of the ID3 tag left little room for expansion so that after the first unsatisfactory attempt (Id3v1.1), there followed a much more flexible new definition: ID3v2.

In 1998, **ID3v2** defined its own container format that consisted of up to 84 individual, different data blocks of each a maximum of 16 MByte long. The maximum length of a ID3v2 tag is limited to 256 Mbytes. In order to take advantage of the possibilities of media streaming, the ID3v2 tag is at the beginning of the MP3 file so that it is available from the beginning. It includes:

- additional predetermined property fields,
- unicode character sets,
- separate files, such as images,
- song lyrics, that can also be produced in sync with the music, such as in karaoke, and
- diverse parameters for the playing of the music.

The additional information contained in the ID3v2 tag can be compressed independently, in this way allowing an efficient storage within the specified MP3 data format.

Further reading:

International Standard, ISO/IEC/JTC1/SC29 WG11: ISO/IEC 13818-3, Information technology – generic coding of moving pictures and associated audio information – Part 3: Audio. International Organization for Standardization, Geneva, Switzerland (1998)

4.5.4.1 MPEG-2

MPEG-2 is an expansion of the MPEG-1 standard. Compatibility with MPEG 1 is guaranteed in both directions, i.e., MPEG-1 and MPEG-2 decoders are capable of interpreting both data formats. The MPEG-2 audio compression method is standardized as ISO/IEC 13818-3 and includes the following addition to MPEG-1:

- the additional sampling rates of 8 kHz, 11 kHz, 16 kHz, 22.5 kHz and 24 kHz.
- 3 extra audio channels that allow a 5 channel surround sound (left, middle, right and 2 spatial channels).
- support of a separate audio channel for low sound frequency effects (<100 Hz).
- support of extra audio information in different configurations (up to 8 multi-lingual channels). These can offer both multiple language transmission support for the hearing and visually impaired.
- use of variable bit rates for compression adjustment to the changing complexity of the audio information to be encoded.

Through the various possibilities of channel encoding new practices of compression open up, e.g.,

- Intensity Stereo Coding (ISC),
- Phantom Coding of Center (PCC),
- Dynamic Transmission Channel Switching,
- Temporal Noise Shaping for good speech quality at low bit rates,
- Dynamic Cross Talk and
- Adaptive Multi-Channel Prediction.

To ensure compatibility, MPEG-2 data must be encoded in such a way that a conventional MPEG-1 decoder is capable of filtering out the left and right stereo channels from the five possible channels. The fixed data format in MPEG-1 is used for the compression of the left and right channel. This implies use of the same compression algorithm for both channels, which is packed in a MPEG-1 data packet with a MPEG-2 expansion field (see Fig. 4.40).

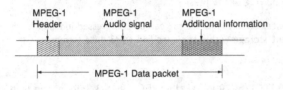

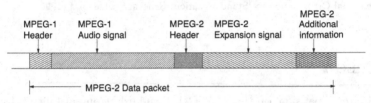

Fig. 4.40 Data format of a MPEG-2 audio bit stream.

4.5.4.2 MPEG-2.5

An non-ISO-certified expansion of the MPEG-2 layer 3 standard was developed by Fraunhofer Institut. This version, known as MPEG-2.5, allows better compression results, especially for low bit rates (8–12 kHz sampling rate for bit rates of 8-160 kbps) with bandwidth limitation. A relatively high sampling rate at a low bit rate must suffice with reduced resolution of the frequency range. If on the other hand the sampling rate is reduced, the temporal resolution of the encoded signal also decreases, however a wider frequency area can be covered. With a combination of both techniques, better sounding results can be achieved with comparable compression.

4.5.4.3 MPEG-2 / MPEG-4 Advanced Audio Coding

Successors of the MP3 standard followed with the 1997 MPEG-2 Advanced Audio Coding (**MPEG-2 AAC**, as ISO/IEC 13818-7:1997) and the 1999 MPEG-4 Advanced Audio Coding (**MPEG-4 AAC**, as ISO/IEC 14496-3:1999) . MPEG-2 AAC is not backward compatible with MPEG-1. The process of advanced audio coding represents the current state-of-the-art in audio compression. Substantial parts of the original MP3 codec have been newly developed. This applies particularly to new predictive algorithms and applied entropy coding. Additionally, the multiple channel capability of MPEG-2 has been expanded to 48 channels in the regular frequency range and 16 channels in the low frequency range. The resolution of the sampling rate was also raised to 96 kHz. MPEG-2 AAC uses almost the same techniques as MP3, only these techniques have been improved in their application:

- the filter bank used is limited to a pure MDCT, while with MP3 it was designed as hybrid (MDCT and FT).
- the window size can be nearly twice as long (2,048 samples) as in MP3 and therefore allows for better resolution.
- at the same time, the window size can also be smaller than in MP3 and enable a better temporal resolution and handling of the pre-echo.
- middle/side and intensity stereo can each be handled based on its own sub-band and not as in MP3 over the entire frequency range.

As it was no longer necessary to ensure compatibility in development, the existing limitations of the MP3 standard could be bypassed. Temporal Noise Shaping (TNS) was also introduced. This is a tool for controlling the quantization noise that occurs in the transfer of coefficients and predictive algorithms. It allows predicting coefficients for every frequency band from each of the two preceding data packets. It increases the efficiency of static signals enormously and improves, in particular, the intelligibility of speech signals, also in the case of low bit rates. MPEG-2 AAC achieves just as good of an audio quality in the encoding of two audio channels as MP3, with approximately 70% of the required bit rate.

MPEG-4 AAC has evolved from the MPEG-2 AAC standard through further improvement, mainly in the transmission of low bit rates. Utilization was therefore primarily intended to target the area of mobile computing, since speech transmission is already possible at bit rates starting at 4 kbps with MPEG-4 . The MPEG-4 AAC standard found widespread application in different Apple products, such as the portable media player iPod as well as the iTunes software for playing, organizing and buying music, movies and games. The improvements of MPEG-4 AAC include the introduction of the Perceptual Noise Substitution (PNS) technique. It allows noise-like passages in the encoded music to be substituted for noise generated on the decoder side. Moreover, an algorithm for long time prediction (LTP) was developed that works with the same performance as the algorithm in MPEG-2 AAC with considerably less encoding complexity. The advanced audio coding concept is characterized by a high degree of modularity. Depending on the complexity of the audio information to be encoded, various profiles can be created that fix which methods and tools should be used from the tool box of the MPEG-2/MPEG-4 AAC standards. Four standard profiles are available:

- Low Complexity (for medium to high bit rates; the simplest and most widespread profile)

- Main Profile (just as low complexity, with the additional possibility of backward prediction)
- Scalable Sampling Rate (also known as MPEG-4 AAC-SSR, enables the uninterrupted possibility of streaming through a lessening of the bit rate if the bandwidth available drops)
- Long Term Prediction (improvement of the main profile with introduction of a forward prediction of low computational complexity)

MPEG-4 is more than just a simple compression mechanism. It also includes multimedia object management that allows a combination of music, speech, noise, synthetic audio or text information and can efficiently encode every one of these sources as an independent media object, according to its specific characteristics. In addition, MPEG-4 has mechanisms for safeguarding and managing copyright and user rights (Intellectual Property Management and Protection).

4.5.5 Other Audio Compression Methods

4.5.5.1 ATRAC

ATRAC stands for Adaptive Transform Acoustic Encoding. It was developed by the Japanese company Sony as the codec for its mini-disc media. The mini-disc is an optical or magneto-optical storage medium with a 64 mm diameter. It has about a fifth of the storage capacity of a standard audio CD. Despite the low storage capacity, it is intended to provide a CD sound quality – with a playing time of 74 minutes, which requires a data reduction of 5 : 1. Just as MPEG, ATRAC is based on a psychoacoustic model used for data reduction. The masking effects of frequency components with low amplitude are exploited by time-dependent, high-amplitude adjacent components An ATRAC data packet is comprised of 512 individual samples. The audio signal is first sub-divided into three individual sub-bands. Each of these is than divided once more via a MDCT: 0–5,5 kHz (128 MDCT), 5,5–11 kHz (128 MDCT) and 11–22 Hz (256 MDCT). ATRAC operates in two different modes, either with one long data block (11,6 ms) or three short data blocks (2,9 ms + 2,9 ms + 1,45 ms). The resulting coefficients are quantized by word length and provided with a scaling factor.
ATRAC supports uninterrupted playback (gapless playback), i.e., the playing of music tracks that merge seamlessly into each other. The decoding effort for ATRAC is relatively low. As a result, longer running times can be achieved on portable playback devices, in contrast to MP3. Unlike MPEG, artifacts creep into ATRAC through cascading, i.e., multiple encoding and decoding. The procedure was nevertheless widely used until 2007.

The various MPEG audio standards

MPEG-1 (1992)

Single channel (mono) and two-channel (stereo) coding of audio signals at sampling rates of 32, 44.1 and 48 kHz and bit rates of 32 kbps to 448 kbps.

Layer 1 was designed for digital compact cassettes (DCC) but did not find wide application.

Layer 2 used by radio because, in spite of the high bit rate, a high quality audio coding can be achieved at low cost. It plays an especially important role in live transmissions.

Layer 3, also known as **MP3**, supplies better audio quality with a low bit rate and is therefore especially interesting for use in live transmissions via the Internet with its (at that time) often quite low bandwidths.

MPEG-2 (1994)

Double-sided compatible extension of MPEG-1 for coding up to five audio channels and one low frequency channel. With the additional support of sampling rates of 16, 22.5 and 24 kHz at bit rates of 8 to 384 kbps.

MPEG-2 AAC

Supports an expanded number of sampling rates (from 8 kHz to 96 kHz) and up to 48 audio channels, including 15 additional low frequency channels and 15 embedded data streams. ACC works with variable bit rates beginning with 8 kbps for speech transmission in mono quality, with more quality than 320 kbps for high-quality multichannel transmission.

MPEG 2.5 (non-standard!)

ISO-based extension of the MPEG-2 standard by the Fraunhofer Institute for Integrated Circuits in Erlangen, which increases low bit rate performance, with the additional support of bit rates 8, 11.025 and 24 kHz.

MPEG-4 (1998/1999)

General coding standard for common multimedia data. Supports coding and composition of natural and synthetic audio signals with a variety of different bit rates. **MPEG-4 version 2** builds on existing MPEG standards, extending them for digital television, interactive graphics and multimedia applications.

MPEG-4 Audio Lossless Coding (2005)

Extension of MPEG-4 standard to a lossless audio encoding version. MPEG-4 ALS supports 32 bit sampling values up to 2^{16} channels, flexible packet rates and streaming.

Fig. 4.41 The various MPEG audio standards.

4.5.5.2 Dolby AC-1, AC-2 and AC-3

The audio compression method from the U.S. company Dolby is designated AC (Audio Code), and numbered according to its level of development. **Dolby AC-1** was developed for satellite links in the field of television and UKW radio. Based on a simple psychoacoustic model, a qualitatively high-value audio signal compression with a 3 : 1 ratio was achieved. The original signal is split up into numerous, overlapping sub-bands on which an MDCT is carried out. Finally, another re-division into sub-bands takes place. Depending on the importance of the sub-band (in relation to human hearing and the proportion of the sub-band containing the total properties of the signal to be coded) it can contain between one (non-significant sub-band) and 15 coefficients (significant sub-bands). Sub-bands with a lower frequency are assigned more pre-allocated bits than sub-bands with a higher frequency. The extra bits necessary for encoding are assigned dynamically. With a sampling rate of 48 kHz, the number of sub-bands is 40 (43 sub-bands at 32 kHz). **Dolby AC-2** is used in PC sound cards and professional audio equipment. It ensures very high audio quality with a data rate of 256 kbps. With a 48 kHz sampling rate, the typical compression rate is 6.1 : 1 (5.4 : 1 at 32 kHz). In addition, Dolby uses a technique called **Time Domain Aliasing Cancellation** (TDAC), a proprietary in-house development targeted at preventing aliasing effects.

The most powerful compression standard developed by Dolby is **Dolby AC-3**. It is suitable for the compression of multi-channel audio streams. Dolby AC-3 was developed as a sound standard for the home theater and can encode up to 6 (5.1) channels, i.e., 5 channels are encoded in full frequency range from 3 Hz up to 20 kHz (left, middle, right and 2 ambient channels). An extra low frequency channel (3 Hz to 120 Hz) is available for effects. Similar to MP3, AC-3 uses masking effects to remove irrelevant information from the input audio signal before compression. Thereby, the input signal can have a sampling frequency of 32, 44.1 or 48 kHz and and a sampling depth of up to 24 bits. Dolby AC-3 is widely used in the cinema, with its very high audio quality at a bit rate of 640 bps, as well as on DVDs, with a bit rate of 384 kbp. A further development of the AC-3 compression process is **Dolby Digital Plus**. It was developed especially for use in HDTV, HD DVDs and Blu-ray discs. Dolby Digital Plus supports data rates of up to 6 Mbps with 14 channels, a 24 bit sampling depth and a sampling rate of up to 96 kHz.

4.5.6 Streaming Techniques

Streaming describes a data transmission method in which reproduction of the transmitted data is already possible during the transmission itself. This means, e.g., that it is already possible to play MP3 files during download. Fast forward, rewind and quality adjustment of the available bandwidth are only possible with the client/server technology from RealAudio. The technology used is called **bandwidth negotiation** : client and server exchange data constantly at the current data transmission rate so that in the case of prolonged low transmission rates it is possible to switch to a file for which the momentary connection quality is sufficient.

- **MPEG-4 TwinVQ**
  This data format, originally the Vector Quantization Format (VQF) of the companies NTT and Yamaha companies, found its way into the MPEG-4 multimedia standard. From a technical point of view it is a method involving a transformation-based encoding of audio data, just as the other procedures. In vector quantization, a complete set (vector) of spectral coefficients or sub-band samples are subjected to a single step of quantization. The vector quantization selects a data set closest to the data set to be quantized from a limited number of predefined vectors. Quantization and irrelevance reduction thus take place simultaneously in one step. In each case only the index of the selected vector is stored which ensures a higher compression. According to the manufacturer details, VQF should be able to reach a bit rate of 96 kbps – already the quality of MP3 at 128kbps. However, in listening tests it has been demonstrated that in VQF the stereo image of the original data suffers and loses clarity. Special transient signal components, e.g., strokes, are clearly washed out. On the other hand, VQF always guarantees a high bandwidth (frequency range) of the reproduced signal.

- **mp3PrO**
  Strictly speaking, mp3PrO is not an independent data format, but rather a combination of MP3 and a technology from the company Coding Technologies called "Spectral Band Replication" (SBR). The resulting development was a special MP3 codec for low bit rates, intended for deployment in the WWW and in portable playback devices. Regular MP3 encoded audio files at a bit rate of 64 kbps, have only a limited frequency spectrum (up to approx. 10,000 Hz). They generate a subjectively duller sound compared to the original. SBR supplements MP3 with additional information during encoding from which the decoder subsequently reconstructs the missing high frequency components. Although not identical to the original, they sound similar and thus lead to the desired effect.

- **Ogg Vorbis**
  Because the MP3 format is patented, the Open Source MP3 Encoder has found itself swimming in a legal gray zone. Because of this situation, the company Xiphophorous Foundation developed within the framework of the Ogg project as carrier, the license and patent-free multimedia format of Vobis audio compression. Like MP3, Ogg Vorbis is based on a transformation encoding that was optimized for transmission at variable bit rates. Due to the free availability of the technology for Ogg Vobis, codecs for it exist on numerous hardware platforms and operating systems. In subjective listening tests, Ogg Vobis averaged clearly better at low bit rates than its chief competitor MP3. Ogg Vorbis supports up to 255 channels with variable bit rates.

Fig. 4.42 Further audio compression methods (part 1).

4.6 Video and Animation – Data Formats and Compression

Based on the previously discussed coding variations for image and audio information, the coding of moving image sequences with synchronous sound presents the biggest challenge from a technical point of view. It is obvious that the bandwidth necessary for transmitting video sequences must be greater than that for audio signals or static images. It was not so long ago that the transmission of video sequences via the Internet was unimaginable. However, today with the advent and widespread use of ISDN, DSL and other

- **Windows Media (WMA/ASF)**
  Microsoft's own development: WMA/ASF uses, just as MP3, a hybrid filter bank, and is designed for transmission at low bit rates. ASF (Advanced Streaming Format) serves as a data container for streaming applications – an area where Microsoft competes with RealAudio and Quicktime. In version WMA9, the Microsofts codec has the ability to encode surround sound (7 regular and one low frequency channel). While CD quality is promised even at very low bit rates (<64 kbps), in subjective listening tests, WMA normally receives only an average rating.

- **MPEGplus (MP+ / MPC / Musepack)**
  MPEGplus (today Musepack) works as a pure sub-band encoder, i.e., it is based on MPEG-1 layers 1 und 2. However, in contrast, there is an improved psychoacoustic model and a more efficient, lossless coding of the quantized and scaled bit stream used. For each quantization, the MPEGplus encoder can draw on two so-called Huffman code dictionaries and chose the more favorable one. These code dictionaries take into account different distribution functions in order to respond more effectively to different types of signals and statistics. Just as Ogg Vorbis, MPEGplus uses variable bit rates to ensure constant quality with the smallest possible file size in each case. MPEGplus supports sampling depths from 1 bit up to 32 bits and sampling rates between 32 kHz and 48 kHz.

Fig. 4.43 Further audio compression methods (part 2).

broadband technologies the necessary bandwidth can be supplied. The rapidly expanding video offering in the WWW is proof of this. Just as with an audio signal, the transmission of video sequences must be largely synchronous (i.e., without time delay) and carried out with a guaranteed bandwidth. If this does not happen, disturbances and data loss occur that effect the desired picture quality in a significant and long-lasting way. Even greater care must be taken in the encoding and transmission of audio signals. Hearing is much more sensitive to interference and transmission errors than vision. In principle, there is not a significant difference between sequential image compression and single image compression. A sequence is – after all – no more then a succession of separate images. The same problems must therefore be dealt with. Besides the occurrence of local redundancies in an image, there is also the possibility of temporal redundancies between images in a sequence. This makes new compression methods necessary. In the following, we will first look at the digitalization of video signals. Subsequently, we will examine their compression and the corresponding methods and file formats used.

4.6.1 Digital Video Coding

In conventional television, a video signal is displayed using a cathode ray tube – or in the modern versions – via LCD or plasma display. The phenomenon of the human eye called **retinal inertia,** and its associated sensory apparatus, is used to an advantage here. An image sensed via the eye's retina is captured for about 1/16 of a second on the retina before it disappears. Film and video exploit this effect. A series of individual images are shown quickly in succession to create the impression of continuous movement of the image sequence (see Fig. 4.44). In a video sequence every single image is formed line by line. The effect of retinal inertia is also used in connection with the echo or afterglow properties of the cathode ray tube where the image is displayed. In spite of conveying the impression of a continuously moving image, classic output devices (screens, projectors, etc.) can only give a limited illusion of natural motion (immersion). The lack of acceleration perception created when the observer moves and the environment passes by at the same time can sometimes result in motion sickness (simulator sickness). In addition, accommodation and vergence (see Fig. 4.44), i.e., movement toward the observer, or away from the observer, do not lead to an adjustment of the focal length of the eye lens or to a alignment of the eyes to each other as in real life. The represented object always remains at a constant distance on the output device, and stereoscopic output devices that allow a three-dimensional display often prove burdensome for the viewer. The use of onerous equipment (e.g., shutter glasses) is necessary in order to achieve the desired viewing effect.

The physiological upper limit of our visual perception is a maximum of 50 to 60 frames per second. Our perception is not able to resolve anything over that (physiological flicker fusion). In contrast, frame series below 25 – 30 Hz are often choppy. A flickering is perceived that leads to fatigue over a longer span of time (psychological flicker fusion). The analog television standard still customary in Western Europe, (**PAL**, Phase Alternating Line), was developed by *Walter Bruch* (1908 – 1990) in 1963. Transmission is at an image repetition rate of 25 Hz, i.e. there are respectively two mutually crossed half frames with a total resolution of 720 × 576 at a repetition rate of 50 Hz. The first field comprises the odd-numbered lines while the second field, which is captured by the camera 20 ms later, includes only the even-numbered sections (see Fig. 4.45). This procedure is known as interlacing. The American **NTSC** system transmits in the same way, except that it uses an image refresh rate of 30 Hz (see Fig. 4.46).

The frame in a video sequence is thus composed by layering – line by line. Every single line is scanned and transmitted one pixel after another. Before transmission, the video signal is broken down into its color components. The color signals recorded by the camera based on the RGB color model, are translated into the YC_rC_b color model based on the CCIR/ITU-R BT.601 recommendation Y describes the luminance components – the greyscale values – and C_rC_b the chrominance components – i.e., the amount of color (cf. Exursus 7, Color and Color systems).

Because the human eye can resolve differences in brightness better than differences in color nuances, luminance and chrominance signals are not encoded with the same resolution. Normally, the luminance signal is encoded with double the resolution of the chrominance signal and an additional distinction is often made between horizontal and the vertical resolution. This technique

Motion perception

The perception of motion is a complex function of the human sensory system. It is made up of the following three components:

1. **Retinal factors**: An object is first sensed as moving when different (adjacent) places on the retina are stimulated in succession by the same catalyst. Other physiological factors of movement perception are **foveal object tracking vergence** and **accommodation**. Foveal object tracking refers to the tendency of the eyes to always want to keep the object of attention in the area of the fovea centralis and to adjust the eyes accordingly. This is the area of the retina with the most sensory cells and the greatest visual acuity. Vergence and accommodation are important for spatial vision. Vergence describes the alignment of both eyes adjusting to objects at different distances. The distance of the object can thus be determined by the angle of the viewing directions of both eyes. Accommodation is the adjustment of the radius curvature of the eye's lens by the surrounding ciliary muscle in focusing on the perceived object .

2. **Physical sensations**: If the person moves but not the surroundings, adjacent sensory cells on the retina are also stimulated by the static objects passing by. We recognize that we are the ones moving, not the objects. The static environment is perceived as such because the other physical sensors (touch, balance, acceleration perception) are set by the brain in connection with visual perception. Subconsciously, the conclusion is drawn from different sensory impressions that it is not our environment moving but us.

3. **Experience**: On a higher level of abstraction, our experience is included in how we perceive movement Our experience teaches us that with a high degree of probability static objects (e.g., houses and trees) do not move, but with a high degree of probability we are the ones who moves. An example of the illusion of movement perception can be observed when one is at a train station seated inside a stationary train and, looking out the window, sees a train on the opposite track start to move. It is only by referring to another stationary object (e.g., the platform) that the perception of movement can be correctly interpreted again.

While the coupling of acceleration perception and the visual awareness are among the best known psychological factors of movement perception, there are other factors initiated by the brain, such as the **elimination of uniform motion**, which are largely generally unknown. If an object is dropped in a uniform motion, the observer has the impression that it falls to the ground in a straight path. Actually the path is not straight but parabolic. The culprit is foveal object tracking, which gives us the impression of uniform movement. This phenomenon made the development of the physical calculation of trajectories difficult for a long time. According to the description of medieval philosopher *Avicenna* (980 – 1037), after leaving the weapon a projectile continues to move straight ahead in the direction of firing until its initial "impetus" has been used up. When this happens, the projectile will immediately come to a standstill and fall to the ground in what seems to be a vertical line. But in fact, the projectile moves in a parabolic curve, as the Italian mathematician *Niccolo Tartaglia* (1499 – 1557) discovered in the 16th century.

Fig. 4.44 Motion perception.

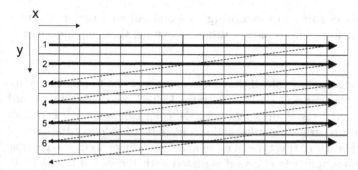

Fig. 4.45 Serialization of a video image in the interlacing procedure.

Analog Color Television Standards

PAL (Phase Alternation Line) The PAL standard was developed by Walter Bruch of the Telefunken company and patented in 1963. The PAL standard is used primarily throughout Western Europe with the exception of France. It is also used in Australia, New Zealand, China as well as the former European colonial states. A characteristic of the PAL standard is the refresh rate of 25 Hz. This corresponds to half of the normal European AC frequency of the public electricity network. The separate images are transmitted as half-fields in the interlace procedure with 50 Hz. The television image is made up of 625 lines, of these 576 lines contain image information. The result is a viewable picture size of 768 × 576 pixels with a aspect ratio of 4:3. For the transmission of image information, PAL uses a quadrature amplitude modulation (QAM, combination of phase and amplitude modulation).

SECAM (Sequential Couleur avec Memoire) The SECAM standard was developed by *Henri de France* (1911 – 1986) in 1956 and has found use primarily in France, the former French colonies and Eastern Europe. Analogous to PAL, SECAM is based on a refresh rate of 25 Hz and a field with 50 Hz transmitted in the interlace procedure. The image size, with 768 × 576 pixels, also corresponds to the PAL standard. SECAM uses a slightly different color model ($YD_B D_R$) – the two color components can each be transmitted alternately by means of frequency modulation.

NTSC (National Television Systems Committee) The NTSC color television standard was developed as the first color television standard in the U.S. in 1953. It is used primarily in North America, Japan, Taiwan as well as parts of the Caribbean and South America. The refresh rate of the NTSC standard is 9,97 Hz and thus corresponds to approximately half of the frequency of the U.S. AC network. In the NTSC interlace procedure, fields with 59,94 Hz and 525 lines per frame are transmitted and of these only 480 lines contain image information. The visible image size in NTSC, with 720 × 480 pixels, corresponds to the VGA resolution and has an aspect ratio of 4:3.

Fig. 4.46 Analog color television standard.

is also known as **chroma subsampling**. A standardized representation for the subsampling format uses integer values to express the sampling ratio:

$$Y : C_r : C_b,$$

Y represents the sampling rate of the luminance signal and C_r, C_b the sampling rate of the chrominance signal. The ratio $4 : 2 : 2$ is considered standard studio quality, i.e., if the sampling rate for the color components is each half the resolution of the grayscale value and can be reduced to 2/3 of the original size. A special feature of this type of chroma subsampling specificaton is that a horizontal subsampling is always designated with the values C_r, $C_b > 0$. If the last component is given as $C_b = 0$, this does not indicate that the color component C_b is not represented, but that both horizontal as well as vertical subsampling take place with the respectively given factors for both color channels C_r, C_b (see Fig. 4.47).

As previously noted, the active resolution of a PAL television image, according to the CCIR/ITU-R BT.601 recommendation, is 720 pixels × 576 lines at a refresh rate of 25 Hz (see Fig. 4.48). If the individual pixels are to be displayed with the color depth of 8 bits represented in the YC_rC_b color mode, the result with a 4:2:2 subsampling is an uncompressed bit rate of

$$720 \times 576 \times 25 \times 8 + 360 \times 576 \times 25 \times (8+8) = 166 \text{ Mbps}.$$

In contrast, HDTV as the current high resolution television standard, works with an increased image resolution of up to $1,920 \times 1,080$ pixels and a refresh rate of up to 60 Hz, resulting in an uncompressed bit rate at a 4:2:2 subsampling of

$$1,920 \times 1,080 \times 60 \times 8 + 960 \times 1080 \times 60 \times (8+8) = 1.99 \text{ Gbps}$$

Digital cinema even offers resolutions of up to 7,680 × 4,320 pixels at 60 Hz refresh rate (UHDV, 8K). This corresponds to 16 times the image resolution of the HDTV format, and, with nearly 33 million pixels, surpasses even the resolution of the traditional analog 35 mm film material. Based solely on the needed rates for transmitting video data, compression algorithms are indispensable for video signals. This is particularly the case when the transmission is to be sent over the Internet or with the digital broadcasting method.

4.6.2 Compression of Video Signals

Video sequences contain a great deal of redundant information. This applies for one thing to spatial redundancy in the individual frames, as previously discussed in the context of image compression. Another area is temporal redundancy. The successive frames of a video sequence differ only slightly from each other – provided that there are no extreme cuts. In this sense,

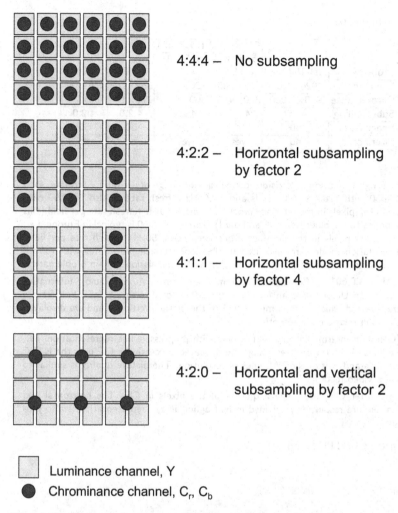

4:4:4 – No subsampling

4:2:2 – Horizontal subsampling
by factor 2

4:1:1 – Horizontal subsampling
by factor 4

4:2:0 – Horizontal and vertical
subsampling by factor 2

☐ Luminance channel, Y
● Chrominance channel, C_r, C_b

Fig. 4.47 The most important variations of chroma subsampling.

video data can be considered a three-dimensional array of pixels. The first two dimensions serve in spatial orientation and the third dimension in temporal orientation. One single image represents all the pixels at a particular point in time. Similarities found in a single image are regarded as **spatial redundancy**. Whereas, **temporal redundancy** defines similarities between several individual images. The reduction of redundancies and irrelevances in several single frames is known as interframe encoding (temporal coding) The reduction of redundancies and irrelevances in a single frame is the process of intraframe encoding (spatial coding). Additionally, the human perceptual system is subject to a variety of limitations – ranging from the optical stimulation of the sensory cells in the eye to the processing in the brain. Those

Standards for digital video

| Property | HD 1080p60 | CCIR/ITU R BT 601 | | CIF | QCIF |
		525/60 NTSC	625/50 PAL		
Luminance	1,920×1,080	720×485	720×576	352×288	176×144
Chrominance	960×1,080	360×485	360×576	176×144	88×72
Subsampling	4:2:2	4:2:2	4:2:2	4:2:0	4:2:0
Images/sec	60	60	50	30	30
Interlace	no	yes	yes	no	no

HDTV   (High Definition TeleVision) defines a wide range of digital TV formats, such as 720p50 with 1280 × 720 pixels and a 50 Hz refresh rate or also 1152i50 with 2048 × 1152 pixels in the interlace procedure with a 50 Hz refresh rate per field (this corresponds to the older HDMAC standard). Today, 1080i50 is typical in Europe, i.e., 1920 × 1080 pixels in the interlace procedure with a 50 Hz refresh rate per field. High resolution modes are also used in the non-interlace procedures with refresh rates of up to 60 Hz, but their reproduction and transmission remain problematic.

CCIR/ITU-R BT.601   (Consultative Committee for International Radio / International Television Union) uses an interlace procedure for display, i.e., two half frames are transmitted which each comprise half of the picture vertically and are displayed staggered in relation to each other.

CIF   (Common Intermediate Format) works with progressive line representation, i.e., all the lines of the transmitted image are displayed successively. CIF uses the NTSC refresh rate and half of the PAL lines of resolution. The picture quality is similar to that of a video recorder.

QCIF   (Quarter CIF) uses only a quarter of the pixels in CIF. The horizontal and vertical picture resolution is divided in half again. Image representation is also progressive.

Fig. 4.48 CCIR/ITU standards.

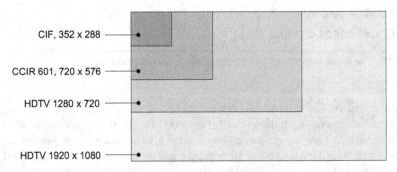

CIF, 352 x 288

CCIR 601, 720 x 576

HDTV 1280 x 720

HDTV 1920 x 1080

Fig. 4.49 Image formats in comparison.

parts of images that are unrecognizable do not have to be encoded, making it possible to further reduce the total amount of data that must be encoded. Video compression uses these factors to bring to a manageable level the huge amount of data necessary for transmitting video sequences. Fig. 4.50 provides an overview of the various types of video compression, which will be discussed here briefly.

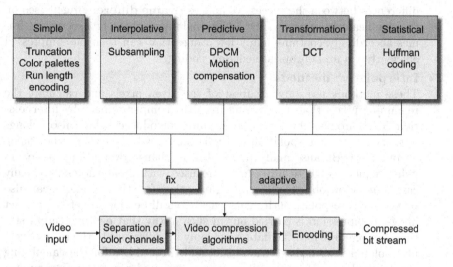

Fig. 4.50 Video compression techniques.

We will proceed from an assumed input for the compression algorithm consisting of a PCM pre-processed uncompressed bit stream in which the individual color components appear separately.

- **Simple techniques**
  The most obvious and simplest form of video compression is the reduction of image information. For example, by reducing the color depth of a given sample the amount of data can be decreased (**truncation**). Although details are lost, the procedure does not contain any complex calculation steps and can therefore be used quite efficiently in real-time processing.
  The entire 24-bit color depth is seldom fully exploited. Therefore, less color depth can be worked out with **color palettes** on which the section of the necessary real color is displayed and given as an index in the respective encoding. It is however a method requiring more complex calculation. If there are sequences containing identical color fields in one of the data streams to be transmitted, these can be compressed very simply with the help of **run length encoding**. Likewise, the refresh rate can be artificially lowered. A reduction can hardly be noticed in the case of static video scenes, however if moving objects are in the field of vision a reduction

quickly affects quality. Relevant data components then get loss because of the lower refresh rate (**relevance reduction**).

By reducing image resolution or cropping the image section, a significant data reduction can also be achieved. Also with this type of relevance reduction a loss of quality quickly becomes evident. Because in a video sequence directly successive single frames are only distinguishable from one another in a few details, it seems an obvious choice to store and encode only the differences between the successive images (**frame differencing**) based on the significant key frames. The differential image of the two successive frames accordingly contains many low values that can then be compressed efficiently via an appropriate entropy coding.

- **Interpolative methods**

  These methods use only a subset of the given pixels and calculate the remaining pixels that are missing from the complete image by interpolation. The chroma subsampling procedure, introduced below, also belongs in this category. Interpolation methods can already be used on the analog output data. Because many frames barely change over a long period in video sequences, these procedures are used with great success. In many cases only a few objects move in a frame, therefore this technique can also be used to interpolate entire cutscenes. To still be able to get the correct image, compression is carried out in such a way that e.g., instead of storing the complete intermediate frame only its difference to the respectively interpolated intermediate frame is stored. Procedures for the calculating the interpolation of intermediate frames are used especially in computer animation (keyframe animation). A further application is increasing the image quality by increasing the refresh rate through the feeding of interpolative intermediate frames. For example, to display a video sequence recorded with a low refresh rate (24 frames per second) on a HDTV output device with a high refresh rate (up to 60 frames per second) and thus to raise the picture quality.

- **Predictive Method**

  Within individual frames of a video sequence there is always a high degree of (spatial) redundancy. **Differential Pulse Code Modulation** (DPCM) is a simple way to exploit this redundancy at the pixel level. Only the difference between successive pixels is encoded in each case. As the difference between adjacent pixels is often quite small, a high reduction is possible. However, with high contrasting images this procedure doesn't have a significant effect. In this case, it is preferable to use the **adaptive DPCM** technique, which in these critical areas increases the resolution and achieves better results. Prediction methods can also be used on successive frames (temporal redundancy). Through an analysis step it is possible to determine which parts of an image already existed in the previous frame. These parts can be referenced from the previous image without having to be calculated again, even if they have changed their position within the image (**motion compensation**).

- **Transformation method**

  By way of transformation, depending on the particular application, data is brought into a favorable position for coding or compression. Crucial for compression is the **decorrelation of image information**, i.e., division into ideally unsymmetrical, image information components that can then be used in a subsequent entropy encoding. In addition, transformation must be reversible so that the original data can be reconstructed. For video and image compression, the **Discrete Cosine Transformation** (DCT) is particularly important. DCT transforms a block of pixels – usually a block of 8 × 8 pixels – into a coeffecient matrix that displays this image section in two-dimensional spatial frequency components. The first value of the matrix (DC) stands for the average value of all coeffecents, while the rest of the values (AC) represent progressively the higher horizontal and vertical frequency components of the transformed block. In practice, many of the high frequencies are near to the value zero and can thus be ignored in encoding, which facilitates compression. For decoding an inverse transformation is carried out. Because calculation of the DCT and its inverse transformation can only be approximated, due to the previously mentioned rounding, this means an information loss. Using the appropriate methods this loss can be kept to a minimum. Transformation methods can also be applied adaptively (**adaptive transformation**). The share of information to be encoded in a certain image section depends on the fineness of the displayed details. Portions of an image with little detail can be compressed to a greater extent than those with substantial detail. In this way further space is gained for storage or the transmission of more detail.

- **Statistical coding (entrophy coding)**

  Here the statistical distribution of pixel values is used to an advantage. Some values consistently appear more often than others. Thus when using codes of variable bit lengths, they can be encoded with shorter code words than those values that appear seldom. An important representative of this method is **Huffman coding**.

4.6.3 Motion Compensation and Motion Prediction

The techniques of so-called **motion compensation** and **motion prediction** are actually included in the family of the previously mentioned prediction method. Just as in other compression techniques, the inherent (temporal) redundancy present in video frame sequences is used to an advantage. Therefore it can happen that in video sequences only the foreground image moves while the background of the scene remains unchanged. Movement can generally be recognized as a change in the position of certain pixels, as recognizable in the brightness alteration of these pixels. Compression methods are thus required that are able to detect changes in brightness of an image sequence and its cause. The procedures for motion prediction can generally be divided into three groups:

- **Context-free prediction**
  A prediction is made here without any semantic information about the image contents. The prediction of the gray scale values of individual pixels is based exclusively on the neighboring relationship to other pixels, or groups of pixels.

- **Model-based prediction**
  Such methods involve certain assumptions about the visual content, for example the typical head-and-shoulder view in video telephony. The image content is modeled using a suitable grid structure and movement is defined by corresponding model parameters.

- **Object and region-based prediction**
  In this method the image is first sliced into separate sections in order to detect the objects in it. The objects are then processed separately from each other. The encoding of separate video objects is part of the MPEG-4 standard.

In typical applications of context-free prediction, the last frame handled is used to predict the next frame and then only the deviation from the actual successive frame and the predicted image is stored. If simply the last frame is used as the prediction image, then only the difference image is kept (**frame differencing**). Improved compression results can be achieved with this simple idea if it is noted that frame changes in video sequences are often only based on the movement of the imaged objects. This can then be used for prediction. If movements of individual objects, or image sections in the successive frames are detected then the object, or image section, is only coded once and the movement stored in the form of a vector (**motion vector**). If the object changes through movement, then the difference to the output object is also encoded. Another cause of motion in a scene is due to a change in the position of the camera. Therefore, the use of a **motion model** is an obvious choice for predicting the next frame, with the aim of further reducing the required information. The technique of movement compensation is however not capable of dealing with abrupt scene changes such as image slices. Designing an efficient motion model means solving various subtasks. These involve, above all, recognizing the important image information necessary for processing. For example, the foreground and background must be separated and straight-line camera movements (**translation**) recognized as well as camera pans (**rotation**) or the use of zoom (**scaling**). The procedure for the detection of movement in the respective motion model situation generally solves these tasks. Initially, the entire image is broken down into separate image blocks. Then each of these image blocks is examined for the presence of motion. If the individual frames examined remain unchanged, there is no motion recognized. A detailed description of movement compensation implementation is given in the following sections discussing MPEG video encoding.

4.6.4 MPEG Compression: Key Problems

As previously mentioned, the MPEG group (Motion Picture Experts Group, see Fig. 4.35) began its work in 1988 on the standardization of a video and audio compression standard at a bit rate of approximately 1.2 Mbps. The application targeted the field of the video compact disc.

Crucial to the development of the MPEG compression standard was a focus on specific key problems and applications requiring a corresponding compression. The most important applications and problem areas in the development of the MPEG standard are:

- **Storage media**
  The starting point for the development of the MPEG video compression standard was to compress a video source in such a way that it could be played at the data rate of an already existing target storage medium (audio CD), which was originally intended for the storage of uncompressed audio information. When using a simple 8 bit sampling, based on the CCIR/ITU-R BT.601 standard, the uncompressed video stream has a bit rate of 210 Mbps. Accordingly, an aggressive compression with a ratio of 200:1 was necessary in order to achieve the data rate of the targeted storage medium at 1.2 Mbps. A further important requirement was the possibility for random access to the storage medium. The video stream should be accessible at any desired location with only minimal time delay.

- **Digital television (terrestrial)**
  Terrestrial television, modeled on radio broadcasting, shares the electromagnetic spectrum with a host of other applications – from conventional analog broadcasting to modern mobile communications. That part of the spectrum available for digital television is therefore extremely limited and requires the most efficient compression of the transmitted contents possible. The intended frequency range is based on the already existing analog media. It is intended to cover a bit rate of 20-40 Mbps. This is sufficient for multiple channels of compressed video and audio information. Channel-based multiplexing procedures are then used to simultaneously broadcast multiple programs via a single digital signal.

- **Digital television (cable operation)**
  Digital cable television requires a continuous, dedicated communication path between the source of the video and the end user. Despite the fact that the most modern optical fiber technology is used here, the data amount alone and the resulting load on the exchanges in the cable network necessitate the use of a powerful compression. Just as important in this regard

is the establishment of a sophisticated standard. This is necessary so that the cable network compatible technology of various manufacturers scattered throughout the geographical and logical distribution areas can be interconnected. Digital video networks often use **ADSL** (Asymmetric Digital Subscriber Line) as their data transmission technology. Via standard telephone cables (twisted pair cabling), the path to the end user at home is bridged and possible bit rates limited to widths of between 1.5 and 10 Mbps.

- **HDTV**
  High Definition Television promises a significant improvement in the detail definition of video transmission. Besides a change in the aspect ration from 4:3 to 16:9 and an increase in image resolution (up to $1,920 \times 1,080$ pixels) this new standard provides a cinema-like television experience. If HDTV is transmitted via a broadcasting operation, only the standard standard television frequencies are available. Substantial compression methods are required to enable a qualitatively high HDTV transmission in this frequency range.

- **Multimedia data transmission in the network**
  A generally accepted standard for video compression would support multimedia developers worldwide in creating multimedia applications. These would then no longer have to rely on existing storage media, such as CD ROMs or DVDs, but would be accessible via the various interconnected networks.

A further target is to enable random access to the video data, with a maximum delay of 0.5 seconds. The quality loss caused by lossy compression should be minimal. Additionally, the possibility of fast navigation within the video data streams, i.e., fast forward and rewind, should be ensured as well as a good editing quality.

4.6.5 MPEG Compression: Basic Procedure

The MPEG compression standard does not define the implementation of an encoder (or a decoder) but only the data format of the coded bit stream and how it is to be decoded. An MPEG encoder must therefore only produce a MPEG compliant bit stream that can be read by a MPEG decoder and decoded back into the original data. The MPEG encoding is dependent on the output material to be encoded, i.e., the encoder decides which compression procedures are to be used. The MPEG decoder, in turn, is controlled entirely by the data contained in the transmitted bit stream. MPEG compression is an asymmetrical encoding, i.e., the encoding effort is markedly higher than that of decoding. The pre-processing and compression of a conventional video sequence that is already in digital form and uncompressed consists of the following main processing steps (see also Fig. 4.51):

- **Conversion of the color space** from 24-bit RGB to 4:2:0-YC_rC_b. In this process a portion of the available information is lost. At the same time a first data compression is accomplished. When decoding, the missing information can be regained to a large extent from the existing data via the interpolation procedure.

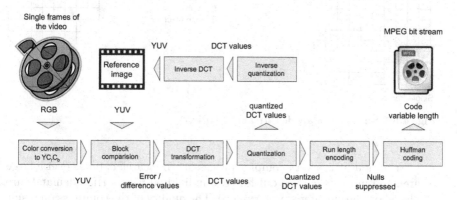

Fig. 4.51 The process of MPEG encoding.

- **Division into slices and macroblocks,** This is a key operation in MPEG compression to detect movement in a frame section. A MPEG coded video sequence is made up of a series of closed groups of pictures. To detect movement, an individual pictures is sectioned off into slices . These slices are further separated into so-called macroblocks. Slices serve in the resynchronization and refreshing of registers with prediction values. All of the necessary calculations for movement detection are based entirely on the luminance components of these macroblocks. Movement over time can be detected by variations in the brightness of adjacent image areas. Macroblocks of 16×16 pixels (396 macroblocks and 16 slices in CIF) are used for the luminance values, while for the chrominance value smaller blocks of 8×8 pixels are used. For a 4:2:0 chroma-subsampling, besides the 16×16 pixel size luminance area, a macroblock also encompasses 2 of these chrominance blocks.

- **A movement prediction algorithms** in MPEG makes it possible to track objects that move across the image. This is performed by a search for multiple blocks of pixels within a given search space Each luminance macroblock is compared to other macroblocks in its surroundings, i.e., in previous or subsequent frames. As soon as a similar macroblock is found, the location change of the respective macroblock is encoded with the help of a vector (motion vector) and stored together with any image difference

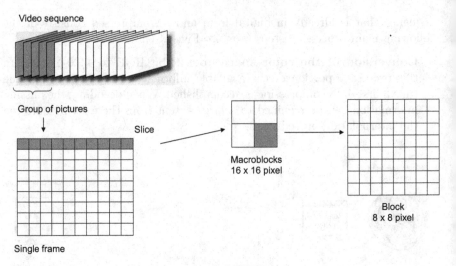

Fig. 4.52 Structure of a video stream in MPEG.

information. It is a very complex process as the search extends over a large area and must be carried out for each individual frame. High demands are placed on the encoder's performance. The quality of the compression result depends largely on the size of the search area. This is in turn determined by the capability of the encoder.

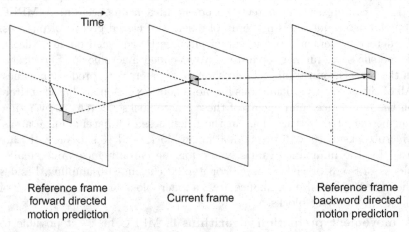

Fig. 4.53 Motion prediction with motion vectors.

- **DCT-Transformation**: Just as JPEG, MPEG uses Discrete Cosine Transformation (DCT). With its qualities corresponding to the human system of perception, it can be used well in image compression. Aided by DCT a block of pixels is transformed based on its spatial coordinates in the frequency domain. In this way, high frequency image components can be easily suppressed whose modifications are perceived less exactly by the human eye. MPEG compression distinguishes between three different types of single image variations (see Fig. 4.54):

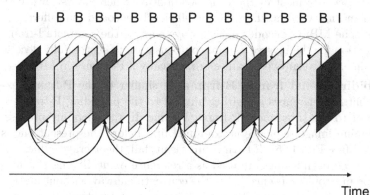

I B B B P B B B P B B B P B B B I

Time

Fig. 4.54 Types of frames in MPEG encoding.

- The **intra-frame (I-frame)** is a complete frame without additional information. For the I-frame no movement prediction algorithms are used. Each I-frame is processed individually and is normally the first image in a sequence of images (Group of Pictures), therefore representing the starting point of a transmission. The encoding of an I-frame follows the same principle as JPEG encoding. In the middle of MPEG-1 after approximately every 15 images is a new I-frame. In MPEG-1 video editing the playback of a segment cannot begin before the first I-frame of that segment. For this to be possible extensive interpolation is necessary. Video editing applications therefore often use so-called I-frame-only MPEG videos. In comparison to standard MPEG-1 videos they need considerably more storage space.

- The **predictive frame (P-frame)** uses a previous I-frame (or P-frame) as the starting point for a motion prediction. For every luminance macroblock in the previous reference image, a search is made in the local area for an image that matches as closely as possible. Motion prediction for chrominance is omitted since it can be assumed that this will also be detected in the luminance area. The MPEG standard does not specify either the spatial exactness or the area where this search should be carried out. This can be determined by the MPEG encoder itself. The larger the search area, the more agreement or similarities can be detected and the higher the compression rate is. On the other hand, an expansion of the search area and a higher search exactness also mean an increased computational complexity. Every macroblock in the P-frame is thus composed of either only a **motion vector** with the associated image difference information (see Fig. 4.55), or – when the comparison in the prediction algorithm was not successful – of a completely pixel encoded macroblock. Motion vectors encode the distance between two images in pixels. In MPEG-1 the accuracy of motion vectors is at half a pixel. Because most of the time neighboring macroblocks have very similar motion vectors, these can be efficiently encoded via differential values. The MPEG decoder must always contain the complete I-frame information for the inverse motion compensation to successfully decode a P-frame. Between two I-frames are typically 3 P-frames in MPEG-1.

- The **bidirectional frame (B-frame)** is similar to the P-frame, except that its references are either aligned to the preceding P-frame/I-frame or to the subsequent P-frame/I-frame. In the encoding process, the coming image sequence is examined first before the present one is accessed (see Fig. 4.55). If both comparisons fail, the average values obtained from both frames are used as a reference point. Should this also fail, the macroblock is encoded in the conventional way without motion prediction. To encode a B-frame, it is necessary that the encoder has numerous I-frames and P-frames in its memory. As the subsequent frames are also needed for decoding, a waiting period may arise. B-frames and P-frames are considered **interframe encoded** because additional information from other frames is needed to carry out the encoding process. There are typically approximately 2-3 B-frames between two pairs of P-frames/I-frames. The main advantage of the bi-directional B-frames is that they allow a more efficient encoding and thus a higher degree of compression. Picture quality is also improved when hidden areas in the frame are revealed through the motion of objects in the course of an image sequence. Reverse motion prediction enables more intelligent and better encoding decisions. As B-frames are not used as reference images for another motion prediction, propagated or image errors that have just occurred are not passed on. The price that must be paid for these advantages is that the image buffers must be dually outfitted on the encoding and decoding sides to be able to accommodate both backward and forward-directed reference images.

- Additionally, so-called **DC-coded picture frames (D-frame)** can be agreed on. In this case, every block of the individual image is only enco- ded by its DC coefficient, i.e., through the (0,0) value of the matrix of a frequency block. These qualitatively poor individual images are only used for special functions, such as "fast forward," and are not permis- sible as reference images for motion prediction.

Through the prediction of picture content, the memory necessary for sto- ring an image can be reduced considerably. The compression rates for B-frames are normally the largest. But at the same time, the computa-

| Previous reference frame | Target frame | Subsequent reference frame |

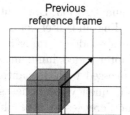 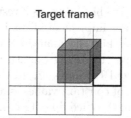 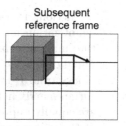

Fig. 4.55 P-frames and B-frames encode luminance macroblocks via preceding and succeeding reference images and motion vectors.

tional effort for B-frames is quite high.Tab. 4.10 provides an overview of typical MPEG-1 compression factors for the individual frame types. The compression achieved always depends on the specific picture content.

Table 4.10 Typical MPEG-1 compression factors

Frame type	Size	Compression factor
I	18 kB	7:1
P	6 kB	20:1
B	2.5 kB	50:1
average	4.8 kB	27:1

The MPEG standard allows the stored frames of a video sequence to be in any order. The display order of the individual frames must therefore not match the transmission sequence but can be sorted based on efficiency criteria. However, a complex reordering of the frames means a correspondingly large memory. MPEG allows random access to the video data so that every sequence must have its own I-frames. Additional possibilities such as e.g., fast-forward, require that an I-frame appear every 0.4 seconds or every 12 frames.

There is no fixed standard that prescribes in what order and in what number of repetitions the various frame types in the MPEG video stream must be implemented. The type of encoding and the use of the different frame types is determined by the respective user. Thus compression rates and image quality are determined based on the application.

- **Quantization**: Just as in the JPEG procedure, in MPEG highly frequented image components are suppressed via a quantization. This is done by rounding to zero the coeffecients from the DCT transformation near zero, which are at the end of the coefficient matrix. While the motion vectors for P-frames and B-frames are stored without loss, an information loss occurs in the storage of I-frames (intra-coding) and the DCT-encoded parts of the P-frames and B-frames (original pixels as well as difference image for prediction, inter-coding). This occurs as a result of quantization. Different quantization matrices are implemented for intra-coding and inter-coding the luminance blocks. While the quantization of intra-coded I-frame luminance blocks is similar to JPEG quantization, inter-coded luminance blocks from P-frames and B-frames are further processed with a quantization matrix made up of constant values, since all frequency components are equally important in the encoding of prediction differences. As a result of the motion prediction in inter-coded luminance blocks, the individual DC coefficients are no longer correlated with each other.

- **Encoding**: In a last phase, a run length encoding of the coefficient matrices is carried out. This proceeds in a diagonal zig-zag fashion passing through the lowest to the highest frequency components. It is followed by a fixed Huffman coding to generate a code of variable length. Depending on the type of image and its content, this type of encoding can have lead to a fluctuating data rate. With the help of a buffer memory at the output of the MPEG encoder, the data is collected and transmitted at a constant data rate. If there is a danger of buffer overflow, the quantization of the DCT coefficients is strengthened thereby achieving higher compression with a lower picture quality.

Since a MPEG data stream is comprised of both video and the associated audio information, the standardized MPEG data format must provide some type of multiplexing to synchronize independent, simultaneous data streams. So-called "lip synchronization" is already lost when there is a time difference of just 80 ms between the audio stream and the video stream. At this point it is noticeable to the viewer that both streams are not synchronized. Besides the simple synchronization between the video and its associated audio stream, MPEG offers the possibility of synchronizing multiple parallel video and audio streams with user-defined data streams.

To synchronize the video and audio data, every single frame has time stamp information. This enables the decoder to provide the correctly associated video sequence when decoding the audio stream and thus ensure lip synchronization. The available time stamps allow an extremely flexible decoding of the existing data streams. It even allows variable data transmission rates. If the necessary computing time for processing is not available, individual frames are simply suppressed and not displayed – without a loss of synchronization. The time stamp is implemented with a reference clock, which operates with a clock frequency of 90 kHz. With random access to the MPEG data stream, the time stamp information contained in the individual images allows an exact identification of the time point of access, which can be reproduced exactly. But since the individual frames do not necessarily exist in a temporally ordered sequence on the decoder side, sophisticated buffer management is necessary to prevent buffer overflow.

MPEG video compression sets a high importance on extreme flexibility regarding the displayed frame size, the bit rates and other key parameters.

However, a full support of the standard by way of simple, low-cost decoder implementations operating in an environment with high throughput often makes little sense and complicates the process unnecessarily. The MPEG group has thus laid out specific restrictions on the parameters to be supported in the so-called **constraint parameter set** (see Fig. 4.56).

MPEG – Constraint Parameter Set (CPS)

This standardized set of parameters must be supported by every MPEG encoder and decoder and applies to software as well as hardware implementations. Otherwise, the implementation is not considered MPEG conform. The MPEG-CPS was defined in 1992 by the MPEG group and primarily served to support a cost-effective VLSI implementation of the then state-of-the-art technology (0.8 µm CMOS).

MPEG-CPS	
Horizontal picture size	$\leq$ 720 pixels
Vertical picture size	$\leq$ 576 pixels
Number of macroblocks/frame	$\leq$ 396
Number of macroblocks/seconds	$\leq$ 396×25 or 330×30
Frames/seconds	$\leq$ 30
Bit rate	$\leq$ 1.82 Mbp/s
Decoder buffer	$\leq$ 376,832

Fig. 4.56 The MPEG Constraint Parameter Set.

4.6.6 MPEG-2 Standard

The original MPEG-1 specification of the MPEG group proved to be so successful that immediately after its release, work began on the standards that followed: MPEG-2, MPEG-3 and MPEG-4. MPEG-2 is today the most commonly used video compression standard. It is used, for example, for DVDs, digital television (Digital Video Broadcasting) via terrestrial antenna (DVB-T), satellite (DVB-S) or cable (DVB-C) or digital video.

The MPEG-1 standard was designed for a data transmission rate of approx. 1.5 Mbps for the storage of multimedia data streams for video sequences with progressive image rendering (non-interlaced) on CD-ROM. Yet at the beginning of the 90s, the MPEG group saw itself increasingly subject to pressure from the media industry. The industry urged the development of a method that would make it possible to effectively compress video sequences encoded according to the conventional television standard – i.e., with higher image resolution and interlace display. Thus the MPEG group began work on a standard for full-screen video compression that would satisfy conditions for the CCIR/ITU-R BT. 601, i.e., 720×480 pixels at 60 Hz interlaced for NTSC and 720×576 pixels at 50 Hz interlaced for PAL. The encoding of fields using the interlaced method is only conditionally suitable for MPEG-1. This is because the algorithms for motion prediction fail to work properly and as a result image components can change dramatically from one field to the next. The development of MPEG-2 should additionally support the transmission of multimedia data streams in networks. The objectives targeted were:

- improving picture quality,
- supporting conventional video formats (interlaced) and
- scalability for different image resolutions and bandwidths.

For the first time the MPEG-2 standard also provided scalable data streams to serve receivers in various performance categories. Based on processing and transmission capability, it was possible to scale down the MPEG data stream to correspond to the available performance resources. Theoretically, the MPEG-2 standard allowed the encoding of video frames up to a size of 16,383×16,383 pixels. The picture dimensions must always be integer multiples of 16 pixels.

MPEG-2 was adopted in November 1996. It was established as international standard ISO/IEC 13818 for digital television with date transmission rates of 4 to 9 Mbps. Its use extended to applications ranging from digital archiving through digital HDTV with data transmission rates of up to 80 Mbps. Nearly 640 patents exist in connection with the MPEG-2 standard. These are held by more than 20 companies and Columbia University in New York .

MPEG-2 defines a range of different **profiles**, which, depending on the application, contain a specific parameter configuration. Each individual profile is divided into a number of layers (levels). These in turn follow a specific parameter configuration (essentially target data transmission rate and image formats). It is therefore possible to implement the MPEG-2 standard for simple video conference applications as well as for high-resolution video based on the HDTV standard. Thus a variety of high-performance decoders may be used. A distinction is made between five MPEG-2 profiles (see also Table 4.11):

- **Main**: supports all main applications and is the most important of the MPEG-2 profiles, uses 4:2:0 chroma subsampling, does not allow for scaling.
- **Simple**: same as Main, only B-frames are not supported (is mainly used in software decoders).
- **SNR**: focus is on increased quality with respect to signal-to-noise behavior, chrominance resolution is scalable.
- **Spatial**: improved Main profile, pixel density is scalable.
- **High**: Stands for the highest quality level, additionally offers 4:2:2 chroma subsampling, pixel density is scalable.

In the **SNR scaled mode** the data is divided into two or more streams of varying quality at the same spatial resolution (pixel density). Similar to the progressive mode in JPEG compression, a base layer with rough information is generated as well as a final layer containing all of the refinements. According to the requirements – or the decoder's capability – it is determined whether all layers are to be decoded or only the first.

A **scaling of the pixel density** is realized by repeated subsampling of the video output data. The result of the last level of sampling is then transmitted as the basic sequence. From the reconstructed images, prediction images are generated by interpolation. The difference between the next respectively higher resolution level and the interpolation result is also encoded. It is transmitted along with the basic sequence in the multiplex procedure, similar to the JPEG hierarchical encoding principle. An extra **time scaling** can also be carried out through the primary encoding of a sequence with a reduced frame rate. Missing pictures are then simply interpolated and the prediction error additionally encoded. Decoders with a low performance ability can evaluate the primary data stream in real-time, while high-performance decoders are able to evaluate the transmitted data for a refinement of the displayed sequence. Furthermore, MPEG-2 is capable of separating the data into important (header, motion vectors, and low frequented DCT coefficients) and less important portions. This serves to improve the picture quality with respect to errors that occur primarily on the transmission path. Four layers are distinguished within the MPEG-2 profile. Essentially, they differ in terms of their target bit rates and potential image formats:

- **Low**
  Comparable to the MPEG-1 standard, the Low layer supports the CIF Format mit 352×240 pixels at 30 images per second (frames per second, **fps**) (352×288 at 25 images per second for PAL) for bit rates of up to 4 Mbps. Applications at the Low level mainly target the general consumer market and qualitatively correspond to the standard video recorder.

- **Main**
  The CCIR/ITU-R BT. 601 standard picture formats are supported in the Main layer, , i.e., up to 720×480 pixels at a refresh rate of 30 fps. Bit rates of up to 15 Mbps can be reached. Applications on the Main level are intended for the high-quality consumer market.

- **High1440**
  As its name indicates, the High1440 layer supports frame formats up to 1,440×1,152 pixels at a refresh rate of 30 fps per frame – four times the image size of the CCIR/ITU-R BT. 601 standard. Bit rates of up to 60 Mbps can be reached. The High1440 level targets the high-resolution television consumer market.

- **High**
  In the High layer, picture formats of up to 1,920×1,080 pixels at 60 fps are supported. Besides the usual ratio of 4:3 in the layers: Low, Main and High

1440, the aspect ratio of 16:9, usual in the HDTV area, is also possible. In this area the bit rates reach up to 80 Mbps. Just as the High1440 layer, the High layer also focuses on the HDTV consumer market.

Table 4.11 MPEG-2 supported profiles and layers

	Simple	Main	SNR	Spatial	High
High	-	1,920×1,152, 60 fps	-	-	1,920×1152, 60 fps 960×576 30 fps
High1440	-	1,440×1,152, 60 fps	-	1,440×1,152, 60 fps 720×576, 30 fps	1,440×1,152, 60 fps 720×576, 30 fps
Main	720×576, 30 fps	720×576, 30 fps	720×576, 30 fps	-	720×576, 30 fps 352×288, 30 fps
Low	-	352×288, 30 fps	352×288, 30 fps	-	-

The MPEG-2 standard requires backward compatibility with MPEG-1, i.e., a MPEG-2 decoder must be capable of correctly decoding MPEG-1 encoded video data. An improved picture quality in comparison to MPEG-1 is achieved through various improvements targeting procedures in MPEG-1 dealing with motion prediction and motion compensation as well as the focused support of interlaced frames that were recorded for interlaced scanning. For example, the motion vectors are always calculated at exactly a half pixel and the encoding of the DC coefficient, following the DCT transformation of an image block, can be selected with up to 11 bits, as compared with the prescribed 8 bits of MPEG-1. Optionally, with MPEG2 there is also a non-linear quantization of the macro blocks possible to achieve an improved dynamic adjustment of the quantization step. Furthermore, in MPEG-2 in addition to 4:2:0 chrominance subsampling, also 4:2:2 and 4:4:4 are possible, whereby the 4:2:0 chrominance value is determined in a different way than in the MPEG-1 procedure. With images recorded in the interlaced method, the special problem is the time offset occurring between the two fields that comprise the complete frame. If both fields are combined into one frame without special precautions being taken, this leads to a comb effect visible on the edges of moving objects. A reduced vertical correlation of the adjacent pixels is the result and accordingly worse compression results. New frame types were therefore introduced in MPEG-2 as well as an alternate sequence of zig-zag encoding of the pixels in a block (see Fig. 4.57).

Horizontal frequencies   Horizontal frequencies

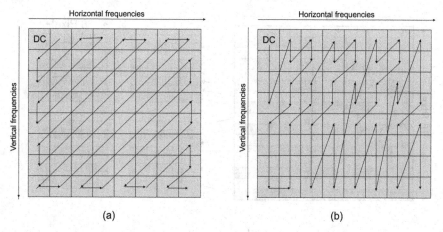

(a)   (b)

Fig. 4.57 MPEG-2: conventional zig-zag encoding (a) and alternative zig-zag encoding (b), to allow better compression for frames in the interlaced scanning procedure.

An I-frame can be a one field frame, consisting of two associated half I-frames or a half field I-frame and a half field P-frame. P-frames and B-frames can compose one full frame or be a mixed pair consisting of a connected half image P-frame and a half image B-frame. Because of this greater possibility of frame types, there is more variety for the motion prediction of macro blocks. Individual macro blocks can be processed either in complete frames using the MPEG-1 progressive method and/or with an interweaving of the individual scan lines (see Fig. 4.58). The preferred variation depends on the respective, achievable compression quality.

Excursus 12: MPEG – Data Format

Syntactic layering in the MPEG data format

The MPEG video stream is structured hierarchically on six different levels. Each of these layers has already been touched on briefly (see also Fig. 4.59). Each level of the hierarchy supports a particular, signal processing- specific (DCT or motion prediction) or logical functionality (resynchronization, random access, etc.). A start code (SC) indicates the layer below. These 32-bit start codes are not encoded or compressed further and are chosen in such a way that they cannot result randomly.

- **Sequence layer**
  The sequence layer defines the context level in the static parameters for the video sequence to be coded, e.g., image size, frame rate or expected buffer size. This layer is responsible for data buffering and is represented by a sequence header. This header contains the static parameters. A sequence code ends a MPEG sequence. The sequence header can be repeated any number of times before a sequence code is generated. While the quantization matrix details can be changed every time, all other data must remain unchanged. This is necessary so that the resynchronization of a decoder is possible in a running MPEG sequence.

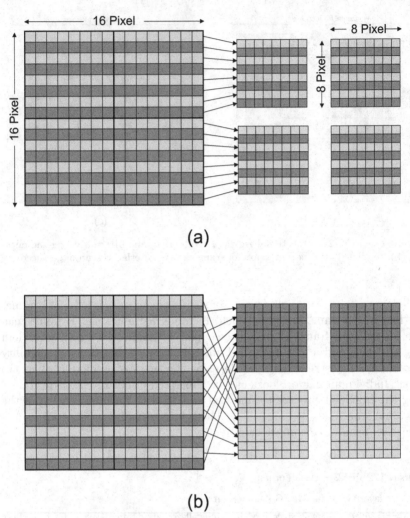

(a)

(b)

Fig. 4.58 MPEG-2: desegmentation of a macroblock with conventional progressive processing (a) and interlaced processing of interwoven fields (b).

- **Group of Pictures (GoP) layer**
  A coherent set of images is defined in the transmission sequence that is necessary for random access to the video sequence, i.e., it must be possible to decode a GoP by itself without information from other GoPs. The first frame in the transmission order of a GoPs must always be an I-frame. The accompanying header section of the data definition contains information as to whether the GoP is opened or closed, whether it is separated from the previous GoP as well as time stamp information relevant to synchronization. Before the actual GoP information, there are video parameters (VidPar), such as image width, image height, pixel aspect ratio and frame rate. This is followed by bit stream parameters (StrPar), e.g., data rate, buffer size, minimum requirements, and then the quantization tables (QT) for intraframes and interframes.

- **Picture layer**

  The position of an image within the GoP is described in the Picture layer. A single image can be defined as an I-frame, P-frame or B-frame. The picture information precedes the picture layer of standardized SMPTE[4] Timecode (TCode) and GoP parameters (GoPPar).

- **Slice layer**

  A slice defines a subunit in a single frame. In case of a transmission error, it is used for resynchronization. A slice consists of a sequence of macro blocks of variable lengths, preceded by a unique resynchronization pattern. The slice information comes before the information about the present frame type (I-frame, P-frame or B-frame) (type). In addition there follows optionally the range of motion vectors used (encode) and information about the minimum capacity of the decoding buffer.

- **Macroblock layer**

  A macroblock defines a unit for motion prediction and motion compensation. It consists of a 16×16 pixel-large area. This is made up, in each case, of 16×16 pixels in the luminance area as well as the two 8×8 pixel areas of both chrominance components. The macroblock information is preceded by the associated start lines (VPos) and, optionally, the steps to be used in the quantization table (QScale).

- **Block layer**

  A block defines the input unit for picture transformation (DCT), which is made up of 8×8 pixels. The block information precedes an address increment (AddrIn), a type specification (Type), scaling specifications for the quantization table (QScale) and information about which blocks are available (CBP). The six individual blocks (4 x luminance block, 2 x chrominance block) are encoded in the fields b0 to b5.

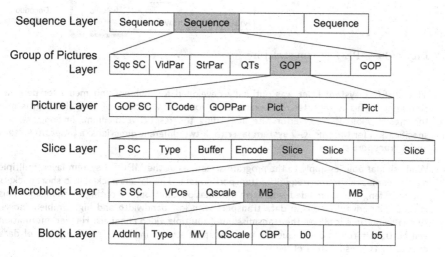

Fig. 4.59 Layers of a MPEG video stream.

---

[4] The SMPTE time code was introduced by the Society of Motion Picture and Television Engineers to the areas of television, radio and studio for the purpose of synchronizing video and audio technologies.

MPEG data streams

The MPEG video syntax works bit-oriented. This means that only a few symbols (for example the start symbols of the different levels) must be oriented on byte boundaries. This ensures an effective use of the available transport resources. In addition, whenever possible the other parameters are displayed with variable code lengths according to the frequency of their occurrence. The MPEG specification provides for the transport of different multimedia data streams in conjunction with the appropriate multiplex and synchronization procedures. The MPEG standards defines how audio and video data is compressed (**compression layer**) and the resulting data streams packed. The so-called **system layer** determines the syntax for the timing and the synchronization of the individual components. Wrapping around the compression layer, it enables shared storage of audio and video data in one single data stream (see Fig. 4.60).

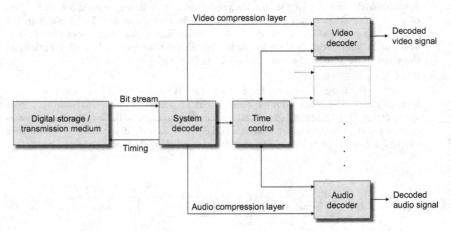

Fig. 4.60 MPEG system structure.

The MPEG-1 **system layer** was optimally developed for memory and media for personal computers. This is reflected, for example, in long data packets of variable lengths and the presumption of a low error rate in reading the respective medium. In contrast, the specification for the MPEG-2 **system layer** took two different directions: a **program stream** and a **transport stream**.

While similar policies apply to the program stream as at the MPEG-1 system layer, multiple data streams are summarized in the transport stream. The data is packed into short packets of a fixed length and provided with extra information and troubleshooting mechanisms. This is especially advantageous in data transport with low bandwidth and high ambient noise. At the same time it allows the transmission of multiple video channels. Header information will be transmitted more frequently in a transport stream in the event of any loss of data caused by the resumption of flow.

Generally, a MPEG data stream (here **MPEG-1 system stream** or **MPEG-2 program stream**) consists of a series of packet blocks (**packs**). Every packet block is, in turn, itself comprised of packets, one from each of the elementary data streams (video, audio or data). The packet block header contains reference information for the system clock — so that resynchronization can take place in case of an error — and other various parameters, some of which are optional. Occasionally so-called system headers are also included in a packet block. These contain the necessary information to configure the decoder for playback of the

MPEG data stream, or to determine whether the implemented decoder is even appropriate for reproduction of the current MPEG stream. This information includes specifications
about the number and type of media streams involved, about the relationship of the system, video and audio clocks to each other, as well as the required size of buffer storage
(see Fig. 4.61).

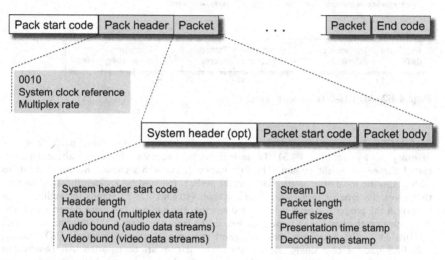

Fig. 4.61 MPEG-1 data stream.

So-called system headers are sometimes included in a packet block. They contain information needed by the decoder to configure reproduction of the MPEG data stream or to
determine if the decoder being used is even suitable for the present MPEG stream. This
information includes the number and type of participating media streams, details about the
relationship between the system, video and audio timer, as well as the necessary size of
buffer storage (see Fig. 4.61).

In contrast, a **MPEG-2 transport stream** consists of packets of a fixed length, each one
188 bytes. The packet header starts with a **synchronization byte**. It always contains the
hexadecimal value 0x47. Because this value can also resurface in the actual payload, packet
boundaries are identified by decoders through multiple checks as to whether this value of
188 bytes is found later in the data stream. After that, a reserved bit follows as an indicator
of possible transport errors (**transport error indicator**) that have occurred during transmission. Then comes a **payload unit start indicator**. It shows that there is corresponding
user data in the payload of this data packet. Another single bit controls **transport priority**,
followed by a packet ID (**PID**). This is a 13-bit address indicating which elementary data
stream is being transported in the data packet. Then comes a **payload unit start indicator**,
showing that the respective user data is in the data transport field (payload). Then comes a
field for transport security – **transport scrambling control**. This field is intended to ensure
an error-free data transport, without a specific security protocol defined by the standard.
The following 184 bytes of the data packet can sometimes also contain a so-called **adaption
field**. This serves as a reference for synchronization with the system clock. This field may
also contain information about possible gaps in the MPEG data stream, the distribution of
MPEG data streams, private user data or padding data (see Fig. 4.62).

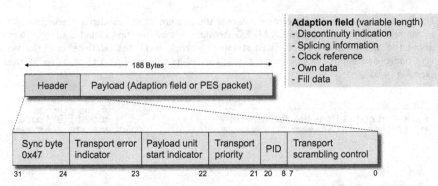

Fig. 4.62 MPEG-2 transport stream.

Both MPEG-2 streams can contain a common sub-element, the so-called **packetized ele-mentary stream packets PES**). These PES packets contain information about an asso-ciated elementary media stream. The PES packet starts with a packets header that begins with a specific fixed start prefix (**start code prefix**), followed by an identification number that gives the type of elementary media stream (**stream ID**, 32 stands for audio, 16 for video). In the program stream it is decided whether the audio or the video decoder contains the packet on the basis of this specification. In the transport stream this information is red-undant. This is because from those transport stream packets with a certain PID number, only PES packets of a single, elementary media stream are transported. Afterwards, the packet length and several optional fields follow. Their most important component is the **presentation time stamp** (PTS). The time stamp information, which only appears in the packet in case a new video frame or audio frame starts, and the **decode time stamp** (DTS) (see Fig. 4.63).

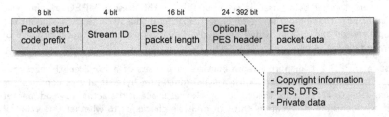

Fig. 4.63 MPEG-2 Packetized Elementary Stream Packets.

The MPEG-2 standard defines a number of tables, which control an association of specific audio and video streams in so-called **programs**. A typical program consists of a video stream, one or more audio streams (e.g., for multilingual transmissions) and, optionally, also several data streams (e.g., for subtitles). Within a transport stream the **program association table** (PAT) always has the PID 0. For each program in the stream it contains the position from the associated **program map table**. This defines the elementary media streams associated with the program. Via PID 0, a special table is defined within the PAT via a wild card program. This is the **network information table**. Besides receiving global information pertaining to the transport stream, it may also receive information about other streams available over the same network.

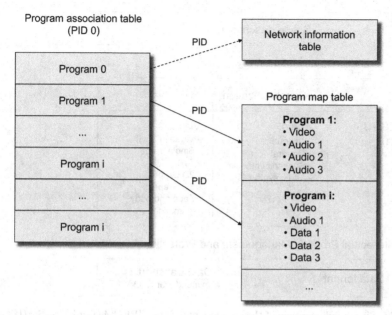

Fig. 4.64 MPEG-2 Program Association Table.

Further reading

Watkinson, J.: MPEG Handbook. Butterworth-Heinemann, Newton, MA, USA (2001)

Mitchell, J. L., Pennebaker, W. B., Fogg, C. E., Legall, D. J. (eds.): MPEG Video Compression Standard. Chapman & Hall, Ltd., London, UK (1996)

Le Gall, D.: MPEG: a video compression standard for multimedia applications. Commun. ACM 34(4), 46-58 (1991)

The **MPEG-3** standard was designed for compression in the area of high-resolution television standards (HDTV) and thus for higher bit rates. However, because support for HDTV was already integrated in MPEG-2, the planned MPEG-3 standard was dropped.

4.6.7 MPEG-4 Standard

The original concept behind the MPEG-4 standard was focused on the transmission of multimedia data streams – particularly videos – at extremely low data transmission rates ($\leq$ 64 kbps), such as in mobile networks. But already during work on its development, the application was extended to general video and audio data. MPEG-4 accomplishes much more than just the compression of multimedia objects. MPEG-4 defines an object model in such a

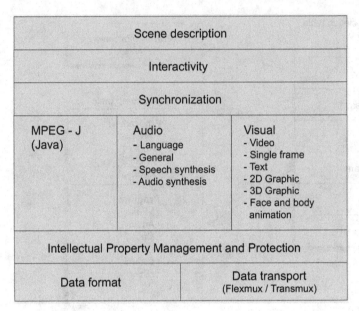

Scene description		
Interactivity		
Synchronization		
MPEG - J (Java)	Audio - Language - General - Speech synthesis - Audio synthesis	Visual - Video - Single frame - Text - 2D Graphic - 3D Graphic - Face and body animation
Intellectual Property Management and Protection		
Data format	Data transport (Flexmux / Transmux)	

Fig. 4.65 Simplified overview of the components of the MPEG-4 standards ISO/IEC 14496.

way as to allow the user to interact with the objects in a displayed scene within the limitations set by the author. In 1998, MPEG-4 was proposed for the first time and later released as the standard ISO/IEC 14496. In certain areas its development has still not been finalized. Presently MPEG-4 is mostly used in the field of media streaming on the Internet and as the data format for video podcasts. Fig. 4.65 shows a simplified overview of the components of the MPEG-4 standards. The core parts are: the system description (Part 1), the visual components (Part 2 including, MPEG-4 AVC, Part 10) and the audio components (Part 3). Delivery multimedia integration framework (DMIF, Part 6) defines an interface between the applications and the network or memory.

Other parts of the MPEG-4 standard include:

- Part 4: Conformance, description of how MPEG-4 applications can be tested
- Part 5: Reference software including reference implementations, which may be used for implementation
- Part 7: Optimized reference software
- Part 8: Transport, defines how MPEG-4 data streams can be sent via IP
- Part 9: Reference hardware
- Part 11: Scene description (BIFS) and application engine (MPEG-J)
- Part 12: ISO base media file format (data format)
- Part 13: Intellectual Property Management and Protection (IMAP)

- Part 14: MPEG-4 file format, container data format for MPEG-4 data, based on Part 12
- Part 15: AVC file format, container data format for MPEG-4 AVC data, based on Part 12
- Part 16: Animation Framework Extension (AFX)
- Part 17: Timed Text subtitle format (subtitles)
- Part 18: Font compression and streaming for OpenType fonts
- Part 19: Synthesized texture stream
- Part 20: Lightweight Scene Representation (LASeR)
- Part 21: MPEG-J Graphics Framework Extension (GFX)
- Part 22: Open Font Format Specification (OFFS) based on OpenType
- Part 23: Symbolic Music Representation (SMR)
- Part 24: Audio and systems interaction
- Part 25: 3D Graphics Compression Model

MPEG-4 breaks a scene down into its individual components – so-called **media objects**, which in turn represent individual, acoustic, visual or audiovisual content. These media objects are encoded individually but in such a way that the original scene can be reconstructed from them. Media objects can be either of a synthetic origin – such as interactive graphic applications – or of a real origin – such as in digital television. For their part, media objects can be combined to become compound media objects. It is determined via the MPEG-4 standard how the media objects are to be prepared for transmission. With the help of suitable multiplex and synchronization procedures the required quality of service can be ensured. As a rule it is however up to the respective application designers to decide what parts of the MPEG-4 standard they take over in their applications. At this time there is still no complete implementation of all the proposed possibilities in the MPEG-4 standard. Like MPEG-2, only a certain number of profiles have been established for fixed types of applications (see Tab. 4.12).

The compilation of a scene, i.e., the information about the spatial and temporal location of the individual objects, is separately encoded with the help of a dedicated description language: **Binary Format for Scenes** (BIFS) Because different media formats are used, different codecs are also necessary. The individual media objects are compressed separately and transmitted with the BIFS data stream in the multiplex procedure, to be reassembled at the receiver side in the reverse manner. BIFS is based on the Virtual Reality Modeling Language (VRML) and used to describe two and three dimensional multimedia, audiovisual interactive contents. The coding of the BIFS scene description is done as a binary data stream. Not only is it specified where and when individual objects appear in a scene, but also their behavior as influenced by potential conditions. In MPEG-4 a genuine interaction with the contents is therefore possible. In a situation where more complex, logical operations trigger certain events in the course of the MPEG-4 data stream, these can be described using the programming language Java via MPEG-J.

It was only recently that the scene description BIFS language was supplemented with the simplified lightweight scene representation (LASeR), in the context of the MPEG-4 standard. LASeR is not based on VRML but on SVG (Scalable Vector Graphics). It is restricted to two-dimensional objects and designed especially for use in resource-limited mobile end devices. To provide the designers of multimedia applications even greater scope in scene compilation and interactive applications, a special programming language was created. This is the Java-based Graphical eXtension Framework (GFX). GFX allows the generation and compilation of audiovisual objects and is especially intended for use in the field of 3D video games. The main advantage of the object-based compression in MPEG-4 is that it is no longer necessary for a compression algorithm to fully compress a complex scene made up of various figures, objects and text. In this way, it is possible to avoid compression artifacts. Once the scene is broken down, it is possible to process each component with the best-suited compression algorithm, thus achieving better results.

Breaking a scene down into its individual components allows an additional **content-based scaling** of the data stream. Depending on the available bandwidth and computing power, the less important components in a scene can be omitted if necessary.

Fig. 4.66 shows an example of the breakdown of a scene that includes various audio and video media objects. While the objects removed from the scene are subject to change in position or size, it can be assumed that the background image remains constant for a time. As all components are individually coded, they must not be retransmitted as long as they do not change.

In the example shown, a person as an object can be removed from the scene and further disassembled into an acoustic speech component and a so-called **sprite**. The sprite is in this case the cut-out video image of the person, which can be compressed separately. Similarly, the voice portion can also be compressed with a suitable voice codec. Because the sprite and language information change constantly they must be transmitted continuously. However, as the background remains static for the most part it must not be transmitted as frequently. If the audiovisual presentation in the example also contains high quality audio components, these can be compressed with a special codec. Fig. 4.67 shows the main components of a MPEG-4 terminal device. These are broken down into a demultiplexing unit, decompression, scene description and composition/rendering. The demultiplexing unit divides the MPEG4 data stream into separate elementary streams (ES). These streams can be decompressed separately and, based on the BIFS scene description, reassembled into a hierarchically structured scene with which the user can interact.

Conversely in the MPEG-4 encoder, separate elementary streams, which have the same priority and service quality requirements, can be combined into so-called FlexMux data streams. First, they are encoded, synchronized and fragmented into a series of data packets. Via multiplexing they are grouped

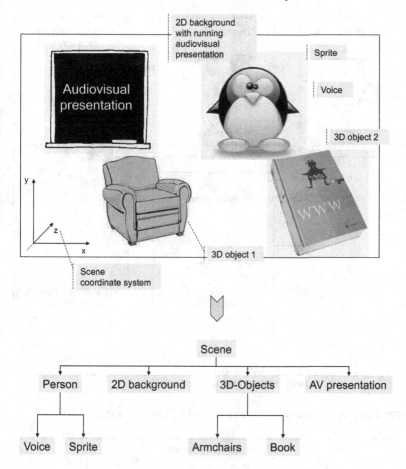

Fig. 4.66 Hierarchical scene description in MPEG-4.

into a FlexMux stream. The FlexMux streams are sent to the transport layer for data transport (Transmux) (see Fig. 4.68).

The MPEG-4 standard supports a wide range of improved video compression variations besides object-based coding. Both progressive and interlaced image representations are supported. Chromiance subsampling 4:2:0 samples the color components both horizontally and vertically with half resolution based on the luminance component. In addition to the possibilities of block encoding provided by MPEG-2 ("zig-zag encoding" and "alternate vertical"), MPEG-4 offers an "alternate horizontal" encoding sequence for the frequency components of an image block. This means a further savings potential for the subsequent run-length encoding of individual images. MPEG-4 was optimized for three different areas of the available bandwidth. These are the areas below 64 kbps, 64 – 384 kbps and 384 kbps – 4 Mbps. Higher bit rates are also supported (see Table 4.12).

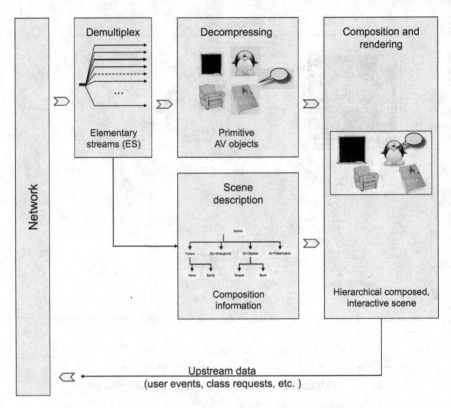

Fig. 4.67 Main components of a MPEG-4 terminal (receiver side).

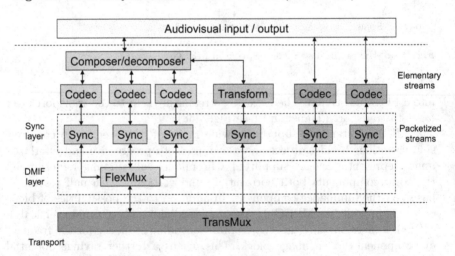

Fig. 4.68 Data flow in the MPEG4 encoder/decoder.

Especially with regard to applications in mobile communication, the error tolerance properties of MPEG-4 are crucial. For one thing, resynchronization markers are included in the transferred data stream. In case of a transmission error the transmitted data in the stream is ignored until a new resynchronization marker follows. Compared to MPEG-2, the number of compressed bits between two resynchronization markers stays relatively constant. In addition, data streams with different degrees of error sensitivity are separated from each other. For example, in MPEG-4 texture and movement compensation streams are separated. Because texture errors are not nearly as noticeable as motion errors to the viewer, the error sensitive data can be outfitted with additional, enhanced error correction mechanisms and then transmitted.

With **MPEG-4 AVC** (Advanced Video Codec, MPEG-4 Part 10) the MPEG-4 standard now contains a highly efficient video encoding component. It is identical to ITU H.264 and needs only half of the bandwidth as MPEG-2 while providing the same picture quality. HDTV satellite transmission, DSL-based video services, video transmission to mobile devices, such as DVB-H, the DVD successor HD-DVD or video game consoles use MPEG-4 AVC. If a limited processing capacity on mobile devices does not allow for use of the MPEG-4 AVC codec, it is possible to use codecs of the more elementary MPEG-4 Simple or the MPEG-4 Advanced Simple Profile (MPEG-4 SP/ASP, MPEG-4 Part 2).

To support the previously described object-based coding of video content, video objects can take any shape and outline to be assembled with other objects in a scene. The particular form of the video object can be encoded as a binary or as an 8-bit transparency mask (shape coding). A further innovation is image coding performed with the help of static **sprites** (sprite coding). For this purpose, a scene is disassembled in the forefront and background. The background is created as a large panoramic image. Every camera movement can be described against this background with the help of motion and scaling vectors (translation, rotation, scaling). In each case, a transformation of the

Table 4.12 MPEG-4 video profile and levels.

Profile and level		Typical image size	Bit rate	Max. number objects	Number maccroblocks
Simple Profile	L1	QCIF	64 kbps	4	198
	L2	CIF	128 kbps	4	792
	L3	CIF	384 kbps	4	792
Core Profile	L1	QCIF	384 kbps	4	594
	L2	CIF	2 Mbps	16	2.376
	L3	CIF	2 Mbps	16	2.376
Main Profile	L2	CIF	2 Mbps	16	2.376
	L3	CCIR 601	15 Mbps	32	9.720
	L4	1.920×1.088	38,4 Mbps	32	43.960

background is calculated that corresponds to the particular camera position. Only the moving objects in the forefront of the scene must be encoded with each camera position. The background image is only encoded one time at the beginning of the scene, or step by step as required (progressive), and transmitted (see Fig. 4.69).

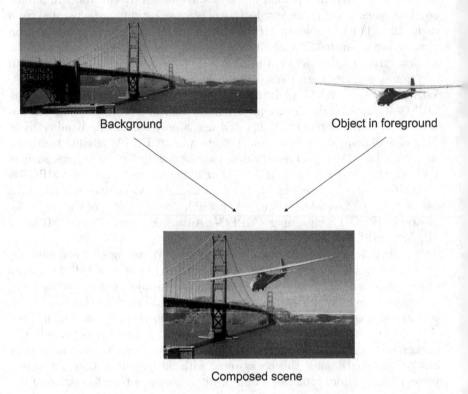

Fig. 4.69 Assembling an MPEG-4 scene from a background image and a moving foreground image.

In contrast to the standards of its predecessors MPEG-1 and MPEG-2, MPEG-4 offers different possibilities for **user interaction**. A general distinction is made between client-side and server-side interaction possibilities. With **client-side interaction**, changes in the properties of one or more media objects in an MPEG-4 scene only take place locally at the client. Attribute values of the relevant object are modified within the graph of the scene description only when the user triggers specific events with the mouse or keyboard. To what extent changes can be made to the scene is decided by the author. In **server-side interaction**, on the other hand, all changes initiated by the user must be forwarded to the server. Most importantly this requires a return channel. For example, in satellite-based digital television (DVB-S), this can be realized via the telephone. A simple example for a server-side interaction would be a change in voice playback. In contrast, more complex interaction primarily involves a change in the viewing perspective of a scene. Both video as well as audio components may be affected.

Main components of the MPEG-4 video compression standard:

Encoding visual objects

Based on MPEG-1 and MPEG-2, MPEG-4 has greater flexibility in low level video compression. It provides extra mechanisms for the assembly of existing image components as well as for the generation of new graphical components. The core of the compression algorithm in MPEG-4 targets the support of video transmission at very low bandwidths. MPEG-4 offers the following extra features which its predecessor did not:

- content-based motion compensation,
- global motion compensation with affine transformations,
- motion compensation with dynamic and static sprites,
- compression of textures,
- texture mapping on 2D and 3D wire frame models,
- compression of closed 2D wire frame models,
- compression algorithms scalable according to

  - content,
  - time,
  - spatial and
  - qualitative criteria.

Coding of audio objects

Compression procedures for very low bandwidths are particularly taken into account as well as the generation of synthetic sound and speech. Natural sound sources are supported by three different compression variations, with different degrees of bandwidth:

- parametric speech coding at a sampling rate of 8 kHz for 2 – 6 kbps,
- a linear prediction algorithm optimized for speech at a 8 kHz or 16 kHz sampling rate, for 6 – 24 kbps,
- starting from 16 kbps, MPEG-4 supports AAC compression (see MPEG-2 AAC) for high quality audio compression.

Scene description and user interaction

Tools are included for the also user-based hierarchical description of a scene and its individual elements. A global coordination system is defined at the top level of the hierarchy. Every one of the nodes in the hierarchy underneath defines its own local coordination system. Its origin within the global coordination system can change within a time frame. MPEG-4 offers the possibility of changing individual objects in a scene, adding objects or deleting them. The scene description in MPEG-4 is based on the concepts of the **Virtual Reality Modeling Language** (VRML).

Fig. 4.70 Main components of the MPEG-4 standards (Part 1).

Main components of the MPEG-4 video compression standard (Part 2):

Scene description and user interaction (2)

Based on the freedom granted to the user by a scene's author, the user has the opportunity to interact with different objects in the scene. For example, the user is able to

- change the viewer's perspective in a scene,
- move objects within a scene,
- trigger events through certain actions or
- choose a specific language in a multi-lingual service.

System-related applications

These include a number of communication protocols to control and synchronize MPEG-4 applications – which can be distributed. The tasks to solve include:

- multiplexing and demultiplexing data streams,
- buffer management and the
- synchronization of data streams.

MPEG-4 streams must additionally be equipped with extra information for the required decoder resources. Among these resources are image size, necessary buffer space and expected quality of service.

Further reading:

Koenen, R.: Overview of the MPEG-4 Standard. International Organization for Standardization, ISO/IEC JTC1/SC29/WG11 N2323, Coding of Moving Pictures and Audio, Geneva, Switzerland (2002)

Fig. 4.71 Main components of MPEG-4 standard (Part 2).

4.6.8 MPEG-7 Standard

MPEG-7[5] is an ISO standard (ISO/IEC 15938) released in 2002. Besides its focus on compression components, it follows the trend already set by MPEG-4 in placing increased emphasis on the inclusion of metadata and coding functionality. In contrast to MPEG-4, MPEG-7 offers a complete multimedia descriptive interface (Multimedia Content Description Interface). It offers data-encoded, multimedia computer-based search functions. Among the main applications of MPEG-7 are

- content-based search and search queries,
- automatically-created summaries of video and audio sequences,
- accelerated retrieval and analysis of web pages,
- personalized news services on the Internet,
- intelligent multimedia presentations and
- monitoring tasks.

---

[5] The numbering of the MPEG standard does not proceed consecutively. For more on the name assignment of the MPEG standards also see Fig.4.72.

Naming of the MPEG standard

The naming of the multimedia standard issued by the MPEG group is often a source of confusion, due to its nonconsecutive numbering (MPEG-1/-2/-4/-7/-21). In the MPEG range of standards, the originally planned MPEG-3 standard was dropped since its functionalities were already integrated in MPEG-2. The MPEG group therefore decided to refer to the standard following MPEG-4 with neither a sequence number (1,2,4,5) nor with a binary sequence (1,2,4,8), but to use the number 7. In this way it should be made clear that the the standard identified as MPEG-7 is strikingly different than the standard that came before it. In contrast to MPEG-1/-2/-4, MPEG-7 does not specify a video compression technology, but defines a metadata standard. It allows structural and content aspects of the multimedia object to be fully described. To add to the confusion surrounding the naming of individual MPEG standards, the standard that came after MPEG-7 – which was intended to form the framework for the whole multimedia infrastructure – was given the number 21. MPEG-21 specifies metadata describing the infrastructure information for the generation, production, release and trade of multimedia contents. For the standards of the supplementary MPEG group to come – which is being worked on currently – numbering is no longer used. Rather identification is carried out using consecutive letters of the alphabet (MPEG-A/-B/-C/-D/-E).

Name	Year of release	Content
MPEG-1	1993	Video and audio compression, etc. for video CD
MPEG-2	1994/1995	Video and audio compression, etc. for DVD and DVB
MPEG-4	1998 – 2001	Improved video and audio compression
MPEG-7	2002	Multimedia metadata
MPEG-21	2004/2005	Multimedia framework
MPEG-A	2004	Multimedia application format
MPEG-B	2005	MPEG systems technologies
MPEG-C	2005	MPEG video technologies
MPEG-D	2005	MPEG audio technologies
MPEG-E	2005	Multimedia middleware

Further information:

MPEG-Homepage: http://www.chiariglione.org/mpeg/

Fig. 4.72 MPEG naming.

While MPEG-1, MPEG-2 and MPEG-4 only encode audiovisual media content efficiently, the description of MPEG-7 allows media content to be located with the help of automated retrieval mechanisms. The quantity of audiovisual information offered is constantly increasing and has already reached a scale that exceeds manageability. As a result, the demand for an efficient and standardized multimedia description interface such as MPEG-7 has become that much greater. The user wants to be able to use audiovisual information in different ways. But it is necessary to search through the available information to find the desired result.

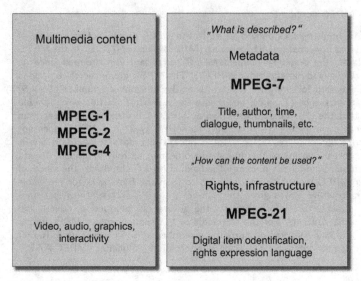

Fig. 4.73 Overview of the various MPEG standards.

The requirements in multimedia retrieval differ significantly from those in traditional text retrieval. This can be clearly seen in the following tasks to be carried out:

- **Music**: A search is initiated by playing several notes on a keyboard. The result delivers a list of music containing the melody that was played (also in different tempos or pitches).

- **Graphics**: A search is triggered by drawing lines on the screen and a set of images returned containing similar graphics, logos or ideograms.

- **Images**: Through the definition of graphic objects that contain specific color ranges or textures, examples are returned to corresponding search queries. The user can choose components from them to add to an image.

- **Motion**: Movement or associations between individual objects can be formulated based on a given set of objects. A list of animations with the required temporal and spatial relationships is issued in response to the search query.

- **Scenarios**: Actions can be described based on a given content. A search query is then formulated from these actions. The result is a list of matching scenarios where similar actions take place.

- **Voice**: A query is formulated based on a sample of a vocal performer. The result is a list of audio or video recordings containing that particular artist.

It is the job of each search engine to formulate the appropriate query from the given examples. The most important support in this context is **metadata**, i.e., data that describes the content of the multimedia data. Metadata can be produced by analytical means or manually by the author or the user (social tagging). MPEG-7 is a XML-based markup language for the description and annotation of multimedia data. The MPEG-7 standard defines a large number of **descriptors** for this purpose, which describe the various types of multimedia content. So-called **schemes (description schemes)** are implemented. They define how new descriptors are to be handled. A higher level of "understanding" by the automated processes should also be obtained with a description language (**Description Definition Language, DDL**), which defines the relationships of individual descriptors with each other.

MPEG-7 provides, for example, metadata schemes for the following tasks:

- management of the creation, production and use of content,
- description of content from a structural and semantic point of view,
- organization of content,
- user-specific data, such as user-profile and
- aspects of access to the multimedia data, e.g., different views and summaries.

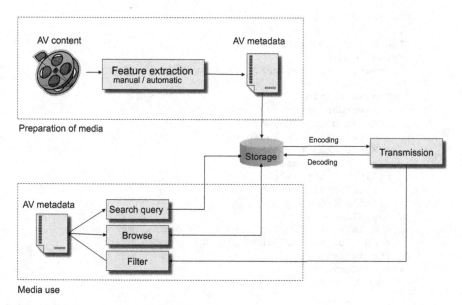

Fig. 4.74 An example of MPEG-7 architecture.

On one hand, MPEG-7 descriptors contain information about the media content, such as recording date and conditions, title, author, copyright information, coding information and classification. On the other hand they contain information that identifies the contents itself. To create a descriptor, the necessary descriptive information must be extracted from the media content.

This can be done manually or, in part, automatically. The descriptor is then stored together with the media content (see Fig. 4.74). In this way, the user is able to use the descriptor later for a search, targeted access or also as the starting point for filter functions. MPEG metadata is saved in the form of one or more XML documents. Besides the XML representation of MPEG-7- data, which is determined by several complex XML schemes, there also exists a space-optimized binary coding. Using the **Description Definition Language** (DDL), descriptors and descriptor schemes can be defined and extended. Fig. 4.75 shows an example of MPEG-7 coded metadata. The individual sections of a video data stream (`<VideoSegment>`) are assigned textual metadata at certain time points (`MediaTimePoint`), for example content-related keywords (`KeywordAnnotation`).

MPEG-7 Metadata Examples of a Video Segment

```
<Mpeg7 xmlns="...">
 <Description xsi:type="ContentEntityType">
  ...
  <MultimediaContent xsi:type="VideoType">
   <Video>
    <MediaInformation>
    ...
    <TemporalDecomposition>
     <VideoSegment>
      <CreationInformation>...</CreationInformation>
      ...
      <TextAnnotation>
       <KeywordAnnotation>
        <Keyword>cat</Keyword>
        <Keyword>mouse</Keyword>
       </KeywordAnnotation>
       <FreeTextAnnotation>
       billy the cat is catching a mouse
       </FreeTextAnnotation>
      </TextAnnotation>
      <MediaTime>
       <MediaTimePoint>T00:05:05:0F25</MediaTimePoint>
       <MediaDuration>PT00H00M31S0N25F</MediaDuration>
      </MediaTime>
     </VideoSegment>
     <VideoSegment>...</VideoSegment>
     ...
    </TemporalDecomposition>
   </Video>
  </MultimediaContent>
 </Description>
</Mpeg7>
```

Fig. 4.75 MPEG-7 metadata example of a video segment.

4.6.9 MPEG-21 Standard

MPEG-21[6] was conceived as a common platform for the standards created until that time – MPEG-1, MPEG-2, MPEG-4 and MPEG-7. Just as with MPEG-7, the core MPEG-21 standard (ISO/IEC 21000) – which is partly still being defined – is a multimedia description language. However, this goal has been expanded to summarize and describe not only the content but the complete infrastructure. In this way all of the elements involved in the process of making available and consuming multimedia contents are summarized and their use is made transparent. This includes representing the different types of media contents across heterogeneous networks and on different end devices and creating largely automatic interoperability. In order to achieve this objective it is of the utmost importance to:

- understand how the individual elements mesh and their interaction,
- determine which new standards are necessary in case there are gaps in the description of the infrastructure and
- carry out the integration of a large variety of standards.

The key elements of the new standard are the **user** and the so-called **digital item**. A digital item is understood as a well-structured digital object for which the MPEG-21 standard provides an appropriate representation, identification and extra metadata. In other words, a digital item is made up of a specific resource, associated metadata describing this resource, and structure information stating how the individual components of this resource interact with one another.

The digital item is the fundamental unit in the MPEG-21 media model. The user is defined as one who interacts with the MPEG-21 infrastructure or who uses digital items. Users can be individuals as well as entire organizations, companies or even governments. Users appear in various roles, whether it be that of the provider, the consumer, the author or the distributor. Each user has specific rights based on this role and bears responsibility in the process of interaction with other users.

Table 4.13 Frame of reference of the individual MPEG standards.

Standard	Frame of reference
MPEG-1,2,4	Coding of audiovisual content
MPEG-7	Definition of metadata for the description of multimedia content
MPEG-21	Provision of a complete framework for the conception, production, provision and marketing of multimedia content. The other MPEG standards can be used within this framework.

---

[6] The numbering of the MPEG standards is not consecutive. For more on the naming of the MPEG standard see 4.72.

MPEG-21 Architectural Elements:

- **Digital Item Declaration**: A worldwide unique and persistent identification of digital items according to the syntactic scheme of an URI, with the possibility of adding annotations to the digital items in the form of metadata based on XML (Digital Item Declaration Language, DIDL).

- **Digital Item Representation**: MPEG-21 provides the necessary technology for efficient representation of any multimedia content. This includes all relevant data types, which can be of a real or synthetic origin. It is additionally capable of scalability and error tolerance.

- **Digital Item Identification and Description**: A standardized system for the identification and description of digital items. It includes a content description that justifies all types of users, e.g., the author, the producer, the application developer and the user. Importance is placed on guaranteeing the persistence of the digital item.

- **Content Management and Usage**: This includes the design of interfaces and protocols for access to MPEG-21 digital items. Here, the search functions of agents should be supported and contents cataloged and archived. The respective user rights should be administered at the same time. In particular, copies of digital contents should be identified and the corresponding user rights managed. It should be possible for users to link their own descriptive information or comments with the specified contents.

- **Intellectual Property Management and Protection**: Intellectual property is to be protected. This is of particular importance at times when information is freely available, e.g. the MP3-file-sharing discussions on the Internet. Protected information has a special value and it should only be possible for those who have acquired the right to have it to do so. For efficient management of the corresponding access rights, the MPEG-21 standard defines its own language – the Rights Expression Language.

- **Terminals and Networks**: With the aim of minimizing the number of user interventions, e.g., in upgrades or extensions in existing installations, and provide stability for existing applications, protocol interfaces are defined that take over a large part of these management tasks.

- **Event Reporting**: Standards are set that define metrics and interfaces as well as capturing performance data and other noteworthy events. Access to this data and its evaluation are also supported.

Fig. 4.76 The seven MPEG-21 architectural elements.

In order to carry out the most efficient implementation of the MPEG-21 standard, the MPEG group works together with 25 other standardization organizations in and outside of the ISO. Their aim is to achieve the greatest possible interoperability and to avoid an overlapping of competing parallel activities.

Excursus 13: Other Video File Formats and Compression Methods

H.261, H.263 und H.264

Two video coding formats emerged from the CCIR/ITU-R BT.601 standard: H.261 and H.263. The **H.261** standard was released in 1990 and is considered the standard of video coding for practical use. H.261 serves primarily for implementation in video conferences and video telephony via the public ISDN network by means of channel bundling, i.e., multiple ISDN lines used in parallel for this purpose so that data transmission rates of integer multiples of the basic ISDN data rate of 64 kbps can be reached. It is designed for data transmission rates of 2×64 kbps for video telephony and a rate of at least 6×64 kbps for video conferences.

The compression in H.261 is based on JPEG still image compression (DCT), with an additional temporal motion prediction. For transmission, a picture sequence is subdivided into four individual layers (single frame, block group, macroblock and block), each of them is given its own header and sent in the multiplex procedure. The corresponding basis image format for H.261 is the CIF format with 352×288 pixels, and the QCIF format with 176×144 pixels, associated with a 4:2:0 or 4:1:1 color subsampling. As a data format, H.261 is less flexible, for example than MPEG, but at the same time also easier to implement. H.261 served as the starting point for the development of MPEG-1 and other video coding standards. H.261 is not suitable for use in packet-switched networks (TCP/IP) via video streaming.

The 1996 video coding standard **H.263** is especially intended for data transmission at lower transmission rates (≤ 64 kbps), where it achieves a better quality than H.261 or MPEG-1. The procedure is more efficient and flexible than the older H.261. In contrast to MPEG, additional motion compensation procedures with an exactness of a half pixel are used in compression. A more efficient mathematical coding is often possible than with Huffman coding. Instead of implementing motion compensation on macroblocks of 16×16 pixels, H.263 uses 4 blocks of 8×8 each, which can also overlap. The motion vectors can also originate from outside of the displayed image. This allows more efficient and more flexible compression. H.263 supports the image formats: CIF, QCIF, 4CIF (704x576 pixels) and 16CIF (1,408x1,152 pixels). An extension of the H.265 standard has also been proposed – **H.263+**. Besides offering further compression improvements it also allows a temporal and spatial scalability of the coded video data.

H.264 is the video compression standard that evolved from H.263. It was also adopted in the MPEG standard as MPEG-4 AVC (MPEG-4 Part 10). The aim of developing H.264 was to support video encoding of high quality – in view of the low compression rates of existing standards. The quality of motion prediction was improved in H.264 allowing up to 16 reference images (and individually weighted motion vectors), in contrast to the frame reference (P-frame) or the forward or backward directed reference images (B-frame) conventional up to that time. The block size used in the motion prediction can also vary between 16x16 and 4x4 pixels. The accuracy of motion prediction was strengthened by a quarter pixel. Therefore, in particular, spatially sharply defined and complex motion can be efficiently encoded. The coding of still images is improved by spatial prediction based on the edges of adjacent image blocks. Instead of a discrete cosine transformation (DCT) being used on 8x8 pixel-size blocks, a derived integer transformation is used on smaller 4x4 pixel blocks. It can be calculated with the help of addition, subtraction and binary shift operations. The decreased block size also reduces the occurrence of compression artifacts. A number of output profiles were additionally established, allowing for a dynamic range of up to 14 bits per channel (in contrast to the 8 bits usual today). H.264 is found today in numerous video codecs such as H.264/AVC High Profile, in the predecessor developments of the DVD-Standard, the Blue-ray Disc, the HD DVD as well as in high-definition digital television (DVB).

AVI, ASF and WMF

The video coding formation known as **Audio Video Interleave (AVI)** was developed by the

Microsoft company and, in contrast to MPEG, is a proprietary data format. The implementation of AVI is therefore limited to MS-Windows systems as a rule. Just as the audio format used by Microsoft, WAV, AVI is a special type of the Microsoft RIFF format (Resource Interchange File Format). AVI is capable of encoding video data in a lossless or lossy form. However, in its proprietary form it does not achieve the performance indicators of MPEG compression rates. AVI is used today mainly in local video editing because it allows the frame accurate synchronization of audio and video information. Images and groups of sound samples are stored in AVI segment-oriented. An AVI file may contain multiple independent, compressed and uncompressed video data. Besides information being given in a file header about length and characteristics of the video information, data is also specified for the video codec in order that the data in the AVI file can be played back correctly The successor of AVI is deemed as the file format known as the **Advanced Streaming Format** (**ASF**) from the multimedia architecture **Windows Media Technologies** (WMT). ASF is used as a kind of container. It is able to accommodate multimedia information coded in different ways, to synchronize it and to transmit it in the streaming method. There are a number of data types supported by ASF and space is provided for independent extensions, scalability and meta-information. The file format **Windows Media Format** (**WMF**) was also introduced with the WMT architecture. It does not differ from the ASF format file except for a search index at the beginning of the file.

QuickTime Movie
Quicktime Movie was developed as a video data format for the Apple operating system MacOS 6 for the Macintosh personal computer as a multimedia extension. Initially, its task was to store video, audio and text information together and synchronized in a single file. QuickTime has been developed throughout the years into a cross-platform multimedia architecture for Windows and MacOS, thanks to the numerous extensions for different media formats. These include the support of MPEG, MIDI, interactive panoramic images and films for 3D objects and streaming. QuickTime Movie does not offer an independent compression procedure but is a single data file format able to accommodate different media formats. Although in the meantime available on different computer and operating system architectures, the further development of the QuickTime standard is still in Apple's hands. QuickTime is especially well-suited to the processing and playback of MPEG-4 data. This is because not only was the ISO standard integrated in QuickTime, but also parts of QuickTime (e.g., the file format) were adopted in the MPEG-4 standard.

Flash Video
The popular Flash Video (FLV) is not an independent video compression procedure, but rather a proprietary container format developed by Adobe Systems. It is primarily used on the Internet for the transmission of video contents. At this time, the Flash Video format supports the video codecs Sorenson Spark (eine H.263-Codec Variante), On2 TrueMotion VP6 and MPEG-4/AVC (H.264) for video compression. The Adobe Flash Player is normally used for playback. In comparison to plugins for QuickTime or RealVideo, it has found widespread dissemination via a large number of hardware platforms and operating systems. Besides providing streaming via the proprietary **RTMP protocol** (Real Time Messaging Protocol), Flash Video offers the possibility of a progressive download via http. Here, the video files are stored via a standard web server in contrast to video streaming. Thus fast random access to the video contents is already possible during transmission. Control of the progressive download is carried out via the client-side scripting language ActionScript. While free use of the FLV container data format is allowed, the proprietary flash codec is patented.

RealVideo
Similar to Flash Video, RealVideo is a proprietary video data format. It was developed by the RealNetworks company in 1997. RealVideo is supported by numerous hardware platforms

and operating systems[7]. RealVideo data is stored in a **RealMedia** data container, together with the audio data format RealAudio, and disseminated throughout the Internet via RTSP streaming (Real Time Streaming Protocol), standardized by IETF. RTSP serves in connection management and control of the transport data stream. The video data itself is sent via the proprietary RDT protocol (Real Data Transport), developed by RealNetworks Inc. Initially RealVideo was based on the video compression standard H.263 until a proprietary, individualized video codecs could be developed for it by RealNetworks. This follows the standard of successor H.264. RealVideo codecs are identified by a four digit code. RV10 and RV20 designate a H.263-based codecs, while RV30 and RV40 a proprietary RealVideo codecs.

To carry out live streaming of video data, RealVideo normally uses coding with a constant data rate. There is also the possibility of a more efficient coding with a variable data rate. It is however less suitable for live streaming as the bandwidth needed by a data transmission cannot be predicted. If the data rate fluctuates too sharply and exceeds the bandwidth available, the result is disturbances and interruptions in transmission.

Further reading:

Côtè, G., Erol, B., Gallant, M., Kossentini, F.: H.263+: video coding at low bit rates. Circuits and Systems for Video Technology, IEEE Transactions on 8(7), pp. 849-866 (1998)

Chen, J. W., Kao, C. Y., Lin, Y. L.: Introduction to H.264 Advanced Video Coding. In: ASP-DAC06: Proceedings of the 2006 conference on Asia South Pacific Design Automation, pp. 736-741. IEEE Press, Piscataway, NJ, USA (2006).

Clarke, R. J.: Digital Compression of Still Images and Video. Academic Press, Inc., Orlando, FL, USA (1995)

Rao, K. R., Hwang, J. J.: Techniques and standards for image, video, and audio coding. Prentice-Hall, Inc., Upper Saddle River, NJ, USA (1996)

Torres, L.: Video Coding. Kluwer Academic Publishers, Norwell, MA, USA (1996)

4.7 Glossary

Aliasing: Term for jagged artifacts that occur when diagonal lines or curves are produced on a pixel-oriented output device. To avoid the aliasing effect, the pixels on the edge of the artifacts are colored with interpolated intermediate color tones to give the impression of a smoother edge. This procedure is known as **anti-aliasing**.

Alpha channel: The proportion of the information contained in a pixel regarding the pixel's characteristics of transparency. In a case where two pixels are superimposed, the alpha channel indicates to what extent the pixel underneath shows through.

Analog: (*ana logum*=[Gk.] in the correct ratio), Designation for technologies/procedures that represent changing values as continuously variable physical qualities.

Animation: A series of two or more individual images that are displayed in rapid succession to create the impression of continuous motion. Animation normally runs at a speed of about 12-15 frames per second.

Artifact: An error caused by a codecs in the encoding and subsequent decoding process. Errors of this type can occur in the compression of audio, image and video data.

---

[7] This property played a key role in the authors' choice of the RealVideo data format for their teleteaching system, "tele-TASK" (URL: http//www.tele-task.de/)

ASCII (American Standard Code for Information Interchange):   This term denotes a character encoding that encodes the letters of the alphabet, numbers and special characters with 7 bits each. The special characters are printable characters belonging to different national alphabets, or control characters. ASCII is standardized in the norms ISO/IEC 646 and DIN 66003 (German variations of the ASCII code), whereby 12 codewords are provided in each case for national characters. The code designated **IA5** and specified by ITU-T/CCITT is identical with ASCII.

Auditory sensation area: Designation for the acoustic apparatus of the ear that perceives and processes sounds in terms of frequency range and volume. The auditory sensation area lies between the absolute threshold of hearing and the pain threshold. All signals that are below the absolute threshold of hearing cannot be perceived by the human ear. Signals above the pain threshold can no longer be distinguished and cause damage to the ear.

Bitmap graphics (raster graphics):   Bitmap images are made up of a set of numerical values representing the color and brightness information of individual pixels or of all pixels. **Pixels** – the smallest physical points of a certain color – are displayed in a raster image arranged on a matrix corresponding to the dimensions of the image. In a historical context, bitmap or raster graphics are associated with the development of the **cathode ray tube (CRT)** as a graphical output device.

Character: A term denoting "something"that stands for something else (that which is "signified"). The relationship between the signifier and the signified object is always a direct one. Syntax defines the relationship of one characters to another and also how they can be combined to form new designations.

Chrominance: Term used to describe information about the color attributes of an image. In order to display a natural image, chrominance must be supplemented with information on brightness distribution (luminance). In the YUV color model (YCbCr model) the components UV (CbCr) provide the chominance information.

Codec: A device (hardware) or a collection of algorithms (software) containing an encoder and a decoder to compress data (encode) – especially audio or video data – and to subsequently display it again in its original state (decode).

Color depth: Specifies the number of possible colors in a graphic file as a result of the number of bits available per pixel, i.e., with a color depth of n bits, a maximum of 2^n F color value can be encoded.

Color model: A mathematical model that describes the creation of new colors based on a mixture (additive or subtractive) of primary colors – the model's foundation. The two best-known models are the **RGB** color model, for the additive color mixing of the primary colors: red, green and blue, and the **CMY(K)** color model, for the subtractive mixing of the primary colors: cyan, magenta and yellow (and black), which plays an important role in the technology of printing.

Complementary color: Designated as complementary (*complementum*=[Lat.] something that completes or fills out/in) are those colors that produce a shade of gray when mixed with each other – whether in an additive or subtractive color mixture. On the color wheel, complementary colors are always exactly opposite one another.

Compression: Compression of the information contents of a message by removing **redundancies (lossless compression)** or non-relevant parts of the information (**lossy compression**). The goal of compression is to reduce the amount of data displayed. It is especially important in cases where the storage space or the bandwidth of the information channel used in transmitting information is limited.

Compression ratio: The ratio between the original information and the compressed information.

Decorrelation: The aim of decorrelation is to modify the sampled data of a signal in such a way that as little as possible symmetric probability distribution of data is achieved. This is important for the later encoding as those values that occur more frequently can be assigned the shortest code possible.

Dictionary-based encoding: See LZW compression.

Difference image: A technique used in video encoding in which only the difference between two consecutive single images is stored as the "difference image." As the frames of two consecutive images often do not differ significantly from one another, considerable compression can be achieved with this procedure.

Digital: (*digitus*=[Lat.] finger) Term for technologies/procedures that only use discrete, discontinuous, i.e., step-like arithmetical sizes. The foundation of this digital technique is the binary number system that contains the two states „true" and „false" and is represented by the numerical values „1" and „0." These binary numbers are called **bits** (**binary digits**) and represent the smallest units of information.

Discrete Cosine Transformation (DCT): DCT is a transformation method used in data compression which, just as the **Fourier transformation**, allows performing a predetermined function from the spatial domain in the frequency domain. The DCT belongs to the family of transformation encoding and was developed in 1970. The DCT transforms data that is in the form of a matrix made up of pixels into a description in which the individual values are represented by frequencies and amplitudes. The frequencies describe how fast the colors change within an image, while the amplitudes describe the strength of the change. Because of its excellent properties for signal decorrelation, DCT is applied in all of the current standards for image and video coding.

Dithering: Dithering (to dither= waver, tremble), also known as error diffusion, is a technique in computer graphics to produce the illusion of more intense color in images with a low color palette. Missing colors can be simulated by a particular arrangement of pixels from the available colors. The human eye thus only perceives the color mixture. In this way, hard transitions between the colors can also be avoided. Dithering is also used in reducing color depth.

EBCDIC (Extended Binary Coded Decimals Interchange Code): An 8-bit character encoding introduced by IBM. It achieved widespread popularity with its application in IBM's mainframe computer system architecture, System/360. Consecutive codes are not necessarily assigned successive characters of the alphabet -reflecting the influence of Hollerith's punched cards on this coding type. There are several variations of EBCDIC that are incompatible with each other. The American variation uses largely the same characters as the **ASCII code**.

Filter bank: Separates the input signal into multiple components. Just as with signal transformations such as DCT, a potentially large decorrelation of the signal may be achieved with filter banks. A filter bank consists of a component for signal separation (analysis) and one for reconstruction (synthesis), to ensure restoration of the complete signal.

Gamma correction: A cross-platform method to adjust image brightness in accordance with the characteristics of the output medium. A gamma correction is especially important if an image is to be output on a monitor (RGB color model) or on paper via a printer (CMYK color model).

GIF (Graphic Interchange Format): A graphic data format that is based on lossless **LZW compression**. The color depth of the original picture is limited to a maximum of 8 bits, which can have a negative effect especially on the picture quality of natural image sources (e.g., photographs).

Huffman coding: Special form of **statistical coding** in which the most common symbols of a string to be encoded are coded with the shortest possible code words. To ensure redundancy-free encoding, the code words chosen must each have their own unique prefix. In 1952, Huffman developed the procedure named after him for the generation of optimal, prefix-free codes.

Interlace technique: If an image is encoded with this technique, the lines of the image are stored in stepped form rather than sequentially. The lines staggered in such a way provide an initial overall impression of the image in a sequential output.

JPEG (Joint Picture Expert Group): The name of a group of experts who developed the graphic compression procedure that was given the same name. JPEG uses lossy compression. The image information is transferred via a local transformation (**DCT**, Discrete Cosine Transformation) in the frequency domain. Through the targeted rounding, highly frequented information (i.e., image portions with a rapid change in contrast) can get lost. JPEG is especially well-suited for the compression of "natural" images, e.g., photography in which low-frequency image components (expressed by continuous color or brightness) dominate. The file format defined in JPEG is designated **JFIF** (JPEG File Interchange Format).

Luminance: Designates the brightness distribution in an image. If luminance is displayed alone, the result is a gray scale image without color components. In the YUV color model (YC_bC_r-Modell) the Y components supply the luminance information.

LZW compression: A dictionary-based compression algorithm named after its three authors: Abraham Lempel, Jakob Zif and Terry Welch. LZW is based on strings (or 8-bit binary words) of an uncompressed data stream **dictionary** (data dictionary, translation table). The occurring data patterns (substrings) of a stream are allocated to separate dictionary entries. If the viewed data pattern does not appear in the dictionary, then a new code word is generated from the content of the data pattern and stored in the dictionary. If this data pattern occurs again, it is replaced by the codeword assigned to the data pattern from the dictionary .

Masking: The covering of one audio signal with another. The quieter signal is still present but is no longer perceptible because it is masked by the other louder signal. For example, an airplane taking off masks a conversation carried on nearby.

MIDI (Musical Instrument Digital Interface): Protocol for the exchange of data between electronic musical instruments. It was also standardized as a file format for data communication. Audio data is not transmitted in the MIDI format in the proper sense of the word, but only the control signals and control instructions for the synthesizer. Sound encoding proceeds in an instrument-focused display that contains a specification of parameters, such as the designation of instruments, beginning and ending of notes, pitch, volume and much more.

Modified Discrete Cosine Transformation (MDCT): The difference between the MDCT and the simple DCT is evident in the overlapping of one data sequence (up to 50%) with the next (critical sampling) in MDCT. This overlapping ensures that artifacts generated through aliasing and redundancies can be avoided to a large extent. MDCT is used in audio compression, for example in MP3, ATRAC or Dolby AC-3.

Motion compensation: Motion compensation signifies a range of predictive procedures used for the compression of moving picture information (video). Thus, in a series of images in a video sequence it is often the case that the forefront of the image changes, while the background image remains constant. Movement of the objects in the forefront can be recognized in an image series by changes in brightness of the object's pixels and be encoded as a simple geometric transformation. In video compression, only the difference image between the actual image and the predicted image is stored for each detected transformation.

MPEG (Motion Picture Experts Group): Designation for a variety of standards for the lossy compression of audiovisual information (moving picture information, video). The video data compression is based on known compression procedures for still images (**JPEG**), the encoding of differential information between neighboring frames in the image sequences and a model of **movement prediction**, whereby only the difference between the predicted and the actual image is stored.

MP3:   Name for a lossy audio compression according to the standard **MPEG 1 Layer 3**. MP3 takes advantage of the psychoacoustic masking effect of human perception. It does this by filtering out parts of the information in the audio signals to be compressed that are not perceptible to humans. The compression is carried out based on a local transformation of the audio signal in the frequency space (**DCT**, discrete cosine transformation) and a subsequent rounding (quantization) of the obtained frequency components.

Multimedia: When different types of media – such as text, image and sound – are employed in presenting information one speaks of multimedia information representation.

Pixel: Short for "picture element," pixels are tiny dots that make up a digitally represented graphic image.

Psychoacoustics: Psychoacoustics is a branch of psychophysics and deals with the description of the link between the human perception of sound as an auditory event and the physical sizes of the sound field. Psychoacoustics creates a model for the auditory impression of a sound event and plays a crucial role in audio compression. With the help of psychoacoustics, filter mechanisms can be developed that filter out sounds that cannot be perceived by the human ear. The inaudibility of these sounds is due to their physiological characteristics or for reasons of masking. The encoded audio data stream can thus be reduced to its significant components without a loss being audible.

Pulse Code Modulation (PCM):   Method of analog-digital conversion that is based on the sampling of an analog signal followed by the discretization of the obtained samples. **Sampling** disassembles the continuous temporal course of a signal into discrete individual time points and captures the current, instantaneous value of an analog signal at each discrete point in time (sampling time). These exact sampling values are rounded to subsequent binary coding within predefined quantization intervals.

Quantization (discretization):   Process in which a continuous output value, e.g., the amplitude of a signal, is transformed into a discrete value for further digital processing. As the discrete set of values is infinite, the continuous output value must be rounded to the nearest discrete value. This leads to so-called **quantization errors**. Because statistically these errors usually occur equally distributed over time, they can be recognized as noise (**quantization noise**). Particularly for signals that are an integer multiple of the sampling rate this takes the form of an unpleasant "tonal" noise. This is because the error rate here is no longer random but follows the phase behavior of the signal.

Redundancy: Term for those parts of a message (signal, code) that do not contain any information that contributes to the message itself. As such they can be removed from the message without reducing the actual information content. Redundant parts of a message are helpful in understanding a message even if errors occur in transmission.

Refresh rate (refresh rate frequency, frame rate):   An indicator of how many individual frames are presented in a video sequence per second. Due to the inertia of the retina, the human eye perceives continuous movement starting at 15 pictures per second. When the refresh rate is lower, the eye perceives the picture as "jerking." A distinction is made between a **progressive refresh rate**, wherein each line of pixels is displayed sequentially and a **interlaced refresh rate**. In the second case, two half images each are displayed alternately. One of the half images is made up of all even-numbered lines of pixels and the other of all the odd-numbered lines.

Retinal inertia: A perceived image remains on the retina of the eye for approximately 1/16 of a second before disappearing. The phenomenon of retinal inertia was already described in antiquity by Ptolemy of Alexandria (85 – 165 AD) and formed the basis for the development of film and television. When still images are shown fast enough one after another in a sequence of 15 frames per second the impression of continuous movement is achieved.

Run Length Encoding: A form of entrophy coding in which the identical symbols of a character string are summarized using code words and compression thereby achieved.

Sampling: Sampling is the measurement of a continuous time signal at predetermined sampling points. The sampling rate provides information on the measurement frequency. A high sampling rate means that the distance between the sampling points is small and that many measurements are taken.

Semantics: Semantics designates a branch of linguistics that deals with the theory of meaning. It addresses the meaning and significance of language and linguistic signs. The focus is on the question of how the sense and meaning of complex sentences and terms are derived from simpler sentences and concepts. Semantics draws upon the rules of syntax.

Shannon's Theorem (Claude Elwood Shannon, 1916–2001):   Shannon's Theorem states that it is not possible to find an algorithm to encode any desired character string into a shorter output string then is defined by its entropy (information content) without a loss of information.

Signal-to-Noise Ratio (SNR):   Describes the relationship between the amplitude of the output signal and the amplitude of the noise. The SNR is measured in decibels (dB). It is also referred to as noise ratio or dynamics and is an important measure of the quality of an audio signal. In lossy audio compression based on a psychoacoustic model, the deterioration of the SNR value is accepted as a given if it goes undetected.

Sound waves: Sound waves are compressions and refractions of the air that spread spherically in all directions. If a sound wave meets the ear, the ear drum vibrates and these vibrations are transmitted through the ear and auditory nerves to the brain. The human ear perceives only sounds with a frequency between 20 Hz and 20.000 Hz.

Sprite: A freely-movable graphic object, which itself can be either static (**texture**) or dynamic (video). It can be freely positioned in a background scene. MPEG-4 uses this graphic representation of objects to compress graphic objects independent of the background. This leads to a significant improvement in compression results.

Streaming: Term for the continuous playback of multimedia contents (audio and/or video) on the Internet in real time. Playback is already carried out during transmission without the need to wait until the contents have been completely delivered. The content to be played can be already be present in stored form or as live data that is constantly available on the Internet immediately after its generation. In contrast to standard data transmission, streaming is delay sensitive, i.e., late data packets lose their relevance. Within a certain framework this causes errors or data loss and as a result a reduction of display quality, however such errors are generally tolerated.

Subsampling: The human system of perception reacts more sensitively to site-specific changes in image brightness than to color changes. The lower resolution in terms of color is taken advantage of in video and image compression. First an image, which is generally in the RGB color model, is transformed into the YCrCb color model with a brightness component (Y) and two color components CrCb. The sampling rate for the color components of the image can now be sampled with a lower resolution than that for image brightness, without the human eye perceiving information loss. As a rule, color subsampling is given in the so-called A:B:C notation, which describes the horizontal and vertical sampling relationships. For example, a subsampling of 4:2:4 means that the luminance is scaled horizontally to the chrominance in the relationship 2:1.

Texture: Two-dimensional image information that is projected onto the surface of 3D objects. This procedure is called **texture mapping** and allows a more realistic representation of graphic objects, which is more efficient in terms of storage space and computational ability.

Unicode: A standard 16-bit coding for multilingual text alphabets that was introduced in 1992. Besides encompassing a wide variety of international alphabets, Unicode includes extra typographical symbols and national characters. Standardized by ISO as ISO10646, with the issuing of the RFCs 2070 and 2077 Unicode became the standard for the WWW language HTML and all future Internet protocols. The transformation rule called UTF-8 ensures backward compatibility for 8-bit applications, it allows all ASCII characters to pass through transparently, while all other characters are transmitted in a unique 8-bit character sequence.

Vector graphics: In vector graphics, the lines, polygons or curves of a graphic image are characterized by specifying certain key points. From these key points a program reconstructs the geometric figure to be displayed. These key points are additionally provided with specific attribute information, such as color or line thickness. Vector graphics developed historically with **plotters** – graphical output devices for computers. A plotter outputs a graphic drawing by way of one or more pens moved across a drawing surface according to predetermined coordinate values.

Wavelet compression: One of the most efficient methods of image compression. The algorithm behind wavelet compression is based on so-called multi-resolution analysis, a method of mathematics that was only developed in the last 15 years. Just as conventional DCT, the wavelet algorithm displays the image as a set of coefficients many of which are close to zero. The image can thus be approximated quite well with a small number of high wavelet coefficients. In contrast to the JPEG procedure, the image is not separated into individual image blocks but analyzed as a whole. Wavelet compression is used in JPEG2000.

Chapter 5
Digital Security

"Certain is that nothing is certain. And not even that."
— Hans Bötticher, called Ringelnatz,
(1883 – 1934)

The global network is an open network. Open means unlimited and available to everyone. It was this openness that was responsible for the Internet's huge popularity in the last century – but it also has its price. There is no central control and this means that it is possible for unauthorized third parties to gain access to the communication sphere of other Internet users. In order to guarantee sufficient protection of privacy and confidentiality it is necessary to use certain cryptology technologies. These enable messages to be encrypted and help to ensure their integrity. Using cryptology methods it is possible to prove the identity of a communication partner and prevent swindlers from wreaking havoc on the Internet under the guise of someone else. After all, Internet communication partners don't sit face to face or communicate in a way as to be identified physically but are normally far away from each other, often on the other side of the globe. The following chapter provides a brief outline of the methods of cryptography. With such methods, digitalized information as well as the digital communication itself, can be protected against multifarious dangers lurking in our new, net-based world. Examples are presented of the most important of these techniques.

5.1 Principles of Security in Computer Networks

Security is an autonomous and crucial factor in the planning and operation of computer networks. Not only are technical aspects of great importance, but also legal and economic factors. Operating a **secure network** is no simple task. Every network user has specific, individual security requirements in terms of communication via a network and the use of that network. From a security point of view there are open and closed networks. **Closed networks** are composed of independent network islands. They cannot be entered from the outside without physical access. The difficulty for unauthorized persons

C. Meinel and H. Sack, *Digital Communication*, X.media.publishing,
DOI: 10.1007/978-3-642-54331-9_5, © Springer-Verlag Berlin Heidelberg 2014

to gain entry goes without saying – it is in any case a feat requiring considerable criminal energy. With **open networks** the situation is completely different. Open networks have a connection to the global Internet so that access from the outside is theoretically possible. Because Internet users are hardly just limited to a circle of trustworthy people, security requirements are essential and have become increasingly important. In many networks, confidential and valuable data resources are available and these must be protected from unauthorized access. On the other hand, companies and firms looking to capture new markets and to jump on the **electronic commerce** bandwagon want to make themselves and their offers known and their services available to everyone via the Internet. Yet this group also includes unknown and potentially unreliable and – from the perspective of network security – "dangerous" users.

Since there is no such thing as a completely secure network – and in principle it cannot realistically exist – network operators must offer the highest degree of network security possible via a specific set of rules, extra components and procedures. Attention must be paid so that this protection is globally and universally valid. This means protection validity at the point of origin and in data transmission via intermediate systems or storage media. This also applies when these resources are outside the area of responsibility. This includes both the local network, in data transport via routers and telephone lines, as well as the end user's local storage or even print form. Also to be considered are the legal regulations for the protection of the private sphere and personal data. The impact of **security risks** are reflected in terms of their financial repercussions. The extent of the potential financial loss is determined by the security relevance of the data to be protected. Losses stemming from unauthorized third parties can begin with something as simple as errors in calculating the connection time to the network provider – i.e., sums amounting to a fraction of a cent – and end with losses in the millions as a result of industry spying or the fraudulent manipulation of electronic financial services – not to mention terrorist attacks. Before turning to the cryptographic principles and methods, let us first look at characteristics and aspects important for secure communication.

5.1.1 Security Objectives

To illustrate security-critical communication scenarios and cryptographic methods, the communication partners involved are normally referred to by the fictive names *Alice* and *Bob* instead of "*A and B.*" In this chapter, *Trudy* is the name given to a fictive intruder who attempts to interfere in the communication between Alice and Bob and whose resources are, theoretically-speaking, unrestricted (see Fig. 5.1).

Alice, Bob and Trudy

Alice and **Bob** are commonly used as synonyms for the sender and receiver of a message and illustrate the communication process in cryptography or physics. The names Alice and Bob serve as metasyntactic variables since the form, "person A would like to send person B a message," would quickly become confusing.

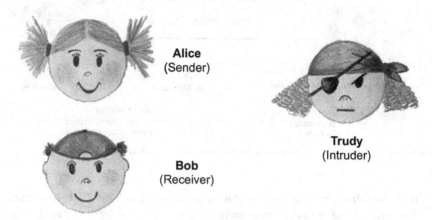

Besides Alice and Bob, other synonyms have been established for specific roles in the communication process. The most important of these is the role of the unauthorized third party who attempts to interfere in the communication between Alice and Bob by spying on them, disrupting or distorting the exchanged messages. This role is often given the name **Trudy** (short for "intruder"). And there are other names as well. For example, active attackers often receive the name Mallory, Marvin or Mallet (all which stem from "malicious"). Eve is likely to be an "eavesdropper"and Oscar an "opponent."Alice and Bob first entered the scene in 1978 in a scientific publication by the renowned cryptography experts Ronald L. Rivest, Adi Shamir and Leonard M. Adleman, who developed the RSA cryptography system named after them.

Literature:

Rivest, R L., Shamir, A., Adleman, L. M.: A Method for Obtaining Digital Signatures and Public-Key Cryptosystems, in Communications of the ACM 21(2), pp. 120–126 (1978)

Fig. 5.1 Alice, Bob and Trudy.

Network operators are solely responsible for deciding where the areas of importance in the layout of network security lie. It is often necessary to make compromises along the way. Not only can different security objectives contradict each other, certain security techniques are very complex and costly. In fact, an open network is exposed to a wide range of threats (see Fig. 5.2). An analysis of individual kinds of threats leads to the formulation of different **security objectives**. The most important of these are addressed in the following.

- **Availability**
  An information provider is dependent on the reliable functioning of the

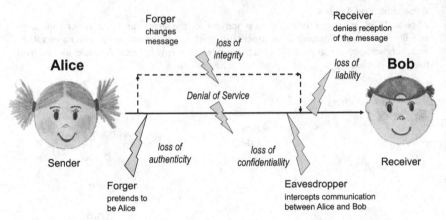

Fig. 5.2 Different types of threats in communication networks.

network infrastructure to to be able to make data available via the Internet. The function of network components can be impaired by accidental errors or targeted attacks from unauthorized third parties. Components can even become paralyzed and as a result the offered information unobtainable. Attacks of this kind are known as **denial of service** (DoS) .

Generally, in such a denial-of-service attack there is so much load generated on the attacked system that it is no longer capable of performing its regular tasks in a proper, functional manner. An example of a denial-of-service attack is so-called **SYN flooding**. The attacker showers its network victim with data segments that have a forged source address. As the attacked computer cannot normally distinguish between legitimate and fake data segments, it opens new connections, allocates all of the requested resources and then waits in vain for continued communication from the side of the forged source address. The number of open, resource-devouring connections increases continually up to the point of overload or even the crash of the computer.

- **Data integrity**
  Data integrity is the assurance that the message received from the sender has not been tampered with along the transmission path. Data that is transmitted from a sender to a receiver should reach its destination unchanged from the original state. If an unauthorized third party intervenes in transmission, the message can be intercepted and changed as desired. The result is a loss of data integrity (**loss of integrity**). The receiver incorrectly assumes that the message it has gotten is complete and unaltered ("integrity").
  The content of the transmitted data must not be changed, either maliciously by an unauthorized third party or randomly though the occurrence of a transmission error. To make sure this is the case, besides using the error

handling procedures provided by regular transport protocols, additional suitable cryptographic procedures must also be applied.

- **Privacy and Secrecy**
  Although the content of the transported digital messages is intended only for the sender and the receiver, in an open network it is possible for a unauthorized third party to gain access to the communication by monitoring the data traffic (**eavesdropping**). The confidentiality of communication is lost as well as the communication partner's associated **loss of privacy**. An unauthorized third party is able to read the transported content as long as it is not protected by the appropriate cryptographic methods. In order to keep a message secret, one must either ensure that unauthorized third parties are not able to copy data packets before the recipient gets them, or encryption techniques must be used that make the data content unrecognizable for the uninitiated.

  The easiest way to spy on data in a computer network is to tap into the transmission lines themselves. This assumes that the attacker either gains direct access to the network, or is able to procure indirect means by taking the appropriate actions. In wireless networks, the spatial proximity to the sender alone is sufficient to gain access, thus without the necessity of direct physical access. Data traffic in the network layer of a local network (LAN) can be monitored with a so-called **packet sniffer**. In diffusion networks, such as most LANs where all computers use a common communication medium, a packet sniffer can easily intercept, read and analyze every data packet. In an Ethernet LAN, every network adapter can be simply reconfigured into the so-called **promiscuous mode** and thus made capable of reading every data packet – regardless of the recipient's address. The packet sniffer was originally developed for a completely different and helpful purpose, namely as a network analysis tool to help network administrators monitor the status of network traffic and discover any possible errors.

- **Authentication**
  The authentication of a message guarantees the sender's identity to the receiver. If an unauthorized third party penetrates a communication process and composes a message for the receiver under a false identify, the authenticity of the message is lost (**loss of authenticity**). The receiver is then no longer able to recognize whether the message in fact comes from the sender claimed. The identity of both the sender and the receiver must be assured without it being possible for an unauthorized third party to masquerade as one of the two communication partners. If communication partners stand face to face in the real world the process of authentication is carried out by visual or acoustic means. But in digital communication the task of authentication is considerably more difficult. Is the received email actually from the named sender? In order to have this assurance, complicated cryptographic authentication procedures have been developed, e.g., digital signatures or a secret password. Every Internet data transfer pro-

ceeds over the Internet Protocol (IP). The header of every IP data packet always contains the addresses of the sender and receiver. If an attacker has complete control over the end system that is available to him (in particular the operating system), he is able to manipulate the protocol software. For example, faking another identity by providing a recipient address other than his own. This form of identity falsification is called **IP spoofing** and, along with packet sniffing, among the most common security infractions on the Internet. Another way of attacking is to manipulate the entries of so-called DNS servers. The Domain Name System (DNS) used on the Internet converts readable, hierarchical host names (domain names) into numeric IP addresses. Through the manipulation of a DNS server it can be fixed that certain computers are no longer reachable via the Internet, or that data packets are re-routed for the purpose of spying and manipulation. This type of attack is referred to as **DNS poisoning**.

- **Non-Repudiation**
  A communication network ideally represents a reliable (binding) transmission medium, i.e., neither sender or receiver can deny the sending or receiving of a message. Without this commitment there is no reliable, legally-binding data transmission and a viable business transaction cannot take place. Similar to authentication, the bindingness of a transaction can be ensured with the help of digital signatures. These not only validate the identity of the sender and the receiver, but provide the transaction with a time stamp so that in hindsight it cannot be withdrawn or denied by one of the parties involved.

- **Authorization**
  After the identity of the communication partners has been established beyond a reasonable doubt, each partner can only access the information and services intended for it. To ensure this, an access authorization is linked to every information resource. In this way it is determined whether the resource is accessible to a specific, authenticated user or not. An attacker who wishes to circumvent such access control must either successfully simulate a false identity or gain authorized entry to the operating system of the computer where the resources are held to then manipulate the access authorizations.

If the named threats become reality and an unauthorized third party attacks the communication network in one of the ways described, the attack can be carried out actively or a passively:

- **Active Attacks**
  A change in the content of digital data communication is carried out in an active attack. The attacker falsifies content, manipulates its authenticity or prevents the use of communication services. Because there is active intervention in the communication process, an active attack is easier to detect than a passive attack.

- **Passive Attacks**
  In a passive attack the communication content is not changed. The unauthorized third party gains access solely to the communication network and eavesdrops on the communicated message, noting it for the purpose of a later analysis or to prepare an attack. Subsequently, such confidential messages can be identified and analyzed or user profiles created. Because no changes are made to the communication contents a passive attack is considerably more difficult to identify than an active one.

5.1.2 Cryptographic Principles

Cryptography (from *"kryptein"*= [Gk.] to understand and *"gráphein"*= [Gk.] to write) has developed into an interesting and independent discipline within mathematics and computer science. It essentially deals with the design and evaluation of encryption procedures implemented to secure the contents of a message from unauthorized access. The art of breaking ciphers, covered by the branch of **cryptanalysis**, focuses on how encryption procedures can be undone and made ineffective. Together, cryptography and cryptanalysis form the science known as **cryptology**. Cryptology plays a central role in computer science, computer security and IT security. The primary object of cryptography is the **encryption** and **decryption** of plaintext information. Through encryption (ciphering, sometimes spelled cyphering), plaintext is transformed into ciphertext. The term **cipher** describes the cryptographic system, i.e., the mapping function, used to transform plaintext into ciphertext. The encryption procedure uses secret information (a **key**) known only to the two communication partners involved. Because this information is selected from an astronomical amount of similar information, guessing the key implemented in each case is practically impossible. With the help of the key the reverse process can also take place: the original plaintext is obtained again from the ciphertext through decryption (deciphering) (see Fig. 5.3).

In this model showing basic encrypted communication, the sender and receiver are given the standard names in cryptography – **Alice** (A) and **Bob** (B). The original message, the so-called **plaintext**, is changed into encrypted information (**ciphertext**) through the implementation of a **transformation function**. The transformation function used – *encrypt* – is normally parameterized (controllable) via a **key**. Therefore *encrypt* uses two arguments to produce the ciphertext E: the key k and the plaintext to be encrypted M.

$$E = encrypt(k, M) \ .$$

The inverse transformation *decrypt*, in contrast, produces the original message M with the help of the key K and the ciphertext E.

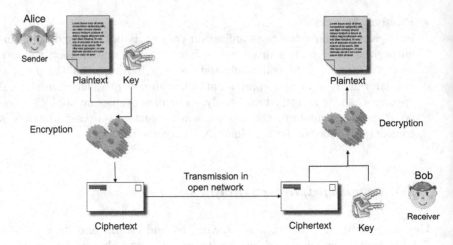

Fig. 5.3 Secure communication through cryptography.

$$M = decrypt(K, E) \ .$$

Normally, the key k consists of a (usually short) string, with which one of the many potential decryption variations of the transformation function is chosen. While the encryption procedure (i.e., the transformation function) is generally known, the real secret of the encryption lies in key k. The number of possible keys is directly related to the key length. It determines the effort necessary to break the cipher text without the secret key via an exhaustive key search (exhaustive key search, brute force attack) From a certain key length on, the methods used are referred to as **strong cryptography** as the effort required to break the key is considered astronomical. With increasing computing power this border shifts to ever-greater key lengths, making the classification of cryptography as strong and weak a relative one.

A computer system for the encryption and decryption of messages is referred to as a **cryptosystem** . In the simple case, a cryptosystem consists of

- a cipher
- the secret key and
- a deciphering procedure.

Cryptocomplexity is the necessary effort for encryption and decryption. While the cipher can always be broken theoretically, the effort to do this is immensely greater than the deciphering effort with the original key. The complexity involved in the asymmetry of deciphering and of breaking the cipher without a valid key ensures the long-term protection of secret information and makes encryption extremely effective.

Ciphering procedures are usually based on the transposition and substitution of certain plaintext characters for other characters. Controlled by the respective key, these operations are repeated in many rounds until the ciphertext is finally generated. The cipher procedures must fulfill a number of criteria to ensure that it is as difficult as possible to break the cipher.

- **Diffusion**
  To complicate the breaking of the cipher to the greatest extent, the individual characters of the ciphertext should depend on as many plaintext characters possible and on the whole key.

- **Confusion**
  The relationship between plaintext, ciphertext and the implemented key should be as intricate as possible.

- **Avalanche/Butterfly Effect**
  A small change in the plaintext results in a large change to the ciphertext later.

The described security objectives can all be achieved through an implementation of different cryptographic methods. Depending on the specific target, other methods or a combination of methods, may be deemed the most appropriate. In an open network, such as the Internet, an unauthorized third party is also able to attack a ciphertext in a secure communication, such as in Fig. 5.3. However, this is useless without knowledge of the right encryption method and key. Nevertheless, **cryptanalysis** has developed a range of methods by which the plaintext content of an encrypted message can be deciphered even without the key. Attempting to decrypt a ciphertext without a key constitutes an **attack**. Cryptanalysis is also described as the science of attacks on the encryption procedure. If the attacker is successful without using a key, the encryption is **broken** or, colloquially speaking "cracked." If the key is retrieved in another way (theft, bribery etc.), it is said to have been **compromised**. A general distinction is made between three types of encryption attacks:

- **Ciphertext-only attack**
  In this variation, the attacker does not know the plaintext of the encrypted message. While this type of attack is by far the most difficult, it is also attempted the most often.

- **Known-plaintext attacks**
  In this variation the attacker knows the plaintext of an encrypted message. The goal is to determine the implemented key to be able to decrypt the ciphertext. Often standard text, such as email headers or greetings, are encrypted along with other information, making it possible to carry out attacks based on the known plaintext.

- **Chosen-plaintext attacks**
  If the attacker himself can choose the to-be-encrypted text in order to prepare an attack on an unknown key, this is called a chosen-plaintext attack. This type of attack is considered the easiest and is used, for example, to break the cipher of pay-TV decoders.

A cost-benefit analysis is always crucial when implementing cryptographic methods, just as compromises must be made in terms of the security achieved. It makes little sense to encrypt harmless private emails using strong cryptography methods. Yet if an email contains, for example, confidential information of economic importance or information that could endanger the sender's life and limb if disclosed, methods of strong cryptography are certainly justified.

In the following, the most important cryptographic procedures and techniques are presented in brief.

5.2 Confidentiality and Encryption

Cryptography is a branch of computer science concerned with the development of encryption methods to protect confidential information from being accessed or from attacks by unauthorized third parties. Its origins reach far back in history. Already in ancient times encryption methods were implemented to protect diplomatic or military information from potential enemies. Even if the enemy succeeded in intercepting this kind of message it still couldn't be read. And even if they were successful in breaking the code and recovering the original text so much time would be lost in this process that the other party could be assured of an advantage. In the Middle Ages a large variety of secret codes existed in Europe for the protection of diplomatic correspondence.

5.2.1 Symmetric Encryption Methods

With **symmetric encryption methods** both the sender and the receiver use the same key, which has been exchanged or agreed on previously. The key must be used together with ciphering and deciphering procedures. The transformation function for most symmetric encryption procedures is based on a combination of simple operations:

Transposition: The position of the individual message characters are exchanged with each other based on a given cipher.

Substitution: The individual characters of a message are replaced with other characters according to a predetermined cipher.

To increase the complexity of the encryption and make it harder to break, transposition and substitution are repeated in numerous rounds and managed with a key. Excursus 13 lays out the basic principles for the simplest encryption techniques. The **rotor-based cipher**, used in the well-known electromechanical code machine from World War II – **Enigma** – was designed on the principle of transposition. Enigma's decryption had an important impact on the outcome of the war, just as it significantly influenced the development of the modern computer.

Excursus 14: Simple Historical Encryption Procedures

Transposition Cipher

In the 5th century BC the Spartans used a transposition cipher (also called permutation cipher) to transfer secret messages during the Peloponnesian War. This was described by the historian *Plutarch* (45 – 125 AD) in his biography of the Spartan general *Lysander* [186]. A so-called **scytale** was used for this purpose. This is a tool consisting of a wooden cylinder of a certain diameter around which a writable leather strap is wound spirally. The band wrapped around the cylinder is written on length-wise. When unwound, only many jumbled letters can be seen on the band. Only when the the band is wound around a cylinder of exactly the same diameter is it possible to read the letters. The scytale changes the position of individual characters based on a fixed pattern and as such is a **transposition cipher**. With a transposition cipher, a k-character key generally determines how k letters of the original text must each be permuted.

Example:

Key: 3 5 2 1 6 4
Plaintext: s e c r e t
Chiphertext: r c s t e e

When the keys are of a short length, transposition ciphers are very easy to break through trial and error. Moreover, via a frequency analysis of characters it is possible to easily determine from the ciphertext in which language the encrypted message was written.

Substitution cipher

Substitution ciphers were also known in ancient times. They are based on the simple principle of replacing each character (or group of characters) in a message with another character (or group of characters) from an alphabet. The simplest form of substitution cipher is one in which all character are shifted by a fixed value. This is exemplified in the so-called **Caesar cipher**, named after the Roman statesman Julius Caesar. In his imperial biographies, Roman author *Suetonius* (70 – 130 AD) writes of Caesar shifting each character of the message to the value 3 (corresponding to the position of Caesar's initial "C" in the alphabet) when transferring secret military intelligence [236].

Example:

Plaintext: a b c d e f g h i j k l m ...
Ciphertext: d e f g h i j k l m n o p ...

The shift is cyclic, i.e., the 26 letters of the alphabet are assigned a numerical value corresponding to their position. After the last letter "z" it starts over again from the beginning with the letter "a." The shift corresponds to an addition *modulo* 26. The operation a *mod* 26 is defined as the remainder of the integer division of a by 26. For $m \in \mathbb{N}\text{-}\{0\}$ applies:

$$a \bmod m = a - \left\lfloor \frac{a}{m} \right\rfloor \cdot m.$$

An effective attack on substitution ciphers can be carried out with a simple frequency analysis. If the message is one that was composed in natural language all characters do not appear with the same frequency. The longer the message the more likely it is that frequency distribution of the characters in the plaintext corresponds to the normal frequency distribution of the letters in that respective language. For example, in English "e " is one of the most frequently used letters at almost 13%. On the basis of such a fact, the attacker can easily determine the key.

Vigenére Cipher

While simple substitution ciphers use only one character of the alphabet for another (**monoalphabetic ciphers**), there are other ciphers that use several different mapping rules at the same time for encryption (**polyalphabetic cipher**). The most famous polyalphabetic cipher was invented by French diplomat *Blaise de Vigenére* (1523 – 1595). Instead of specifying a single substitution, several substitutions are described in the form of a key word. Each character of the keyword defines a substitution specification and each character of the plaintext is shifted by the "letter value" (i.e., the position of the letter in the alphabet) of the current character in the keyword. To encrypt the entire plaintext, the keyword is repeated as many times as necessary.

Example:

Keyword: A L I C E

Key: A L I C E A L I C E A

Plaintext: g e h e i m n i s s e

Cipher: h q q h n n z r v x f

The Vignére cipher is virtually composed of several substitution ciphers. Therefore the same character can be encrypted in different ways. It is more difficult to crack a Vignére cipher than a simple substitution cipher. But if the key length is known, the problem can be easily broken down into a solution consisting of several substitution ciphers. To determine the key length, a search is made in the ciphertext for sequences of identical characters. The intervals between these strings must then be divisible by the key length.

A special form of the Vigenére cipher is called **Vernam cipher**, named after *Gilbert Vernam* (1890 – 1960). Vernam cipher is characterized by the corresponding length of the keyword and the plaintext. Therefore this cipher cannot be broken using a simple frequency analysis. But if the plaintext and the ciphertext are composed in natural language, an attacker can use each different occurrence of letters, or groups of letters – depending on the language – to find an analytical solution.

Disposable Cipher (One-Time Pad)

In contrast to the encryption methods introduced thus far, which can be cracked relatively easily, there exists a very simple procedure that can (theoretically) not be broken. It is called the **one-time pad**, and was developed in 1917 by *Gilbert Vernam* and *Joseph Mauborgne* (1881 – 1971). Along with the plaintext (in the form of a bit string) a randomly generated key (also in the form of a bit string) of the same length is created. Both sequences are linked bit by bit via the binary operation XOR ($0\,\text{XOR}\,0=0$, $1\,\text{XOR}\,1=0$, $0\,\text{XOR}\,1=1\,\text{XOR}\,0=1$). The ciphertext generated does not reveal any hint of the plaintext, which cannot be discovered without knowledge of the key.

Example:

Plaintext:	1 0 1 1 1 0 1 1 0 1 0 1 1 0 1 0 1
XOR Key	1 0 1 0 1 1 1 0 0 0 1 0 1 1 1 1 0
Ciphertext:	0 0 0 1 0 1 0 1 0 1 1 1 0 1 0 1 1

In contrast to the related Vernam cipher, the distribution of the key bits in one-time pad has to be random and they can only be used once. It is necessary that sender and receiver use the same sequence of key bits. Mathematical procedures are normally used for the generation of the key. It should be noted that it is considerably more difficult to generate large amounts of random bits than is generally believed. The quality of the respectively selected procedure is responsible for the encryption achieved.

Rotor Cipher and Enigma

The most important electromechanical encryption machines were based on the principle of the rotor cipher (see Fig. 5.5). The heart of the machine was the metal discs (rotors) with 26 metal contacts each (for each letter of the alphabet) on both sides. Each contact on one side was connected with a contact on the other side. Different rotors were switched several times in succession and arranged in a tachometer fashion.

Fig. 5.4 The encryption machine Enigma.

When a contact on the left side of the left rotor was activated by pressing a typewriter key, an electrical current passed through the wires and mechanical parts of the machine to the rotors switched in succession. This caused the lamps linked to one of the 26 contacts on the right side of the right rotor to light up. The keys and lamps had letters on them. Every rotor was responsible for a wired transposition in the cipher machine. After every strike of a key, the left rotor advanced one notch. When a complete revolution had taken place, the second rotor then moved one notch etc., just like a tachometer.

The **Enigma** was a rotor cipher-based electromechanical encryption machine developed in 1918 by the German engineer *Arthur Scherbius* (1878 – 1929). It was patented in 1926 (see Fig.5.4). The Enigma had three – and later four – rotors, each with 26 letters. Before an encryption all the rotors were set in a starting position based on a predetermined key. The to-be-encrypted message was entered on the keyboard and the ciphertext could then be read on the flashing lights. A large part of German radio traffic in World War II was encrypted with the help of this machine.

Under the direction of the leading mathematician *Alan Turing* (1912 – 1954), the allies invested a great amount of personnel and time in deciphering these messages. To speed up the decryption process the first cryptanalysis computer was developed in Bletchley Park near London. The so-called **Bombe** is considered a predecessor of the modern computer.

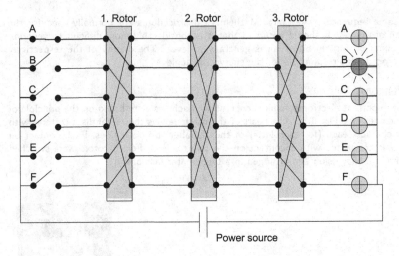

Fig. 5.5 Simplified demonstration of the principle of the rotor-based cipher: if key "A" is pressed, the corresponding wiring of letter "B" lights up.

Fig. 5.6 The cryptanalysis computer "Bomb"
used in deciphering Enig-
ma's encryption.

Further reading:

B. Schneier: Applied Cryptography: Protocols, Algorithms, and Source Code in C, John
Wiley & Sons, New York, NY, USA, (1995)

As mentioned, the (decryption) key is the decisive instrument for gaining access to the information in plaintext. It must therefore always remain secret.
An unauthorized third party who obtains the **secret key** is able to decrypt
the ciphertext with no trouble. When the same key is used for encryption as well as decryption ($k = K$), it is called a **symmetric encryption
procedure** (secret key encryption). The distribution of the secret key (**key
management**) to the recipient of a symmetrically encrypted message must

always proceed under the most stringent conditions – a task that has been the stuff of many suspenseful spy and detective novels (see Fig. 5.7).

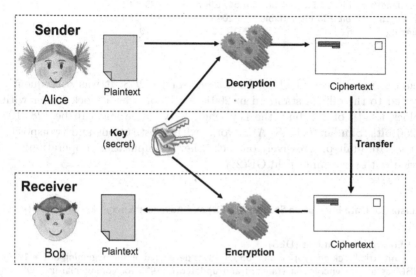

Fig. 5.7 Symmetric encryption (secret key encryption).

A distinction is made between two types of ciphers:

- **Block encryption method (block cipher)**
  In this method the plaintext is divided into individual blocks of a fixed length. The individual blocks are encrypted independently with the same key and together form the ciphertext.

- **Stream encryption method (stream cipher)**
  This procedure treats the entire plaintext as a text stream, i.e. an arbitrarily long sequence of plaintext characters. An equally long stream of key characters is also generated – just as in the one-time pad encryption, described in Excursus 12. Decryption is carried out character by character based on this stream.

The most important representatives of symmetric block encryption are **DES** (**Data Encryption Standard**), **IDEA** (**International Data Encryption Algorithm**), the different variations of the so-called **Rivest Cipher** (**RC2** to **RC6**) and the **Advanced Encryption Standard** (**AES**). As seen in Table 5.1, the various procedures differ in complexity and safety.

The most important symmetric encryption procedure at this time is considered to be the **Advanced Encryption Standard**. Called **Rijndael** (a combination of the names of its two Belgium developers *Vincent Rijmen* and *Joan Daemen*), this method was the winner of the 1988 competition held by the US standardization authority NIST (National Institute of Standards and

Table 5.1 The symmetric block encryption procedure.

Procedure	DES	IDEA	RC2	RC5	RC6
Block length	64 bit	64 bit	64 bit	24/64/128 bit	128 bit
Key length	56 bit	128 bit	variable	0 - 2040 bit	128/192/256 bit
Rounding	16	8		0 - 255	20

Technology) who were looking for a successor to DES. It was subsequently elevated to the official standard in 2001. AES works as a block cipher with a block length of 128 bits, the key length is variable and can be 128, 192 or 256 bits. Similar to DES, AES works with substitutions and transposition that are built progressively on each other. Computational operations are carried out over a finite field $GF(2^8)$.

Excursus 15: Data Encryption Standard (DES) and Advanced Encryption Standard (AES)

Data Encryption Standard (DES)
The symmetric block encryption method DES was developed at the beginning of the 1970s by IBM as a data encryption standard and updated in 1993 for commercial use. DES is considered the first efficiently feasible encryption via only one computer. It combines easy to implement transposition-substitution and one-time pad ciphers in a multi-level complex encryption. DES encodes blocks of 64 bits each with an equally long key. The effective DES key length is however only 56 bits because each of the 8 bytes of the key contains a parity bit. The DES method runs through a total of 19 rounds, whereby the 16 inner rounds cover repeated use of the key.

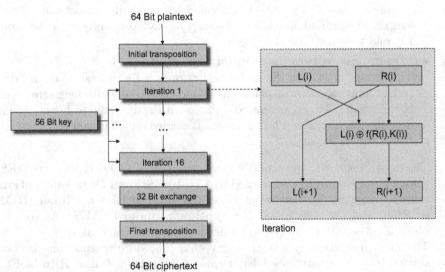

- **Level 1**: Key independent 64 bit transposition (initial permutation).

- **Level 2 – 17**: Functionally identical application of the key.
  64 bit block M(i) on level i is split into two 32 bit words L(i) and R(i). R(i) is passed on to the next level unchanged as L(i+1), while R(i+1) is calculated as XOR via L(i) and a function, which is applied to R(i) and the key K(i) of level i. It ensures that in every level key and data change through permutation and substitution. The result of L(i+1) and R(i+1) together is the new 64 bit block M(i+1).
- **Level 18**: Interchange of the two 32 bit words of the 64 bit blocks.
- **Level 19**: Key independent 64 bit transposition.

Although DES's relatively short key length of 56 bits was a point of criticism initially, it was the only proven weakness of the method that had been able to withstand a cryptanalysis exhaustive key search until 1997. The IT security company RSA held the DES Challenge in 1997, offering a $10.000 prize for the decryption of a ciphertext encrypted with DES. One of the participating teams did in fact carry out a successful brute force attack less than 4 months later. The challenge was repeated the following two years. Whereas in 1997 it took 96 days to break the key, 41 days were needed in 1981 and just 22 hours in 1999. In the meantime it is possible to break a DES key in a matter of hours with the IT technology commonly available.

To increase security, a multiple application of DES using different keys each time is strongly recommended – for example **Triple DES**. A double DES encryption that works with two different 56 bit keys, would theoretically offer a search space of 2^{112} different keys and could be sufficiently safe even by today's standards. However, there is a possibility to get around an exhaustive search with the help of a **meet-in-the-middle attack**. This attack is a variation of the known-plaintext attack. Trudy (the attacker) takes the known plaintext and encrypts it with all 2^{56} possible DES keys. She then takes the ciphertext and likewise decrypts it with all possible 2^{56} DES keys. If a match of intermediate ciphertext (in the "middle") is evident when comparing the results of the first encryption round with those of the decryption round, it is highly probable that the respectively associated DES keys have been found.

Applying the DES algorithm three times (Triple DES, 3DES), offers a adequate degree of security even if this procedure is also not immune to the meet-in-the-middle attacks. In triple DES, the plaintext is first DES-encrypted with key K_1, the ciphertext is DES-decrypted with K_2 and then DES-encrypted again with K_3. In practical application it is even sufficient to use just two different keys K_1 and K_2 (i.e., $K_1=K_3$).

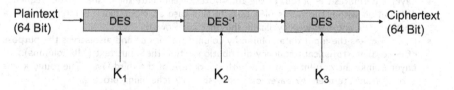

Triple-DES was specified in the standards X9.17 and ISO 8732. However, in comparison to DES, Triple-DES needs triple the computational effort. Until this time weaknesses have not been identified in Triple-DES.

Advanced Encryption Standard (AES)

As weaknesses became known in DES encryption, the wish for a new, secure encryption method eventually took the concrete form of an open competition. A contest for the development of new, secure "Advanced Encryption Standard" (AES) was announced in 1997. The call for proposals stipulated the following criteria:

- Block cipher

- Minimum block length: 128 bits
- Key lengths: 128, 192, 256 bits
- Efficient implementation in terms of hardware as well as software
- Resistance to known methods of cryptanalysis
- Low resource consumption for use on e.g., smart cards
- Free use with no patent law restrictions

Of the 15 algorithms proposed in the competition, five (MARS, RC6, Rijndael, Serpent and Twofish) fulfilled all of the criteria and were subsequently shortlisted. After additional theoretical weaknesses had been examined as well as resource consumption in respect to the algorithm performance analyzed, a winner was announced at the end of 2002. This was the **Rijndael** encryption algorithm, which received the name AES.

While the block length for AES is 128 bits, a key length of 128, 192 or 256 bits can be chosen. Similar to DES, AES encryption runs through multiple rounds in the encryption process. The number of rounds depends on the key length selected.

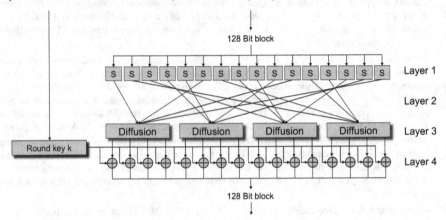

- **Layer 1** consists of 16 substitution boxes (S-box), an 8-bit long input from a statistical table is assigned an 8-bit long output. The S-boxes were designed in such a way as to withstand various methods of linear and differential cryptanalysis.
- **Layer 2** permutes the output of the 16 S-boxes to eliminate the characteristic frequency distribution within the words of a text. In this case an input block is interpreted as a (4x4) matrix and row-wise cyclically shifted (ShiftRows).
- **Layer 3** mixes the input data column by column (diffusion) and also serves the purpose of concealing statistical frequency distribution within the input text (MixColumns).
- **Layer 4** links the current round key with the output of the third layer. The round key is derived from the user key based on a recursive key scheduling process.

Before a certain number of rounds is carried out, a key expansion based on the key scheduling procedure takes place. The encryption ends with a final round that is only carried out on layers 1,2 and 4. Decryption is possible with the same algorithm if the rounds are run in the reverse order with inverse transformation. Until this time there have been virtually no successful attacks on AES.

Further reading:

J. Daemen, V. Rijmen: The Design of Rijndael: AES – The Advanced Encryption Standard. Springer Verlag, Berlin, Heidelberg, New York (2002)

B. Schneier, Applied Cryptography: Protocols, Algorithms, and Source Code in C, John Wiley & Sons, New York, NY, USA (1995)

Even if today adequate safety is offered by AES, the problem of passing the secret key remains. The receiver of an encrypted message needs the key in order to convert the message back into plaintext. The problem becomes even more difficult if the communication channels of multiple parties need to be secured independent of one another. Each potential pair of participants must then have its own secret key, i.e, the number of secret keys needed increases quadratically with the number of participants. A solution is offered by asymmetrical key procedures in which only two keys are necessary per participant – a public key and a secret key.

5.2.2 Asymmetric Encryption Methods

In symmetric encryption procedures a secret key that cannot be compromised is exchanged between each pair of communication partners for encryption and decryption ($k = K$). In contrast, **asymmetric encryption procedures (public key encryption)** always use two different keys ($k \neq K$): a public key and a secret key. This form of decryption, together with the use of digital signatures, was presented for the first time in 1976 by *Whitfield Diffie* and *Martin Hellman*. It was to prove crucial for the further development of cryptography and Internet security as a whole. Some years ago it was brought to the attention of the public that already in 1970 a parallel procedure had been developed for the British secret service (Government Communications Headquarters, GCHQ) by British cryptographers *James H. Ellis, Clifford Cocks* and *Malcolm Williamson*. However at that time the economic significance of this discovery was not recognized nor could it be made public for reasons of confidentiality.

Asymmetrical key procedures are characterized by specific features. The secret, private key is not accessible to anyone except the user. After a complicated, non-reversible procedure the public key is generated from the secret key and made accessible to everyone under the user's name. A characteristic of the transformation function is that a message encrypted with user A's public key kp_A can only be decrypted again with its private key ks_A. As it is virtually impossible to trace the private key from the corresponding public key, the often problematic secret key exchange required in conventional symmetric procedures can be omitted. A message is encrypted with the (available to anyone) public key of the message receiver. The receiver alone is able to decrypt the original plaintext from the ciphertext with the private, secret key known only to him (see Fig. 5.8). Making the public key known does not present a security risk if a so-called one-way function is used as the transformation function in this procedure. With this function, calculating the inverse transformation, and thus the determining the private key, is virtually impossible (with reasonable effort).

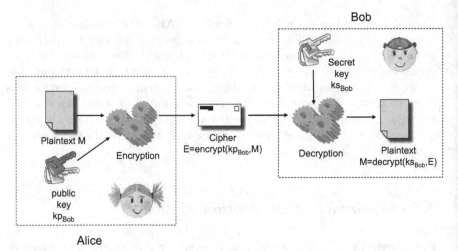

Fig. 5.8 Asymmetric Encryption (Public Key Encryption)

This type of procedure to solve the key exchange problem by using the discrete logarithm[1] as the transformation function was published for the first time in 1976 by *Whitfield Diffie* and Martin Hellman. It played a decisive role in the popularity of the science of cryptology, which until that time had been carried out away from the public eye (see Fig. 5.9). The Diffie-Hellman key exchange protocol forms the basis for the ElGamal cryptosystem.

The Diffie-Hellman procedure was solely intended for the safe exchange of a private key between two communication partners via a public network. In contrast, the 1977 **RSA procedure** for encryption, named after its developers *Adi Shamir, Ronald L. Rivest*[2] and *Leonard M. Adleman,* goes one step further and offers a complete asymmetric encryption procedure that can also be implemented as a digital signature. The RSA procedure uses a secret key from which a public key is calculated. The reverse calculation is impossible to obtain with a reasonable effort using today's technology. The messages to be transmitted are encrypted with the public key of the receiver, who alone can decrypt the ciphertext with the help of his private key. In this way it is ensured that only the receiver and no one else can read the plaintext. The RSA procedure, based on facts from number theory, is described in Excursus 15. It is founded on the current state of knowledge that the factoring of a large number, i.e., its breakdown into prime factors, requires an extremely high calculation effort, while generating a number through the multiplication of two prime numbers is very simple. Whereas attacks on breaking the key

---

[1] Also known as the modulo logarithm reversal operation of the modular exponentiation. If $a, b, n \in \mathbb{N}$ are given, then the discrete logarithm is number x, and the following applies: $a^x = b \bmod n$.

[2] Ronald L. Rivest also developed the well-known symmetric encryption procedures RC2, RC4, RC5 and RC6.

Diffie-Hellman Key Exchange

Alice and Bob want to communicate via an insecure medium encrypted with a conventional symmetric encryption procedure. To do this both need a shared secret key. With the help of the Diffie-Hellman key exchange they can both safely gain possession of such a key.

Sequence:

1. Alice and Bob agree to a prime number p and a primitive root g *mod* p with $2 \leq g \leq$ p-2. It is not necessary for these parameters to be kept secret.
2. Alice and Bob each generate for themselves a random number to keep confidential, a or b with $1\leq a, b \leq$ p-2. Both random numbers a and b are only known to Alice or Bob respectively. They are not transfered, i.e. they cannot fall into the hands of a potential attacker.
3. Alice calculates $A = g^a$ mod p, Bob calculates $B = g^b$ mod p. A and B can be safely transmitted over the insecure medium because a and b can no longer be simply calculated from A and B.
4. Alice and Bob now calculate the identical private key $K = B^a$ mod p, or $K = A^b$ mod p, which can be used for the subsequent communication.

Without special precautions being taken the Diffie-Hellmann key exchange can be compromised by a **man-in-the-middle attack** if the attacker is in a position of changing the data packets transmitted. Trudy intercepts the message sent by Alice and Bob during the key exchange and instead of sending it sends her own message $Z = g^z$ mod p. It is calculated from a random number z and the publicly known numbers g and p. After conclusion of the key exchange, Alice and Bob have different keys – K_A and K_B, because unknowingly Alice and Bob have in fact each exchanged a key with Trudy. Consequently, Trudy has knowledge of both keys K_A and K_B. This attack can however be thwarted by using a public key infrastructure.

Further reading:

W. Diffie, M. E. Hellman: New Directions in Cryptography, in IEEE Transactions on Information Theory, no.6, pp. 644–654 (1976)

Fig. 5.9 Diffie-Hellman key exchange.

in symmetric encryption are primarily ciphertext-only, known-plaintext and chosen-plaintext based, the following attacks dominate asymmetric encryption:

- **Public-key-only attacks**: Attacker Trudy only has access to Alice's public key. Trudy can encrypt any plaintext with this key and generate text pairs from plaintext and the accompanying ciphertext, which can then be used for determining the private key.

- **Chosen-cyphertext attacks**: In this variation Trudy can choose a ciphertext freely and then Alice can decrypt it. In contrast to public-key-only attacks, in which Alice's known public key is the basis, the chosen-cyphertext attack can only be carried out in certain situations. For example, when Trudy has direct access to a RSA hardware module

Theoretically, Trudy can also try to determine the private key via an exhaustive search. However with key lengths of up to 4,096 bits this is fruitless with RSA. In comparison to symmetric procedures such as DES or Triple-DES, asymmetric RSA encryption is slower by a factor of 1,000 because of the much more complex calculation required. Therefore, practically-speaking, so-called **hybrid-encryption methods** make sense for the encryption of larger amounts of data. With these methods a sufficiently longer private key can be exchanged between the communication partners with the help of an asymmetric encryption procedure. The actual message itself can then be symmetrically encrypted with this key.

Excursus 16: The RSA Public-Key Procedure

The best known and most widely used asymmetric key procedure **RSA** is named after its inventors *Ron Rivest*, *Adi Shamir* and *Leonard Adleman*. The RSA procedure, developed in 1977, is considered the first encryption method by which not only asymmetric encryption can be implemented but also digital signatures. In 1983 RSA was registered for a patent, although it was not the first asymmetric encryption. The patent expired on September 21, 2000.

Preparation on Bob's side

Alice and Bob want to communicate with each other via the RSA procedure. Before Alice can encrypt message M and send it to Bob, it is necessary that Bob generate a private and a public key. This takes place as follows:

- Selection of two, different very large prime numbers p and q.
  Both prime number should be approximately the same magnitude. RSA recommends the selection of p and q so that their product has a length of 768 bits for the encryption of private communication and 1024 bits for commercial use. Key lengths of 2048 bits, 4096 bits or longer are also possible. The determination of large prime numbers generally represents a very difficult problem. The calculation complexity for checking whether a randomly chosen number is indeed a prime number rises exponentially with the length of the number to be checked. Therefore, for this purpose, fast, probabilistic primality tests are carried out. While these do not give an absolutely accurate indication, they offer a correct assessment of primality with a high degree of probability.

- Calculation of the RSA modulus $n = p \cdot q$ and
  Euler's ϕ function $\phi(n) = z = (p-1) \cdot (q-1)$.

- Selection of the encryption exponents $e < n$, $e \neq 1$, so that e (just as n) has no shared prime factors with z, i.e., $ggT(e,z)=1$.

- Calculation of the encryption exponent d as multiplicative inverse from e *mod* z, i.e., e $\cdot$ d $\equiv$ 1 *mod* z applies. Calculation of the partial secret key d can proceed with help of the expanded Euclidean algorithm as $d=eggT(e,z)$ [51].

- Bob's public key kp_B is the number pair (n,e), Bob's secret key ks_B is the number pair (n,d).

Encryption by Alice

- Bob has made his public key $kp_B=(n,e)$ available for Alice and the public. Alice would like to send Bob a message M (encoded as a bitstring), for the interpretation of M as a number applies: $M < n$.
- To encrypt from the plaintext M with the public key from Bob $kp_B=(n,e)$ Alice calculates the ciphertext c as

$$c \equiv M^e \bmod n.$$

- Alice sends the encrypted message c to Bob.

Decryption by Bob

- To decrypt the ciphertext, Bob calculates with the help of his secret key $ks_B=(n,d)$ the original plaintext message

$$M \equiv c^d \bmod n.$$

The Security of the RSA Public Key Method

The security of the RSA method is based on the difficulty of solving the so-called "RSA problem." Trudy, the attacker, has the public key $kp_B=(n,e)$ from Bob and the ciphertext c. Trudy wants to reconstruct the original plaintext M from it . This corresponds to the task of extracting the eth root from c, when c is made up of two unknown factors – a task that remains virtually insolvable to date. However, it must be critically noted that there is currently no mathematical proof that confirms this assumption.

The RSA method is based on prime numbers that can be found relatively easily with the help of probabilistic methods (e.g., prime tests based on Rabin-Miller [51]) and multiplied with each other. However, if an attacker only knows the product of the two prime numbers, identifying the factors involved (the so-called "factorization problem") with reasonable effort is virtually impossible. Factorization is currently the only way known to solve the RSA problem. More efficient methods of solving the RSA problem – and subsequently breaking the RSA encryption – are not known.

The RSA Security company held a contest between 1991 and 2007 known as the RSA Challenge. It was intended to demonstrate the security of the RSA procedure. Mathematicians and computer scientists were called to find the prime factorization of given numbers of different lengths (from 330 to 2048 bits). In the first years of the RSA challenge several of the listed numbers were factorized. However the limit of 530 bits could only first be broken in 2003. The two mathematicians Jens Franke and Thorsten Kleinjung, from the Mathematical Institute in Bonn and the Institute for Experimental Mathematics in Essen succeeded in separating a number of 576 bits in length into its prime factors and thereby winning a prize of 10,000 US\$. In November 2005 the same team succeeded in factoring a number of 640 bits in the RSA Challenge. In May 2007 when a 1039 bit-long number was factorized (the 1039 Mersenne number[3]) that was not among the numbers listed in the RSA Challenge, RSA security declared the contest over with the security of the procedure verified. Since key lengths of 2048 bits, 4096 bits and longer are also possible there are no doubts regarding the security of the RSA procedure over a longer time span, at least as long as no scientific breakthrough in regard to efficient solutions to the RSA problem can be found.

Further reading:

Cormen, T. H., Leiserson, C. E., Rivest, R. L., Stein, C.: Introduction to Algorithms. The MIT Press, Cambridge, MA, USA (2001)

Kaufman, C., Perlman, R., Speciner, M.: Network Security, Private Communication in a Public World, Prentice Hall, Englewood Cliffs NJ, USA (1995)

Rivest, R. I., Shamir, A., Adleman, L.: On a Method for Obtaining Digital Signatures and Public Key Cryptosystems, in Communications of the ACM, vol.21, pp. 120-126 (1978)

---

[3] A Mersenne number is a number in the form $2^n - 1$, $M_n = 2^n - 1$. It is referred to as the nth Mersenne number after the French mathematician Marin Mersenne (1588 – 1648).

5.2.3 Authentication

In order to establish the identity of the communication partner, and to be sure that the communication partner is not an impostor, a procedure for **authentication** is necessary. In a computer program that can grant access to a secure area, the user first validates his identity by giving his user name. The user also authenticates himself by giving a password or secret information known only to him and his partner. The program can then identify the user based on this information and subsequently authenticate identity. The password proves that the user is indeed who he claims to be, thereby establishing the identity of the communication partner for the program. The identified user is granted **authorization** for access to the secured resources immediately.

Because authentication via the Internet is not possible in the manner of face-to-face partners whose mutual recognition is based on biometric characteristics, it is necessary to rely on the help of electronic messages exchanged over the network. Special **authentication protocols** have been developed for this purpose. Information is exchanged between the communication partners intended to prove their identification conclusively. Only if this process is carried out successfully and the identity of the partners established beyond a reasonable doubt can the actual communication take place. The development of reliable authentication procedures is more difficult than one might imagine. For a better understanding, we will look briefly at this development as well as the difficulties that must be overcome. Alice and Bob are the two communication partners. Alice attempts to authenticate herself reliably over the network. The third party, Trudy, tries to feign Alice's identity to Bob.

- The simplest way of authentication is for the communication partner to give her name, i.e., identity. Therefore before the actual communication begins, Alice transmits the message to Bob: *"Hi, this is Alice."* However, there is no way for Bob to verify whether this notification is actually from Alice. It would be easy for Trudy to send Bob the same message and successfully feign Alice's identity.

- If Bob knows Alice's IP address for communication, it follows that he assumes the message is from her when the received data packet contains Alice's address as the sender. It is easy for Trudy to manipulate the return address in the data packet to make it look like it was sent from Alice's IP address (**IP spoofing**) if Trudy has control over the operating system and network software of Alice's computer. IP spoofing can be avoided if the first router via which Trudy forwards the data on the Internet is configured in such a way that only Trudy's data containing her original IP address as sender is forwarded (see RFC 2267). But as such a configuration cannot be assumed, the verification of the IP addresses alone does not offer secure authentication.

- The classic approach to authentication proceeds via the use of a secret password. Alice sends a secret password together with the message *"Hi, this is Alice."* Only Bob and Alice are privy to this password. Bob can therefore be sure that his communication partner is only Alice. But it is also possible for Trudy to spy on the entire data traffic between Alice and Bob (**packet sniffing**). Alice's secret password can be captured and used later for unauthorized communication with Bob (**playback attack**). Because Internet protocols such as telnet transmit passwords in plaintext this scenario presents a real threat.

- Next, Alice and Bob can agree on a common symmetric encryption procedure to transfer Alice's password in encrypted form. Because Alice is not only using her password now but also the shared secret key, Bob believes all the more strongly in her identity. But also here Trudy has the possibility to spy on the communication between Alice and Bob, recording the encrypted password from Alice and using it in a subsequent attack in the communications with Bob (not understood) (**replay attack**). The situation has not improved much regarding Alice's authentication.

- The playback attack can only succeed if the same password is always used. A simple defense for Alice and Bob against such an attack is that they do not have just a single password each, but in advance have agreed with each other on a whole series of passwords to be used one after another. The prerequisite is of course a secure exchange of the password list.

A solution to the problem is found in the use of a technique similar to the three-way handshake of the TCP protocol . To ensure that in a connection setup (SYN), via the TCP protocol, no old SYN segment (retransmission) from an earlier connection is being used, every segment receives a sequence number. At the start of a connection a random value is generated as a sequence number for the sender's SYN segment. The answering receiver responds with an ACK segment with the same sequence number. A random value used in the way is referred to as a **nonce** (or "salt"). This value may only be used once. An authentication with a nonce value proceeds as follows (see Fig. 5.10):

1. Alice sends the message *"Hi, this is Alice"* to Bob.
2. Bob chooses a nonce value R and sends it back to Alice, to determine is Alice is indeed present "live."
3. Alice encrypts R with the symmetric secret key k, which Alice and Bob have previously agreed upon, and sends $k(R)$ back to Bob.
4. Bob can decrypt $k(R)$ and recognizes the nonce value R. Because Alice knows and uses k, Bob is assured that Alice's identity is correct. Since Alice sends back the value $k(R)$, Bob can assume that Alice is also answering "live" and that this is not a playback attack. Bob has successfully authenticated Alice.

Instead of using a symmetrical encryption procedure in this scenario, an asymmetrical encryption procedure with a public key may be performed. The new protocol looks like this (cf. Fig. 5.11):

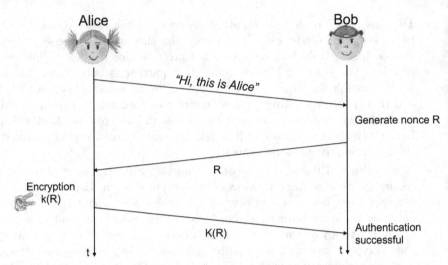

Fig. 5.10 Authentication with the help of a nonce value and a symmetrical encryption procedure.

1. Alice sends Bob the message "*Hi, this is Alice.*"
2. Bob selects a nonce value R and sends it back to Alice to determine if Alice is indeed a "live" communication partner.
3. In order to encrypt R, Alice uses the asymmetrical encryption algorithm (cf. Excursus 16) with her private key ks_A on R and sends $ks_A(R)$ back to Bob. Since only Alice knows her private key, no one except for Alice can generate the value $ks_A(R)$.
4. Bob obtains Alice's public key kp_A, uses the asymmetrical encryption algorithm on the received message and calculates $kp_A(ks_A(R))$. If $kp_A(ks_A(R)) = R$ is valid, then Alice has been successfully authenticated.

In this case, just as in other asymmetrical applications, there is however the problem of secure access to the public key. The following scenario illustrates this problem. Trudy succeeds in carrying out a man-in-the-middle attack , successfully authenticating herself to Bob as Alice.

1. Trudy sends Bob the message "*Hi, this is Alice.*"
2. Bob selects a nonce value R and sends it back to Alice to determine if Alice is actually participating "live" in the communication. The message is intercepted by Trudy.
3. For encrypting R Trudy uses the encryption algorithm with her own private key ks_T on R and sends $ks_T(R)$ back to Bob. As the received value presents an unknown bit string, Bob cannot decide if is comes from Alice or Trudy, i.e., if it is $ks_A(R)$ or $ks_T(R)$.
4. In order for Bob to decrypt the received value he needs the public key kp_A from Alice. While it might be assumed that he has access to the

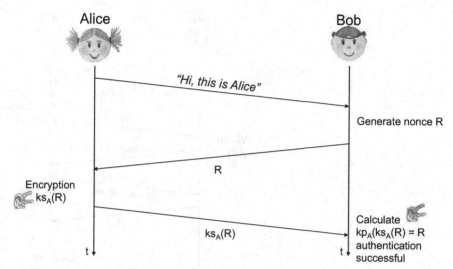

Fig. 5.11 Authentication using a nonce value and an asymmetric encryption procedure.

key, he actually first must request it from Alice. This request can also be intercepted by Trudy and she can answer Bob with her own public key kp_T. Bob uses the decryption algorithm together with the obtained public key kp_T on the received message and calculates $kp_T(ks_T(R)) = R$. He mistakenly believes to have correctly authenticated Alice, while unknowingly communicating with Trudy.

Such an attack can be detected, however, when Bob reports to Alice that they communicated with each other, when Alice knows that this was not the case. But if Trudy carries out the same actions in her contact with Alice that she has with Bob, she can succeed in remaining unnoticed by both, i.e., **transparent**. She can then cause interference in Alice and Bob's communication session. Trudy pretends to be Alice to Bob. At the same time, she pretends to be Bob in her contact with Alice (see Fig. 5.12). Another possibility for securing the authentication of a message in the face of the described attack is so-called **second channel communication**. Here, part of the identification data is sent over a separate, second channel. For example, the sending of a text message (SMS) in a mobile TAN (mTAN) procedure.

5.3 Digital Signatures

In daily life a handwritten signature is used to confirm the contents of a document or as proof of agreement with the contents of a document – e.g., a contract. On the Internet and in the digital world there is also a wish to

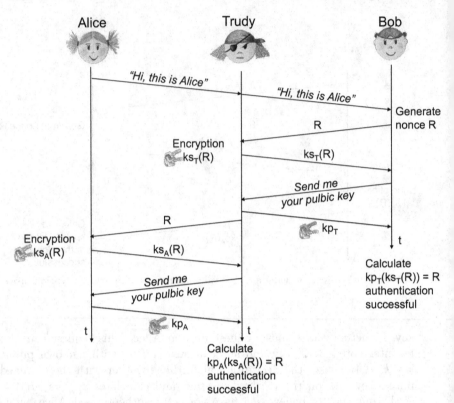

Fig. 5.12 Man-in-the-middle attack in the authentication phase of a communication session.

unequivocally provide agreement with contents of a document, confirm its correctness or to prove the document's authorship or ownership. So-called **digital signatures** are used for this purpose.

Just as with a normal signature in everyday life, there are specific requirements for a digital signature. It must be:

- verifiable,
- tamper-proof and
- binding.

There must be an assurance that the one who signs the document is indeed the person he or she claims to be. At the same time it should not be possible for the signer of a document to later be able to dispute having signed the document in question. These qualities can also be fulfilled with a digital signature via modern cryptographic methods based on asymmetric encryption.

5.3.1 Data Integrity and Authenticity

Let us assume that Alice wants to use a digital signature for proof of the integrity of message M and its authenticity. Additionally, Bob, the receiver of message M, wants to be assured that it was in fact Alice who sent him message M (see Fig. 5.13).

- To sign message M digitally Alice simply uses an asymmetrical encryption algorithm together with her own secret key ks_A and calculates $ks_A(M)$, the so-called digital signature of message M.
- Alice sends $ks_A(M)$ to Bob, who with Alice's public key kp_A, can decrypt the message $M = kp_A(ks_A(M))$.

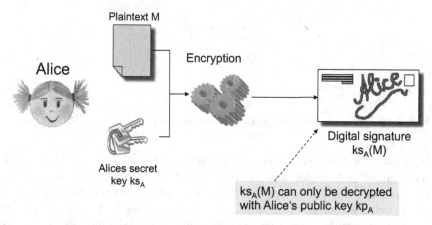

Fig. 5.13 Generating a digital signature for a message.

This simple form of the digital signature does in fact satisfy the requirements for the equivalent of a handwritten signature named above. Bob can verify whether Alice was actually the sender of the message by using the decryption algorithm with Alice's public key kp_A and calculating $kp_A(ks_A(M))$. If the result is then readable as message M, Bob can be sure that Alice is the originator and signer of the received message. $kp_A(ks_A(M)) = M$ applies namely only is the received digital signature $kp_A(M)$ is encrypted with Alice's secret key ks_A. However, the only person who has access to this key (according to prescribed use) is Alice. Therefore, Alice is the only one who could have generated the digital signature. To additionally ensure that the sent message was not manipulated during transmission, besides sending the digital signature Alice can also send Bob the message M. Alice can protect message M from being seen by third parties by encrypting M with Bob's public key kp_B and transmitting it as $kp_B(M)$. Upon receipt, Bob decrypts $kp_B(M)$ with his secret key ks_B and obtains the original message $M = ks_B(kp_B(M))$. By comparing message M with the decrypted digital signature $M = kp_A(ks_A(M))$,

Bob can tell whether the content of the original message M was manipulated in any way during the course of transmission (see Fig. 5.14).

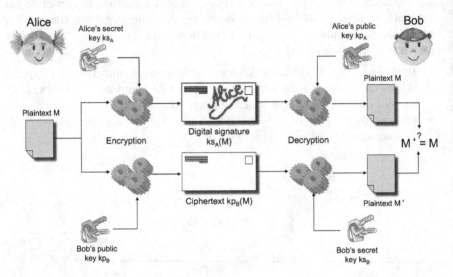

Fig. 5.14 Verification of the integrity of a message with the aid of a digital signature.

If an unauthorized third party has forged the original message M as a new message M' before Bob has received it, Bob recognizes in encryption that $kp_A(ks_A(M)) \neq M'$ now applies. Bob then realizes that something has gone wrong and the content of the message is no longer reliable. However, there are two serious problems with this variation of the digital signature. First, the calculation complexity of asymmetrical encryption procedures increases when compared to symmetrical encryption procedures by a factor of 1,000. The calculation of a digital signature, which is based on encryption of the whole document, is extremely complex in the case of a large document. Second, it cannot be guaranteed that the message content remains secret. It is namely always possible to decipher Alice's digital signature with Alice's public key. Because this key is accessible to everyone there is an ever-present danger that the contents of the original message might be disclosed. The starting point of a digital signature should thus not be the original message itself, but a derivative of the message. This derivative should uniquely identify the message without making it possible to drawn any conclusions about its content.

5.3.2 Message Digest

The encryption of an entire message in order to generate a digital signature is in many cases an extremely cumbersome process. The necessary data transfer alone is doubled thus hindering an effective encryption of the content. In addition, there are a lot of messages regularly exchanged by a large number of network components and processes that do not need encryption, e.g., routers or email agents. Solely the identity of the sender must be secured and the receiver assured that the message content has not been tampered with by an unauthorized third party. In these cases the application of a **hash function** is recommended to generate a so-called **message digest**. Such hash functions calculate from the content of the message to be sent M a short as possible "fingerprint" $h(M)$ of the message of fixed-length, known as a message digest. It is sent together with the message to the receiver. With the help of the message digest it is possible to check whether the contents of the received message M' have arrived intact and therefore if $M = M'$ is valid. To do this, using the same hash function the receiver calculates the fingerprint $h(M')$ of the received message M' and verifies whether it matches the received fingerprint $h(M)$. If $h(M') = h(M)$, then (at least with overwhelming probability), due to the requirements placed on the hash function, $M = M'$ is also valid. The received message is thus identical with the message originally transmitted.

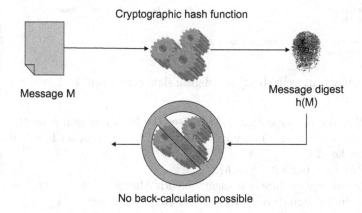

Fig. 5.15 Hash function for generating a message digest.

From this point of view it makes sense to use the message digest for the digital signature. Namely, if Alice carries out encryption with her secret key ks_A on the message digest $h(M)$, instead of encrypting the whole message it is sufficient to transfer $ks_A(h(M))$ with the original message instead of $ks_A(M)$. This fulfills all the requirements of a digital signature. At the same time the message digest function must fulfill the following requirements to qualify as forgery-proof:

- With a given message digest value d it is not possible to reconstruct the original message M with a reasonable effort so that $h(M) = d$ applies.
- It is impossible to find two different messages M and N with a reasonable effort so that $h(M) = h(N)$ applies.

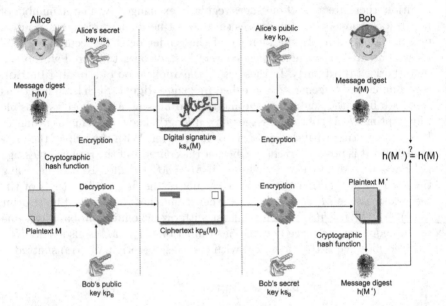

Fig. 5.16 Use of digital signature and message digest.

Fig. 5.16 shows how a message bearing a digital signature is sent and received via a message digest .

- For generating the message digest, Alice uses the hash function h on the message to be sent M and encrypts $h(M)$ with the encryption function and its secret key ks_A.
- Alice sends M together with $ks_A(h(M))$.
- Bob uses the decryption function together with Alice's public key kp_A on the received digital signature $ks_A(h(M))$ of Alice's message.
- Bob applies the hash function h on the received message M' and compares whether $h(M') = kp_A(ks_A(h(M)))$ applies.
- If both values are identical, Bob can assume that the received message is really from Alice and has not been altered during transmission.

Generating a message digest today is usually carried out with the **MD5** algorithm developed by Ron Rivest. As specified in RFC 1321, a 128 bit-long message digest is calculated from the document. Another algorithm, specified as a standard for U.S. federal government communication, is called the **secure hash algorithm (SHA-1)**. It is based on a principal similar to MD5's predecessor, MD4, and generates a 160 bit-long message digest. Cryptographic hash functions are described in detail in Excursus 17.

Excursus 17: Cryptographic Hash Functions

A **hash function** is a function or mapping that generates a smaller target amount of output (a **hash value**) for a large amount of data input. A hash value is also referred to as a message digest or fingerprint. Just as a human fingerprint is a virtually unique way to identify a person, a hash value also provides unique identification of the input. In cryptography, a hash value has the purpose of preserving the integrity of a document. This means its authentication can be proved without the contents being revealed.

Definition of a Hash Function

The amounts K and S are given, whereby K represents the data amount for which a hash value is to be determined and S the quantity of the available hash values (also keys). In certain contexts the quantity S is also referred to an address space. A mapping $h:K \rightarrow S$ is called a hash function if $[\#S] \leq [\#K]$ applies. Typically, in practical application the hash value is only determined for a small subset $K' \subseteq K$. The amount $S' := \{h(k)|k \in K'\}$ is thus the amount of hash values actually used. A **collision** occurs if $h(k)=h(k')$ applies for two different data sets $k, k' \in K$, $k \neq k'$. A hash function is called **perfect** if it does not produce any collisions.

Quality Criteria for Hash Functions

The following criteria characterize the quality of a hash function:

- The lowest possible likelihood of collisions, i.e., the most uniform distribution of hash values that can be achieved.
- Considerably smaller storage requirements for the hash value than those of the data represented (data reduction)
- Similar data should result in completely different hash values, i.e. ideally, the flipping of one bit of the data should change half of all bits of the associated hash value
- Potentially, every possible hash value in the value range should be possible (surjectivity)
- Implementation of the hash function should be carried out in the most efficient way in terms of calculation and storage (i.e., in polynomial time) and, as far as possible, the source data read only once.

Cryptographic Hash Functions

If hash functions are to be used for calculating a digital signature, even higher demands must be placed on them in order to meet the necessary safety criteria. The most important of these conditions is the virtual impossibility of drawing conclusions about the source data from the hash values. A cryptographic hash function must therefore be a **one-way function**. So-called **one-way hash functions** (OWHF) fulfill this requirement. It is next to impossible to trace the original value x from a given output value of the hash function $h(x)=y$ (preimage resistance), i.e., the calculation of the inverse cannot be done in polynomial time with the help of a probabilistic algorithm. Additionally, it must not be possible for an attacker to intentionally cause collisions. Otherwise Trudy would be able to produce her own message with the same hash value and pretend that it was signed by Alice. One-way hash functions must be able to satisfy the conditions of weak collision resistance. Accordingly, for a given value x it should be virtually impossible to find a different x' with the same hash value $h(x)=h(x')$ (2nd-preimage resistance). If a one-way hash function also fulfills the condition of strong collision resistance, i.e., two different input values e x and x' cannot be found with the same hash values $h(x)=h(x')$, the hash function is referred to as a **collision resistant hash function** (Collision Free Hash Function, CFHF).

A special class of one-way hash functions are so-called **trapdoor functions**. These can only be reversed efficiently if one has additional information (e.g. a specific key). In cryptography, key-independent hash functions are also called **message authentication codes** (MAC). In contrast to digital signatures, MACs work according to the principle of symmetrical encryption. Accordingly, a secret key must first be exchanged between the sender and the receiver so that both can calculate a MAC from the transmitted message, thus verifying the authenticity of the transferred message. While an attacker can change the message, because he does not know the secret key he cannot produce a valid MAC for the manipulated message and a subsequent manipulation can therefore be recognized.

Construction of Cryptographic Hash Functions

The majority of cryptographic hash functions are iterated compression functions. The message M to be processed is divided into blocks of a fixed length $M(1), \ldots, M(n)$ and, if necessary, filled with additional (padding) bits so that the input length is always a multiple of the block length. The compression function used in each case receives as input a block of data and the output of the previous implementation of the compression function. The hash value of the total data is represented as the output of the last data block $M(n)$:

- $H(0) = IV$, IV (Initial Value) indicates a start value
- $H(i) = h(M(i), H(i-1))$, for $i=1,\ldots,n$
- $h(M) = H(n)$

Some of the best known cryptographic hash functions are briefly described in the following.

SHA-1

The **Secure Hash Algorithm** (SHA-1) is one of the most important cryptographic hash functions. Specified in RFC 4634, it was developed starting in 1991 by the NSA, under the direction of the US standardization authority NIST. The flow of SHA-1 follows the generally given construction scheme of cryptographic hash functions. The data is divided into 512 bit blocks. The central element of SHA-1 are five string variables. The compression function is applied sequentially to all blocks, whereby the content of the string variables changes with each step. At the end, the contents of the five string variables form the 160 bit-long SHA-1 hash value.

SHA-1 Algorithm in Pseudo-Code:

```
// Initialize variables
var int h0 := 0x67452301
var int h1 := 0xEFCDAB89
var int h2 := 0x98BADCFE
var int h3 := 0x10325476
var int h4 := 0xC3D2E1F0



// Pre-processing of the message:
var int messageLaenge := bit_length(message)
extend the message  bit to "1"
extend the message bits to "0" until the length corresponds to 448 mod 512
extend message to message length

// Process the message in successive 512-bit blocks:
for all 512-bit blocks of message
   divide each block into 16 32-bit words w(i), 0 <= i <= 15
   // extend the 16 32-bit words into 80 32-bit words:
   for all i from 16 to 79
      w(i) := (w(i-3) xor w(i-8) xor w(i-14) xor w(i-16)) leftrotate 1
   // Initialize hash value for this block:
   var int a := h0
   var int b := h1
   var int c := h2
   var int d := h3
   var int e := h4

   // Main loop:
```

```
for all i from 0 to 79
    if 0 <= i <= 19 then
        f := (b and c) or ((not b) and d)
        k := 0x5A827999
    else if 20 <= i <= 39 then
        f := b xor c xor d
        k := 0x6ED9EBA1
    else if 40 <= i <= 59 then
        f := (b and c) or (b and d) or (c and d)
        k := 0x8F1BBCDC
    else if 60 <= i <= 79  then
        f := b xor c xor d
        k := 0xCA62C1D6

    temp := (a leftrotate 5) + f + e + k + w(i)
    e := d
    d := c
    c := b leftrotate 30
    b := a
    a := temp

// Add this block's hash value to the result of the hash so far:
h0 := h0 + a
h1 := h1 + b
h2 := h2 + c
h3 := h3 + d
h4 := h4 + e

hashwert = h0 append h1 append h2 append h3 append h4
```

Among other things SHA-1 is supported by all major web browsers, is part of the Pretty Good Privacy protocol (PGP) for secure email data traffic, and part of the network protocols SSL, IPsec and S/MIME. However, in 2004 a weakness of the SHA-1 hash function was made known. This could make it possible to break a SHA-1 hash value with the computing power available in the near future. NIST therefore no longer recommends future use of SHA-1. Based on SHA-1, the (still) secure hash functions **SHA-224**, **SHA-256**, **SHA-384** and **SHA-512** have been developed. The number after the hyphen indicates the bit length of the hash value generated.

MD-4
The **Message Digest Algorithm 4** (MD4) was released in 1990 by *Ronald L. Rivest* and specified in RFC 1320. MD4 provides a 128 bit hash value and is easily implementable and computationally efficient. The procedure is very similar to SHA-1 (SHA-1 is based on the MD4 algorithm), however it could be demonstrated that MD4 has serious deficiencies [4].

MD-5
The identified safety deficiencies in MD4 led *Ronald L. Rivest* to present an improved version of his Message Digest Algorithm already in 1991. This was the MD5 hash procedure, described in RFC 1321. SHA-1 as well as MD5 are further developments of MD4 and are therefore very similar. Both methods disassemble the data to be processed into 512-bit size blocks. They use string variables with a length of 32 bits and go through four rounds each in the compression function. In contrast to SHA-1, MD5 provides a hash length of just 128 bits. Although 128 bits is considered today the lowest limit for safe hash value calculation, due to its short hash length MD5 is seldom used anymore.

RIPEMD-160
An important alternative to SHA-1 at this time is RIPEMD-160. It is a further development

---

[4] In RSA's "CryptoBytes" journal, a method was published of generating two messages in an hour that are identical to each other except for one character and have the same MD4 hash value.

of the RIPEMD hash function, which was developed in 1992 as part of an EU project. The hash value lengths for RIPEMD-160 is 160 bits. Just as SHA-1, RIPEMD-160 works with data blocks of 512 bits, one compression function and five string variables. The main loop of the compression algorithm consists of five rounds, each with 16 steps. The algorithm runs parallel in two variations. After the execution of a block, the results of both variations are added to the string variables. Besides RIPEMD-160, there are also the variations **RIPEMD-120 RIPEMD-256** and **RIPEMD-320**. As RIPEMD-160 has not revealed any cryptographic weaknesses until now it is considered the first choice among the cryptographic hash functions.

Other Cryptographic Hash Functions

- **TIGER**
  Released in 1995, the TIGER hash method is a genuinely new development rather than a further development of an already existing procedure. It calculates 192-bit hash values. Up to this time it has not been widely distributed.
- **WHIRLPOOL**
  A cryptographic hash function released in 2000 which was proposed by the AES co-developer *Vincent Rijmen* with *Paulo Barreto*. WHIRLPOOL operates with 64 string variables and provides a 512 bit-long hash value. The compression function used is based on AES encryption. So far no weaknesses of this method are known.
- **SNEFRU**
  A method proposed in 1990 by cryptography pioneer *Ralph Merkle*. SNEFRU provides a variable number of rounds and is based on the block cipher system Merkle developed called Khafre. Depending on the number of rounds SNEFRU is considered either too slow or too uncertain today.

There are a variety of other cryptographic hash functions but they are not relevant in practical application today.

Attacks on Cryptographic Hash Functions

Attacks on cryptographic hash functions can ignore the respective algorithm completely, which can be treated as a black box. The concentration can be placed exclusively on the length of the hash value delivered by the hash function. Trudy, the attacker, chooses a message randomly and compares its hash value to that of a given message. In detail, this attack – called a **substitution attack** – proceeds as follows. Trudy intercepts a message with an extra cryptographic hash value from Alice to Bob. The cryptographic hash function used has a hash value with a length of n bits. Trudy now generates her own message that she wants to pass off to Bob. Through simple, sense-preserving substitutions, Trudy generates 2^n variations. This is done, for example, by substituting n individual words in the faked message or by adding meaningless filler words. Trudy generates the associated 2^n hash values until a fake message is found with the same hash value as the originally intercepted message. Trudy sends the fake message variant with the hash value to Bob, who is not able to detect the forgery. If it is assumed that for a successful attack Trudy must generate an average of half of all the possible hash values/message pairs, i.e. she must generate 2^{n-1} hash values, then with a hash length of 160 bits an astronomically high number of hash values to be made, namely $2^{159} = 7,3 \cdot 10^{47}$. This method can be used in all cryptographic hash functions and with any kind of message.

If Trudy also has the possibility of passing off to Alice a variation of her own message before its signing, the number of necessary hash calculations is dramatically reduced. This phenomenon is also known as the **birthday paradox**[5]. For this purpose, Trudy must generate $2^{n/2}$ different equal message variations to pass off to Alice and $2^{n/2}$ forged variations. If

---

[5] How many people need to be brought together so that the probability of at least two of them having their birthdays on the same day is greater than 50 percent? The startling answer to this question is just 22.

she finds a hash value equivalence between an original and a fake version, she gives the original version to Alice to sign and send, intercepts the signed message and and replaces it with her own fake message with the same signature. On the other hand, attacks on cryptographic hash functions can also be directed against the compression function itself. Hash functions that are based on a block cipher can direct an attack against the underlying block cipher. Because there are often different implementations of the individual hash procedures, an attack can take advantage of mistakes made in the respective implementation and compromise them.

Further reading:

Menezes, A.J., Vanstone, S.A., Oorschot, P.C.V.: Handbook of Applied Cryptography, pp. 321–384, CRC Press, Inc., Boca Raton, FL, USA, (1996)

Preneel, B.: Cryptographic primitives for information authentication – state of the art. In: State of the Art in Applied Cryptography, Course on Computer Security and Industrial Cryptography – Revised Lectures, pp. 49–104. Springer-Verlag, London, UK (1998)

Stinson, D.: Cryptography: Theory and Practice, 2nd Edition, pp. 117–154. Chapman & Hall, CRC, London, UK (2002)

5.4 Public Key Infrastructures and Certificates

Symmetric encryption methods with private keys as well as asymmetric encryption methods can only work reliably if a secure key exchange is guaranteed. While in symmetric procedures it is necessary that the secret key of both partners be exchanged in order to decrypt the transmitted messages, this is not necessary in the asymmetric process. Here it must instead be ensured that a communication partner's public key does indeed belong to him and not to an unauthorized third party who tries to sneak into a confidential communication under a false identity.

Secure key exchange or secure key assignment can be ensured by using a **trusted intermediary** (**trusted third party**). In a symmetric encryption procedure this trusted third party is also called the **Key Distribution Center (KDC)**. The KDC manages the private, secret keys necessary for secure communication via a symmetric encryption procedure. It creates secure and reliable distribution thereby preventing unauthorized third parties from gaining access to the private keys. In an asymmetric encryption procedure it is necessary for a communication partner to provide assurance that the public key indeed comes from him. This is done by way of certificates. These are issued and digitally signed by a trusted third party who provides the guarantee of a **certificate authority (CA)** or a **trust center (TA)**. Generally, such certification authorities form a hierarchical structure with a root authority at the top, and various subordinate bodies and users below. Such a hierarchy of certification authorities and all the associated data technology (e.g., certificate formats) and organizational requirements (**security policy**) is called a **public key infrastructure (PKI)** . This infrastructure is necessary to perform an asymmetrical key procedure securely.

5.4.0.1 Key Distribution Center (KDC)

Let us assume that Alice and Bob want to communicate with each other via an encryption procedure and do not have the possibility to exchange the necessary private, secret key securely. They must then rely on a KDC. Prior to use, those who use the KDC must register there. They must prove their identity upon registration and at that time deposit a private key. A KDC has authority over the secret key of every registered user. But how do Alice and Bob, who are both registered with the KDC, get a shared private session key in a secure way via the KDC? Initially both know only their own private key, i.e., Alice has key k_A and Bob key k_B. Fig. 5.17 shows the process of generating and securely distributing a shared private session key for Alice and Bob.

- Alice takes the initiative and sends a message $k_A(A, B)$ encrypted with k_A to the KDC, that she (A) wishes to communicate with Bob (B).
- The KDC has Alice's secret key k_A and can therefore decrypt Alice's message $k_A(A, B)$. The KDC then randomly generates key $R1$, which can be used for Alice and Bob's subsequent communication as a **unique session key**. The KDC sends a message to Alice encrypted with t k_A containing the following:

  – the unique session key $R1$ and
  – a pair of values consisting of Alice's name A and the session key $R1$, which is encrypted with Bob's secret key k_B: $k_B(A, R1)$.

  The KDC sends the encrypted message $k_A(R1, k_B(A, R1))$ to Alice.
- Alice receives and decrypts the KDC's message. She extracts the unique session key $R1$ and saves it for the subsequent communication with Bob and then directs the second part of the message $k_B(A, R1)$ (not understood) to Bob.
- Bob receives $k_B(A, R1)$, decrypts the message with his own secret key k_B and thereby learns of Alice/A's communication wish and the shared unique session key $R1$. The encrypted communication between Alice and Bob can now begin. If necessary, Alice and Bob can agree upon their own shared key in the first communication round, which is now securely encrypted by $R1$. This key is not known to the KDC.

The authentication service **Kerberos**, developed at the Massachusetts Institute of Technology (MIT) and specified in RFC 1510, provides such a key distribution center for symmetric keys – the so-called Kerberos server. At the request of registered users in a network, the Kerberos server provides a certificate file (ticket) with a limited time validity. This can serve as identification for the protection of data traffic. Beyond the services of the KDC, the Kerberos server additionally manages access rights of registered users to specific network resources. It also provides the issued session key with an expiration date. The key will no longer be accepted by Bob after this date.

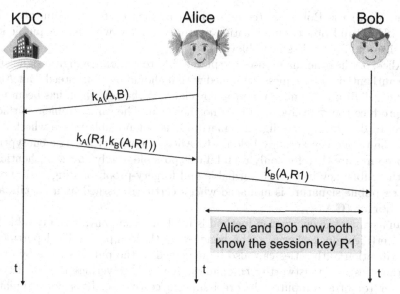

Fig. 5.17 Generation and secure distribution of a shared, secret session key for Alice and Bob via a key distribution center (KDC).

5.4.1 Certification Authority (CA)

The big advantage of encrypting with the asymmetric encrypting procedure is that private keys are not necessary. The public keys required are freely distributed by their owners and made available, e.g., on a homepage in the WWW. At the same time, in asymmetric encryption it is essential that a communication partner is able to trust that the public key offered to him is indeed the public key of his communication partner. This is where the difficulty lies. Authentication can easily be undermined by a malicious third party who assumes a false identity, (e.g., man-in-the-middle attack in Section 5.2.3).

Suppose Alice would like to send Bob an encrypted message that she wants to encrypt with Bob's public key. But if Trudy succeeds in passing off her own public key to Alice by pretending it is Bob's, she is able to read Alice's encrypted message with its associated private key. If Bob has sent his public key to Alice, then Trudy only needs to replace it with her own. Or if Trudy gains access to Bob's web server she can replace Bob's public key with her own there. The crux of the problem is the fact that one is not able to see the owner of the public key, i.e., its authenticity is not clear. Another problem is that public keys can lose their validity. For example, in the case that Bob's key pair is compromised, he can generate a new one. He leaves the new public keys at his web server, but Alice and other communication partners have no way of knowing that Bob has blocked his old key pair. As a result they continue to use Bob's old (compromised) public key to communicate with him. How are Bob's communication partners to know whether his public key is still valid or if it has been blocked?

If Alice, on the other hand, uses her private key to generate a digital signature, the authenticity of the message signed with it should be guaranteed. But Alice could still dispute signing a message by claiming the key which has been used to produce the digital signature is not her own. The same problem surfaces here. In decrypting the digital signature it is not possible to see whether or not the public key actually belongs to Alice or not. Asymmetric encryption procedures are therefore only useful if it is possible to rely on the authenticity of the public key used. The verifiable and forgery-proof, binding nature of a user's public signature is managed with a certificate issued by a **certificate authority (CA)**.

If an asymmetric encryption method is used in a company, it is advisable for the certification authority to be handled by the company's IT department. Certification authorities can also be managed in the public sphere by other authorities and trustworthy companies. A CA first verifies the identity of a user (or of a computer) before issuing a certificate. It is not stipulated how the CA must perform identity verification. But, for example, if identity verification is done based on email notification, then the certificate that is issued later is not of much value – email messages can be easily forged. On the other hand, if a publicly recognized CA fulfills the standards of the signature law, the certificate issued can be trusted without hesitation. In any case, the CA must make known its own certification guidelines. A user can then assess the quality of the certificate and – accordingly – the reliability of the transmitted public key.

After the CA has verified the user's identity, it creates a digital **certificate**, which connects the public key with the user's identity (name, address or IP address). The certificate is signed by the CA (see Fig. 5.18). The signing of a certificate is referred to as **certification**. Besides containing the identity and the public key of a participant, a digital certificate has other information, e.g., period of validity, serial number and information on the use of the public key. But the digital certificate of a CA can only be trusted if Alice and Bob are in a position to verify the signature of the CA. Alice and Bob have to know the public key of the CA to do this. Here again the problem crops up of not being able to identify whether or not the CA's public key is authentic and valid. The public key of a CA is also often verified based on a digital certificate (CA certificate). This means that the same problem is just shifted over once more – this time to the CA who signed the CA certificate. It is therefore necessary to find other more secure methods to safely issue a CA's public key. One possibility is for the company who distributes the software to already provide the CA's public key on user's PCs. In case Alice did not trust the public key, she could then have it personally verified, e.g., by calling the company. Another possibility is for the CA's public key to be made known through an announcement in a a reputable (=trustworthy) daily newspaper or to even receive the key personally directly at the CA.

To ensure that a public key passed by a user in fact corresponds to its specified identity, the following steps are taken:

- If Alice would like to communicate with Bob via an asymmetrical encryption procedure, she sends him her message together with her certificate (the certificate can also be requested by the CA).
- The respective CA has made its own public key accessible to all users in a secure manner (e.g., published in a prominent place in a reputable newspaper). Using this public key from the CA, Bob decrypts the certificate from Alice.
- If Bob is able to decrypt the certificate and if the information it contains corresponds to the information from Alice, Bob can be sure that he is really in contact with Alice and then uses her public key for further communication.

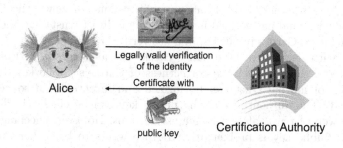

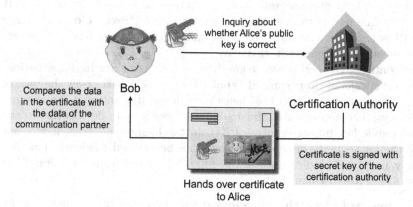

Fig. 5.18 Alice and Bob using a CA to verify the public key.

5.4.2 Trust Models

It's not only possible for digital certificates to be issued by CAs. The signing of a certificate can also be done by a body that both communication partners trust. In fact, there are a variety of **trust models**. The simplest variation, known as **direct trust**, is designed so that Bob can personally confirm the authenticity of his public key to Alice. This can be done by issuing a certificate. But to prevent manipulation by Trudy, Alice and Bob have to use a second channel for transmitting the certificate (e.g., via the telephone). Thus the authenticity and the validity of the public key can be guaranteed – at least within a small user group. As the number of communication participants grows, this procedure can quickly become inefficient. It is also not possible to to ensure that this method is binding as Bob could theoretically deny a public key as his own at any time.

If the number of participants increases, besides using the direct and personal verification of public keys it is also possible to rely on an indirect variation. In other words: if Alice trusts Bob and Bob trusts Carol then it is also possible for Alice to trust Carol. From a technical point of view, Alice knows Bob's public key and has verified it (e.g., through direct trust). On the other hand, Bob knows Carol's public key and has verified it. Bob now signs Carol's public key with respect to Alice. Alice checks the authenticity of Bob's signature and can thereby infer the correctness of Carole's public key. In this way a chain of mutual trust can be formed and, eventually, a so-called **web of trust**. The authenticity of the public key can be efficiently determined in the web of trust, also in larger user groups. However, checking the validity of a public key is problematic. If Alice wants to block her public key she has to inform all of the members in the web of trust. In contrast to direct trust, the binding nature of a public key cannot be denied easily as there is always at least one guarantor who can prove the authenticity of a key. It is worthwhile noting that secure communication in **Pretty Good Privacy** (PGP) is based on a web of trust. The web of trust model has achieved its widespread dissemination in this way.

If, in contrast, the certificates come from a CA, as in our initial situation, then one speaks of **hierarchical trust**. Here, the CA takes over the task of determining unambiguously the identities of the participants and of managing their keys. The appropriate infrastructure is necessary to do this (hence the name public key infrastructure – PKI). In the hierarchical trust model not only the authenticity of the public keys can be realized efficiently but also their validity and binding nature. The following variations in the hierarchical trust model are distinguished:

- **Single-level hierarchy**: the simplest variation with just a single CA; its public key must be held by all participants. All certificates can be verified with this public key.

- **Web model:** Since many different CAs exist, each CA has a specific, mostly overlapping group of participants. If secure communication is to take place between participants of different CAs, the members must first check at which CA the communication partner is registered and which CA key is needed to verify a corresponding certificate. Web browsers today are already pre-configured with numerous CA certificates for this purpose and delivered to the customers.

- **Cross certification:** If two participants from different CAs want to communicate with each other securely without their membership in a CA overlapping, the respective CAs can certify each other.

- **Multilevel hierarchy:** If a reciprocal cross certification proves too complex, CAs can also certify themselves at a superordinate CA. In this case, a communication participant only needs the public key of the superordinate CA to verify the certificate of the subordinate CA. When certification takes place reciprocally between superordinate and subordinate CAs, the hierarchy is no longer considered multilevel. A CA that is part of a network of reciprocal cross certification is also referred to as a **bridge CA**.

5.5 Glossary

Asymmetric encryption (public key encryption):   In the cryptographic method referred to as "public key" each communication partner has a key pair consisting of a so-called **public key** and a **secret private key**. The public key is made available to all participants with whom communication is desired. Participants who wish to communicate with the owner of the public key, encrypt their message with his public key. The owner of the public key can only decode a message encrypted this way with the help of his corresponding, and securely held, private key.

Authentication   Serves to prove the identity of a user or the integrity of a message. Certificates from a trusted body are used to verify identity in authentication. Digital signatures are created and sent with a message to verify its integrity.

Authorization: Access to certain sensitive information resources is often limited to a restricted group of people. When a user requests a secure information resource or its service it is necessary to verify whether he is authorized to use or gain access to the resource or not.

Certificate: Digital certificates are the electronic counterpart of a personal ID. They assign their owner a unique **public key** and therefore a **digital signature**, which can only be generated by way of the corresponding private key. Certificates must be issued and signed by a trustworthy third party called a Certificate Authority.

Certificate Authority (CA):   A **certificate authority** authenticates public keys from registered users based on certificates corresponding to Internet standard RFC 1422. In this way, the user's identity is verified. The public key of the user is digitally signed along with the user's name and control information from the CA and issued in this form as a **certificate**.

Cryptanalysis: Unlike cryptography, in cryptanalysis an attempt is made to break cryptographic procedures, i.e., to determine the contents of the encrypted message without knowing the key. Together cryptanalysis and cryptography are referred to as **cryptology**

Cryptography: A branch of computer science and mathematics that involves the design and evaluation of encryption procedures. The aim of cryptography is to protect confidential information from being accessed by unauthorized third parties.

Cryptography procedure: A procedure for the encryption and decryption of data. A distinction is made between **weak** and **strong** cryptography procedures, depending on the effort that must be exerted for unauthorized decryption. This effort increases dramatically as the key length grows. Cryptography procedures can be symmetric or asymmetric. Symmetric encryption is based on a secret key used for both encryption and decryption. On the other hand, with asymmetric encryption each participant holds two keys, one is public and other is private and known only to the key holder.

Data integrity: While cryptography cannot prevent data or messages from being altered by unauthorized third parties during transmission, the changes can however be made recognizable through the use of so-called hash functions. These provide a digital fingerprint of the sent data.

Denial of Service (DoS): This is an Internet attack intended to overload the victim's system through targeted manipulation so that it can no longer conduct its normal communication tasks or even fails completely. The known weaknesses and errors of Internet services are often used to an advantage in such attacks. To hide the attacker's identity, the attack is normally carried out from many different, alien computers where the attacker has previously planted his malware. Later at his discretion the actual attack is conducted in a coordinated manner (**distributed denial of service**). The system administrators of the affected computers are misled concerning the existence of the attack programs that are brought in illegally and stored hidden in the local file system.

Data Encryption Standard (DES): Symmetric block encryption methods were introduced in 1977 and updated for commercial use in 1993. DES encodes blocks of 64 bits each with an equally long key (56 bits effectively). The DES procedure is composed of 19 rounds altogether, whereby the 16 inner rounds are controlled by the key. The DES procedure presents a 64 bit substitution encryption procedure. This code can be broken today by relatively simple means. A multiple application of DES is carried out with different keys to increase security, for example **triple DES** (3DES).

Diffie-Hellman procedure: The first publicly known asymmetric encryption procedure, developed in 1976 by W. Diffie, M. Hellman and R. Merkle. Quite similar to the RSA procedure, a mathematical function is used in Diffie-Hellman whose reversal — specifically the problem of the discrete logarithm — is virtually impossible to calculate with a reasonable effort.

Digital signature: Used to authenticate a document, it consists of the digital fingerprint of the document that has been encrypted with the private key of the originator.

DNS poisoning: A targeted, active attack on a DNS server in which the domain names and IP addresses managed there can be manipulated. In this manner, entire domains can be cut off from network traffic, for example, or a targeted re-routing of the data traffic forced.

Identification: The recognition process of a user or a message is called identification. Once identity is established, it can be verified with authentication. Certain authorizations are connected with an identity.

IP spoofing: The targeted manipulation of the IP header of an IP datagram. Most of the time the sender's IP address is changed by the attacker so he can "spoof" a false identity or further prevent the transmitted datagram from being traced back to him. IP spoofing is the starting point for many further attacks.

Key: A message can be transmitted securely over an insecure medium when its content is concealed from unauthorized third parties by using an encryption procedure (**cipher**). The original message, the so-called **plaintext**, is transformed into the encrypted message (ciphertext)by way of a **transformation function**. The transformation function used for encryption can be parameterized with a key. The size of the key space is a measure of the difficulty involved in an unauthorized reversal of the transformation function.

Man-in-the-middle attack: An attack at a secured connection between two communication partners, whereby the attacker interacts with both partners (man-in-the-middle attack). The communication is intercepted or forged without it being noticed.

MD5 (Message Digest 5): A one-way hash function used in many cryptographic algorithms that generates a digital fingerprint of the input data. It was developed by Ron Rivest to succeed the MD4 hash function. MD5 uses a key length of 128 bits and is implemented in e.g., PGP and SMTP.

Message digest: A short digital fingerprint of a message that is generated by using a hash function on the message to be transmitted. If the message digest is encrypted with the sender's private key via an asymmetric encryption procedure, one receives a digital signature of the original message. This can be used to help check the sender's identity and the authenticity of the message.

Nonce (aka **salt**): Randomly selected unique value that can be used in a secured communication to prevent so-called **playback attacks**. In such attacks an unauthorized third party attempts to exert influence by using a previously recorded and later duplicated message. A nonce value may be used only once in the communication.

One-way function: A simply calculated mathematical function whose inverse function is virtually impossible to calculate with a reasonable effort. The one-way function is used in cryptography as an encryption procedure or for the generation of so-called **digital fingerprints**, via the use of **one-way hash functions**. A one-way hash function is also referred to as a **message authentication code** (MAC), **data authentication code** (DAC), **digital signature** or **message d gest** (MD).

Packet filter: Special software or dedicated hardware that filters the data traffic in a network or between an internal LAN and the global Internet. IP datagrams are analyzed and a determination made as to whether the datagram is forwarded or blocked depending on the given source or target address, packet type or other parameters. Packet filters are used as access control systems, e.g., in firewalls.

Packet sniffer: A network application or dedicated hardware with the task of monitoring data traffic on the network layer of a LAN. In a diffusion network in which all computers use a shared communication medium, a packet sniffer can read and analyze every single packet. The actual purpose of packet sniffers is to monitor and analyze the network data traffic, yet they can also be misused for the purpose of break-ins and spying.

Playback attack: Simple attack on a computing system. By monitoring data communication the encrypted passwords are recorded and then used in a later attack to break into the system being monitored.

Pretty Good Privacy (PGP): A system for the secure handling of email traffic developed in 1991 by Phil Zimmermann. PGP is freely available for most hardware platforms and operating systems. It offers email encryption with symmetric encryption procedures (Triple DES, IDEA, CST), securing the symmetric key via an asymmetric encryption procedure (RSA) as well as securing the integrity of emails (MD5 message digest) and preserving the authenticity of the communication partner (digital signatures). PGP is the most widely used system for the safe transport of emails.

Privacy: Only the sender and the receiver are allowed access to the contents of a confidential message. If an unauthorized third party spies on communication (**eavesdropping**), confidentiality can no longer be guaranteed and results in a **loss of privacy**.

Public Key Infrastructure (PKI): In the application of asymmetric public key encryption, each participant needs a **key pair**. It consists of a **public key,** which is available to everyone, and a secret (**private key**), which is only accessible to the holder. To prevent abuse, the assignment of the participant's public key must be verified by a trusted third party – the **certificate authority CA)** – by means of a **certificate**. The rules as to how this certificate is created (**security policy**) must be established in a a way that is publicly accessible. A PKI includes all organizational and technical measures that are necessary for the secure use of an asymmetric encryption procedure for encryption or for digital signatures.

Request for Comments (RFC):   New Internet technologies that develop in the course of expert discussion are retained in so-called RFCs (Request for Comments). As part of the Internet standardization process a sequentially numbered group of documents has arisen from this, in which technologies, standards and other items pertaining to the Internet are documented and standardized.

RSA procedure: The most well known asymmetric encryption procedure, it is named after its developers Rivest, Shamir and Adleman. Just as Diffie-Hellman encryption, the RSA procedure works with two keys. One is accessible to everyone – the public key – and the other is a private key that must be kept secret. RSA is based on number theory and the prime factorization problem. Encryption with a reasonable effort is not possible without knowledge of the private key.

Secret key encryption: The oldest family of encryption procedures in which both the sender and the receiver have an identical, private key for the encryption and decryption of a message. A distinction is made between **block ciphers**, in which the message to be encrypted is broken down into blocks of a fixed length before encryption, and **stream ciphers**. In the latter case, the to-be-encrypted message is treated as a text stream for which a one-time key of identical length is generated. Encryption of the message is carried out character by character with this key . One problem with secret key encryption involves the exchange of the key, which must be kept secret from third parties.

Steganography: A special type of encryption whereby the message to be encrypted is concealed inside another message with information irrelevant to the hidden message. The primary aim is to hide the fact that encrypted information is being transmitted.

Strong cryptography: Designation for encryption procedures with the highest level of security, for which no known practical methods for breaking the encryption exist. The necessary calculation for breaking a key typically depends on the length of the key used. Thus a method with a specific key length is referred to as a strong cryptographic procedure. This limit however shifts constantly with the ever-growing power of computing systems.

Transport Layer Security (TLS):   TSL is waiting in the wings to become the potential successor to SSL. This protocol, at the transport layer of the TCP/IP communication model, promises even more security in Internet communication. The TLS specification has been raised by the IETF to Internet standard RFC 2246.

Trapdoor function: This is a one-way function whose inverse can be calculated relatively easily with knowledge of additional – so-called trapdoor – information. Without knowing the trapdoor information this however proves virtually impossible.

User authentication: Proving a user's identity is done via special authentication methods, e.g., a password mechanism or a biometric authentication procedure such as fingerprinting.

Chapter 6
Epilogue

> *"...and what is writ, is writ"*
> *– Lord Byron (1788–1824)*

Digital communication has become one of the driving forces behind technical and cultural advancement in the 21st century. This volume has primarily focused on the historical development and technical foundation of digital communication. The associated key media, the "Internet " and the "World Wide Web," have only been given a cursory treatment here due to space considerations. In addition to summarizing the contents of the present book, we would like to present a brief look ahead in this epilogue to the topics discussed in the other volumes of our trilogy, comprised of: "Digital Communication,""Internetworking" and "Web Technologies."

The rising digitalization and virtualization of our environment and the digital communication associated with it has been the point of departure for our study. For a better intuitive understanding of the subject of our investigation, we have chosen the historical development of communication and its technical resources as the place to launch our tour through the world of digital communication, which began with prehistoric cave painting and continues up to today's World Wide Web. The information-theoretic implementation of communication is discussed with an initial focus on the coding of messages. Before information can be transmitted over the communication medium from one partner to the other, it must first be brought into a suitable form. This means digitally encoding the information and then sending it in message form via a digital communication medium.

Because information can exist in different medial forms, such as text, image, audio or video recording, it is necessary to consider these forms in encoding. Different types of encoding are needed for efficient technical implementation. "Efficient" in this sense, applies primarily to the required data memory space. The more storage space necessary, the longer message transmission takes. Compression practices help to reduce this needed space by eliminating redundancy in a message, i.e., removing those components that do not play a role in the information content of the delivered message. The Shannon criterion indicates the maximum extent of lossless message compression. This is

C. Meinel and H. Sack, *Digital Communication*, X.media.publishing, DOI: 10.1007/978-3-642-54331-9_6, © Springer-Verlag Berlin Heidelberg 2014

determined by the entropy of a message (information content). If the message is to be reduced beyond this point, lossless compression is no longer adequate and information-bearing elements must be removed from the message (lossy data compression).

The system of human perception offers approaches on how to do this. Certain limitations are set by our sensory organs and the information processing that takes place in the brain. Based on these physiological factors, it is possible to determine components of information that can be left out in compression because they have little or no bearing on our perception. This fundamental principle forms the basis for MPEG audio coding, JPEG image coding as well as MPEG video compression.

Our previously coded messages are nowadays transmitted via digital communication channels whose scope ranges from the pico networks of one's personal environment to the worldwide spanning, heterogeneous network system of the Internet. For the success of worldwide digital communication in computer networks, all participants must follow strict rules. These are dictated to them in a communication protocol specifying message format as well as rules for message exchange.

Many computer networks, and particularly the worldwide Internet, are based on the paradigm of "open networks." This means that in principle every communication participant is in a position to receive all of the messages sent over the network. Digital communication networks share the security risks of their analog predecessors, for example, the telephone network, where lines or exchange locations were "tapped," or the postal system, where letters could be intercepted and opened undetected. However, the dimensions of security problems in digital communication are in fact far more diverse. In order to guarantee a sufficient level of security and privacy in the digital communication process, secure symmetrical and asymmetrical encryption procedures with public keys have been developed. These may be implemented today by everyone for private communication, and their reliability is officially guaranteed by recognized certification authorities.

The book at hand is dedicated to digital communication from the technical perspective of computer science. The topic as a whole spans a further range of areas that could not be addressed in greater detail here for lack of space. Neither the physical/electronic foundation of data transmission could be examined in depth nor could the media-technical basis of the devices and networks involved in data transmission. A detailed treatment of the philosophical, psychological and sociological aspects of communication also had to be left out. In the latter discipline the change in perspective should also be noted, depending on whether taken from the standpoint of the communication medium and the exchanged messages, from the transmitter or receiver and their handling of messages and the effect on those involved in the communication process, or even society at large. The philosophy of language in this sphere investigates the functioning of human communication. It reveals the boundaries between syntax and semantics and addresses decisions that must be made by the acting and communicating person and the responsibility connected with it.

In contrast, our technical-informatics perspective, attempts to illuminate the functioning of modern, digital communication media. This includes fundamental observations on message encoding, the data formats exchanged as well as the protocols deployed. At the same time, the technical-physical side also has to be considered. This is what determines the construction and design of the devices used in communication. While in the present book we have already examined general aspects of encoding, the efficient encoding of multimedia data and the foundation of communication in computer networks, it is still difficult, even with this level of knowledge, to answer basic questions such as: How does an email get from my computer to the recipient's at the other end of the world in a matter of seconds? How does the World Wide Web function anyway? How is it possible to reliably link millions of computers via different technologies so that our "Internet"appears to be one big unified whole? The volumes following "Digital Communication "in the trilogy, "Internetworking" and "Web Technologies," are dedicated to these questions and their contexts will be presented here briefly.

Volume 2 "Internetworking" is devoted to the the technical foundation of the Internet and provides the reader with a detailed background. The Internet is a global amalgamation of diverse computer networks. Company networks, scientific networks, military networks, municipal networks or supra-regional operators based on the most diverse carrier media, whether it be copper cable, fiberglass or radio waves, and network technologies all make up "the Internet"– the name given to the virtually linked new world. Nearly four decades passed before a trial network, comprised of only four computers in 1969 – the year of the moon landing, developed into a comprehensive network of hundreds of millions of computers from many different networks. This technology described as **Internetworking**, with its fixed set of rules founded on the communication protocols of the TCP/IP protocol suite, is capable of making digital communication possible via a large number of different networks, which are not compatible per se. Internet technology is capable of completely concealing details of the implemented network hardware. In this way, the connected computers can communicate with each other independent of their physical connection to the Internet.

Before a computer can be linked to a network, it must have special network connection components available. Such network adapters take over the processing effort of the central computing unit of the connected computer, translating the message to be transmitted into a network-conform format. Additionally, intermediate systems must be provided in a network. These are installed at node locations and carry out a relay function. They decide in which direction a data stream is to be guided and often carry out an additional amplification function to expand the physical range of the network.

The logical interconnection of the individual network components, the rules according to which they communicate with each other and the implemented data formats are determined via the Internet protocols. Internet protocols are subdivided into hierarchical layers one on top of the other, based on their degree of abstraction and respective "closeness"to the physical output medium Such a communication layer is required on both the side of the sender as well as the receiver and in such a way that both computers can communicate with each other on every one of the layers. This communication is however only illusionary. In reality, each layer only communicates with the one directly above or below it. Instructions and data are received from above and instructions and data are passed below. Today's generally accepted layer model is the so-called **TCP/IP reference model** (TCP/IP stack). While 20 years ago these terms from the TCP/IP world were only know by a handful of specialists, there can be no doubt today that TCP/IP rules the Internet.

With the TCP/IP reference model as the starting point, each of the five layers that build on one another will be looked at and the technologies and protocols employed at each layer explained in detail. The initial focus is on **physical data transmission** via different types of wired or wireless media. Every physical data transmission medium has specific characteristics that must be taken into account both in message encoding as well as in the coordination of the employed protocols. Examined in detail are modulation procedures specifying how the characteristics of the physical media can be used for information transfer as well as multiplex procedures enabling the shared use of a physical medium by many communication partners.

The **data link layer** built on the physical layer provides the communicating hosts a physical connection and ensures their constant operational readiness. Basically, the two most important categories here are the **Local Networks** (**LANs**), whose geographic extension is limited to individual rooms or buildings, and the **Wide Area Networks** (**WANs**), which support greater distances up to intercontinental connections. Different technologies are employed in both categories. LANS distinguish themselves in terms of the topology realized, i.e., the arrangement of the computers in the network. Besides the popular Ethernet LAN technology, wireless network technologies, such as WLAN, Bluetooth or WiMax, are also examined in detail. Individual networks may be extended and interconnected by means of special intermediate systems using repeaters, bridges and switches. These intermediate systems are distinguished by their implemented layer in the TCP/IP reference model. Yet to transport data over widely separated geographical distances the technology used has to take other aspects into account than those implemented in the close range of the LANs. In the framework of these wide area networks a detailed look is taken at the technologies of the Asynchronous Transfer Mode (ATM), Distributed Queue Dual Bus (DQB) and Synchronous Digital Hierarchy (SDH), as well as focusing on the necessary conditions for access to the wide area networks (modem, ISDN, DSL, etc.).

In order to create a homogeneous-appearing network from the multiple number of network technologies, the protocols at the Internet layer TCP/IP reference model are used. Above all, the **Internet Protocol** (**IP**), aided by logical addressing, makes communication possible across network borders from the source computer to the target computer. On the basis of different criteria, such as maximum throughput, reduced cost, uniform load distribution or the best possible security, the **routing** process located here chooses the best path through the network. Besides giving a detailed presentation of the current IP protocol IPv4, its addressing, data formats and functionality, different routing procedures are described as well as the Internet protocol of the next generation IPv6, along with its advantages and the problems associated with its implementation.

The Internet layer only provides an unreliable, wireless data transport service. To make reliable communication possible, protocols such as the **Transport Control Protocol** (**TCP**) are deployed in the transport layer structured above it. TCP provides a universal transport service, i.e., an explicit (per software) switched connection with assembly and disassembly procedures, as well as secured quality criteria. Among these are error correction methods or the correct arrangement of the transmitted data packets. Data flow algorithms are responsible for a uniform load on the network infrastructure. In case of overload, the transmission volume is throttled accordingly, or if a free medium is involved its performance capacity is fully exploited. TCP therefore represents the most complex of the protocols in the TCP/IP reference model and is supplemented by the connectionless (unreliable) transport protocol **User Datagram Protocol** (**UDP**).

The real meaning and purpose of the Internet can be found in the **Internet applications**. These are based on the communication services of the Internet. These services, an extension of the network operating system, are provided for application programs at the upper layer of the TCP/IP reference model. Many protocols that have achieved great popularity in data transmission are here, such as HTTP (Hypertext Transfer Protocol), FTP (File Transfer Protocol) or SMTP (Simple Mail Transfer Protocol). The applications themselves, e.g., the email client or HTML browser, are not part of this layer. They are outside the communication model and only avail themselves of the functionalities at the application layer. Applications such as email, IRC or WWW are the ones that influence our idea of the Internet. They are responsible for helping us forget how many technological tricks and details are necessary in getting this network of networks up and running.

Among the most important Internet services are: directory services, message exchange and information services, as well as data transfer services. Directory services is the term used for service programs that supply information about technical resources or people who are reachable within the network. The most well-known Internet directory service is the DNS (Domain Name Service). It is able to transform logical names for network end systems into the numerical IP addresses fixed by the Internet communication protocols. Electronic mail (email) is one of the best-known message exchanges and among the oldest Internet service offered. For the user, electronic mail is a digital reproduction of standard mail. The email client is the application program that provides the user an interface to read, create and forward messages to the email server. In turn, the email server takes over communication with remote email servers along the path and at the location of the addressee of the sent email. In the Internet protocol stack, SMTP (Simple Mail Transfer Protocol) is provided as the standard protocol for email applications. Along with the SMTP protocol for transmitting text-based messages, the MIME (Multi-Purpose Internet Mail Extension) coding standard was introduced in order to send all types of multimedia messages. Using the corresponding utilities (plugins), MIME encoded multimedia documents can be decoded and displayed by the client. In the chapter examining the application layer, a detailed look is also taken at audio and video communication in Internet-connected technologies and protocols. In contrast to asynchronous email communication, synchronous audio and video communication connection are subject to strict time requirements. For this to be implemented reliably, streaming technologies are deployed along with different real-time transport protocols. Further topics explored in the "Internetworking" volume are file transfer services (FTP, NFS, etc.), remote login (Telnet, SSH, etc.), network management (SNMP), Usenet, Internet Relay Chat, instant messaging, peer-to-peer networks, grid computing and Internet security.

Volume 3 "Web Technologies" focuses specifically on the foundation of the World Wide Web. The World Wide Web is a huge, comprehensive collection of information and data distributed across the whole world that we are able to access via the Internet, or more precisely with the help of the HTTP protocol situated on the Internet protocol and a web browser. The Internet has gained its enormous popularity and dissemination today thanks to the WWW. A large part of this success is due to the simple access interface. Owing to the browser it is also possible for laypeople to have fast and simple access to the vast range of information on the WWW.

The WWW, the world-spanning Internet in the form it offers today for the general public, has come of age. When at the end of the 80s Tim Berners-Lee and Robert Cailliau were contemplating a simple document exchange and administration system via the Internet, they never could have guessed that their idea – a byproduct of their actual work at the European Organization for Nuclear Research – CERN (Centre Européenne pour la Recherche Nucléaire) – would be the impetus for the Internet revolution. With the creation of a easy to use graphic user interface, it was possible at the beginning of the 90s for the general population to use the Internet as a new communication and information medium. The number of computers connected to the Internet in order to use the WWW began to grow phenomenally. This development continues unabated until today.

The information itself is contained in the WWW in the form of so-called hypermedia documents. Connected with each other by so-called hyperlinks, they build an information network where the user can navigate fast and easily. So that a certain document can be found in the WWW it must be uniquely identified worldwide by an address called a **Uniform Resource**

Identifier (URI). A detailed look is taken at the URI address scheme and its subtypes URL, URN, IRI, persistent URL and openURL. Access to the user desired WWW resources, distributed across countless servers, proceeds over the **Hypertext Transfer Protocol (HTTP)**. This works according to the client/server paradigm. A very simple and, most importantly, fast protocol, it has been continually extended since its introduction. It offers a flexible and secure infrastructure for efficient data transfer in the WWW today supplemented by components such as SSL (Secure Socket Layer) or TLS (Transport Layer Security).

As well as allowing access to hypermedia documents, modern browsers also act as multifunctional clients to access alternative Internet services such as FTP, email or video. The sometimes complex mechanisms behind the individual services and protocols remain completely hidden from the user. The user is only confronted with the simple to use graphic user interface of the browser. Along the transmission path between the WWW server and the user's browser, proxy servers, caches and gateways ensure a smooth and efficient data transfer as well as considerably increasing the performance ability of the HTTP protocol. The special feature of WWW documents is the possibility of the cross-linking via so-called hyperlinks to a distributed hypermedia system. Unlike a book or a document in the traditional sense, it is possible for the user to gain direct access from one place in the document to a marked place in another document. This does not have to be even stored at the same WWW server, but in fact can be stored at the other end of the world.

It is not only possible to link every type of text with each other in the WWW but also every type of multimedia document. This includes pictures, audio and video clips and interactive contents. The hypermedia documents of the WWW are written in a special descriptive language called **Hypertext Markup Language (HTML)**. This language makes it possible for the author to determine the structure of his or her document, i.e., the layout of the headings, paragraphs and tables, as well as to highlight certain parts of the document. This structuring is carried out via special "markups." These are recognized by the browser as separate from the actual document and processed accordingly.

The graphic form (formatting) of a HTML documents is carried out via separate files – so-called **Cascading Style Sheets (CSS)**. Via CSS, depending on the graphic features of the respective output device (mobile telephone, computer monitor, printer etc.), different formatting can be determined for the individual structural elements of a HTML document. The desire for greater flexibility and the establishment of individualized identifying markings and a markup language led to the development of **XML**, the **Extensible Markup Language**. With the ability to establish new identifying elements, XML, as a meta-markup language, soon became the starting point for a whole series of application-specific markup languages tailored to special applications. The corresponding XML language definitions are fixed with the help of a Document Type Definition (DTD) or the data definition language schema XML. The principles of the XML, DTD and XML schema, as well as expanded object identity using XPath and XPointer are explored in detail against this background. The reader is also introduced to the advanced hyperlink concept XLink, form processing with XForms, XML queries with XQuery and XML transformation with XSLT.

Up to this point it was only necessary to provide prerecorded content at a WWW server that the user could access with the help of a browser (static Web documents). At the same time, in the professional area Content Management Systems (CMS) have prevailed. CMS enables the dynamic generation of communicated contents (**dynamic Web documents**). This means, the contents are only taken from a data bank based on need and according to predefined style sheets.

Up to this point it was only necessary to make pre-recorded contents available at a WWW server, which the user could access with the help of a browser (static Web documents). At the same time, Content Management Systems (CMS) prevailed in the professional area. CMS enables the dynamic generation of communicated contents (**dynamic Web documents**). This means, the contents are only taken from a data bank on demand and according to predefined style sheets. A CMS offers the possibility of creating style sheets independent of the frequently-changing information they offer. If there is a layout change, only the respective style sheet must be adapted, which accommodates the actual information content stored separately in a data base. In this case, WWW servers work together with special server application programs. Their task consists of immediately generating the desired Web documents based on the information that was sent to the WWW server. The documents are then encoded as HTML documents and conveyed to the WWW server, who delivers them to the user.

To be able to request dynamically generated web documents from WWW servers, it is often necessary to transmit special parameters that indicate exactly which information is to be sent back. In this context, WWW servers offer multi-faceted possibilities for the interaction with server-side application programs, e.g., Common Gateway Interface (CGI), Server Side Includes, Java Servlet, Enterprise JavaBeans or Web Services.

On the client's side, the activities can therefore involve much more than the simple display of HTML pages. User involvement in the areas of user feedback and interactivity extend far beyond pure information consumption with "genuine" participation in the WWW taking place. HTML is however then no longer adequate as a basic display language of the web document as HTML only allows a static display of information with a "simple" return channel (e.g., via so-called web forms). Early in the development of the WWW, the idea therefore arose of not only transmitting static information from the WWW server but also programs. These could then be executed at the client side. Naturally special security regulations are necessary to prevent software transmitted this way from causing any damage. The program code loaded by the client, e.g., a JavaScript program or a so-called Java Applet, may only run within a specially secured environment – the "sandbox." It is not possible here to gain access to sensitive computing resources. The chapter **Web Programming** provides an in-depth look at client-side and server-side web programming. It also explores, e.g., the Document Object Model, Java Servlets, Web Frameworks, distributed applications with Remote Procedure Call (RPC), Remote Method Invocation (RMI), Enterprise Java Beans (EJB) and introduces the world of Service-Oriented Architecture (SOA).

Today the WWW has grown into the largest information archive worldwide. Because the billions of web documents make it impossible for users to maintain their orientation, the first directories and search services emerged soon after its launch. Only with the development of powerful **search engines**, such as Google, is possible for us today to gain (usually) targeted and efficient access to the desired information. Google administers a gigantic search index that accesses the relevant web documents in a matter of seconds on the input of a search word. Based on the sheer size of the WWW this only works with the help of automatic index compilation procedures. Using statistical methods this procedure evaluates and indexes all terms within a web document and puts the relevant documents in a ranked order with respect to a certain key word.

The WWW has also changed a great deal with respect to content since its birth in 1990. With the advent of e-commerce in the mid 90s, the focus shifted from the WWW as a specialized personal communication and publication medium to a mass communication medium. The medium of mass communication – information production and information consumption – remained strictly separate areas. Only a specialist was able to put personal content online in the WWW. The general public consumed the information offered just as they had the offerings from providers in the traditional broadcast medium. In the meantime the WWW continued to evolve. Interactive technologies operating under the name **Web 2.0** provided laypeople with the possibility of publishing their own information content in a simple way. Blogs, chat rooms, file-sharing, social networks, tagging systems and wikis have conquered WWW and opened up a path of true interaction in the digital word to a broad base of users.

The resources communicated in the WWW are generally present in the form of text documents or multimedia documents in which the information is described in natural language. The person as receiver and user of this document can understand the content (most of the time) without a problem. The situation changes completely, however, when this content is submitted for automatic processing. This can already be seen in WWW search engines, for example, which are often not able to deliver documents with synonymous search words (different words with the same meaning). This is because search engines rely solely on the occurrence of a certain string of characters in carrying out a search. Consequently, paraphrases and synonyms cannot be found.

To make the terms behind the words of the natural language accessible for automatic processing they must be made "machine understandable," encoded and linked to the natural language document. The contextual semantics, i.e., the meaning of the terms and how they relate to one another, must also be described in a machine-readable, standardized format. This type of a formal knowledge description is known as ontology and can be read by a program, such as a search engine, and processed. The tools necessary to do this have already been standardized and are the starting point for the new **"Semantic Web,"**and its ontology descriptive languages with their various semantic strengths, such as RDF, RDFS or OWL. Semantically annotated websites make it possible for autonomously acting agents to collect targeted information and, building on that, to reach decisions independently as defined by their client and trigger self-initiated actions. A scenario that not only changes the Web but also the real world.

List of Persons*

Ramses II,   (ca. 1290 – 1214 BC), Egyptian pharaoh of the 19th Dynasty of the New Kingdom who established one of the first libraries in his memorial temple, the "Ramesseum," as reported by historian Diodorus Siculus. Under his reign, Egypt reached an economic and cultural prosperity that no other pharaoh afterwards could achieve.

Assurbanipal,   (669 – 627 BC), Assyrian king who founded the first large-scale library in world history with over 20,000 inscribed clay tablets.

Thales of Miletus,   (640 BC – 546 BC), Greek philosopher, mathematician and astronomer (also merchant, statesman and engineer), he is generally considered to be the founder and progenitor of Greek philosophy and science. Among his many contributions was an important work on geometry (Thales Theorem). He calculated the height of the pyramids from the length of their shadows and is said to have predicted the solar eclipse of 585 BC (in all probability relying on Babylonian knowledge of the so-called Saros Cycle, which states that an eclipse can occur every 233 lunar month). He was the first to describe the magnetic effect of static electricity produced by rubbing amber with a cloth (frictional electricity).

Cyrus II,   (601 – 535 BC), founder of the ancient empire of Persia who established one of the first fixed postal services in his kingdom, including stations for mounted messengers to change horses at intervals of a day's journey.

Aeschylus,   (525 – 456 BC), Greek poet who described the first torch telegraphy in his tragedy "*Agamemnon*." This method of communication was purportedly used to report the Fall of Troy in Greece, in approx. 1184 BC.

Cratinus,   (520 – 423 BC), Greek comedy writer in whose work the term "library," to mean a collection of books, was found for the first time. He also introduced the rule that in a comedy three actors should always share the stage .

Panini,   (5th c. BC), Indian scholar who wrote the oldest surviving textbook on the grammar of Sanskirt, which is therefore recognized as the oldest grammar book ever written. In the 19th century his work on grammar, containing nearly 4,000 rules, was also known in European countries as a result of the British colonization of India and inspired grammar studies in other languages.

Socrates,   (approx. 470 – 399 BC), Greek philosopher who was concerned with the study of humankind and the possibilities of self-knowledge. None of his own writings

---

* in chronological order

C. Meinel and H. Sack, *Digital Communication*, X.media.publishing,
DOI: 10.1007/978-3-642-54331-9, © Springer-Verlag Berlin Heidelberg 2014

have survived. His pupils Plato and Xenophon reported on Socrates' life and philosophy as well as his criticism on the invention of writing. Convicted on the charges of impiety and corrupting the minds of the youth, he was sentenced to death.

Lysander,   (†395 BC), Spartan statesman and general in the Peloponnesian and Corinthian Wars. The ancient historian Plutarch describes in his Lysander biography the use of a scytale to encrypt messages during the Peloponnesian War.

Thucydides,   (ca. 460 – 399 BC), Greek general and historian, who founded with his manuscript " *The Peloponnesian War*" the scientific historiography in which he reported on communication via smoke signal from the Peloponnesian War (431 – 404 BC).

Plato,   (427 – 348 BC), Greek philosopher and Socrates' pupil who, with his own pupil Aristotle, is considered as the most influential Greek philosopher. Between 387 and 367 BC he founded the "Academy," an educational institution in Athens that existed until 529 AD when it was abolished by Byzantine emperor Justinian. Above the entrance to his school was the epithet he had commissioned reading: "Let no one ignorant of mathematics enter here". (actually geometry is meant). Plato considered mathematics to be the foundation of all eduction and training. He founded the school of thought known as Platonism, in which mathematical objects and structures have an existence independent of human thought. Beside making important contributions to the areas of philosophy, logic and the ideal state, Plato outline his criticism on the development of writing in his dialogue "*Phaedrus.*"

Aristotle,   (384 – 322 BC), Greek mathematician, zoologist and philosopher. He is considered the founder of modern scientific work and was the first to describe, among other things, the principle of the pinhole camera. In 343 BC King Phillip of Macedonia entrusted him with the education of his thirteen-year-old son who was later to become Alexander the Great. In 334 BC he founded his own school of philosophy at the Lyceum, a group of buildings and gardens dedicated to the god Apollo. It was known as the Peripatetic school, a name that was derived from the colonnades ([Gk.] peripatoi) where lessons were held. The canonical view of Aristotle's zoological, anatomical and physiological writings held in the Middle Ages has affected advancement in these areas until modern times.

Polybius,   (208 – 120 BC), Greek historian who described using torch telegraphy as a means to transmit freely formulated messages. After achieving a leading political position, Polybios was deported to Rome. There he advanced in his station and eventually became advisor to the general Scipio the Younger, whom he accompanied on his campaigns. His most important work is the 40-volume history of Greece and Rome. Five volumes of this history exist today.

Gaius Julius Caesar,   (100 – 44 BC), Roman statesman and autocrat, he led Rome out of the age of revolutions and paved the way for the Roman Empire. The reforms he introduced include the Julian calender in 45 BC. Modified by Pope Gregory XIII in 1582 (with the support of the astronomer Sosigenes of Alexandria), it retained its validity within the Gregorian calender. He introduced the first daily newspaper in the western world, the "Acta Diurna."The Roman historian Suetonius reported in his imperial biographies about Caesar's implementation of a simple substitution encryption method that was named after him. It was used to transport military messages. Each letter of the alphabet was substituted for another letter three positions away in the sequence.

Marcus Vitruvius Pollio,   (1st c. BC), Roman architect and writer. He is perhaps best known for his 10-volume work on the foundation of the Greek and Roman architecture, which had a considerable influence on the great architecture of the European Renaissance. In addition, Vitruvius was the first to compare the propagation of sound to the propagation of waves in water.

Augustus, (31 BC – 14 AD), born Gaius Octavius, great-nephew and principal heir to Gaius Julius Caesar. Since 31 BC sole ruler of the Roman Empire and first Roman emperor, he institutionalized the "cursus publicus" as the first regular postal service throughout the entire Mediterranean region.

Plutarch, (45 – 125 AD), Greek writer and historian. In his biography of the Spartan commander Lysander he described the use of the scytale for transporting encrypted messages in the Peloponnesian War in the 5th century AD. Plutarch became famous for his imperial biographies, dual biographies – in which he juxtaposed a Greek biography with a Roman biography – and his moral writings.

Gaius Suetonius Tranquillus, (45 – 125 AD), Roman writer and civil servant. In his imperial biography *"De Vita Caesarum"* he describes how Julius Caesar used the simple substitution cipher, named after him, for the transmission of secret military messages.

Ptolemy of Alexandria, (85 – 165 AD), Egyptian astronomer, mathematician and geographer. Among many other things he described the phenomenon of retina inertia, an essential concept for modern media such as film and television. His *"Almagest"* is viewed as a ground-breaking work in astronomy and was a standard work until the 17th century. The geocentric world view, postulated in this work, prevented advances in astronomy for a considerable time due to the prevailing canonical position.

Q. Septimius Florens Tertullianus, (approx. 160 – 220), was the first important Christian church writer in Latin. In around 205 he joined the early Christian movement of Montanism, named after its founder Montanus, at which time he composed theological and apologetic writings. He takes credit for being the first to use the word "alphabetum" to describe the sum of all letters.

Lucius Domitius Aurelianus, (214 – 275), Roman emperor who contributed in large part to the destruction of the great library of Alexandria while waging a campaign against Zenobia, the ruler of Palmyra (in modern-day Syria).

Theophilus of Alexandria., (†412), Christian patriarch of Alexandria. Acting on a decree of Emperor Theodosius, who ordered all pagan cults to be banned in the Roman Empire, he was responsible for having what remained of the Great Library of Alexandria torn down and the manuscripts burned as a testament to pagan beliefs.

Theodosius I, (346 – 395), Christian Roman emperor, who was the last emperor to rule the Roman Empire in its entirety. He took strong measures against paganism, ordering the banning of all pagan cults and the closing of all pagan temples in 391. In an act of overzealousness, Theophilus, the patriarch of Alexandria, ordered what remained of the Great Library of Alexandria to be torn down. Its collection of manuscripts, seen as evidence of pagan beliefs, was burned. In the course of this imperial decree the Olympic Games were also declared a pagan cult and banned in 393.

Publius Flavius Vegetius Renatus, (approx. 400), Roman veterinarian and war theorist who described the Roman version of an ancient optical telegraphic system. Movable wooden beams were fastened to towers and messages exchanged by way of prearranged signals. His main work *"Epitoma rei militaris"* deals with the art of war and siege technology. Its maxims have met with great interest throughout history and up to modern times.

Omar of Damascus,   (592 – 644), (Umar ibn al-Chattab) the second "rightly guided" Caliph of Islams. In 642 he conquered Egypt and was blamed by Christian propaganda for the destruction of the Great Library of Alexandria, which had been destroyed two centuries previously.

Gregory II,   (669 – 731), the pope who arbitrated the iconoclastic controversy that had flared up in the Church as a result of an edict by Byzantine emperor Leo III. Pope Gregory II also became noteworthy through his commission of Boniface as missionary to Germany in 719.

Leo III,   (685 – 741), East Roman emperor who supported the ban in the Byzantine Church on worshiping sacred images. He appeared to have interpreted a major volcanic explosion in the year 726 as a warning from God and subsequently had an image of Christ removed that had been affixed to gateway of the imperial palace. In the iconoclastic controversy he is viewed as an opponent of Pope Gregory II. According to historical sources this conflict was actually triggered by disputes concerning tax payments.

Abu Ja'far Mohammed Ibn Musa Al-Khowarizmi,   (approx. 780 – 850). In 820, Persian mathematician, astronomer, geographer and historian from Khowarizm (Khorasan), wrote the book called *"About the Indian Numbers,"*, in 820. In this work he explains the use of the decimal system. He also wrote *"Al-Jabr Walmukala,"* an examination of equation solving. Its title contains the source for our modern-day word "algebra," while the word "algorithm" can be traced back to the author's name. In the Latin translation, *"About the Indian Numbers"* begins with the words *"Algoritmi dicit ..."*, which means roughly *"Al-Khowarizmi says ..."*.

Kung-Foo Whing,   (10th c.), Chinese scholar who was the first to describe the "string telephone"– made up of two bamboo cylinders connected by a long, taut string. The cylinder into which is spoken works as a microphone and the other as a loudspeaker.

Ibn Al-Haitham (Alhazen),   (965 – 1040), Arab mathematician and physicist who first described the principle of the camera obscura, the predecessor to the modern photo camera, and who concerned himself with questions about the effect of curved (spherical and paraboloidal) mirrors as well as those of magnifying lenses.

Ibn Sina (Avicenna),   (980 – 1037), Persian doctor, physicist and philosopher is considered one of the most important scientists of medieval Islam. His main work the *"Canon,"* had a significant effect on the development of medicine up through the 17th century. His impetus theory, taken from Aristotle, however inhibited advances in physics, especially in ballistics. According to this theory, a projectile should follow a straight path until its "impetus" is used up. After that it should stop and fall straight to the ground – however this path to the ground is actually a parabolic one. The trajectory of a thrown or projectile object was first described correctly by Niccolo Tartaglia in the 16th century.

Bi Sheng,   (†1052), Chinese blacksmith who is credited with the invention of printing with movable type made of clay in the year 1040.

Nur-Ed Din,   (1118 – 1174), Emir of Damascus. He set up the first scheduled transport service by carrier pigeons in the Middle East. He thus managed the administration of his kingdom, which extended from Egypt to the Iranian highlands.

Roger Bacon,   (1214 – 1294), English Franciscan monk and philosopher who was the first to turn away from the prevailing scientific method of the Middle Ages that blindly followed the authority of the past (Scholastic): He propagated experimental gains in science based on personal experience (empiricism). Among his publications are works on optics, in which he deals with color theories, reflection and refraction laws.

Marco Polo,   (1254–1324), Venetian merchant's son and the "founding father of tourism."Together with his uncles Niccoló and Maffeo Polo he traveled to the Far East, getting as far as China to the court of Kublai Khan. The well structured postal system he found there particularly merited his praise as expressed in his travelogues.

Johannes Gensfleisch zum Gutenberg,   (1397 – 1468), goldsmith from Mainz who in 1440 developed a new method of book printing using movable type and simultaneously created the springboard for the launch of the printed book as the first mass medium.

Johannes Fust,   (1400 – 1466), Mainz banker who financed Gutenberg's development of the printing trade for the huge sum of 800 gulden (equivalent to 100 oxen). Five years later he demanded repayment of the money from Gutenberg at a court hearing, but in the meantime Gutenberg had accumulated more debt. Fust took over Gutenberg's company and together with his son-in-law Peter Schöffel continued its success.

William Caxton,   (1424 – 1491), president of the English trading company in Brügge (Flanders). During a diplomatic mission to Cologne he learned the printing trade and in 1476 introduced it to England. There, he operated a printing trade shop in Westminster until his death. He is still erroneously considered by some to be the inventor of the printing trade.

Berthold von Henneberg,   (1441 – 1504), archbishop-elector of Mainz, who established the first book censorship in 1485. It involved a ban on the printing and sale of all Bible translations under threat of excommunication.

Innocent VIII,   (1432 – 1492), Giovanni Battista Cibo who as pope lamented the abuse of the printing and dissemination of heretical writings as harmful to society in his Bull of 1487. He transferred the preventive censorship for all printed works to local bishops. Under the threat of excommunication and heavy fines, the printing, binding and reading of books that had not previously received episcopal approval was prohibited.

Alexander VI.,   (1430 – 1503), Rodrigo Lanzol, who as pope initiated a general book censorship with his 1501 Bull "*Inter multiplices.*" It affected all (not yet printed and all previously printed) writings that are "impious, scandalous and contrary to the true faith."

Leonardo da Vinci,   (1452 – 1519), Italian scientist, artist and inventor, produced countless design sketches, among them for mechanical devices such as flying machines or architectural plans ranging from churches to channel systems and even entire fortresses. His famous works as a painter include "Mona Lisa" and "The Last Supper.".

Leonardo Loredan,   (1459 – 1516), (Leonhard Lauredan), Doge of Venice. In one of his letters translated into German, the German word for newspaper"Zeitung"can be read for the first time.

Maximilian I,   (1459 – 1519), German king (emperor from 1493 on), who had the first modern postal route set up in 1490 between his courts in Innsbruck and near Brussels. The postal route was maintained by the Thurn and Taxis family.

Leo X (Giovanni de Medici),   (1475 – 1521), elected pope in 1513, he forbid translation of the Scriptures from Latin into the vernacular in 1515, which he saw as a threat to the supremacy of clerical interpretation. Leo misunderstood Luther's revolt and accusations of abuse in the Catholic church and excommunicated him in 1520.

Martin Luther,   (1483 – 1546), German religious leader and founder of the Reforma-
tion. Ordained to priesthood and a professor for biblical studies at the University of
Wittenberg, he criticized the selling of indulgences for the forgiveness of sins by the
Catholic Church. In exchange for a fee the church issued a letter of indulgence that
promised forgiveness of past sins. Luther believed that guilt, remorse and forgiveness
were solely dependent on the sinner's change of heart. In the 95 Theses, which he
nailed to the door of the castle church in Wittenberg, he vehemently attacked the
selling of indulgences and expressed doubt in the Church's power to forgive sins.

Francis I,   (1494 – 1547), King of France. In 1536 he set up the first national library
in the world, the "Bibliothèque du Roi." It was an obligation that a copy of every
book published in France be sent to this library. In this way it was possible for the
entire literature of a country to be completely archived and cataloged for the first
time.

Niccolo Fontana Tartaglia,   (1499 – 1557), Italian mathematician who is considered
the father of ballistics and was the first to find a solution for cubic equations. In
1573 he researched the trajectory of a fired cannonball and developed a concept of
compound movement that later became the foundation of ballistics.

Blaise de Vigenére,   (1523 – 1596), French diplomat and cryptographer. Based on
the ideas of Benedictine monk Johannes Trithemius, he developed the polyalphabetic
Vigenére encryption. Considered unbreakable for a long time, Vigenére cipher was
only first cracked in 1850 by British mathematician Charles Babbage

John Napier,   (1540 – 1617), Scottish mathematician who introduced logarithms and
the decimal point in math. He developed one of the first slide rules, the so-called
"Napier's Bones,"which could be use to carry out mechanical multiplication.

Rudolf II of Habsburg,   (1552 – 1612), German emperor, he raised postal service to
a sovereign right in 1597 and thereby created the foundation for a general postal
system.

Jan Lipperhey,   (approx. 1570 – 1617), Dutch spectacle maker who is considered
the inventor of the telescope. He did not receive a patent for his invention however
because fellow spectacle makers Jacob Adriaanszon, called Metius from Alkmaar,
and Zacharias Janssen also later claimed to have invented the telescope.

Johannes Kepler,   (1571 – 1630), German astronomer and mathematician, his friend
Willhelm Schickard set out to build Kepler one of the first mechanical calculating
machines, which was intended to facilitate the tedious calculation necessary in determining the position of planets. However, during its construction the calculating
machine was destroyed in a fire. On the basis of the Copernican model of the solar
system, Kepler developed the laws of planetary motion named after him.

Marin Mersenne,   (1588 – 1648), French theologian and mathematician who established the theory of the Mersenne (prime) numbers. He was also engaged in the
study of music theory, acoustics and physics. He undertook the first measurments
of the speed of sound and supported the natural science theories of Galileo and
Descartes.

Willhelm Schickard,   (1592 – 1635), German astronomer, mathematician and artist,
he conducted the first land surveys based on his own cartographic methods. He
additionally constructed the first mechanical, gear-driven calculating machine on
which the four basic operations of arithmetic could be performed.

Johannes Marcus Marci,   (1595 – 1667), Bohemian physician and physicist whose
work focused on mechanics and optics. He carried out the first experiments involving
the refraction of light through a prism, although it was first Newton who succeeded in

explaining the nature of the phenomenon. He shared a long friendship with the Jesuit, mathematician and natural scientist Athanasius Kircher, who introduced Marci to knowledge of writings from the orient.

Athanasius Kircher, (1602 -1680), Thuringian, Jesuit, mathematician and natural scientist. He was the first to use the camera obscura with a converging lens and startled his audiences with the projection of frightening images. The improved camera obscura was soon marketed under the name Laterna Magica (magic lantern).

Timotheus Ritzsch, (1614 -1678), editor of the first regularly published daily newspaper in Leipzig, the "*Neueinlaufende Nachricht von Kriegs- und Welthändeln*" (1650).

Blaise Pascal, (1623 -1662), French mathematician who made important contributions to number theory, geometry and the calculation of probability. In 1642 he developed a mechanical calculating machine that made possible the addition and subtraction of decimal numbers.

Robert Hooke, (1635 – 1703), English scientist who developed the law named after him describing the elasticity of a mechanical spring. Besides biology, physics and mechanics he also occupied himself with telecommunication and supplied the first European description of the "string telephone."In 1684 Hooke also described the possibility of an optical telegraph for message transmission between London and Paris.

Isaac Newton, (1643 – 1727), English physicist, mathematician and astronomer who discovered the law of gravity. He proved the axioms named after him – the so-called classic mechanics – and researched light as it enters matter. He wrote fundamental works in the areas of electrical theory and differential and integral calculus.

Gottfried Willhelm von Leibniz, (1646 – 1716), German mathematician and philosopher, he developed integral and differential calculus independent of Newton. He introduced the binary system and constructed the first mechanical calculating machine that directly supported all 4 basic arithmetic operations. Leibniz attempted to create a unification of all philosophies into one universal philosophy. Through his deliberations he developed the theory of the monads – non-objectified units – from which the world was to have been constructed.

Guillaume Amontons, (1663 – 1705), French physicist and inventor of the barometer who demonstrated for the first time in 1695 a viable possibility of optical signal transmission using the wing telegraph. The physicist, who had lost his hearing in early youth, used the windmills of Belleville because of their slowly turning blades. He had large pieces of cloth painted with the letters of the message to be transmitted attached to the blade tips. After one revolution, the clothes were replaced. The transmitted letters were read at a remote location in the vicinity of Paris with the aid of a telescope.

Stephen Gray, (1666 – 1736), English physicist and amateur astronomer who discovered that almost all material can conduct electrical current, in particular copper wire.

Heinrich Schulze, (1687 – 1744), German doctor and pioneer of photography; he discovered that the blackening of silver compounds is caused by exposure to light energy from the sun.

Petrus van Musschenbroek, (1692 – 1761), Dutch physicist and developer of the predecessor of the electrical battery, the "Leyden jar,"a form of capacitor for the storage of electrical energy.

Antonio Caneletto,   (1697 – 1768), Venetian painter of the renown 18th century cityscapes. He often used the camera obscura for his work as an aid to capturing the natural image of a scene.

Denis Diderot,   (1713 – 1784), French philosopher, writer and central figure in the European Enlightenment. Together with d'Alembert he published the great French encyclopedia (*"Encyclopèdie, ou dictionnaire raisonnè des sciences, des arts et des mètiers"*), which is seen as a forerunner of the hypertext system.

Jean le Rond d'Alembert,   (1717 – 1783), French mathematician, physicist and philosopher. Together with Dennis Diderot he published the great French encyclopedia (*"Encyclopèdie, ou dictionnaire raisonnè des sciences, des arts et des mètiers"*). It is considered the predecessor of the hypertext system principle.

Johann Gottfried Herder,   (1744 – 1803), German philosopher, poet and aesthete, in 1771 he wrote *"Über den Ursprung der Sprache"*(On the Origin of Language). Herder is regarded as a humanist and trailblazer of the German historical periods of "Sturm und Drangs"and"Romanticism."In his writings he emphasizes the profound connection between nature and man – only by exposing this bond can true culture (humanity) be achieved.

Richard Lovell Edgeworth,   (1744 – 1803), British inventor, politician and writer. In 1767 he developed a telegraph that was set up for "private" operation between Newmarket and London. It was not until 1796, after Claude Chappe had already debuted his French semaphore telegraph, that Edgeworth proposed his system to the British admiralty.

Alessandro Volta,   (1745 – 1827), Italian physicist who produced works on electrolysis. In 1800 with his invention called the Voltic pile Volta presented the first reliable electrical energy source and precursor of the modern battery.

Johann Wolfgang von Goethe,   (1749 – 1832), the greatest German poet, whose work probably had the most formative influence on European literature and intellectual history in modern history. Besides his poetic works and numerous autobiographical writings he also wrote many treatises with a scientific content. Among other things he dealt with anatomy, zoology, botany, optics, mineralogy and color theory.

Francisco Salva y Campillo,   (1751 – 1828), Spanish physician and natural scientist. He developed the first electrolyte telegraph.

Joseph Marie Jacquard,   (1752 – 1834), French engineer. The son of a weaver, in 1790 he received the commission to improve the mechanical loom that had been invented 50 years earlier by Jacques de Vauconson. He separated the loom control from the actual machine itself with the help of punched cards. His invention was so revolutionary that weavers in fear of losing their jobs burned his machine and personally attacked him. The unrest however soon settled when the invention led to a huge economic boom.

Samuel Thomas von Sömmering,   (1755 – 1830), German anatomist and physiologist who advanced the development of the electrolyte telegraph.

Claude Chappe,   (1763 – 1805), French physicist. He developed the semaphore wing telegraph as the first modern and practically usable optical telegraph for the transmission of freely formulated messages.

Nicéphore Niepce,   (1765 – 1833), French officer and private teacher who is considered to be the inventor of photography. Using the photogravure process he was the first to produce permanently fixed photographs.

Charles Barbier de la Serre,   (1767 – 1841), French officer who developed a predecessor of braille called "night writing." Barbier's night writing served the purpose of providing soldiers on the front with their written orders in such a way that they could be read without the light of a lantern, lowering the risk of enemy fire. Due to its complexity, Barbier's night writing however did not prevail It was later taken up by Louis Braille and became the basis for braille writing.

Jean-Baptiste Joseph Baron de Fourier, (1768 – 1830), French mathematician and physicist. In 1822 he developed his analytic principle of the expansion of periodic functions in trigonometric series. With the help of the procedures named after him (Fourier analysis, Fourier transformation), a periodic function can be represented as an overlapping of sinus and cosinus vibrations of different amplitude and frequency.

Napoleon Bonaparte, (1769 – 1821), French emperor and general, he recognized early on the use of modern telecommunications procedures in warfare. He supported the expansion of the French semaphore telegraph line and also carried portable semaphores into his campaigns to enable communication between his headquarters and troops. This allowed him the fastest possible coordination of his military and logistic organization and gave him a strategic advantage over his opponents.

Thomas Wedgewood, (1771 – 1805), English pioneer of photography. He experimented with silver nitrate images on ceramic, which, however, did not remain permanently affixed.

Thomas Young, (1773 – 1829), English ophthalmologist and philologist, who determined the wavelength of light visible to humans with the help of diffraction. Through his experiments he recognized light waves in the form of transverse waves and developed a color model based on a mixture of the three primary colors (trichromatic vision). He made significant contributions to deciphering Egyptian hieroglyphics and was therefore considered the main rival of Jean-François Champollions, who finally achieved the decryption breakthrough based on Young's findings.

André Marie Ampère, (1775 – 1836), French physicist who worked on electromagnetism and developed the electro-magnetic needle telegraph.

Georg Friedrich Grotefend, (1775 – 1853), German philologist and classical scholar who was the first to decipher the cuneiform in 1802.

Nathan Mayer Rothschild, (1777 – 1836), British banker and founder of the Rothschild dynasty. According to legend he was said to have laid the cornerstone for his immense fortune after learning of Napoleon's defeat at Waterloo via carrier pigeon. Using this information to his advantage, he was able to make a significant profit on the London stock exchange.

Hans Christian Oerstedt, (1777 – 1851), Danish physicist and chemist. He founded the theory of electromagnetism, thus laying the foundation for modern electromagnetism.

Carl Friedrich Gauss, (1777 – 1855), German mathematician famous for his pioneering work in algebra, number theory and differential geometry. Together with Wilhelm Weber, he developed one of the first electromagnetic pointer telegraphs, which linked the physics building next to the Göttingen Pauline church to the Göttingen observatory.

Francois Dominique Arago, (1786 – 1853), French physicist and director of the Paris Observatory, he also invented a wide range of optical instruments. In 1839 he spoke in front of Louis Daguerre at the Paris Academy of Science about the invention of photography, becoming its first and most important proponent.

Louis Jacques Mandé Daguerre, (1787 – 1851), painter, actor and photographer he further developed Niépce's heliography procedure into the daguerreotype technique named after him. The process permanently fixed photographs on silver iodine plates.

Jean Francois Champolion, (1790 – 1832), French Egyptologist. In 1822 he deciphered hieroglyphics with the help of the "Rosetta Stone." This basalt stone tablet, found July 1799 by Napoleon's troops in the western Nile Delta, contained the same text inscribed in hieroglyphics as well as in demotic and Greek writing.

Michael Faraday, (1791 – 1867), American physicist who besides discovering diamagnetism also discovered the magneto optic effect and electromagnetic induction, which played a crucial role in the development of the telephone.

Charles Babbage, (1791 – 1871), British professor of mathematics, he developed concepts for the construction of the first, freely programmable calculating machine – the "Analytical Engine." The machine was already capable of carrying out logical program branching, program loops and jump instructions and thus anticipated many of the concepts of today's computer. For a lack of precision engineering at the time, a technical implementation of his machine was not yet feasible. Babbage had previously constructed a calculating machine for mechanically solving differential equations – the 1822 "Difference Engine," which could only be partially completed.

Samuel Morse, (1791 – 1872), American portrait artist and inventor whose pioneering work in the advanced development of the telegraph led to the major breakthrough of the "writing " telegraph and the Morse code, an encoding used in electrical telegraphy and named in his honor.

James Gordon Bennet, (1792 – 1872), American publisher, editor and reporter. He was the first Anglo-Saxon to receive the designation "press baron." In 1835 he founded the "*New York Herald,*" based on the yellow press newspaper "*The Sun,*" which had begun publication two years earlier as a cheap newspaper for the masses. A variety of journalistic innovations can be traced back to Bennet, for example, his early use of the telegraph in 1846, maintenance of a system of European correspondents, writing in interview form, and pioneering use of illustrations.

William Fox Talbot, (1800 – 1877), philologist and mathematician, he succeeded in developing the first procedure in photography to make paper prints – the calotype, making it possible to produce multiple copies of one image.

Willhelm Weber, (1804 – 1891), German physicist who researched and published studies on the measurement of the earth's magnetic field together with Carl Friedrich Gauss. In 1833 he developed the electromagnetic pointer telegraph.

Alfred Louis Vail, (1807 – 1859), American engineer and inventor, who as assistant to Samuel Morse made important contributions to the development of the Morse method. Whether the invention of Morse code can be attributed to him or to Morse remains a subject of much controversy.

Louis Braille, (1809 – 1952), inventor of the braille writing named after him. In early childhood Braille lost his eyesight in an accident. He refused to resign himself to only being read to and began early trying to develop writing for the blind. In 1825 he published his easy to learn script for the blind. He had developed it from the extremely complex "night writing" devised by artillery captain Charles Barbier for military use.

Frederick Scott Archer, (1813 – 1857), British sculptor and photographer. In 1851 he developed the collodion wet process for the photographic exposure of negatives on glass plates. For the first time the exposure time necessary was reduced to just a few seconds.

Augusta Ada King,   Countess of Lovelace, (1815 – 1842), daughter of the famous English poet Lord Byron and Charles Babbage's assistant. She contributed to the conception of Babbage's "Analytical Engine," the first freely programmable computer, and thereby developed programming concepts that are still valid today. The programming language commissioned by the American Department of Defense was named ADA in her honor.

George Boole,   (1815 – 1864), British mathematician and inventor of what is now known as Boolean algebra. Boole found that the symbolism of algebra is not only useful for statements between numbers and numerical variables but could be extended to the realm of logic.

Richard Leach Maddox,   (1816 – 1902), English physician and photography pioneer. In 1871 he developed a drying process for photography based on silver bromide and gelatin. Gelatin plates could be stored for long periods of time before they were exposed.

Cyrus W. Fields,   (1819 – 1892), American entrepreneur and businessman who acquired the exclusive right to the laying of a transatlantic cable from America to Europe. He was finally succeeded in this venture in 1858 and 1866. In 1871 he also promoted the laying of the cable in the Pacific Ocean that was to connect the United States with Japan and China via Hawaii.

Hermann von Helmholtz,   (1821 -1894), German physiologist and physicist who is considered to be the last universal genius. Independent of J. P. Joule and J. R. Mayer, he formulated the principle of energy conservation, he produced works on hydrodynamics, electrodynamics, thermodynamics and further developed the three-color theory of Thomas Young.

Étienne Jules Marey,   (1830 – 1904), French physiologist and film pioneer, he developed chronophotography – serial photographic stroboscope images used by scientists to study the movement pattern of subjects in motion.

James Clerk Maxwell,   (1831 – 1879), Scottish physicist, who developed a standardized theory for electricity and magnetism. He postulated the existence of electromagnetic waves, creating the foundation of radio technology. He proved that light is produced by electromagnetic oscillation of a specific wave length.

David Edward Hughes,   (1831 – 1900), American music professor who occupied himself with improving and advancing the development of the telegraph. With the invention of his "Hughes telegraph" in 1855 he succeeded in developing a printing telegraph where the transmission signals are directly output as punch code. We still know this today in the form of the "stock ticker." The invention earned him a great fortune. In 1878 Hughes constructed the first carbon microphone – an essential step on the way to the development of the telephone.

Phillip Reis,   (1834 – 1874), German teacher and inventor, in 1861 he constructed the first precursor of today's telephone.

Elisha Gray,   (1835 – 1901), American inventor who invented the telephone and had it patented at the same time as Alexander Graham Bell. Based on a court decision, it was however Bell who was later ultimately awarded the telephone patent. In 1886 Gray made the first proposal for a multiple use of telegraph lines via frequency-division multiplexing.

Louis Ducas Du Hauron,   (1837 – 1920), French physicist who made important contributions to the development of color photography. In his 1869 book, "*Les Couleurs en Fotografie,*" he presented the subtractive color mixing theory, which however at that time could not be technically implemented due to a lack of suitable material.

Almon Brown Strowger,   (1839 – 1902), American funeral director who was responsible for developing the first automatic telephone exchange and subsequently the rotary-dial telephone.

Charles Cros,   (1842 – 1888), French poet and inventor. Cros made fundamental contributions to the development of color photography and the phonograph. He was however unable to contend with Edison (phonograph) and Hauron (color photography) and did not achieve success financially with either invention.

Emile Baudot,   (1845 -1903), French engineer and telecommunications pioneer who invented the eponymous Baudot code for the encoding of letters and numbers. The unit of measure, a **baud** (character transmitted per second) is named after him.

Eduard Branly,   (1846 -1940), French physicist. Branly discovered the possibility of converting radio waves into electrical power. He developed a detector for electromagnetic waves – the coherer, a glass tube containing metal filings that change their conductivity based on how they are influenced by electromagnetic fields and therefore can be used for detecting the same.

Thomas Alva Edison,   (1847 – 1931), American inventor and organizational talent. Among other things, Edison developed the phonograph, improved the telephone, developed the light bulb, kinetograph and kinetoscope. In 1876 he had his own research lab built in Menlo Park, New Jersey. Along with a team of specialists, he dedicated himself to his epoch-making inventions. Edison registered up to 400 patents a year. He became an idol in the U.S, representing the classic example of a self-made man.

Alexander Graham Bell,   (1848 – 1922), American physiologist who, based on a US Supreme Court decision, is the acknowledged inventor of the telephone and subsequently received the patent.

Karl Ferdinand Braun,   (1850 – 1918), German physicist and Nobel laureate. Braun developed the cathode ray tube and discovered the possibility of frequency tuning by coupling a radio circuit with an antenna circuit.

Emil Berliner,   (1851 – 1929), German-born electrical engineer. He developed the gramophone, which, in contrast to Edison's phonograph, had no recording ability but supplied a sound storage medium in the form of a record. The record could be reproduced on a large scale in a simple way.

George Eastman,   (1854 – 1932), American inventor, who developed flexible roll film and was the first to offer the complete photography infrastructure – from film to camera to a developing service for the mass market.

Heinrich Hertz,   (1857 – 1895), German physicist, who applied Maxwell's theories and constructed devices for sending (resonator) and receiving electromagnetic waves. He thus proved the validity of Maxwell's theories and succeeded in carrying out the first wireless message transmission. The physical measurement to describe the frequency of a wave (one cycle per second = 1 Hz) was named after him and has been established in the international metric system since 1933.

Alexander Stephanowitsch Popov,   (1858 – 1906), Russian naval engineer and inventor who – based on the work of French inventor Branly – developed antennas and radio receivers to detect natural electrical phenomena such as thunderstorms. He established the first wireless Morse connections across a distance of 250 m.

Albert Henri Munsell,   (1858 – 1918), American painter who in 1915 presented his color atlas – a very popular color system based on visual sensation, whereby colors are ordered along a black and white axis.

Michael Idvorsky Pupin, (1858 – 1935), American engineer who developed the self-induction coil named after him. The Pupin coil was used in phone amplification technology before the development of the electron tube or transistor amplifiers.

Emil and Max Skladanowsky, (1859 – 1945) and (1863 – 1939), German showmen and film pioneers. Together they developed the film camera and film projector. The Skladanowsky brothers are credited with the first public film screening in history, which took place in November 1895. They were passed up later by the Lumière brothers due to a lack of financial resources for further developments and later fell into oblivion.

Hermann Hollerith, (1860 – 1929), American inventor who in 1890 developed a punch card machine for the US Census. In this way, the census evaluation could be sped up considerably and carried out with lower costs. To market his product Hollerith founded the "Tabulating Machine Company" in 1896. After several company mergers it eventually evolved into the "International Business Machines" (IBM) company.

Paul Nipkow, (1860 – 1940), German engineer and television pioneer. Nipkow developed the Nipkow disk. It is used to break up a single image into individual pixels that are then converted into electric voltage and transmitted using a selenium cell.

Auguste and Louis Jean Lumière, (1862 – 1954) and (1864 – 1948), French film pioneers who further developed Edison's kinetoscope into the Cinématograph Lumière. It combined a camera, copier and projector in one.

Paul Andre Marie Janet, (1863 – 1937), French physicist who was the first to propose using thin steel wire for electro-magnetic sound recording.

Reginald Aubrey Fessenden, (1866 – 1932), Canadian inventor and engineer. He was the first to invent a method for speech transmission in approx. 1900. On Christmas 1906 he sent the first radio transmission in history. Fesseden received over 500 patents as an inventor, among them for sonar, voice encryption based on an electronic chopper circuit, and the radio compass.

Charles Francis Jenkins, (1867 – 1934), American inventor. In 1925 he developed an electromechanical television system.

Boris Iwanowitsch Rosing, (1869 – 1933), Russian physicist who proposed the implementation of Braun's cathode ray tube for displaying a television picture. In 1907 he was already transmitting simple geometric figures, although he was not successful in displaying halftone images.

Kurt Stille, (1873 – 1957), German engineer who improved the procedure of magnetic recording by the use of extremely thin steel tape.

Lee De Forest, (1873 – 1961), American engineer. De Forest developed the electron tube into an amplification element – the so-called Audion. This was a gas-filled triode that could amplify telegraphic and radio signals. In 1908 De Forest received a patent for this "grandfather of all radio tubes." It was considered one of the most valuable patents that had ever been issued by the US Patent Office. De Forest still thought that gas was necessary in the tube for signal amplification, but later it was proven that performance could be increased even more with the help of a vacuum.

Guglielmo Marconi, (1874 – 1934), Italian engineer and physicist who advanced the field of wireless communication building on the work of Hertz, Branly and Popow. He experimented with marine radio and created the first transatlantic radio link.

Jòzef Tykociński-Tykociner, (1877 – 1969), Polish engineer, inventor of the optical sound recording process that aided in the breakthrough of sound-on-film technology. In 1922 he screened the first film with a soundtrack at the Institute of Electrical Engineering in Urbana, Illinois. The patent application was however delayed due to differences with the then president of the University of Illinois. The patent was first granted in 1926, three years after a patent had been received by Lee de Forest, who produced the first commercial sound-on-film picture.

Robert von Lieben, (1878 – 1913), Austrian physicist. In 1905/06 he invented the amplification electron tube with magnetic control named after him and in 1910 debuted his incandescent tube with grid control (triode). Both inventions were fundamental in developing radio and telephone technology.

Arthur Scherbius, (1878 – 1929), German electrical engineer and entrepreneur. In 1918 he developed a rotary cipher machine called the "Enigma." The Enigma was one of the most important encryption machines of World War II. In order to decrypt its transmission, the allies built what was to become a predecessor of today's computer.

Sir Isaac Shoenberg, (1880 – 1963), Russian emigrant to England. Leading a research group at the British company Electric and Musical Industries (EMI), Shoenberg developed a new type of camera tube and a picture tube for receivers between 1931 – 1935. His system was implemented by the BBC between 1939 and 1962.

Joseph Oswald Mauborgne, (1881 – 1971), American general and engineer. In 1917 together with Gilbert Vernam he invented the secure One Time Pad encryption method. It is based on a stream cipher with a random number stream and may be used only once.

Max Dieckmann, (1882 – 1960), German physicist. In 1906 he patented his invention entitled "A Method for the Transmission of Written Material and Line Drawings By Means of Cathode Ray Tubes. "

John Logie Baird, (1888 – 1946), Scottish inventor who in 1926 developed an electromechanical television system in England.

Ralph Vinton Lyon Hartley, (1888 – 1970), American electrical engineer and cofounder of information theory with Claude E. Shannon. The Shannon-Hartley law named after them describes the maximum data transmission rate of a data transmission channel, depending on its bandwidth and the signal-to-noise ratio. The Shannon-Hartley law is considered one of the most important principles of message and communication technology.

Harry Nyquist, (1889 – 1978), born in Sweden, an American physicist who made important contributions to information theory. In the course of his investigation into the necessary bandwidth for information transmission, he published the Nyquist-Shannon theorem in 1928. Named after him and Claude Shannon, it states that an analog signal with more than twice the signal frequency must be sampled in order to reconstruct the analog output signal from the digital image of the signal.

Vladimir K. Zworykin, (1889 – 1982), Russian television pioneer. Zworykin developed the first completely electronic television camera and picture tube.

Gilbert Sandford Vernam, (1890 – 1960), American electrical engineer who invented the process of the stream cipher and was involved afterwards in the development of the One Time Pad decryption method.

Vennevar Bush, (1890 – 1974), American engineer, inventor and science administrator, whose most important contribution was as head of the U.S. Office of Scientific Research and Development (OSRD) during World War II, through which almost all wartime military R&D was carried out, including initiation and early administration of the Manhattan Project. He is also known in engineering for his work on analog computers, for founding Raytheon, and for the memex, an interactive microfilm viewer with a structure analogous to that of the World Wide Web.

David Sarnoff, (1891 – 1971), American radio pioneer of Russian descent. In 1912, as a young radio operator, he received the emergency transmission from the sinking Titanic and thus gained early fame. While working at Marconi's company, in 1916 he presented the idea of "radio for the masses." He later became president of the Radio Corporation of America (RCA), which emerged from Marconi's original company and supported the development of television.,

August Karolus, (1893 – 1972), German physicist who developed the so-called Kerr cell, used in recording sound on film soundtracks, for optical telephony and fast transmission of still and moving images. His contributions were crucial in initiating the emergence of German television technology.

Fritz Pfleumer, (1897 – 1945), German engineer who developed the first magnetic tape – a paper tape layered with steel powder – for the electromagnetic recording of audio signals.

Paul VI., (1897 – 1978), Giovanni Battista Cardinal Montini, Pope from 1963 to 1978, he carried out the reforms began by his predecessor John XXIII, as well the Second Vatican Council he had initiated. In 1967 he officially lifted the Index Librorum Prohibitorum and with it the censorship of books by the church.

Alec A. Reeves, (1902 – 1971), British engineer who in 1938 developed pulse code modulation – a procedure for the transformation of analog signals into single pulses of constant amplitude that may be recorded digitally and transmitted.

Walter House Brattain, (1902 – 1987), American physicist whose work at Bell Laboratories focused on problems of surface properties in solid state physics. Brattain was co-developer of the first transistor.

John von Neumann, (1903 – 1957), mathematician and computer pioneer of Hungarian descent. Neumann was a member of the development team of the first completely electronic universal computer, ENIAC. The principle named after him states that the memory of a computer can be used for both the program code to be executed and for storing data. Among other things, Neumann made important contributions to game theory, quantum mechanics and to the theory of cellular automata.

John M. Whittaker, (1905 – 1984), British mathematician and son of the famous mathematician Edmund Taylor Whittaker. In 1929 Whittaker expanded the sampling theorem developed by Harry Nyquist (Nyquist-Shannon theorem).

John W. Mauchly, (1907 – 1980), American physicist and computer pioneer, belonged to the development team of the first completely electronic universal computer, ENIAC.

Walter Bruch, (1908 – 1990), German electrical engineer and television pioneer. In 1962 he developed the PAL (Phase Alteration Line) color television technology at the Telefunken company, for which he subsequently received a patent in 1963.

John Bardeen, (1908 – 1991), American physicist who carried out research work on semiconductors at Bell Laboratories and was co-developer of the first transistor. He developed the theory of the superconductivity of certain metals close to absolute zero.

Vladimir A. Kotelnikov, (1908 – 2005), Russian engineer in the area of radio technology and pioneer of information science. In 1933 he discovered the sampling theorem independent of Harry Nyquist (Nyquist-Shannon theorem).

Konrad Zuse, (1910 – 1995), German inventor and constructor of the first functioning, freely programmable, computer in the world based on the binary number system. The Z3 was completed in May 1941 in Berlin.

William Shockley, (1910 – 1989), British physicist and co-developer of the first transistor at the American Bell Laboratories.

Herbert Marshall McLuhan, (1911–1980), Canadian writer, media theorist and visionary. According to his theory, electronic media can have a far greater impact than the content it transports ("The medium is the message").

Henri de France, (1911 – 1986), French engineer and television pioneer, in 1956 he developed the European SECAM color television standard as an alternative to the United States NTSC color television system. Henri de France was an officer in the French Legion of Honor.

Alan Turing, (1912 – 1954), British mathematician and cryptographer, who is considered the "father" of modern information and computer technology. The predictability model – the Turing machine – developed by him and named after him, investigates the hypothetical limits of mechanical computation and is one of the foundations of theoretical computer science. Turing played a leading role in deciphering the radio messages encrypted with the German cipher machine Enigma during World War II. One of the most prestigious awards in computer science – the Turing Award – was named after him.

Herman H. Goldstine, (1913 – 2004), American mathematician and computer pioneer. Part of the development team of the first fully electronic universal computer, ENIAC.

Joseph Carl Robnett Licklider, (1915 – 1991), American visionary and co-developer of the ARPANET. Licklider developed the idea of a universal network and realized his vision in a practical sense as director of the Information Processing Techniques Office at ARPA.

Richard Wesley Hamming, (1915 – 1998), American mathematician and pioneer of coding theory, he worked on error-correction codes, numerical integration methods and digital filters. Hamming received the Turing Award in 1968.

Claude Elwood Shannon, (1916 – 2001), American mathematician who made fundamental contributions to mathematical information and coding theory.

Robert Mario Fano, (*1917), American computer scientist and engineer of Italian descent. Fano became known because of the theory named after him, stating that in a prefix-free code, no code word may be the prefix of another code word.

John P. Eckert, (1919 – 1995), American mathematician and computer pioneer member of the development team of the first fully electronic universal computer, ENIAC.

Robert William Bemer, (1920 – 2004), American computer pioneer and programmer who developed the ASCII character code and was co-developer of the COBOL programming language. In 1971 and then again in 1979, Bemer first brought attention to the the so-called millennium bug (occurrence of errors in computer programs at the turn of the century due to insufficient dimensions of variable declaration).

Charles P. Ginsburg, (1920 – 1992), American engineer who developed the first video recording procedures for the Ampex company.

Jack St. Clair Kilby, (1923 – 2005), American physicist. In 1958 Kilby developed the first integrated circuit in the world at Texas Instruments. He received the Nobel Prize in physics in 2000 for his work.

Joseph Weizenbaum, (1923 – 2008), German-born, American professor of computer science at Massachusetts Institute of Technology (MIT). Between 1964 – 1967 Weizenbaum developed computer programs for language analysis. The best-known was "Eliza," which imitated the behavior of a psycho-therapist in dialog.

James H. Ellis,   (1924 – 1997), British mathematician and engineer who together with Clifford Cocks and Malcolm Williamson discovered the possibility of public key encryption in 1970. This asymmetric encryption method was developed for the British secret service (General Communications Headquarters) and could therefore not be published. It was not until 1976 that Martin Hellman and Whitfield Diffie were able to publish the procedure named after them – the Diffie-Hellman method.

Donald W. Davies,   (1924 – 2000), British computer scientist who with Paul Baran and Leonhard Kleinrock developed the principle of packet switching as a fundamental principle of the computer network. It was Davis who first coined the term "packet switching."

David A. Huffman,   (1925 – 1999), American computer scientist who developed the eponymous Huffman code, for the efficient (compressed) coding of information.

Douglas C. Engelbart,   (1925 – 2013), American engineer who in 1973 developed a hypertext system with a graphic user surface (NLS) at the Augmentation Research Center, Stanford Research Institute. Among other technologies, he was responsible for the computer mouse as an input device.

Paul Baran,   (1926 – 2011), American engineer of Polish ancestry. Baran developed the concept of packet switching with Donald Davies and Leonhard Kleinrock as a fundamental principle of computer networks.

Jacob Ziv,   (*1931), in 1977 he developed a simple, dictionary-based data compression procedure (LZ procedure) together with Abraham Lempel. Improved by Terry Welch in 1984, it went on to achieve great popularity as the **LZW** procedure.

Leonard Kleinrock,   (*1934), professor at the University of California Los Angeles. With Paul Baran and Donald Davies, Kleinrock developed the concept of packet switching and is considered to be the author of the first message sent over the Internet.

Abraham Lempel,   (*1936), director of HP Labs, Israel and professor at the Israel Institute of Technology. In 1977 he developed a simple, dictionary-based data compression method with Jacob Ziv (LZ procedure). It was improved by Terry Welch in 1978 and went on to achieve great popularity as the **LZW** procedure.

Ted Nelson,   (*1937), American scholar who is considered to have originated the term "hypertext." In 1967 he created a worldwide publishing system called "Xanadu," which already anticipated the idea of the WWW 20 years before its birth.

Lawrence Roberts,   (*1937), American engineer regarded as one of the "fathers" of the ARPANET. In 1966 Lawrence became ARPA chief scientist and founded the Network Working Group. The ARPANET became the precursor of the Internet under his leadership.

Robert E, Kahn,   (*1938), American engineer and member of the development team at the BBN company, which under contract for ARPA designed the first communication processor (Interface Messenger Processor, IMP) for the ARPANET. In 1973 Kahn and Vinton Cerf began their work on the Internet protocol TCP/IP. Kahn has also served as director of the Internet Society (ISOC). Kahn was awarded the Turing Award with Vinton Cerf in 2004, and in 2005 both scientists received the "Presidential Medal of Freedom" – the highest civilian award in the US.

Terry Welch,   (1939 – 1988), who in 1984 improved the dictionary-based data compression procedure developed by Jacob Ziv and Abraham Lempel (LZ procedure). It went on to attain its great popularity as the **LZW** procedure.

Ray Tomlinson,   (*1941), American engineer who sent the first email in the world in 1971 (to his own account from a computer in the next room) via the ARPANET.

He used the "@"symbol for the first time to separate the name of the user from the name of the target computer.

Vinton Cerf,   (*1943), American mathematician and computer scientist, member of the development group for the ARPANET. Together with Robert Kahn he developed the Internet protocol **TCP/IP** in 1973, which in 1983 became the standard protocol of the Internet worldwide. Today, Cerf is vice president and Chief Internet Evangelist for Google. He and Robert E. Kahn received the Turing Award in 2004, and in 2005 the "Presidential Medal of Freedom" – the highest civilian award in the US.

Jon Postel,   (1943 – 1998), American computer scientist and Internet pioneer who as RFC editor had been responsible for the organization and publication of Internet standards since the start of the ARPANET. He also played a leading role in the IANA in the allocation and organization of Internet addresses. Postel was further involved in the development of the basic Internet protocols FTP, DNS, SMTP and IP.

Whitfield Diffie,   (*1944), cryptography expert, co-developer of the **Diffie-Hellman** procedure named after him. This is a cryptographic procedure based on the use of a public key, which makes the exchange of secret key information – necessary in standard, symmetric key exchange – superfluous. Diffie is politically active and committed to the rights of the individual in the cryptographically secure private sphere.

Friedemann Schulz von Thun,   (*1944), German psychologist, communications scientist and professor at the University of Hamburg, he developed the "four ears" communication model. In addition to the factual information exchanged in verbal communication, there is always additional information involved, such as a self-revelation from the speaker, an indication of the relationship between the dialog partners and/or an appeal to the receiver.

Phil Zimmermann,   (*1944), cryptography expert and developer of the **PGP** procedure for the secure exchange of emails (Pretty Good Privacy, 1991). PGP includes secure authentication of the communication partners and encryption of the transmitted email messages via an asymmetric encryption procedure. At the same time, the integrity of the transmitted messages is safeguarded with the help of digital signatures. At the time of the Cold War, the US government saw its export restrictions violated by the free availability of Zimmerman's software. As a result, Zimmerman was involved in a three-year legal battle that was finally resolved.

Leonard M. Adleman,   (*1945), professor of computer science at the University of Southern California, Los Angeles, co-developer of the RSA cryptographic procedure (Rivest-Shamir-Adleman, 1978) for asymmetric encryption. Adleman invented the procedure to solve the simple Hamiltonian circuit problem and also built the first DNA computer. He received the Turing Award with Adi Shamir and Ron Rivest in 2003.

Martin Hellman,   (*1945), cryptography expert and co-developer of the Diffie-Hellman procedure named after him. The procedure is based on use of a public key, which makes the exchange of the secret key information necessary in the encryption procedure superfluous.

Robert Metcalfe,   (*1946), American engineer who developed the Ethernet LAN technology at the Palo Alto Research Center of the Xerox company. On his initiative, Ethernet became the product standard of the Digital, Intel and Xerox companies in a joint campaign, and then went on to become the most widely used LAN standard today. In December 1973, he wrote the RFC 602 "*The Stockings Were Hung by* *the Chimney with Care,* "describing the first attack by a hacker on the still young ARPANET.

Robert Cailliau, (*1947), Co-developer of the World Wide Web (1990). At the European Organization for Nuclear Research, CERN, Cailliau and Tim Berners Lee came up with the design for the World Wide Web as a simple hypertext-based document exchange system.

Ronald L. Rivest, (*1947), professor of computer science at the Massachusetts Institute of Technology (MIT), co-developer of the **RSA cryptography procedure** (Rivest-Shamir-Adleman, 1978), developer of the symmetrical encryption procedures RC2, RC4, RC5 and co-developer of RC6. Along with Adi Shamir and Leonard Adleman, Rivest was honored with the Turing Award in 2003.

Ward Cunningham, (*1949), American programmer and developer of the first Wikis of the WikiWikiWeb. He is also considered a pioneer of the software development procedure known as Extreme Programming (XP).

Stephen Wozniak, (*1950), founded the Apple company with Steve Jobs in 1975, after having quit his engineering studies. Apple was the first company in the world to put personal computers on the market.

Steven Sasson, (*1950), American electrical engineer who developed the first practical digital camera in 1975 at Eastman Kodak. The camera weighed almost 4 kilograms, had a picture resolution of 100 x 100 pixels and could take a black and white picture in 23 seconds and save it on magnetic tape.

Clifford Christopher Cocks, (*1951), British mathematician and cryptologist. In 1970 Cocks had already discovered the possibility of public key encryption – an asymmetric encryption procedure – along with Malcolm Williamson and James H. Ellis. Because the method was developed for the British secret service (General Communications Headquarters) it could not be made public. First in 1976 Martin Hellman and Whitfield Diffie published the equivalent method bearing their names – the Diffie-Hellman procedure.

Ralph C. Merkle, (*1952), American computer scientist and pioneer in cryptography who together with Martin Hellman and Whitfield Diffie developed the Diffie-Hellman key exchange procedure. Merkle also designed the block ciphers Khufu and Khafre and the cryptographic hash function SNEFRU.

Adi Shamir, (*1952), professor at the Weizmann Institute of Science in Tel Aviv, co-developer of the RSA cryptography procedure (Rivest-Shamir-Adleman, 1978) for asymmetric encryption. He received the Turing Award in 2003 together with Leonard Adleman and Ron Rivest.

Tim O'Reilly, (*1954), Irish software developer, author and publisher, who played an important role in the development of the scripting language Perl. Together with his co-worker Dale Daugherty, O'Reilly coined the term "Web 2.0".

Karlheinz Brandenburg, (*1954), German electrical engineer who in 1982 began development of the world-famous MP3 audio compression procedure with his research group. The project was carried out at the Fraunhofer Institut for Integrated Circuits (IIS) in Erlangen, in the framework of an EU project with the University of Erlangen-Nuremberg, and further involved the companies: AT&T Bell Labs and Thomson.

Christoph Meinel, (*1954), director of the Hasso Plattner Institute for Software Systems Engineering at the University of Potsdam, visiting professor at Luxembourg International Advanced Studies in Information Technology and at the Beijing University of Technology. Meinel's work has dealt with issues addressing communication complexity, e.g., as inventor of the high security network lock system "Lock-Keeper," which facilitates message exchange between physically separated networks, and as developer of the internationally implemented teleteaching system "tele-TASK." Meinel is chairman of the German IPv6 Council and one of the authors of this book.

Steve Jobs,   (1955 – 2011), American entrepreneur. After quitting his engineering studies, Jobs founded the Apple company with Steve Wozniak. Apple succeeded in putting the first personal computer on the market – the Apple II – even before IBM.

William Henry "Bill" Gates III.,   (*1955), American entrepreneur who founded the Microsoft company in 1975 with Paul Allen. Gates is currently considered to be the third richest person in the world. The success of his company Microsoft started with the deployment of the operating system for the IBM PC – MS-DOS. In the 1990s the graphic operating system Microsoft Windows and Microsoft's software for offices, simply called Microsoft Office, became the market leader.

Tim Berners Lee,   (*1955), professor at MIT and Father of the World Wide Web (1990), he currently serves as director of the W3C (World Wide Web Consortium). Founded by Berners Lee in 1994, the Consortium coordinates and directs the development of the WWW. Berners Lee collaborated with Robert Caillieau to develop the first WWW server at the European nuclear research center CERN, thereby laying the foundation for the WWW. In 2004, he was knighted by Queen Elizabeth II as a "Knight Commander of the Order of the British Empire" (KBE) for his service to science. Tim Berners Lee sees the future of the World Wide Web today in the Web of Data.

Paulo S. L. M. Barreto,   (*1965), Brazilian cryptographer, he developed with Vincent Rijmen the cryptographic hash function WHIRLPOOL. Additionally, both jointly developed the block ciphers Anubis and KHAZAD.

Joan Daemen,   (*1965), Belgian cryptographer who with Vincent Rijmen developed the Rijndael encryption procedure. It was standardized as the Advanced Encryption Standard (AES) 2001 and is regarded as one of the most important symmetric encryption procedures today.

Harald Sack,   (*1965), computer scientist and senior researcher at the Hasso Plattner Institute for Software Systems Engineering at the University of Potsdam. Sack is a founding member of the German IPv6 Council, co-founder of the video search engine Yovisto.com and one of the authors of this book. After working in the field of formal verification, his research today is focussed on on multimedia retrieval, the semantic web technology, and knowledge mining.

Vincent Rijmen,   (*1970), Belgian cryptographer. With Joan Daemen Rijmen he developed the Rijndael encryption procedure. It was standardized as the Advanced Encryption Standard (AES) 2001 and is viewed today as the most important symmetric encryption procedure. Rijmen also developed the cryptographic hash function WHIRLPOOL with Paul Bareto.

Abbreviations and Acronyms

3DES	Triple-DES
4CIF	4 times Common Intermediate Format
AAC	Advanced Audio Coding
ABR	Available Bit Rate
AC	Audio Code
ADSL	Asymmetric Digital Subscriber Line
AES/EBU	Audio Engineering Society / European Broadcasting Union
AFX	Animation Framework Extension
AIFF	Audio Interchange File Format
AJAX	Asynchronous JavaScript and XML
AM	Amplituden-Modulation
ANSI	American National Standards Institute
ARPA	Advanced Research Project Agency
ASCII	American Standard Code for Information Interchange
ASF	Advanced Streaming Format
ASK	Amplitude Shift Keying
ASP	Advanced Simple Profile
ATM	Asynchronous Transfer Mode
ATRAC	Adaptive Transform Acoustic Coding
AVC	Advanced Video Codec
AVI	Audio Video Interleave
BCD	Binary Coded Digits
BDSG	Bundesdatenschutzgesetz
BIFS	Binary Format for Scenes
Bit	Binary Digit
bit	Basic Indissoluble Information Unit
BMP	Basic Multilingual Plane
BMP	Bitmap Format
bps	Bits per Second
BSC	Bit Synchronous Communication

C. Meinel and H. Sack, *Digital Communication*, X.media.publishing,
DOI: 10.1007/978-3-642-54331-9, © Springer-Verlag Berlin Heidelberg 2014

b/w	Black and White
CA	Certification Authority
CAP	Carrierless Amplitude Phase
CBR	Constant Bit Rate
CC	Creative Commons
CCIR	Comité Consultatif International des Radiocommunications
CCITT	Comité Consultatif International de Telegraphique et Telefonique
CCD	Charge Coupled Device
CD	Compact Disc
CD-DA	Compact Disc Digital Audio
CD-ROM	Compact Disc Read Only Memory
CERN	Conseil Européen pour la Recherche Nucléaire
CERT	Computer Emergency Response Team
CHAP	Cryptographic Handshake Authentication Protocol
CIE	Commission Internationale d'Eclairage
CIF	Common Intermediate Format
CMS	Cryptographic Message Syntax
CMY	Cyan, Magenta, Yellow
CPU	Central Processing Unit
CR	Carriage Return
CRC	Cyclic Redundancy Check
CRT	Cathod Ray Tube
CSNet	Computer Science Network
DAB	Digital Audio Broadcasting
DARPA	Defense Advanced Research Projects Agency
db	decibel
DCC	Digital Compact Cassette
DCE	Data Communication Equipment
DCT	Discrete Cosine Transform
DDCMP	Digital Data Communications Message Protocol
DECT	Digital Enhanced Cordless Telecommunications
DES	Data Encryption Standard
DFN	Deutsches Forschungsnetzwerk
DFT	Discrete Fourier Transform
DIN	Deutsche Industrie Norm
DIT	Directory Information Tree
DMIF	Delivery Multimedia Integration Framework
DNS	Domain Name Service
DoD	Department of Defense
DoS	Denial of Service
DPCM	Differential Pulse Code Modulation
dpi	dots per inch
DRM	Digital Rights Management
DSA	Digital Signature Algorithm
DTE	Data Terminal Equipment

DVB	Digital Video Broadcasting
DVB-T	Digital Video Broadcast - Terrestrial
DVB-S	Digital Video Broadcast - Satellite
DVB-C	Digital Video Broadcast - Cable
DVD	Digital Versatile Disk
EBCDIC	Extended Binary Coded Decimals Interchange Code
EOB	End of Block
EOF	End of File
EOI	End of Image
EOT	End of Text
Exif	Exchangeable Image File Format
FFT	Fast Fourier Transformation
FLV	Flash Video
fps	Frames per Second
FT	Fourier Transformation
GAN	Global Area Network
GFR	Guaranteed Frame Rate
GFX	Graphical Framework Extension
GIF	Graphic Interchange Format
GOP	Group of Pictures
GPS	Global Positioning System
HDCL	High Level Data Link Protocol
HD DVD	High Density Digital Versatile Disc
HDTV	High Definition Television
HSV	Hue, Saturation, Value
Hz	hertz
IC	Integrated Circuit
IDCT	Inverse Discrete Cosine Transformation
IDEA	International Data Encryption Algorithm
IFF	Interchange File Format
IMP	Internet Message Processor
IP	Intellectual Property
ISDN	Integrated Service Digital Network
ISO	International Standards Organisation
ITC	International Telegraph Code
ITU	International Telecommunications Union
JFIF	JPEG File Interchange Format
JPEG	Joint Photographic Experts Group
KDC	Key Distribution Center
KEA	Key Exchange Algorithm
kHz	kilohertz
LAN	Local Area Network
LAPD	Link Access Procedure D-Channel
LASeR	Lightweight Scene Representation
LLC	Logical Link Control

LZW	Lev Zipf Welch
MAC	Message Authentication Code
MAN	Metropolitan Area Network
MD5	Message Digest 5
MDCT	Modified Discrete Cosine Transformation
MIDI	Musical Instrument Digital Interface
MIME	Multimedia Internet Mail Extension Format
MPEG	Moving Pictures Experts Group
NSF	National Science Foundation
NTSC	National Television Systems Comitee ("Never the same color")
OSI	Open Systems Interconnect
PA	Preamble
PAL	Phase Alternating Lines
PAN	Personal Area Network
PAP	Password Authentication Protocol
PARC	Palo Alto Research Center
PCM	Pulse Code Modulation
PDF	Portable Document Format
PGP	Pretty Good Privacy
PKI	Public Key Infrastruktur
PNG	Portable Network Graphics
QAM	Quadrature Aperture Modulation
QCIF	Quarter Common Intermediate Formate
RAM	Random Access Memory
RC	Rivest Cipher (Ron's Code)
RDF	Resource Description Framework
RFC	Reverse Path Forwarding
RGB	Rot - Grün - Blau
RIFF	Resource Interchange File Format
RLE	Run Length Encoding
ROM	Read Only Memory
RSA	Rivest, Shamir, Adleman - Verschlüsselungsalgorithmus
RTMP	Real Time Messaging Protocol
RTSP	Real Time Streaming Protocol
SECAM	Systéme Électronique pour Couleur avec Mémoire
SHA	Secure Hash Algorithm
SIP	Supplementary Ideographic Plane
SMR	Signal-to-Mask Ratio
SMR	Symbolic Music Representation
SMS	Short Message Service
SNR	Signal-to-Noise Ratio
S/PDIF	Sony/Philips Digital Interconnect Format
SSL	Secure Socket Layer
SSP	Supplementary Special-purpose Plane

TA	Trust Center
TCP	Transmission Control Protocol
TDM	Time Division Multiplexing
TIFF	Tagged Image File Format
UBR	Unspecified Bit Rate
UCS	Universal Character Set
UDP	User Datagram Protocol
UHDV	Ultra High Definition Video
URI	Uniform Resource Identificator
USB	Universal Serial Bus
UTF	Unicode Transformation Format
VBR	Variable Bit Rate
VC	Virtual Container
VGA	Video Graphics Array
VHS	Video Home System
VoIP	Voice over IP
VPN	Virtual Private Network
VRML	Virtual Reality Modeling Language
WAN	Wide Area Network
W3C	World Wide Web Consortium
WLAN	Wireless LAN
WMA	Windows Media Audio
WMF	Windows Media Format
WMT	Windows Media Technologies
WPAN	Wireless Personal Area Network
WWW	World Wide Web
WYSIWYG	What You See Is What You Get
XLink	eXtended Lokales Informatik Netz
XML	Extended Markup Language

Image References

Abb. 2.3:   Marie-Lan Nguyen / Wikimedia Commons
Abb. 2.4:   A. Frankenhäuser, Hieroglyphs
Abb. 2.5:   A. Frankenhäuser, Greek and Phoenician Writing
Abb. 2.7:   Jost Amman, Ständebuch (1568) [6]
Abb. 2.8:   Jost Amman, Ständebuch (1568) [6]
Abb. 2.9:   Leaflet against indulgences (16th Century), from [194]
Abb. 2.10: Johann Carolus, Relation aller Fürnemmen und gedenckwürdigen Historien (1609)
Abb. 2.11: Wikimedia Commons
Abb. 2.12: Sketch of the first Morse telegraph (1886) , from [246]
Abb. 2.14: Brady-Handy Photograph Collection, Library of Congress (1877)
Abb. 2.13: Die Gartenlaube, Ernst Keil's Nachfolger, Leipzig (1863)
Abb. 2.15: Athanasius Kircher: Athanasii Kircheri Ars magna lucis et umbrae (1646) [135]
Abb. 2.16: Scientific Identity: Portraits from the Dibner Library of the History of Science and Technology, Smithsonian Institute, SIL14-M001-13
Abb. 2.17: Th. Audel: Hawkins Electrical Guide (1917), [46]
Abb. 2.18: Gregor Reisch: Margarita Philosophica (1504)
Abb. 2.19: The Mechanic's Magazine, Museum, Register, Journal and Gazette, October 6, 1832-March 31, 1833. Vol. XVIII
Abb. 2.21: U.S. Army Photo / Wikimedia Commons
Abb. 2.24: W3C, URL: http://www.w3.org/People/Berners-Lee/WorldWideWeb.html
Abb. 5.1:   A. Frankenhäuser, Alice, Bob and Trudy
Abb. 5.4:   K. Sperling / Wikimedia Commons
Abb. 5.6:   U.S. Air Force Photo / Wikimedia Commons

C. Meinel and H. Sack, *Digital Communication*, X.media.publishing,   373
DOI: 10.1007/978-3-642-54331-9, © Springer-Verlag Berlin Heidelberg 2014

Bibliography

1. Abrahamson, A.: The history of television, 1880 to 1941. McFarland, Jefferson, N.C. (1987)
2. Abrahamson, A.: The history of television, 1942 to 2000. McFarland & Co., Jefferson, N. C. (2003)
3. Abramson, N.: Development of the alohanet. Information Theory, IEEE Transactions on **31**(2), 119–123 (1985)
4. Accredited Standards Committee: X9: American National Standard X3.17-1985: Financial Institution Key Management (Wholesale) (1985)
5. Aischylos: Die Orestie: (Agamemnon, Die Totenspende, Die Eumeniden): deutsch von Emil Staiger, mit einem Nachwort des "Übersetzers. Reclam, Stuttgart (1986)
6. Amman, J., Sachs, H.: Eygentliche Beschreibung Aller Stände auff Erden / hoher und niedriger / geistlicher und weltlicher / aller Künsten / Handwercken und Händeln / u. vom größten bis zum kleinesten / Auch von ihrem Ursprung / Erfindung und gebreuchen. Georg Raben / Sigmund Feyerabents, Frankfurt a. M. (1568)
7. Anderson, C.: The Long Tail: Why the Future of Business is Selling Less of More. Hyperion, New York, NY, USA (2006)
8. Assmann, J.: Zur Entwicklung der Schrift im alten Ägypten. In: L. Engell, B. Siegert, J. Vogl (eds.) Archiv für Mediengeschichte – Medien der Antike, pp. 13–24. Universitätsverlag Weimar, Weimar (2003)
9. Badach, A., Hoffmann, E.: Technik der IP-Netze - TCP/IP incl. IPv6 - Funktionsweise, Protokolle und Dienste, 2. erw. Aufl. Carl Hanser Verlag, München (2007)
10. Baier, W.: Geschichte der Fotografie. Quellendarstellungen zur Geschichte der Fotografie. Schirmer und Mosel, München (1977)
11. Baran, P.: On distributed communication networks. IEEE Transactions on Communication Systems **12** (1964)
12. Baran, P.: Reliable digital communication systems using unreliable network repeater nodes, report p-1995. Tech. rep., Rand Corporation (1965)
13. Bauer, F.: Das Gießinstrument des Schriftgießers. Ein Beitrag zur Geschichte der Schriftgiesserei. Genzsch & Heyse, Hamburg; München (1922)
14. Bauer, F.L.: Entzifferte Geheimnisse. Methoden und Maximen der Kryptologie. Springer Verlag, Berlin, Heidelberg, New York (2001)
15. Beauchamp, K.: History of Telegraphy. The Institution of Electrical Engineers, London, UK (2001)
16. Beck, K.: Computervermitelte Kommunikation im Internet. Oldenbourg Verlag, München (2006)
17. Berlekamp, E.R.: Key Papers in the Development of Coding Theory (IEEE Press Selected Reprint Series). IEEE Press (1088)
18. Berlekamp, E.R.: Algebraic coding theory. Aegean Park Press, Laguna Hills, CA, USA (1984)
19. Berners-Lee, T., Cailliau, R., Groff, J.F., Pollermann, B.: World-wide web: The information universe. Electronic Networking: Research, Applications and Policy **1**(2), 74–82 (1992)
20. Bertsekas, D., Gallagher, R.: Data Networks, 2nd edn. Prentice Hall, Englewood Cliffs, NJ, USA (1991)
21. Beutelspacher, A.: Kryptologie : eine Einführung in die Wissenschaft vom Verschlüsseln, Verbergen und Verheimlichen. Vieweg Verlag, Braunschweig (1993)
22. Beutelspacher, A.: Geheimsprachen: Geschichte und Techniken. C. H. Beck, München (1997)

C. Meinel and H. Sack, *Digital Communication*, X.media.publishing,
DOI: 10.1007/978-3-642-54331-9, © Springer-Verlag Berlin Heidelberg 2014

23. Bierbrauer, J.: Introduction to Coding Theory. Chapman and Hall/CRC Press, Boca Raton, FL, USA (2004)
24. Binder, F.: Die Brieftaube bei den Arabern in der Abbassiden- und Mamlukenzeit. Journal of Ornithology **95**(1), 38–47 (1954)
25. Black, U.: OSI: a model for computer communications standards. Prentice-Hall, Inc., Upper Saddle River, NJ, USA (1991)
26. Black, U.: Emerging communications technologies (2nd ed.). Prentice-Hall, Inc., Upper Saddle River, NJ, USA (1997)
27. Blanck, H.: Das Buch in der Antike. Beck, München (1992)
28. Bless, R., Mink, S., Blaß, E.O., Conrad, M., Hof, H.J., Kutzner, K., Schööller, M.: Sichere Netzwerkkommunikation. ISBN 3-540-21845-9. Springer Verlag, Berlin, Heidelberg (2005)
29. Bradner, S.: The internet standards process – revision 3 (1996)
30. Brockhaus (ed.): Der Brockhaus in einem Band. 10., vollständig überarbeitete und aktualisierte Auflage. Bibliographisches Institut F. A. Brockhaus AG, Mannheim (2005)
31. Buchmann, J.: Einführung in die Kryptographie. Springer Verlag, Berlin, Heidelberg, New York (2001)
32. Buddemeier, H.: Von der Keilschrift zum Cyberspace: Der Mensch und seine Medien. Verlag Freies Geistesleben & Urachhaus GmbH, Stuttgart (2001)
33. Buford, J.F.K.: Multimedia systems. Addison-Wesley Publishing Company, Reading, MA, USA (1994)
34. Bush, V.: As we may think. interactions **3**(2), 35–46 (1996)
35. Bußmann, H.: Lexikon der Sprachwissenschaft. Alfred Körner Verlag, Stuttgart (1983)
36. Cailliau, R., Gillies, J.: How the Web Was Born: The Story of the World Wide Web. Oxford University Press (2000)
37. Cassin, E., Bottero, J., Vercoutter, J.: Die Altorientalischen Reiche III - Die erste Hälfte des 1. Jahrtausends. Fischer Weltgeschichte, Band 4. Fischer Taschenbuch Verlag, Frankfurt a. M. (1967)
38. Cavalli-Sforza, L.: Gene, Völker und Sprachen. Die biologischen Grundlagen unserer Zivilisation. Carl Hanser Verlag, München (1996)
39. Cavalli-Sforza, L.L., Menozzi, P., Piazza, A.: The History of Geography of Human Genes. Princeton University Press, Princeton, NJ, USA (1994)
40. Chen, J.W., Kao, C.Y., Lin, Y.L.: Introduction to H.264 Advanced Video Coding. In: ASP-DAC '06: Proceedings of the 2006 conference on Asia South Pacific design automation, pp. 736–741. IEEE Press, Piscataway, NJ, USA (2006)
41. Chomsky, N.: On certain formal properties of grammars. In: R.D. Luce, R. Bush, E. Galanter (eds.) Handbook of Mathematical Psychology, vol. 2, pp. 323–418. Wiley, New York, NY, USA (1963)
42. Christopoulos, C., Skodras, A., Ebrahimi, T.: The JPEG 2000 still image coding system: An overview. IEEE Transactions on Consumer Electronics **46**(4), 1103–1127 (2000)
43. Churchhouse, R.F.: Codes and Ciphers: Julius Caesar, the Enigma, and the Internet. Cambridge University Press (2001)
44. Clarke, D.: The ingenious Mr. Edgeworth. Oldbourne, London, UK (1965)
45. Clarke, R.J.: Digital Compression of Still Images and Video. Academic Press, Inc., Orlando, FL, USA (1995)
46. Co., T.A.&.: Hawkins Electrical Guide, Volume 6. Hawkins and staff, New York, NY, USA (1917)
47. Comer, D.E.: Computernetzwerke und Internets. Prentice Hall, München (1998)
48. Compaine, B.M. (ed.): The digital divide: facing a crisis or creating a myth? MIT Press, Cambridge, MA, USA (2001)

49. Compuserve Incorporated: GIF Graphics Interchange Format: A standard defining a mechanism for the storage and transmission of bitmap-based graphics information. Columbus, OH, USA (1987)

50. Compuserve Incorporated: GIF Graphics Interchange Format: Version 89a. Columbus, OH, USA (1990)

51. Cormen, T.H., Leiserson, C.E., Rivest, R.L., Stein, C.: Introduction to Algorithms. The MIT Press, Cambridge, MA, USA (2001)

52. Corsten, S.: Die Drucklegung der zweiundvierzigzeiligen Bibel. Technische und chronologische Probleme. In: W. Schmitt (ed.) Johannes Gutenbergs zweiundvierzigzeilige Bibel. Faksimile-Ausgabe nach dem Exemplar der Staatsbibliothek Preußischer Kulturbesitz Berlin. Idion Verlag, München (1979)

53. Corsten, S.: Die Erfindung des Buchdrucks im 15. Jahrhundert. In: V. der Maximilian Gesellschaft, B. Tiemann (eds.) Die Buchkultur im 15. und 16. Jahrhundert, Bd. 1, pp. 125–202. Maximilian-Gesellschaft, Hamburg (1995)

54. Côté, G., Erol, B., Gallant, M., Kossentini, F.: H.263+: video coding at low bit rates. Circuits and Systems for Video Technology, IEEE Transactions on **8**(7), 849–866 (1998)

55. Coulmas, F.: The Blackwell Encyclopedia of Writing Systems. Blackwell, New York, NJ, USA (1996)

56. Crowcroft, J., Handley, M., Wakeman, I.: Internetworking Multimedia. Morgan Kaufman Publishers, San Francisco, CA, USA (1999)

57. Crowley, D., Heyer, P.: Communication in History: Technology, Culture and Society (Fourth Edition). Allyn and Bacon, Boston, MA, USA (2003)

58. Crystal, D.: Dictionary of Linguistics and Phonetics. John Wiley and Sons, Hoboken, NJ, USA (2011)

59. Daemen, J., Rijmen, V.: The Design of Rijndael: AES - The Advanced Encryption Standard. Springer Verlag, Berlin, Heidelberg, New York (2002)

60. Daigle, J.D.: Queueing Theory for Telecommunications. Addison-Wesley, Reading, MA, USA (1991)

61. Davies, D.W., Barber, D.L.A.: Communication networks for computers. John Wiley, London, New York (1973)

62. Day, J.D., Zimmermann, H.: The OSI reference model. Proceedings of the IEEE **71**(12), 1334–1340 (1983)

63. Deutscher, G.: The Unfolding of Language: The Evolution of Mankind's greatest Invention. Henry Holt and Company, New York (NY), USA (2006)

64. Dietz, M., Popp, H., Brandenburg, K., Friedrich, R.: Audio compression for network transmission. Journal of the Audio Engineering Society **44**(1-2), 58–72 (1996)

65. Diffie, W.: The first ten years of public-key cryptography. In: Innovations in Internetworking, pp. 510–527. Artech House, Inc., Norwood, MA, USA (1988)

66. Diffie, W., Hellman, M.E.: New directions in cryptography. IEEE Transactions on Information Theory **IT-22**(6), 644–654 (1976)

67. DIN 44302: DIN 44302: Datenübertragung, Datenübermittlung: Begriffe. Deutsches Institut für Normierung DIN, Berlin / Köln (1979)

68. DIN 66020: Funktionelle Anforderungen an die Schnittstellen zwischen Datenendeinrichtung und Datenübertragungseinrichtungen - Teil 1: Allgemeine Anwendung. Deutsches Institut für Normierung DIN, Berlin / Köln (1999)

69. DIN 66021: DIN 66021-9: Schnittstelle zwischen DEE und DÜE für Synchrone Übertragung bei 48000 bit/s auf Primärgruppenverbindungen. Deutsches Institut für Normierung DIN, Berlin / Köln (1983)

70. Eckschmitt, W.: Das Gedächtnis der Völker. Hieroglyphen, Schriften und Schriftfunde. Heyne Verlag, München (1980)

71. Eco, U.: From Internet to Gutenberg, a lecture presented at the Italian Academy for Advanced Studies in America, nov. 12, 1996 (1996). URL http://www.italynet.com/columbia/Internet.htm

72. Engell, L., Siegert, B., Vogl, J.: Archiv für Mediengeschichte – Medien der Antike. Universitätsverlag Weimar, Weimar (2003)
73. Erb, E.: Radios von gestern. M + K Verlag Computer Verlag, Luzern (1993)
74. Essinger, J.: Jacquard's web. Oxford University Press, Oxford, UK (2004)
75. Evenson, A.E.: The Telephone Patent Conspiracy of 1876: The Elisha Gray - Alexander Bell Controversy. McFarland, Jefferson, NC, USA (2000)
76. Falk, D., Brill, D., Stork, D.: Seeing the Light: Optics in Nature, Photography, Color, Vision and Holography. John Wiley & Sons, New York, NY, USA (1986)
77. Faulmann, C.: Schriftzeichen und Alphabete aller Zeiten und Völker, Reprint der Ausgabe von 1880. Augustus Verlag, Augsburg (1990)
78. Faulstich, W.: Das Medium als Kult: von den Anfängen bis zur Spätantike. Vandenhoek & Ruprecht, Göttingen (1997)
79. Fickers, A.: „Politique de la grandeur" vs. „Made in Germany". Politische Kulturgeschichte der Technik am Beispiel der PAL-SECAM-Kontroverse. Oldenbourg Verlag, München (2007)
80. Flichy, P.: Tele: Die Geschichte der modernen Kommunikation. Campus Verlag, Frankfurt a. M. (1994)
81. Fluhrer, S.R., Mantin, I., Shamir, A.: Weaknesses in the key scheduling algorithm of RC4. In: SAC '01: Revised Papers from the 8th Annual International Workshop on Selected Areas in Cryptography, pp. 1–24. Springer-Verlag, London, UK (2001)
82. Földes-Papp, K.: Vom Felsbild zum Alphabet. Die Geschichte der Schrift von ihren frühesten Vorstufen bis zur modernen lateinischen Schreibschrift. Chr. Belser Verlag, Stuttgart (1966)
83. Freyer, U.: Nachrichten-Übertragungstechnik, 4. Aufl. Carl Hanser Verlag, München (2000)
84. Fritsch, A.: Diskurs über den heutigen Gebrauch und Mißbrauch der Neuen Nachrichten, die man Neue Zeitung nennt (Discursus de Novellarum quas vocant Neue Zeitunge hodierne usu et abusu). In: K. Kurth (ed.) Die ältesten Schriften für und wider die Zeitungen (Quellenhefte zur Zeitungswissenschaft), 1, pp. 33–44. Rohrer, Brünn/ München/ Wien (1944)
85. Fuglèwicz, M.: Das Internet Lesebuch - Hintergründe, Trends, Perspektiven. Buchkultur Verlagsgesellschaft m.b.H., Wien (1996)
86. Füssel, S.: Johannes Gutenberg. Rowohlt Taschenbuch Verlag GmbH, Reinbeck bei Hamburg (1999)
87. Füssel, S. (ed.): Gutenberg-Jahrbuch 2006. Harrassowitz, Wiesbaden-Erbenheim (2006)
88. Gage, J.: Kulturgeschichte der Farbe. Von der Antike bis zur Gegenwart, 2. Aufl. E. A. Seemann Verlag, Leipzig (2004)
89. Gantert, K., Hacker, R.: Bibliothekarisches Grundwissen, 8., vollst. neu bearb. und erw. Aufl. Saur, München (2008)
90. Gellat, R.: The fabulous phonograph. From tin foil to high fidelity. Lippincott, Philadelphia, NY, USA (1954)
91. Gessinger, J., v. Rahden (Hrsg.), W.: Theorien vom Ursprung der Sprachen. de Gruyter, Berlin - New York (1989)
92. Gibson, J.D., Berger, T., Lookabaugh, T., Lindbergh, D., Baker, R.L.: Digital compression for multimedia: principles and standards. Morgan Kaufmann Publishers Inc., San Francisco, CA, USA (1998)
93. Goldstein, E.B.: Wahrnehmungspsychologie: Der Grundkurs, 7. Aufl. Spektrum Akademischer Verlag, Heidelberg (2007)
94. Gööck, R.: Radio, Fernsehen, Computer. Sigloch, Künzelsau (1989)
95. Görne, T.: Tontechnik. Carl Hanser Verlag, Leipzig (2006)
96. Grimm, R.: Digitale Kommunikation. Oldenbourg Verlag, München (2005)
97. Gunther, R.W.T. (ed.): Early science in Oxford. Dawsons, London, UK (1966)

98. Haarmann, H.: Universalgeschichte der Schrift, 2. Aufl. Campus Verlag, Frankfurt a. M. (1991)

99. Haarmann, H.: Early Civilization and Literacy in Europe, An Inquiry into Cultural Continuity in the Mediterranean World. Mouton de Gruyter, Berlin - New York (1996)

100. Haase, F.: Mythos Fackeltelegraph – Über die medientheoretischen Grundlagen antiker Nachrichtentechnik. In: L. Engell, B. Siegert, J. Vogl (eds.) Archiv für Mediengeschichte – Medien der Antike, pp. 13–24. Universitätsverlag Weimar, Weimar (2003)

101. Haaß, W.D.: Handbuch der Kommunikationsnetze: Einführung in die Grundlagen und Methoden der Kommunikationsnetze. Springer Verlag, Berlin, Heidelberg, New York (1997)

102. Hacker, S.: MP3: The Definitive Guide. O'Reilly & Associates, Sebastopol CA, USA (2000)

103. Hadorn, W., Cortesi, M.: Mensch und Medien - Die Geschichte der Massenkommunikation. AT Verlag Aarau, Stuttgart (1985)

104. Hafner, K., Lyon, M.: Arpa Kadabra: Die Geschichte des Internet. dPunkt Verlag, Heidelberg (1997)

105. Hahn, H., Stout, R.: The Internet Complete Reference. Osborne McGraw-Hill, Berkeley CA, USA (1994)

106. Hambling, D.: Weapons Grade. Carroll & Graf, New York, NY, USA (2005)

107. Hamilton, E.: JPEG File Interchange Format. Tech. rep., C-Cube Microsystems, Milpitas, CA, USA (1992). URL http://www.w3.org/Graphics/JPEG/jfif3.pdf

108. Hamming, R.W.: Error detecting and error correcting codes. Bell System Technical Journal 26(2), 147–160 (1950)

109. Hammond, N.G.L., (Hrsg.), H.H.S.: The Oxford Classical Dictionary, 2nd Ed. Oxford University Press, Oxford, UK (1992)

110. Hanebutt-Benz, E.M.: Gutenbergs Erfindungen. In: Mainz (ed.) Gutenberg - Aventur und Kunst: Vom Geheimunternehmen zur ersten Medienrevolution, pp. 158–189. Schmidt, Mainz (2000)

111. Harris, M.H.: History of Libraries of the Western World. Scarecrow Press, Lanham, MD, USA (1991)

112. Harris, R.: The Origin of Writing. Duckworth, London, UK (1986)

113. Hartley, R.V.L.: Transmission of information. Bell Syst. Tech. Journal 7, 535–563 (1928)

114. Hauben, M., Hauben, R.: Netizens: On the History and Impact of UseNet and the Internet. Wiley-IEEE Computer Society Press, Los Alamitos, CA, USA (1997)

115. Hiebel, H.H., Hiebler, H., Kogler, K., Walitsch, H.: Die Medien - Logik, Leistung, Geschichte. W. Fink Verlag, München (1998)

116. Hiltz, S.R., Turoff, M.: The Network Nation. Addison-Wesley Professional, Boston, MA, USA (1978)

117. Horstmann, E.: 75 Jahre Fernsprecher in Deutschland. 1877–1952. Ein Rückblick auf die Entwicklung des Fernsprechers un Deutschland und auf seine Erfindungsgeschichte. Bundesministerium für das Post- und Fernmeldewesen, Bundesdruckerei, Bonn (1952)

118. (Hrsg.), J.G.: The communications Handbook. CRC-Press, Boca Raton, FL, USA (1996)

119. (Hrsg.), J.G.: Multimedia Communications - Directions and Innovations. Academic Press, Inc., San Diego, CA, USA (1996)

120. (Hrsg.), J.L.C.: A History of Algorithms: From the Pebble to the Microchip. Springer Verlag, Berlin, Heidelberg, New York (1999)

121. (Hrsg.), W.K.: Propyläen Technikgeschichte. Ullstein Buchverlag GmbH, Berlin (1997)

122. Huffman, D.A.: A method for construction of minimum-redundancy codes. Proceedings IRE **40**(9), 1098–1101 (1952)
123. Huffman, W.C., Brualdi, R.A.: Handbook of coding theory. Elsevier Science Inc., New York, NY, USA (1998)
124. Hyman, A.: Charles Babbage, Pioneer of the Computer. Prineton University Press, Princeton, NJ, USA (1982)
125. International Organization for Standardization: ISO/IEC 10918-1:1994: Information technology — Digital compression and coding of continuous-tone still images: Requirements and guidelines. International Organization for Standardization, Geneva, Switzerland (1994). URL http://www.iso.ch/cate/d18902.html
126. International Organization for Standardization: ISO/IEC 10918-2:1995: Information technology — Digital compression and coding of continuous-tone still images: Compliance testing. International Organization for Standardization, Geneva, Switzerland (1995). URL http://www.iso.ch/cate/d20689.html
127. International Standard, ISO/IEC/JTC1/SC29 WG11: ISO/IEC 13818-3, Information technology – generic coding of moving pictures and associated audio information – Part 3: Audio. International Organization for Standardization, Geneva, Switzerland (1998)
128. Jochum, U.: Kleine Bibliotheksgeschichte, 3. verbesserte und erweiterte Aufl. Reclam, Stuttgart (2007)
129. Jossé, H.: Die Entstehung des Tonfilms. Beitrag zu einer faktenorientierten Mediengeschichtsschreibung. Alber, Freiburg/München (1984)
130. Kahn, D.: The Codebreakers. The Macmillan Company, New York (1967). xvi + 1164 pages
131. Kahn, D.: An Enigma chronology. In: C.A. Deavours, D. Kahn, L. Kruh, G. Mellen, B.J. Winkel (eds.) Selections from Cryptologia: history, people, and technology, pp. 423–432. Artech House, Inc., Norwood, MA, USA (1998)
132. Kasner, E., Newman, J.R.: Mathematics and the Imagination, 24th ed. Simon and Schuster, New York, NY, USA (1967)
133. Kidwell, P.A., Ceruzzi, P.E.: Landmarks in digital computing: A Smithonian practical history. Smithonian Institute Press, Washington, D.C., USA (1994)
134. Kippenhahn, R.: Verschlüsselte Botschaften: Geheimschrift, Enigma und Chipkarte. Rowohlt Taschenbuch Verlag GmbH, Reinbeck bei Hamburg (1997)
135. Kircher, A.: Athanasii Kircheri Ars magna lucis et umbrae, in X. libros digesta. Quibus admirandae lucis & umbrae in mundo, atque adeo universa natura, vires effectusque uti nova, ita varia novorum reconditiorumque speciminum exhibitione, ad varios mortalium usus, panduntur. Scheus, Rom (1646)
136. Kleinrock, L.: Information flow in large communication nets, ph.d. thesis proposal. Ph.D. thesis, Massachusetts Institute of Technology, Cambridge, MA, USA (1961). URL http://www.cs.ucla.edu/~lk/LK/Bib/REPORT/PhD/
137. Kleinrock, L.: Queueing Systems, Volume 1: Theory. John Wiley & Sons, Hoboken, NJ, USA (1975)
138. Koenen, R.: Overview of the MPEG-4 Standard. International Organization for Standardization, ISO/IEC JTC1/SC29/WG11 N2323, Coding of Moving Pictures and Audio, Geneva, Switzerland (2002)
139. Kollmann, T.: E-Business : Grundlagen elektronischer Geschäftsprozesse in der Net Economy, 3., überarb. und erw. Aufl. Gabler, Wiesbaden (2007)
140. König, W. (ed.): Propyläen der Technikgeschichte, Bd. 1-5. Propyläen, Berlin (1990)
141. Krcmar, H.: Informationsmanagement, 4th ext. & rev. edn. Springer Verlag, Berlin, Heidelberg, New York (2005)
142. Kuckenburg, M.: ...und sprachen das erste Wort. Die Entstehung von Sprache und Schrift. Eine Kulturgeschichte der menschlichen Verständigung. Econ Verlag, Düsseldorf (1996)

143. Kuhlen, F.: E-World – Technologien für die Welt von morgen. Springer, Berlin, Heidelberg, New York (2005)
144. Kuo, F.F., Effelsberg, W., Garcia-Luna-Aceves, J.J.: Multimedia communications protocols and applications. Prentice-Hall, Inc., Upper Saddle River, NJ, USA (1998)
145. Küppers, H.: Das Grundgesetz der Farbenlehre, 10. Aufl. DuMont Literatur und Kunst Verlag, Köln (2002)
146. Kurose, J.F., Ross, K.W.: Computer Networking - A Top-Down Approach Featuring the Internet. Addison-Wesley Professional, Boston, MA, USA (2001)
147. Kyas, O., Campo, M.A.: IT Crackdown, Sicherheit im Internet. MITP Verlag, Bonn (2000)
148. Laue, C., Zota, V.: Klangkompressen – MP3 und seine Erben. c't - Magazin für Computertechnik, Verlag Heinz Heise, Hannover 19, 102–109 (2002)
149. Le Gall, D.: MPEG: a video compression standard for multimedia applications. Commun. ACM 34(4), 46–58 (1991)
150. Leroi-Gourhan, A.: Hand und Wort. Die Evolution von Technik, Sprache und Kunst. Suhrkamp, Frankfurt a. M. (1984)
151. Leuf, B., Cunningham, W.: The Wiki Way: Collaboration and Sharing on the Internet. Addison-Wesley Professional, Boston, MA, USA (2001)
152. Lewis, N.: Papyrus in Classical Antiquity. Oxford University Press, Oxford, UK (1974)
153. Licklider, J.C.R., Taylor, R.W.: The computer as a communication device. Science and Technology 76, 21–31 (1968)
154. Luther, A.C.: Principles of Digital Audio and Video. Artech House, Inc., Norwood, MA, USA (1997)
155. Luther, A.C., Inglis, A.F.: Video Engineering. McGraw-Hill, Inc., New York, NY, USA (1999)
156. Marcellin, M.W., Bilgin, A., Gormish, M.J., Boliek, M.P.: An overview of JPEG-2000. In: DCC '00: Prof. of IEEE Data Compression Conference 2000, pp. 523–542. IEEE Computer Society, Washington, DC, USA (2000)
157. Martin, E.: Die Rechenmaschine und ihre Entwicklungsgeschichte. Bd. 1. Burhagen, Pappenheim (1925)
158. Maxwell, J.C.: A dynamical theory of the electromagnetic field. Philosophical Transactions of the Royal Society of London 155, 459–513 (1865)
159. Meinel, C., Sack, H.: WWW - Kommunikation, Internetworking, Web-Technologien. Springer Verlag, Heidelberg (2004)
160. Menezes, A.J., Vanstone, S.A., Oorschot, P.C.V.: Handbook of Applied Cryptography. CRC Press, Inc., Boca Raton, FL, USA (1996)
161. Meschkowski, H.: Denkweisen großer Mathematiker – Ein Weg zur Geschichte der Mathematik. Vieweg Verlag, Wiesbaden (1990)
162. Miano, J.: Compressed image file formats: JPEG, PNG, GIF, XBM, BMP. ACM Press/Addison-Wesley Publishing Co., New York, NY, USA (1999)
163. Miller, A.R.: The cryptographic mathematics of enigma. Cryptologia 19(1), 65–80 (1995)
164. Miller, G.: The magical number seven, plus or minus two: Some limtis on our capacity for processing information. Psycological Review 63, 81–97 (1956)
165. Mitchell, J.L., Pennebaker, W.B., Fogg, C.E., Legall, D.J. (eds.): MPEG Video Compression Standard. Chapman & Hall, Ltd., London, UK, UK (1996)
166. Mitterauer, M.: Predigt - Holzschnitt - Buchdruck. Europäische Frühformen der Massenkommunikation. Beiträge zur historischen Sozialkunde 28(2), 69–78 (1998)
167. Moffat, A., Neal, R.M., Witten, I.H.: Arithmetic coding revisited. ACM Trans. Inf. Syst. 16(3), 256–294 (1998). DOI http://doi.acm.org/10.1145/290159. 290162

168. Möller, E.: Die heimliche Medienrevolution – Wie Weblogs, Wikis und freie Software die Welt ver"andern. Heise Verlag, Hannover (2004)
169. Moore, G.E.: Cramming more components onto integrated circuits. Electronics **38**(8) (1965)
170. Murray, J.D., vanRyper, W.: Encyclopedia of graphics file formats. O'Reilly & Associates, Inc., Sebastopol, CA, USA (1994)
171. Naumann, F.: Vom Abakus zum Internet : die Geschichte der Informatik. Primus-Verlag, Darmstadt (2001)
172. Nettle, D.: Linguistic Diversity. Oxford University Press, Oxford, UK (2001)
173. Newhall, B.: History of Photography: From 1839 to the Present. Bulfinch; Revised edition (1982)
174. Oertel, R.: Macht und Magie des Films. Weltgeschichte einer Massensuggestion. Volksbuchverlag, Wien (1959)
175. O'Regan, G.: A Brief History of Computing. Springer Verlag Ldt., London, UK (2008)
176. O'Reilly, T.: What is web 2.0: Design patterns and business models for the next generation of software (2005). URL http://www.oreillynet.com/pub/a/ oreilly/tim/news/2005/09/30/what-is-web-20.html
177. Painter, T., Spanias, A.: Perceptual coding of digital audio. Proc. of the IEEE **88**(4), 451–515 (2000)
178. Parsons, E.A.: The Alexandrian Library, Glory of the Hellenic World; Its Rise, Antiquities, and Destructions. Elsevier, Amsterdam - New York (1952)
179. Patel, P., Parikh, C.: Design and implementation of AES (Rijndael) algorithm. In: K.E. Nygard (ed.) CAINE, pp. 126–130. ISCA (2003)
180. Pennebaker, W.B., Mitchell, J.L.: JPEG Still Image Data Compression Standard. Kluwer Academic Publishers, Norwell, MA, USA (1992)
181. Peterson, L.L., Davie, B.S.: Computernetze - Ein modernes Lehrbuch. dPunkt Verlag, Heidelberg (2000)
182. Picot, A., Reichwald, R., Wigand, T.R.: Die grenzenlose Unternehmung : Information, Organisation und Management ; Lehrbuch zur Unternehmensführung im Informationszeitalter, 4., vollst. überarb. u. erw. Aufl. Gabler, Wiesbaden (2001)
183. Pierce, J.R., Noll, A.M.: Signale - Die Geheimnisse der Telekommunikation. Spektrum Akademischer Verlag, Heidelberg (1990)
184. Platon: Kratylos. In: Sämtliche Werke, vol. 1, pp. 541–617. Lambert Schneider, Berlin (1940)
185. Platon: Phaidros. In: G. Eigler (ed.) Werke in acht Bänden, vol. 5. Wissenschaftliche Buchgesellschaft, Darmstadt (1983)
186. Plutarch: Große Griechen und Römer, eingeleitet und übersetzt von Konrad Ziegler, Bd. III. Artemis und Winkler, Zürich (1955)
187. Pohlmann, K.: Compact-Disc-Handbuch: Grundlagen des digitalen Audio; technischer Aufbau von CD-Playern, CD-ROM, CD-I, Photo-CD. IWT, München bei Vaterstetten (1994)
188. Pohlmann, K.C.: Principles of Digital Audio. McGraw-Hill Professional, Berkeley CA, USA (2000)
189. Powell, B.B.: The History of Geography of Human Genes. John Wiley and Sons, Hoboken, NJ, USA (2012)
190. Poynton, C.A.: A technical introduction to digital video. John Wiley & Sons, Inc., New York, NY, USA (1996)
191. Preneel, B.: Cryptographic primitives for information authentication - state of the art. In: State of the Art in Applied Cryptography, Course on Computer Security and Industrial Cryptography - Revised Lectures, pp. 49–104. Springer-Verlag, London, UK (1998)
192. Pullan, J.M.: The History of the Abacus. Hutchinson, London, UK (1968)

193. Rao, K.R., Hwang, J.J.: Techniques and standards for image, video, and audio coding. Prentice-Hall, Inc., Upper Saddle River, NJ, USA (1996)

194. am Rhyn, O.H.: Kulturgeschichte des deutschen Volkes, Zweiter Band, p. 13. Baumgärtel, Berlin (1897)

195. Richardson, I.E.G.: H.264 and MPEG-4 Video Compression: Video Coding for Next-generation Multimedia. John Wiley & Sons, Inc., New York, NY, USA (2003)

196. Rivest, R.L., Shamir, A., Adleman, L.: A method for obtaining digital signatures and public-key cryptosystems. Commun. ACM **21**(2), 120–126 (1978). DOI http://doi.acm.org/10.1145/359340.359342

197. Robinson, A.: The Story of Writing. Thames and Hudson Ltd, London, UK (1995)

198. Rochlin, G.I.: Trapped in the Net: The Unanticipated Consequences of Computerization. Princeton University Press, Princeton, NJ, USA (1998)

199. Rock, I.: Wahrnehmung: vom visuellen Reiz zum Sehen und Erkennen. Spektrum der Wissenschaft Verlagsgesellschaft, Heidelberg (1985)

200. Roelofs, G.: PNG: The definitive guide. O'Reilly & Associates, Inc., Sebastopol, CA, USA (1999)

201. Rosenthal, D.: Internet - schöne neue Welt?: Der Report über die unsichtbaren Risiken. Orell Füssli Verlag, Zürich, Schweiz (1999)

202. Rück, P. (ed.): Pergament. Geschichte - Struktur - Restaurierung - Herstellung. No. 2 in Historische Hilfswissenschaften. Thorbecke, Sigmaringen (1991)

203. Salus, P.H.: Casting the Net: From ARPANET to Internet and Beyond... Addison-Wesley Longman Publishing Co., Inc., Boston, MA, USA (1995). Foreword By-Vinton G. Cerf

204. Sandermann, W.: Papier. Eine Kulturgeschichte, 3. Aufl. Springer Verlag, Berlin, Heidelberg, New York (1997)

205. Schenkel, W.: Die ägyptische Hieroglyphenschrift und ihre Weiterentwicklungen. In: H. Günther, O. Ludwig (eds.) Schrift und Schriftlichkeit – Writing and its Use. Ein interdisziplinäres Handbuch internationaler Forschung, 1. Halband, pp. 83–103. de Gruyter, Berlin - New York (1989)

206. Scherff, J.: Grundkurs Computernetze. Vieweg, Wiesbaden (2006)

207. Schmeh, K.: Die Welt der geheimen Zeichen. W3L Verlag, Bochum (2004)

208. Schmeh, K.: Kryptografie – Verfahren, Protokolle, Infrastrukturen, pp. 199–234. dPunkt Verlag, Heidelberg (2007)

209. Schneier, B.: Applied Cryptography: Protocols, Algorithms, and Source Code in C. John Wiley & Sons, Inc., New York, NY, USA (1993)

210. Schöning, U.: Ideen der Informatik – Grundlegende Modelle und Konzepte. Oldenbourg Verlag, München (2002)

211. Schubert, H.: Historie der Schallaufzeichnung. Deutsches Rundfunkarchiv, Frankfurt a. M. (1983)

212. Schulten, L.: Firefox - Alles zum Kultbrowser. O'Reilley (2005)

213. Schwarze, J., Schwarze, S., Hoppe, G.: Electronic commerce : Grundlagen und praktische Umsetzung. Verl. Neue Wirtschafts-Briefe, Herne / Berlin (2002)

214. Schwenk, J.: Sicherheit und Kryptographie im Internet. Vieweg Verlag, Wiesbaden (2002)

215. Sedgewick, R.: Algorithms, 2nd Edition. Addison-Wesley, Boston, MA, USA (1988)

216. Servon, L.J.: Bridging the digital divide: technology, community, and public policy. Blackwell, Malden, MA, USA (2002)

217. Shannon, C.E.: A Mathematical Theory of Communication. The Bell System Technical Journal **27**, 379–423 (1948)

218. Shannon, C.E.: Communication in the presence of noise. Proceedings of the IRE **37**(1), 10–21 (1949)

219. Shannon, C.E., Weaver, W.: The Mathematical Theory of Communication. University of Illinois Press, Urbana, Illinois (1949)
220. Shapiro, C., Varian, H.R.: Information rules: a strategic guide to the network economy. Harvard Business School Press, Boston, MA, USA (1998)
221. Siegert, B.: Translatio Imperii: Der cursus publicus im römischen Kaiserreich. In: L. Engell, B. Siegert, J. Vogl (eds.) Archiv für Mediengeschichte – Medien der Antike, pp. 13–24. Universitätsverlag Weimar, Weimar (2003)
222. Singh, S.: Geheime Botschaften. Carl Hanser Verlag, München (2000)
223. Solari, S.J.: Digital Video and Audio Compression. McGraw-Hill Professional, New York, NY, USA (1997)
224. Stamper, D.A.: Essentials of Data Communications. Benjamin Cummings, Menlo Park, CA, USA (1997)
225. Stein, E.: Taschenbuch Rechnernetze und Internet. Fachbuchverlag Leipzig, Carl Hanser Verlag, München (2001)
226. Steinmetz, R.: Multimedia-Technologie: Grundlagen, Komponenten und Systeme, 3. Aufl. Springer Verlag, Heidelberg (2000)
227. Steinmetz, R., Nahrstedt, K.: Multimedia: Computing, Communications and Applications: Media Coding and Content Processing. Prentice Hall PTR, Upper Saddle River, NJ, USA (2002)
228. Stelzer, D.: Digitale Güter und ihre Bedeutung in der Internet-Ökonomie. Das Wirtschaftsstudium (WISU) **29**(6), 835–842 (2000)
229. Stelzer, D.: Produktion digitaler Güter. In: A. Braßler, H. Corsten (eds.) Entwicklungen im Produktionsmanagement. Franz Vahlen, München (2004)
230. Stetter, C.: Schrift und Sprache. Suhrkamp Verlag, Frankfurt a. M. (1999)
231. Stinson, D.: Cryptography: Theory and Practice,Second Edition, pp. 117–154. Chapman & Hall, CRC, London, UK (2002)
232. Stöber, R.: Mediengeschichte. Die Evolution neuer Medien von Gutenberg bis Gates, Eine kommunikationswissenschaftliche Einführung. Band 1: Presse - Telekommunikation. Westdeutscher Verlag, GWV Fachverlage, Wiesbaden (2003)
233. Stöber, R.: Deutsche Pressegeschichte: Von den Anfängen bis zur Gegenwart, 2. überarb. Aufl. UKV Medien Verlagsgesellschaft, Konstanz (2005)
234. Störig, H.J.: Weltgeschichte der Wissenschaft. S. Fischer Verlag, Frankfurt a. M. (1982)
235. Strutz, T.: Bilddaten-Kompression. Grundlagen, Codierung, MPEG, JPEG, 2. Aufl. Vieweg Verlag, Braunschweig/Wiesbaden (2002)
236. Sueton: Leben der Caesaren übersetzt von Andre Lambert. Artemis und Winkler, Zürich (1955)
237. Tanenbaum, A.S.: Computer Networks. Prentice-Hall, Inc., Upper Saddle River, NJ, USA (1996)
238. Taubman, D.S., Marcellin, M.W.: JPEG2000 : image compression fundamentals, standards, and practice. Kluwer Academic Publishers, Boston (2002)
239. Thom, D., Purnhagen, H., Pfeiffer, S.: MPEG-Audio Subgroup: MPEG Audio FAQ,. ISO/IEC JTC1/SC29/WG11 Coding of Moving Pictures and Audio (1999)
240. Thukydides: Geschichte des Peloponnesischen Krieges. Bücherei Tusculum, Darmstadt (1993)
241. von Thun, F.S.: Miteinander reden: Störungen und Klärungen., vol. 1, 35 edn. Rowohlt (2001)
242. Timmerer, C., Hellwagner, H.: Das MPEG-21 Multimedia-Framework. Informatik-Spektrum **31**(6), 576–579 (2008)
243. Torres, L.: Video Coding. Kluwer Academic Publishers, Norwell, MA, USA (1996)
244. Tschudin, P.F.: Grundzüge der Papiergeschichte. No. 12 in Bibliothek des Buchwesens. Hiersemann, Stuttgart (2002)

245. Unser, M.: Sampling – 50 years after Shannon. Proceedings of the IEEE **88**(4), 569–587 (2000)
246. von Urbanitzky Alfred, R., Wormell, R.: Electricity in the Service of Man: A Popular and Practical Treatise on the Applications of Electricity in Modern Life. Cassell & Company Ltd., London, UK (1886)
247. Vise, D., Malseed, M.: The Google Story: Inside the Hottest Business, Media, and Technology Success of Our Time. Random House Inc., New York, NY, USA (2006)
248. Wallace, G.K.: The JPEG still picture compression standard. Communications of the ACM **34**, 31–44 (1991)
249. Watkinson, J.: MPEG Handbook. Butterworth-Heinemann, Newton, MA, USA (2001)
250. Webers, J.: Handbuch der Film- und Videotechnik. Film, Videoband und Platte im Studio und Labor. Franzis, München (1983)
251. Welch, T.A.: A technique for high performance data compression. IEEE Trans. on Computer **17**(6), 8–19 (1984)
252. Wiegand, T., Sullivan, G.J., Bjntegaard, G., Luthra, A.: Overview of the H.264/AVC video coding standard. Circuits and Systems for Video Technology, IEEE Transactions on **13**(7), 560–576 (2003)
253. Wilkinson, E.: Chinese History – A Manual, Havard-Yenching Institute Monograph Series, 52. Harvard University Press, Cambridge, MA, USA (2000)
254. Winston, B.: Media Technology and Society, A History: From the Telegraph to the Internet. Routledge, London, UK (1988)
255. Witten, I.H., Neal, R.M., Cleary, J.G.: Arithmetic coding for data compression. Commun. ACM **30**(6), 520–540 (1987)
256. Wolf, L.: Essays in Jewish history. With a memoir by Cecil Roth (ed.). The Jewish Historical Society of England, London, UK (1934)
257. Ziegenbalg, J.: Elementare Zahlentheorie. Verlag Harri Deutsch, Frankfurt a. M. (2002)
258. Zimmermann, H.: OSI Reference Model–The ISO Model of Architecture for Open Systems Interconnection. Communications, IEEE Transactions on [legacy, pre - 1988] **28**(4), 425–432 (1980)
259. Ziv, J., Lempel, A.: A universal algorithm for sequential data compression. IEEE Transactions on Information Theory **23**, 337–343 (1977)
260. Zotter, H.: Die Geschichte des europäischen Buchdrucks; Grundausbildung für den Bibliotheks-, Dokumentations- und Informationsdienst, 4. revidierte Aufl. Österreichische Nationalbibliothek, Wien (1992)
261. Zuse, K.: Der Computer - Mein Lebenswerk. Springer, Berlin, Heidelberg, New York (1984)

Index

8K, 240

Abacus, 65
Absolute threshold of hearing, 216
Accommodation, 192, 238
Acknowledgement, 145, 146
Acoustic masking, 215
Acta Diurna, 38
ActionScript, 282
Adaption, 192
Adaptive transformation, 245
Adleman, Leonard M., 293, 310, 364
ADSL, 248
Advanced Encryption Standard, see
    AES
AES, 305, 307
AES/EBU, 210
Aeschylus, 42, 347
AIFF format, 211
Aiken, Howard A., 68
Al-Haitham, Ibn, 51, 175, 350
Al-Khowarizmi, Abu Ja'far Mohammed
    Ibn Musa, 350
Alexander VI, 37, 86, 351
Alexandria, 27
Alias effect, 172
Aliasing, 221, 283
Alice and Bob, 292, 293
Alpha channel, 189, 190, 283
Alphabet, 19, 85, 157
Alternating current, 195
Amber, 44
Amber Road, 30
Amontons, Guillaume, 43, 353
Ampère, André Marie, 45, 355
Amplitude, 203
Analog, 85, 283

Analog to digital conversion, 204
Analytical engine, 67
Andreesen, Marc, 80
Animation, 283
ANSI X3.102, 119
Anti-aliasing, 283
Application Layer, 138
Arago, Francois Dominique, 52, 355
Archer, Frederick Scott, 53, 356
Archive, 27
Aristotle, 51, 174, 175, 348
Arithmetic coding, 196, 200, 201
ARPA, 102
ARPANET, 74, 85
Artifacts, 172, 189, 196, 207, 219, 283
ASCII-Code, 162, 284
ASF, 282
Aspect ratio, 173
Assurbanipal, 27, 347
ATRAC, 232
Attack, 299
Attacks
    active, 296
    passive, 297
AU format, 210
Audio, 155
Audio recording, 63
Auditory sensation area, 215, 216, 284
Auditory threshold, 204
Augustus, 29, 349
Aurelianus, Lucius Domitius, 27, 349
Authentication, 295, 314, 333
Authentication protocol, 314
Authenticity, 123
Authorization, 296, 314, 333
Availability, 120, 124, 293
Avalanche effect, 299

C. Meinel and H. Sack, *Digital Communication*, X.media.publishing,
DOI: 10.1007/978-3-642-54331-9, © Springer-Verlag Berlin Heidelberg 2014

Printed in the United States
By Bookmasters